The Fatal Alliance

ALSO BY DAVID THOMSON

The Fatal Alliance

A CENTURY OF WAR ON FILM

David Thomson

HARPER

An Imprint of HarperCollins*Publishers*

HarperCollins books may be purchased for educational, business, or sales promotional use. For information, please email the Special Markets Department at SPsales@harpercollins.com.

FIRST EDITION

Designed by Kyle O'Brien

Library of Congress Cataloging-in-Publication Data has been applied for.

ISBN 978-0-06-304141-7

23 24 25 26 27 LBC 5 4 3 2 1

for Isaac, Grace, and Joe

"A war doesn't merely kill off a few hundred or a few hundred thousand young men. It kills off something in a people that can never be brought back. And if a people goes through enough wars, pretty soon all that's left is the brute, the creature that we— you and I and others like us—have brought up from the slime."

—John Williams, *Stoner* (1965)

"The film is like a battleground. Love . . . hate . . . action . . . violence . . . death. . . . In one word, emotion."

—Samuel Fuller, in *Pierrot le Fou* (1965)

A little panic-fear grew in his mind. As his imagination went forward to a fight, he saw hideous possibilities. He contemplated the lurking menaces of the future, and failed in an effort to see himself standing stoutly in the midst of them. He recalled his visions of broken-bladed glory, but in the shadow of the impending tumult he suspected them to be impossible pictures.

—Stephen Crane, *The Red Badge of Courage* (1895)

"The enemy is anybody who's going to get you killed, no matter which side he's on, and that includes Colonel Cathcart."

—Joseph Heller, *Catch-22* (1961)

Houdini thought the boy comely, fair like his mother, and tow-headed, but a little soft-looking. He leaned over the side door. Goodbye, Sonny, he said holding out his hand. Warn the Duke, the little boy said. Then he ran off.

—E. L. Doctorow, *Ragtime* (1975), describing an impossible event that seems to have occurred in 1909

"Tyger, tyger, burning bright."

—William Blake (1794)

"Contains scenes that some viewers may find disturbing."

—CNN, every now and then

CONTENTS

I

MOBILIZATION

In which, getting ready for this big subject—fashioning
the board, some rules, and attitudes; and finding appealing
tokens to play with (a top hat, a machine gun, and a Scottie
dog?)—the idea gathers that war has become a game.

IMITATE THE ACTION OF THE TIGER

No, I cannot hear the growling, not yet. But the other day, on Inisherin, I heard gunfire plodding across the sea, from the mainland.

This is a book about war, an attempt to describe the dynamic in film that has been so infatuated with battle. But battle and war are not the same: war is a malignancy in our nature and society, the deep expression of our fear; while battle aspires to adventure and a thrill, like going to a movie, and trying to believe that we can handle fear.

The book will be a history and a commentary, moving forward from the marker of 1914, as world war and world cinema came into being in the same burst of change. Like an explosion. It will try to tell our story while observing many of our finest war films. But we are as much intent on the future as the past, and this book is dedicated to grandchildren. Strict chronology can be a fallacy, so the book moves sideways sometimes, from one theater to another, taking in backstory along with speculation. Nineteen fourteen cannot be separated from 2023. For there are three lessons to start with on this project.

One is that war steadily repeats and digests its melodrama, not just in tactics and technology, but in the pattern of misguided hopes and brutal reality. War drags us down, so that we forget peace.

Another lesson—for a book written and published first in the United

States—is the way America has seldom understood how marginal it is in this dark history. In two world wars, the American homeland was calm; its industry thrived; its stories swelled in grandeur. But it longs to be the leader and a star in war studies. So America has had few rivals in the making of exciting war movies, or in the ingenuity and expressiveness of its military expenditure. As if the young nation wanted to romance combat or make an advertisement for it.

The third lesson is the most far-reaching: as time has passed since 1914, it becomes clearer that, for so many of us, the most available sense of history is reappraisal through a movie. Later in this book, I will note how some potential viewers complained that *The Vietnam War* on television, a chronicle by Ken Burns and Lynn Novick, was too long. Whereas even at over seventeen hours it is too short. Because an attempt at understanding believes a war of thirty years deserves a lifetime of research. (And if you think it wasn't thirty years, then you are victim to Hollywood condensation.) But there are many who think Vietnam was *Platoon*, or *Apocalypse Now*, or *We Were Soldiers*, three spectacular films that squeezed the totality to fit a glib story line. If we let the movies be our history book, we will only repeat the movies.

Still, it does seem exciting, doesn't it, war on film, like butter on hot toast? Who could resist that side order with your scrambled eggs? As quick as a flash there will be images and sounds in your heads: the arachnoid churning of helicopters from *Apocalypse Now* and Colonel Kilgore's surfer exuberance over the smell of napalm in the morning—just hope your scrambled eggs weren't cooked in that oil.

The highlights are so many. Talk about coming attractions: the brilliant rearguard action for that bridge in *Saving Private Ryan* and the stress on Ryan earning the sacrifice that saved him; the incoherent skirmishing in the streets of Mogadishu in *Black Hawk Down* as bold adventure turned to chaos; the suave Russian captain in *The Hunt for Red October* asking for "just one ping" on the brink of a very bad bang; the way the sweet grassy hill is taken on Guadalcanal in *The Thin Red Line*; and even the pageant of knights on horseback whose green fields of Ireland masquerade as the mud patch of Agincourt for Olivier's *Henry V*. These are spectacles in what has always been a dynamic for the film business. The slaughter of our fellows was big box office from the start—so long as it was done with an elegance fit to please pacifist audiences. For something in us has always delighted in the imitation of war's tiger. So long as we don't throw up in horror when we see its teeth.

Can you hear him yet?

That tiger comes from Shakespeare's *Henry V*: "But when the blast of war blows in our ears, then imitate the action of the tiger." Will could not have met too many tigers in his life, but he knew about pretending. That martial encouragement comes right after this appealing homily: "In peace there's nothing so becomes a man as modest stillness and humility." I hope that can cover the steady concentration with which film craftsmen, artificers at the big computer, compose scenes of immense battle (still elegant) that were not possible when you needed extras, uniforms, gunpowder, horses, and soft ground to soak up the blood.

That stillness before the tiger makes a riddle: It is there in the heartfelt way in which battle has been our thing, even if it terrifies us, as if we might be shot to pieces today, or as if our entire enterprise—the civilization project—could be charred debris before dinner. How do we stand that contradiction? Are we crazy?

Well, yes, of course, you say. But just calm down, so we can get on with good stories of battle.

WHEN WAR HAPPENS, IT EXPECTS TO BE EVERYTHING, NOT A GAME PLAYED in the next valley but a plan to rewrite geography. It is aiming a gun and determining the direction of life. In the twentieth century we learned that war unified the world, pressured it and accelerated it. We realized that "a state of war" affected every item of how we thought and what we hoped for. When world war "finished"—in 1945, we say—some preparedness lingered in the air, not just dread but purpose, a potency that would not subside. The tiger's growl.

So we would have wars on poverty, forever; and others on racism, violence, intolerance, and even tolerance. Why not a war on guns? We had to rearm, and make movies that set out an absurd protocol for having a successful war. So hungry for war we invented combat games to play on Xboxes, and that audience soon surpassed the old fogies loyal to movies about war. The sofa-bound hostilities, wearing out triggers with kill counts, left actual war and casualties seeming archaic and humbled. Is it all theater now?

The war in Afghanistan might have been declared "over" at the end of summer 2021, but the previous two centuries showed how it only kept coming back, first as the romance of British cavalry patrols in the Khyber Pass, and then as whispering drone strikes and the damage that would be omitted from official reports. To go to war, sooner or later, is to realize that your government is lying to you. By the time you read this, there may be "boots on the ground" again in that sad, available territory. We may have gone back "in" just to end the landscape of starvation and inhumanity. We are sentimental about such things.

Of course, war is a cold, ugly game. I'm sure you want to be clear about that, even if the endless insistence may spell out our derangement. We feel that disapproving way every time combat is posited, in parts of the world we still hardly know. It is a source of immense destruction, of cities and nations, lives and hopes. So you wonder sometimes where our race and civilization might have been without war.

Or is that too great a stretch, and too close to a world possible for the common people who may be buried or lost statistically in centuries of rich mud? In going to war and giving up your life you will be complicit in a plan to overlook the rights of man. Is the stuff about "a bad thing" formulaic now, a cliché? Just our humbug habit?

Then ask why this terrible thing so entertains us that we cannot stop looking at it. This fun has gone so far beyond diligent attempts to record or re-create combat—the way real land is won and lost; the frailty of brave, uniformed men wilting under fire. That early stress on the physicality of war has given way to a cinematic takeover of combat in which the labor of engines and men in the mud has been supplanted by the smoothness of computers, the soaring of lethal flight, and the simplification of destroyed lives as animated shapes. This is how the acknowledged catastrophe in *All Quiet on the Western Front* (1930, and now again) turned into the childish zest of *Star Wars* (begun in 1977). But *Star Wars* was a long time ago already, and we have found new ways to do war that are as fabulous and exciting as a son et lumière of the Somme or Stalingrad. Do you know what those places looked like—or are they all movie now?*

Do you remember (this was only August 2021), the newsreel sight of some large military transport aircraft trying to take off from Kabul's airfield, but having to tread delicately because of the desperate lives around the plane, striving to get on board, longing to escape? And weren't there tiny figures clinging to the structure of the plane itself, when surely they knew they would have to fall away in the next few seconds? Were those human beings or digital leaves? Can you tell the difference?

Immediately, that image was recognized not just as a journalistic coup but as a summary of the misguided war in Afghanistan—or of the latest mishap in that battered nation. It was clear immediately—in the moment of seeing it—that that footage would be as much the emblem of American humiliation as those helicopters being tipped into the ocean at the close of the Vietnam affair.

Within a year of the desperate departure from Kabul, we had no easy escape from Matthew Heineman's *Retrograde* (2022). That was a documentary in which the film and American support had been embedded with Afghan army forces fighting the Taliban. The Americans were Green Berets, young men, gaunt, scorched, and older than their years, having to listen to their president tell them that the Afghan project had been accomplished, so go home now, in honor. The guys do not smile, but we know how clearly they see their betrayal of the Afghan leader, General

---

* From time to time I have used the word "movie" as being like "music" or "painting" or "writing." It signifies the overall cultural place of film, as a practice, a language, and a way of thinking.

Benny Sadat, and the political convenience that has wiped away decades of service. *Retrograde* is a major work, one that teaches soldiers not to trust war or those pale faces who schedule it. You have to wonder how far the pale faces will continue to let people like Matthew Heineman be embedded.

BUT THERE'S MORE TO AGONIZE OVER. I DO NOT DOUBT THE DEPICTED events in that Kabul coverage. I am not seeking to undermine its tragedy or the panic. But I know that shots like these can be contrived and manipulated, without need of actuality. You have known this for years now. And that means you cannot exactly trust what you see, because the sophistication of movie has humbled and tricked our tragedies. In hurrying to keep up with the slaughter we have had to make a concession: that tragedy doesn't quite happen anymore—we've had too much of it, or worn out our grief. That which can be duplicated and passed around for fun begins to lose its power. Did two million or *x* million perish at Stalingrad? Would it make a difference seventy-five years later?

We used to be so trusting. In our sleep we murmured, "Warn the duke." But when Archduke Franz Ferdinand and his wife, Sophie, were shot dead in Sarajevo on June 28, 1914, there was no film or photograph of the killing. There is a picture of the hapless couple earlier on that day; they are middle-aged gentry in their Gräf & Stift phaeton enjoying the feel of summer and looking forward to lunch, even if a rude grenade had been tossed in their direction by inept members of the Black Hand movement. They were parked on a back street to catch their breath, or feel safe. Then, by accident and providence, Gavrilo Princip happened to leave a café on the side street, and since he had a pistol in his pocket he thought, *Why not?* Give a lost soul a gun and he'll fire it—isn't that a movie law? When a group calls itself the Black Hand you guess it will drop the ball. Truly that Sunday was a mess, as if unscripted.

Still the world believed the telegraphed reports of the killings and began to act on them: a locomotive of hostilities was set in motion. Everyone soon knew it was the Great War. This spasm educated us in the existence of "everyone."

A hundred or so years later, we are not as confident. There is ample coverage of what happened at the battle for the Washington Capitol on January 6, 2021, but political paranoia has made a ferment of dispute over that violence and its scripts. The factual images are repeated, but our culture is bored by how easily such things can be fabricated. Photography is no longer a record; it is an unsound assertion. The technological subterfuges of "recording" have made the morality of the real back off. Those who control the media have taken over the rights on history. The most influential innovation in the process of war was the onset of the movies because their smile said the damage didn't quite matter.

I'm warning you. This book will not be comfortable; the tiger is not a kitten. Ask yourself whether you are up for it. Or are you one of those armchair generals who watches a massacre like a football match?

What can we do, then, in the name of decency? If you are reading a book, I feel you have the seeds of optimism within you. But if you're writing it, you know the shadow of pessimism, and the inescapable conclusion that war is a big show.

Warn the duke. Don't say it's too late.

But in June 1914, the duke *had* been warned. He wasn't quite the idiot we sometimes make him in our stories. The people—leaders and led—on the brink of catastrophe often seem sensible and diligent. Franz Ferdinand had thoughts on the governance of the empire and wanted to give more fairness to the Slavs. So he went to Sarajevo knowing the danger, and accepting the risk. He was one of us, waiting on fortune.

The point about warn the duke is that somehow or later we'll feel like idiots, or worse, like the Green Berets sick at Kabul.

2

AT EASE

By the end of this book we will come to a moment where a man and a woman in an expensive hotel room observe what seems to be a war outside. "Looks like there's a war on," the woman says, and I think we understand that worry. It has a numb menace that seems disconcerting, but which really is quite normal, or one of our things. So be wary of growing indignant or soulful over war and its damage. Casual horror happens now, still ghastly but so matter-of-factly we take it for granted. Once its novelty wears off, horror humiliates the theory of our intelligence.

You will be saying, *But that casualness is terrible*, and of course you're right. But that propriety gets staler year by year, as we prepare for the show. Isn't war (as depicted, as viewed from our movie distance, as action on our screen) our game now, a rash way of signaling that we would like to be brave?

It is the custom of war movies to see combat as a field for courage and its prowess. But isn't that dynamic pretentious now? I am not doubting that here and there in battle some of us do astonishingly brave Audie Murphy things, saving lives, winning a hill, or rescuing the princess. But don't take that as orthodoxy. Wars are fought by people who are constantly afraid, and that state deserves to be honored and accepted. How many wars are started to deny fear? How many war movies share that delusion? The white lie in war movies is that we are willing fighters, deserving victory and validation. War is also the system in which poor and underprivileged people are ground down, and shamed for being afraid. To be incontinent at the threshold of a gas chamber is not indecent or unreasonable.

For nearly all our lives, we have wondered over the irrepressible urge of cataclysmic war to break out (as if it was the tiger). We fear it, and think of our young ones in jeopardy, but we have always been the dominating infants eager for inviting triggers. What bliss, to open fire—that sounds insane. But it is a steady pressure. You have to think the worse of us because of it, but we are so bad at closing down fire. So we labor on in the philosophy that war is a very bad thing. Yet we hunger for its banquet. Even now, I daresay, you are a touch impatient with this introduction and itching to get on to *Black Hawk Down*, *The Thin Red Line*, or . . . please add in your favorites, the ones you always pause for if they come up on TV.

AS I WAS WRITING THIS BOOK, I MIGHT FIND MYSELF AWAKE BEFORE DAWN calculating some fresh outbreak of hostilities in the world. There are many sites to consider as one imagines the board set up for Risk. I did think of Ukraine. But Taiwan seemed the next available flash point. Toss a coin? Or admit that that offshore island feels such a natural part of China that we can understand the Chinese wanting to keep their union in place? Without it, where would we be? Moreover, it is evident in any strategic military estimate that China could retake Taiwan quicker than Germany took Holland in 1940.

Are you shaky on the facts and the names—or as uncertain as millions were in 1939–40 about what and where the impregnable Maginot Line was? As you get into world war you have to appreciate how ignorant you were all along about most reaches of the world, as if you have never been to school.

Taiwan (or, as it calls itself, the Republic of China) is about 13,800 square miles and 23.4 million inhabitants, a little over a hundred miles offshore from the People's Republic of China (1.4 billion people; 3.7 million square miles). Taiwan has an army of about 130,000; for China the number is over 2 million.

Taiwan (formerly known as Formosa) became the escape ground for the regime in China ousted by the Communist revolution of 1949. If it's helpful, think of a cartoon movie (a kind of Tom and Jerry) where Mao Tse-tung boots Chiang Kai-shek off the mainland. In the time since, Taiwan has become prosperous and a significant part of Western economic life. It is in our world. No nation has done more to sustain that status than the United States, and we are treaty-bound to protect it if ever the People's Republic of China thinks to invade. President Biden has the habit of saying "Of course" when asked if the US would really—truly, madly, deeply—do that. It is said we have a few military people there, "helping." You hear the number 70. Warn the president?

But what could happen? Why did General Mark Milley (chairman of the Joint Chiefs of Staff) seem so impressed in October 2021 by a Chinese hypersonic weapons test that "changed the game"? What happened when the French army and the British Expeditionary Force faced the German blitzkrieg attack of May 1940? The probability in warfare was amended with shocking speed as the constipation of the Great War blew up in military academic faces. With a similar thrust against Taiwan, the United States and the diplomatic fraternity would be deeply distressed. There could be brief, heroic resistance on the island and emergency debates at the United Nations, along with protest marches in many countries. But there's not much more that the US or anyone else could do. Think of what has happened recently in Hong Kong, and ask whether anyone sees an alternative to some abrupt reunification of the two Chinas.

Unless . . . I am going to make a more modest proposal. Suppose (in the spirit of our board game Risk) the US and China resolved to go to war, but with a gentlemen's agreement whereby the conflict would abjure the use of nuclear weapons. Instead, there would be combat by dice tossing, and the modern mayhem possible with computer-generated imagery—those soldiers made by a computer are never exactly killed; they are deleted (but with full cinematic conviction, bodies erupting, heads in smithereens, the full et cetera). This saving grace would come not just from humanitarian idealism or a wish to stop short of the unthinkable, but from the practical objection that you can't have a satisfactory world war (with season ticket involvement) unless you draw the line at a level of conventional armament such as existed in 1945.

You are deciding that your author is preposterous—warn the publisher? But consider what a lengthy conventional war could do for two large yet insecure economies. Wasn't 1939–45 (for all its catastrophes) the dynamic that replaced the Depression with modern prosperity? And we surely understand that modern prosperity can be more compelling than many rights of mankind, including fair play for all. So think about how a World War 3 (we need a better title) might do so much to reorganize this jittery world of ours. Full productive employment? Entertainment for all? Health care for the wounded and for all? Wouldn't such a war promote our search for renewable natural energy? Think how it would galvanize artificial intelligence, and help us get rid of the antiquated human version.

I've no idea how it would conclude. I suppose the key to such a war would be that it *not* conclude, that a state of harmonious and profitable industrial hostility goes on, and on. What I am envisaging is a full-bodied war culture, exciting but regulated, destructive yet safe, as full of victory as defeats, a show for those of us who really don't want to fight ourselves, but who are thoroughly exercised by the show of war, such as seems to dominate our most popular movies.

Am I dreaming, or do we have this already?

My guess would be that instead of invading China (the practicality of which is so far-fetched) a more beckoning theater of war might be what we still call the Middle East (as if we presided over the world and mapped it), and the territory to the east of it. I will not be astonished if we reinvade Afghanistan for an eventual battleground that might extend to Kashmir and the north of India. Even to Siberia, which has always seemed promising for a robust campaign in which artillery fire sets off outbursts of permafrost gases. This is spectacular open country for large troop movements—indeed, it is the kind of terrain already familiar not just from "realistic" films like *Courage Under Fire* (shot outside El Paso) or *The Hurt Locker* (filmed in Jordan), but from the multiplicity of futuristic, computer-generated combat epics. Just as in the old Westerns where a man wanted a prairie where his horse could gallop, now he delights in an unencumbered expanse where tanks and machines play. Where drones simmer in the skies.

There will be casualties? Of course. But don't we do those numbers? Warn the casualties? Why spoil their last days? We are going to have to be grown-up about the casualties. That word turns on "casual," as if the losses came by chance. Let's give that up. Generals and presidents were counting them on their fingers—one for fifty thousand—in the dark.

It's notable how far movies have reveled in this indefinite sandscape territory—it goes from *Star Wars* and *Mad Max* to *World War Z* and *Warcraft* to *Dune*—providing inviting desolation where rambunctious machines and demons may growl and swoop. The technology seems modern, but the atmosphere is as archaic as Risk or John Buchan's *Greenmantle* (a novel published in 1916) where the English gentleman Richard Hannay (recovering from wounds suffered at the Battle of Loos in 1915) ventures into the broad area of "the East" to scupper nasty German plans for a jihad to put a cat among the Great War pigeons. (Mix metaphors to taste.)

I'm being facetious, to stress the degree of lived-out fantasy in that Great War, but Hannayism does resemble the theater of T. E. Lawrence, an Englishman in dress-up who could be close to forgotten now but for a movie.

Isn't it still the case that even the educated among us don't properly know where the places are, let alone the nature of the lives led there? How fatuous it was in 1962 to have Alec Guinness (born in the suburb of Maida Vale) playing Prince Faisal of Arabia—but how daft is it still to feel the thrill of Peter O'Toole's ecstatic charge on "Aqaba!" in *Lawrence of Arabia* when I could not find that city on the map? Movie is too often a mask for ignorance, just as so many wars owe their energy to our knowing too little about faraway places. They thrive on the refusal to take history seriously. Thus the dilemma of a book that wants to be a history, not just in the chronology of what happened, but in trying to understand how the technology of film as a medium and its narrative constructs drove and directed our understanding of war.

So being playful with the thought of a war over Taiwan is not simpleminded or cynical. It is guiding us toward what has happened to war movies in, say, the past thirty years. I mean an inflation and a trivialization occurring in concert. We exist now in a culture of battle films where damage, death, and disaster are not much graver than tossing the dice to see how Risk armies can be destroyed over Kamchatka, Irkutsk, and Yakutsk.

Consider this example: In 1990, *The Hunt for Red October* opened. It was an engaging adventure movie, with a plausible sense of submarine warfare as it then existed. Taken from a Tom Clancy novel, scripted by Larry Ferguson and Donald E. Stewart, and directed by John McTiernan, it concerns a Soviet submarine captain, Marko Ramius, who wants to sail his missile-armed vessel to the Maine shore and defect. But only one headstrong American intelligence analyst, Jack Ryan, understands this motivation. The story is complicated, yet icy clear, and if you haven't seen the picture I urge you to do so. It's as if Gary Cooper was still running our high-tech show. You'll feel better.

Red October (the sub and the film) depends on Sean Connery as Ramius: he is taciturn, Scottish-Russian, noble, and one of the most endearing officers ever put on film. With the US Navy's encouragement, the project was able to photograph the most modern submarines to create credible sets for its cramped interiors. We feel as if we are seeing the real thing. That is a sweet trick in movies, and it matches Ramius's dry candor. It made a rousing entertainment, well written and adroitly played—the impetuous Alec Baldwin is Jack Ryan, and there is excellent work from Scott Glenn, Sam Neill, and Courtney B. Vance in a laconic Hawksian world. But it seems old-fashioned now, like a Second World War picture dedicated to the steely nerves and professional acumen of our reliable guys.

The film is cunning: It has a Russian hero, but it arranges itself so that a "bad" Soviet sub can be outmaneuvered and blown to pieces. That's the wow moment. It has an air of authenticity (and a trust in the real thing) so great that American naval security was alarmed that a few secret devices in their subs might have been let slip. Moviegoers love that genuine flourish (it stimulates our dreaming), and you may be amused to hear that the urbane Connery took the part of Ramius at about forty-eight hours' notice after other actors had melted away. Of course, he could have done it in twenty-four. Minutes.

But there's a deeper lesson, in hindsight. *Red October* was released just as the Soviet empire ended—I mean the Communist bloc we had grown up with in a mood of fear and loathing. With glasnost, the Berlin Wall (an old movie prop) came down. So the Cold War was "over," and there were many reasons to rejoice and relax. As well as one large worry still not settled: For in cold triumph we, the West, were left to puzzle out what we were doing in the geopolitical world and where the future would take us. What was the story? Were we freer now to solve racism and poverty at home? Or could we put those things off? Can we say that in the thirty years since the wall came down, the US has done a good job at defining its new identity? Would Russia need war again?

Then add this: the benefits and the puzzle of the Cold War ending coincided with the rapid evolution of what I will call CGI cinema, or our ability to show anything we could imagine, as opposed to the state of nature. Thus in the thirty years since, our battle films have become teeming fantasies, lyrically violent, so that our sense of war gets closer to a reckless, uninhibited make-believe. Well, of course, you say, that is progress. But that complacency doesn't let us off the hook. It is in our glorying over fanciful wars that we are losing touch with the Ramius ethos and integrity, and his looking forward to some quiet fishing if he can get *Red October* through all the bureaucratic barriers of homeland security.

Hannay and Lawrence now look like gaudy puppets on an exotic stage. But the cool Ramius may be closer to that ancient confidence than we suppose. Are we really smarter or more realistic when it comes to getting out of (or into) Kabul? Or in wondering whether to be there in the first place? Being in all these remote places is hard—not just getting there and establishing our own familiar eateries, but researching the factual texture of Somalia or Nova Zembla and deciding what to do with it. It may be easier to live in the dark, or in the air.

3

OPEN FIRE

I was at 34,000 feet, doing 520 miles per hour, coming in from Kennedy on JetBlue. It sounds like a mission, skipper. You can tell yourself your aircraft is sailing along, riding the clouds and the turbulence like a yacht at sea. But sitting in ticketed aspic you don't feel the real friction of traveling or the cold outside; inside the plane you are breathing the air that, they say, is renewed every two minutes. No one disputes that claim, or tells the flight attendant offering theoretical pretzels that we will settle for nothing less than a dish of English trifle with fresh cream and black currant sauce.

This is not an aside. It is the heart of the matter.

Flying in a commercial aircraft is a form of military service, or doing as one is instructed to make sure everything will be "all right." (The pressure in us to stay "all right" deepens as so many things go wrong.) You sit in your seat, belted up under orders; you do not get out of line—for the sake of the flight and its calm. Even now, the crew wears a kind of uniform, and the pilot is called a "captain." There is talk about what to do in the unlikely case of an emergency.

In any event, flying along as part of the unit, at ease but paying attention, I thought I'd watch a movie on the screen in the back of the seat in front of me.

The available selection had titles I had never heard of, and I thought,

Why not pick one of them? So many of the well-known pictures nowadays turn out so bad. There was this item, *Nobody*. The title meant nothing to me, but its star, its ragged face, was Bob Odenkirk, an actor I like. His face was suffering because for most of *Nobody* Odenkirk, as Hutch, is beaten up and treated badly. His life becomes a constant emergency in which his energy and identity are pitted against the unkind world. He plays an apparently plain family man (with a fond son and a lovely wife). But his inertia is broken one night when hoodlums enter his home intent on taking money, or whatever. And Hutch rather lets this happen. You can say he is timid or circumspect—afraid of violence, or simply a nobody, like us.

He regrets his reticence enough to recall that once upon a time he was an enforcer, an assassin or discourager hired by respectable intelligence agencies. Odenkirk was Arnold? So many white lies hover over this scheme: intelligence agencies, for instance, when "unintelligence" might be more credible; the notion that this expert in violence has become meek and dull without undue medication; or the proposition that the role is fit for Bob Odenkirk and his bitter, victimized view of life. He is not an actor who has faced the world with AK-47s in his hands. So *Nobody* draws on a forlorn but ubiquitous fantasy, known to every stooge sitting in seat 12D or whatever, that his compressed, dutiful, and uncomfortable service might be cover for valiant outlawry. Ready to open fire.

Nobody may not be "good," as in a seal of approval, but it has stayed with me long after landing. In an hour and a half Hutch takes the wicked world of Russian gangsters apart, not just to protect his family and innocent women on the subway, but to get into an orgy of firing. I sat there in 12D entranced by the flare and the rattle of Hutch's gunfire as he trashed every enemy he could see. You can say that *Nobody* is not really a war film, but tread carefully. We typecast oligarchs and thugs from Russia now in a way that would be vetoed if those guys were Welsh or Zulu. It is a film in which the humble and abashed viewer is granted the liberty of opening fire endlessly in his dreams. At 34,000 feet, my trigger fingers were flexing to keep up with Hutch's kill count: it was like playing *Call of Duty: World at War* as a video game with one's son and being wiped out by his nonchalant speed.

And even if the quantity of licensed firearms in the United States is unseemly (and evidence of fear in the home of the brave), I do not believe your everyday JetBlue flight is crowded with shootists. It's just that in the darkness of the enclosed flight (perversely shutting out the glow of the West) so many of us could jerk off in our minds at the glee of opening fire.

Here is a structure in understanding that is vital to the disconnect movie has always indulged between what we do in life and what we might want to do, despite knowing that the dream could be dangerous, and illegal. It has never seemed coincident that films and guns are both shot, and that they concern contained explosions. It may seem an awkward proposition, but in taking a picture and firing a weapon there is a level of sexual metaphor, a kind of self-expression that is heady but risky. Both cases contain an attempt to take over reality, to make it our play. Our sexual explosions are, similarly, plans to possess nature and a moment with our desire. The passion of one seems more creative or wholesome than the urge in the other. But sometimes the results are as mixed as motives. So often the storm of power is in play. That affinity goes all through this book, and we may find it embarrassing having to reconsider this beside such things as the Second Amendment and the philosophy that Americans believed they were so surrounded with dangers that they had to be armed. And ready to open fire. "Opening" fire is so suggestive and liberating. Makes you feel good to be alive.

I understand that some readers may be perturbed by the equation of sexuality and shooting. So I will offer the link in a broader way: Suppose shooting is an expression of individualism and the urge to be oneself. Is it just a spurt of ego or the liberty in which a man can stand up? That is where movie has been so influential, for it has made shooting a source of fun for people who would not think of belonging to the National Rifle Association or indulging in open carry. And there we are again with this pickle: that we who hope to be enlightened and unarmed can make six-shooters of our fingers in a trice for our kids.

Do moms do that as easily as dads? One vacuum in war films is the nonparticipation of women. This is not constant, and I will make as much as I can of women at war. But isn't it extraordinary that so popular a genre should depend so little on female agency? We should not forget the possibility that wars are declared and fought as a blunt projection of male necessity, with rape as one of the regular spoils of war.

As such, we are at the brink of asking ourselves about the deepest gendered impulse in film itself. More or less, the history of movies indulged a pattern of our longing (or the male urge) to see sex and violence. The various censorship measures meant to restrain that withered in the sixties and seventies. It seemed as if we might have our fair share of both. But that didn't work out. Sexuality on movie screens has receded: Was it an embarrassment to large family audiences? Were ardent filmmakers disappointed that the new orgasms (or last tangos) didn't change the world or their endorphins? Was the access to tenderness and intimacy against the manly grain? Did pornography (a generally power-driven genre) take up the slack? But violence has known no limits, and the computerization of film fantasy has become its energy and its madness.

Back at 34,000 feet, I finished *Nobody* with fatigue but was sure that the busy film had met its targets. The carnage of its story "worked," and one could conclude the film, in some exhausted faith, at how law and order are meant to operate. So why not have retired enforcers as avenging angels (and flight attendants)—even if the face of Bob Odenkirk (or Saul Goodman) is not quite angelic?

Still, I was surprised to discover that *Nobody* had done so well. Costing $16 million, *Nobody* had earned over $56 million. That prosperity affected Odenkirk in ways beyond simply acting in a hit: he was a coproducer on the film, which meant he had decided to accommodate its brutal subject matter.

Now, here's the bonus of coincidence—like that phaeton stopping where Princip would see the Duke. Heading into San Francisco, my Jet-Blue flight was crossing the West on Thursday, October 21, 2021. I don't think we got into the airspace of New Mexico, but we came close. And the day of my flight—even the moment—was the one on which 34,000 feet beneath us, a mishap occurred on the set of a film called *Rust*, in Bonanza

City, New Mexico, when the actor (and coproducer on the project) Alec Baldwin accidentally fired off a prop gun and killed the movie's director of photography, Halyna Hutchins. Also, the director, Joel Souza, was injured.

I won't explore what happened on *Rust*, a matter destined for the courts, where Baldwin's role as a coproducer could be more significant than his inadvertent firing of a gun. But the revelation of elaborate protocols on film sets for the use of guns and ammunition reminded us of how much firing there is in modern cinema—which means that those explosions are reckoned to bring us gratification and a kind of fulfillment.

After the *Rust* accident, there was talk of real guns and props, hot guns and cold. At the same time, news was breaking of a surge in "ghost guns" in America, weapons assembled out of spare parts purchased online, without serial number or old-fashioned identification. Wild guns meant to express desire and need.

It was in the sixties and seventies—before computer imagery, but thanks to the new craft of implanted blood and membrane sachets—that fictive bodies began to erupt to satisfy another desire. You can trace that in *Bonnie and Clyde* (1967) and the films of Sam Peckinpah. Morsels of wild flesh in the air, all approved, but seldom splashes of ejaculate. If that contrast is indelicate, which item is most problematic, the coming or the going? Perhaps those questions require cross-examining our own pleasure and the medium's mix of peril and entertainment. The film business will protest that such solemnity spoils the fun. But for a century that business has gotten away with murder.

We are accomplices, screen gazers who play the tricky game of watching immediacy from a safe distance. It's a matter of technical superiority, the essential military advantage. In his 1955 novel, *The Deer Park*, Norman Mailer has his hero reminisce about his air force days:

Sometimes on tactical missions we would lay fire bombs into Oriental villages. I did not like that particularly, but I would be busy with technique, and I would dive my plane and drop the jellied gasoline into my part of the pattern. I hardly thought of it any other way. From the air, a city in flames is not a bad sight.

That was Korea, but the stress on technique covers so many other theaters.

This is not an aside: you have to ask what your hand is thinking reaching for a gun, and what provides satisfaction.

4

BLACK HAWK DOWN

Here is a favorite, a film that leaves one feeling like Mailer's flier in *The Deer Park*, so many thousands of feet above the pattern of life below. Warn Somalia.

Say "black hawk down" and feel the ambiguity. You can hear it as the urgent report of a loss, one of ours plucked out of the sky. But the cry can be exultant, too. It could come from an untrained fellow on the African street who got off a lucky shot with his antique antitank gun, and shouts with triumph, "Black hawk down!" as the whirlybird spirals to the ground. Of course, the phrase goes both ways: a black hawk may be a trusted scout, or a bird of prey. Isn't it poetry to call a helicopter a "Black Hawk" instead of a Sikorsky UH-60 (estimated unit cost $5.9 million)? Hasn't war always been a breeding ground for poetry (and engineering), as if creativity is spurred by fear? Wasn't that helicopter named after a warrior chief in the Sauk nation from the nineteenth century?

In every taking aim there is an implicit desire for accuracy and lucidity. That can amount to poetry. To make a movie is to frame and focus, to select and arrange, to fix an instant; and in that pressure of exactness, eloquence and meaning may emerge. It is like aiming a gun and hoping to hit the target. The accuracy can be beautiful. Just read this passage slowly, and feel its heartbeat of intent:

His head low, he swung the gun on a long slant, down, well and ahead of the second duck, then without looking at the result of his shot he raised the gun smoothly, up, up ahead and to the left of the other duck that was climbing to the left and as he pulled, saw it fold in flight and drop among the decoys in the broken ice. He looked to his right and saw the first duck a black patch on the same ice. He knew he had shot carefully on the first duck, far to the right of where the boat was, and on the second, high out and to the left, letting the duck climb far up and to the left to be sure the boat was out of any line of fire. It was a lovely double, shot exactly as he should have shot, with complete consideration and respect for the position of the boat, and he felt very good as he reloaded.

I know, you are ready to sigh for those birds, put the book down, and abandon Julia Child's recipe for roast duck—and this is just page 5 from what for its first seventy pages is a piercing novel about military paranoia, the besieged mind-set of an old soldier. Don't read past that, because Hemingway's *Across the River and Into the Trees* (1950) then introduces a fantasy heroine who reduces the aiming to dreamy blindness. Tough colonels and earnest authors can turn to mush. But understand the passion for order and prowess that exists in shooting.

IF I PRESENTED YOU WITH AN OUTLINE MAP OF THE WORLD—THE CONTI-nents and the countries as unnamed shapes—could you find Somalia? Do you have a secure idea of how "old" Somalia is and what life was like there, centuries before Christ or Netflix? If that seems facetious, can you appreciate how easily "ancient" and "primitive" are steps in our dark? Do you take refuge in the theory that Somalia is somewhere on the eastern shoulder of Africa, troubled, unstable, a likely hot spot for *Madam Secretary* or the latest American administration?

Now consider 1993 in Somalia. Do you know what was happening, beyond the "instability" that we often assign to remote places in an imperialist and racist way? Not that Somalia believed it was remote. It felt sure it was the center of activity that might quickly be converted into "action"—that movie scan of life. Of course, thirty years later, with everything passing on, it's hardly useful to spend the time it would take to understand what Somalis felt in 1993. Haven't we given up on researching and fretting over what was happening there in '93, or a thousand years before that? During the Second World War, it was called "British Somaliland," though it was occupied by the Italians.

There was more turmoil or political conflict within Somalia in 1993 such that the rest of the world—or the parts prepared to take responsibility—called it "a failed state." Somalia had split, north and south, and Mohamed Farah Aidid and Mohamed Ali Mahdi were rivals for control. There was fighting between their factions, and what communiques call human distress. So the United Nations passed resolutions (733 and 746) calling for humanitarian relief and for restored order in the country.

That was an urge to redirect the nation, to give it a new, or positive, story. So long as the positivism matched Western requirements. But see how that feeling comes close to the desire to make a new movie out of a muddled world. The military impulse often aims at the appearance of order instead of untangling the confusion of a situation. Soldiers say they can't be expected to do that difficult thing. So in a movie you're going to get the show in two or three tidy hours. That's a package for denying that some issues require many years. Thus movie narrative structure has done a lot to dictate the popular sense of history.

Aidid challenged Pakistani troops who were under UN charge, and thus American forces (Rangers and Delta Force) were inserted in Somalia, leading to a raid on the capital, Mogadishu, that was meant to isolate and extricate advisers to the troublesome Aidid. This climaxed in October 1993 in an action where nineteen US troops and over a thousand Somalis were killed. That was hectic and regrettable; the United Nations soon withdrew its forces, largely at the behest of an embarrassed President Clinton.

In other words, *Black Hawk Down.*

I love this film, but I marvel at my pleasure over its clarity and its absurd grace.

I have never done any military service; I have not aimed, let alone fired, a gun. (I only responded to the prose of Hemingway's Colonel Richard Cantwell at dawn in the marshland near Venice.) But that aspiration is strong and a current learned in childhood.

I like to believe I am averse to physical cruelty or force of arms. I am timid every day and climatically apprehensive. At the same time, I was born in February 1941, in a London being bombed, and I was told by everyone in my childhood that it was a good thing "we" had won the war. Because, otherwise . . . ? To the extent that I understand the political situation in Somalia leading up to October 1993, I suspect it was a dubious thing that United States troops were sent there ready to fight. It has been a steady part of our education to weigh the impertinence of sophisticated white armies going all over the world to impose order on countries of color, other languages, and dissenting views of history.

Yet I am always thrilled at this movie's view of Black Hawk helicopters flying low over the shoreline of Somalia, basking in the late sunlight and the authority of overview. There is a kinship between the advance of those Hawks and the tide of time and story. It is the motion in cinema that prompts emotion. And when the time comes, I will be gratified by the way a shooting can take out an enemy. He may be shot to pieces, in anguish, but I feel no pain, except theoretically. And that is only a minor offset to the contentment of firing accurately and being adept enough to counter an ambush and protect my buddies. Those men who had no life for me to know or share in. Except as being a vicarious member of their group, the unit.

We may be fighting for "liberty"; that has a good track record. But in going into battle we will pick up the same weapons and the clothing—the garb we call uniform, as if aware that service involves the dissolution of independence and becoming part of the group project. *Black Hawk Down* will end up rueful about what Americans were doing in Somalia. But it never backs down from its constitutional faith in the unit, and its avoidance of responsibility.

I am talking about accomplishment or prowess, things that seem far away in mundane life—though I can come close to its well-being if I write a clear sentence or just type out a word correctly on my keyboard. I sometimes think of the keypad as the inward model of my being, my weapon, and admire its chance of targeted accuracy—take aim and fire, as opposed to numb fingers reducing "vicissitude" to "vcisssiturd." That example seems foolish, but small details of accuracy are close to our pulse in the new age of technology. Trying to live up to the ethos of our best machines, we take quiet pride in getting our password right.

Are you the same way?

AFTER THE ACTUAL GUNFIRE, *BLACK HAWK DOWN* BEGAN AS A BOOK, SUBTItled *A Story of Modern War*, written by Mark Bowden and published in 1999. This is a coherent narrative of the frenzied events in Mogadishu. Not that Bowden served there, but he was a journalist who researched the action carefully and talked to many of its participants. His book was a finalist for the National Book Award. Then the producer Jerry Bruckheimer purchased the film rights and oversaw the complicated scripting process. Several people did drafts or versions—from Bowden himself to Steven Zaillian and Stephen Gaghan—but the final credit went to Ken Nolan, who had lasted the longest of the writers. Even so, the film is about action, so its authorship can also be found in how it was cast, set, shot, and edited. Many of the best films are "written" as a plan ready to be executed. Or a weapon waiting to be fired.

Ridley Scott was engaged to direct *Black Hawk Down*. There may have been argument on who should get that job, but the decision now seems obvious, as if to say, well, Scott was the man for the job—or for any tough job. He was the son of an army officer. By 2001, when the film was made, Scott had acquired a reputation for getting difficult and novel adventure pictures done. That did not mean his every picture had been a commercial success, or flawless. But they had been delivered, and many had been widely enjoyed and appreciated: from 1977 to 2001 he had made *The Duellists*; *Alien*; *Blade Runner*; *Legend*; *Someone to Watch Over Me*; *Black Rain*; *Thelma & Louise*; *1492: Conquest of Paradise*; *White Squall*; *G.I. Jane*; *Gladiator*; *Hannibal*—those are his films before *Black Hawk Down*. His flag hangs in the regimental hall.

I like many of those movies, but I appreciate how their reliability and fluency amount to impersonality. Anyone would appreciate Scott's capacity for showing brave men in dangerous action—*Blade Runner, Gladiator, Black Rain*—but he is as comfortable watching women in similar situations: *Alien, Thelma & Louise, G.I. Jane*—without reaching for a "feminist" label. In most of these films, there is a respect for service and a code of honor; the unit has a certain glamour. That honor is the obligation that consumes the two hussars (Keith Carradine and Harvey Keitel) in the superb and demented *The Duellists*.

Scott does not reveal himself, or believe in that egotistical need. You cannot watch his films and sum up the nature of the man. Rather, it is as if he has decided that exposure is as foolishly vain in directing a film as it would be in carrying out a military mission. Decades later, with Scott at eighty-six, I don't feel I know him, or that he needs to believe I know him. There have been directors in the history of film as self-effacing as they are efficient and open to nearly anything—Michael Curtiz, who made *The Charge of the Light Brigade* and *Casablanca*; William Wyler, who did *Mrs. Miniver* and *The Best Years of Our Lives*, and Ridley Scott. So Scott handles *Black Hawk Down* in a way fitting two of its characters—Sam Shepard as General Garrison at the US base trying to reconcile the plans with the emergency radio messages of mishaps from the city; and Tom Sizemore as the sergeant hacking his way out of the labyrinth of Mogadishu. Those men are unsentimental and committed: they mean to get a dirty job done as well as possible, and they do not reflect on whether they and the men should be there in Mogadishu.

They had faith in maps of that city, in Intelligence, and their orders; they know not to trust strangers; and they will fight with those that confront them. But Mogadishu is a city like all the others a soldier has to fight through, and not so different from the Normandy town in *Saving Private Ryan* (1998) where Sizemore played another sergeant trying to fall back on a crucial bridge. There is a code of service in which the sergeant is a saving link, a model, and Sizemore could be that man in many circumstances. This is an attitude to cinema that sees the sergeant as a kind of director, expert and committed, yet uninterested in the nature of the mission. This works very well, and leaves us feeling that battle is mere weather.

Filming a battle is so demanding—you have to manage the men, the actors and the extras, the gunfire and the explosions, as things seen and heard; the uniforms and the equipment; and you have to organize those elements so that the tender audience at home or in the dark can follow the whole thing, and be excited, without having one hair out of place. I am talking about the congruency of danger and safety that affects every combat film.

Black Hawk Down concerns a failed mission by our guys, and it is faithful to what happened and went awry. But take a step back and recognize how (like any movie) the order of battle resembles the process and the scheduling of a film. To make *Black Hawk Down* required the correct uniforms and equipment; it called for a daily schedule where streets, extras, costumes, and gunfire were all on call; the explosions had to be vivid but safe; it necessitated physical damage to its characters, but not to its players—the rhetoric of blood and body parts—while making sure that everyone on call got a hot lunch and the proper rest periods. To say nothing of the budgetary provisions: invading Mogadishu and doing it on film both had bottom lines, with clerical officials nagging at the loose edges of infrastructure and per diems. In short, the mishap of the Mogadishu raid looks and feels tidy and brilliant.

I have seen *Black Hawk Down* half a dozen times. I do not watch it because I support war, or recognize it as a trenchant antiwar statement. But something is gratified by the film's resolve to make shape out of disorder. The operation in Mogadishu turns into a miscalculation, with two helicopters down, some men isolated or lost in the dense city, and an overriding urge to get the hell out without leaving casualties or prisoners, and doing your best to keep some scrap of honor intact. Not that this is a rowdy patriotic film that asserts Americans are the best of men. Let's settle for their dogged instinct for cleaning house after spoilage. In defeat, the American effort seems to succeed.

Black Hawk Down is a job for which the shooting script has to be translated into filmed shots cut together so that they are lucid and frightening without being hideous. We are talking about grave wounds, the cause of death, and shattered bodies, and Scott and his crew must deliver those things without being what is called stomach-turning or beyond the limit of an R rating. He cannot upset civilian ticket buyers so deeply as to frighten them away. But he must stay true to the experience of veteran soldiers who may see the picture and be wary with their approval. After all, the army provided Black Hawks for the picture and took the cast in hand for a week of basic training so that the actors could get a taste of esprit de corps. The army had confidence that even with this famous fuck-up event, Ridley Scott was going to make you proud of the armed forces in which you had no intention of serving.

I will not glamorize the army, its leaders, or its servants. But I am trying to acknowledge the appeal of authority and action in war films. I need to see how it works in my own response to this film. The American mission quickly breaks apart: Was it always naive or unrealistic? It becomes hard for General Garrison back at headquarters to understand what is happening. There are Somalis in the streets who are terrified onlookers, men, women, and children who have no choice but to live in the cockpit city; and there are soldiers of Aidid who long to bring down helicopters and kill Americans (because these visitors have had the temerity to invade their home).

In 1993, let me ask you, was Mogadishu a city of 1.3 million people, 2.8 million, or 5.5 million? I didn't know the answer until I looked it up, and I don't expect better of you. Mogadishu was simply a place, a question mark, a warren for impoverished people trying to survive, whether Stalingrad or Bramley End, the fictional village in the 1942 film *Went the*

Day Well? That description fits most invaded communities. And they are places you do not want to be, even if the fifty or so feet separating you from the movie screen may seem like an effective buffer.

As I began watching *Black Hawk Down*, I had difficulty identifying many of the soldiers, or the actors. I recognized Sam Shepard and Tom Sizemore, but most of the guys wore helmets and goggles, so they felt identical or interchangeable. I gave up on distinguishing Ewan McGregor, Josh Hartnett, Ewen Bremner, Hugh Dancy, Jason Isaacs, Tom Hardy, William Fichtner, Eric Bana, and many others. This is not to say those actors give insipid or invisible performances. They all move as intently as footballers in a key game. But the movie believes in their uniformity and the way they are atoms in a body of water or iron. Isn't that the imperative of corps ideology? Isn't it the impacted anonymity of ourselves, the audience?

The implications of this condition are immense. For they suggest linkage between the technology of movie and the fantasizing or the conscience behind war.

But what do we know or care about Somalia, and its need for humanitarian assistance? Just as you may have been uncertain over the population of Mogadishu (go for two million eight), you are likely confused over what is happening in Somalia today, thirty years after the failed raid on Mogadishu. How can we care about every city and failed state? The situation in Mogadishu may be changed now, as we keep watching the movie. But if we have given up the ghost about concern for Somalia, that is a disgrace. It leaves the feeling that the movie was never more than a game.

Do we care about the picture more than the place? Is *Black Hawk Down* an imperialist gesture? Was the justification for the troubles in Somalia toward the end of the twentieth century that they should provide for the pleasure of *Black Hawk Down*? How do we live with that grim conclusion? This feels outrageous, but if I say "Somalia," don't you think of this movie?

You are probably not surprised to hear that the movie was spun off as a first-person shooter video game, *Delta Force: Black Hawk Down*, developed by NovaLogic and sold for Microsoft Windows. It did well, though not as well as some other combat games. Still, you should digest this approbation from *Maxim* magazine:

> Drink in your fill of military realism in crowded, confusing war zones where you can drown in rivers, kill civilians, and partake in friendly fire—just like we did—before heading to boot camp to apologize. If that's not enough carnage, you can also engage in 32-player (50 on Xbox Live) online deathmatch missions, which is technically twice the bloody chaos of *Halo 2*. See, foreign policy can be fun!

BREAKING NEWS: BEING BRANDED WITH A FAMOUS ADVENTURE MOVIE HAS not brought rest or quiet progress to Somalia. By October 2021, it was revealed that the US and its CIA were still caught up in that country, doing whatever they could to contest al-Shabab, "one of Africa's deadliest militant groups," and a branch of al-Qaeda. On October 25, the *New York Times* ran a lengthy article, starting on the front page but extending to two inside pages, on the new troubles in Somalia. I read it carefully, but it was not easy to follow. I felt that labels were being employed to cover journalistic hedging. The *Times* story had this subheading: "Long After 'Black Hawk Down' Disaster, U.S. Battles Offshoot of Al Qaeda."

I'm not complaining: few other papers attempted to be as thorough, or aware, and the story made it clear that no one had reason to relax over Somalia. Not that the causes of the upset were examined. So many angry indigenous peoples are still written off as bloody-minded extras instead of living characters.

Of course, it would have seemed comical for Hollywood to do *Black Hawk Down* again. *Been there, done that* would be every moviegoer's refrain. In the years after the classic film, Ridley Scott (a knight since 2003) had turned his eye to other battles—*American Gangster, Robin Hood, Prometheus*, and still valiant with *The Last Duel* (2021, even if without much audience). He seemed forever embattled and still an authoritative commander of big action movies. He might smile to think his films now stand as markers, not just box-office events but signposts for digesting history. Yet he did have what seemed like an elderly episode with *House of Gucci* where command gave way to lavish lack of control. Even our best captains can be secret nervous wrecks and closeted laughingstocks.

5

IN THE HEART OF NATURE

There is something natural about war. Or beyond reason. Why are eggs the way they are, not spherical, not oval, but asymmetrical? As if they are people, or beautiful? If eggs seem insignificant or whimsical, or unworthy of war, just ask yourself about the whole damn purpose of the Great War—I mean the reasoning behind 1914–18—to get a better grasp on how triviality or silliness can rule the day. Don't let war get you down. If all is lost, guard your sense of humor and remember that eggs are good eating.

Lilliput and Blefuscu are small islands in the south Indian Ocean. They are only eight hundred yards apart, close enough for shouting contests, though the inhabitants of the two islands are six inches tall, which reduces the noise level. Both islands are egg-shaped, so the two nations are rivals in many aspects of ovoid thought. This is from *Gulliver's Travels* (1726, a key year in the development of the slave trade), in which Jonathan Swift marveled at the human habit of conflict.

What has the slave trade got to do with this? What has it not got to do with?

In a hotel room in Japan, a French woman notices the arm of her Japanese lover as he lies in bed asleep. This seems ordinary, but then the film cuts to the rhyming arm of her German lover, a soldier killed fifteen years earlier. How can our woman have two arms and two lovers in her head? That was *Hiroshima Mon Amour* (1959), where the title of the film urged us to scramble seemingly opposed strands: terrible and lovely, the conjunction that movies had uncovered.

On the screen, when two people look at each other, we may imagine harmony or love at first sight, as if the act of seeing generates fondness. That exists in the nature of crosscutting, or film's capacity for going from one wonder to another quicker than we can close our eyes. So I am imply-ing, in this chapter, that the tale of Lilliput and Blefuscu may be enriched by a glimpse of *Hiroshima Mon Amour*. In sentences, reading traces the line of a scene. But movie puts unalike things together instantly, so we are driven to find a link, if only in the poetic subconscious.

There can be violence in this scheme, and not just the trite impact of shock cuts from horror or suspense. Beneath that, there is a tension within movies between flow and passing time and our realization that this flow can stop short, dead in its tracks, and suffer the drastic beginnings of an-other flow. That dialectic of cutting, or the potential for interruption, can be more decisive than any war events being depicted.

Or put it this way: if every cut reminds us of violence or warring urges, then every shot is like a breath of peace. Tolstoy might have worked this out: that cinema did war and peace so many times in every second.

Eggs seem alike. We say we can't tell one from the other—apart from that funny variation in their ends. But that can start an argument. Think of two faces in love—Alfred and Klara in *The Shop Around the Corner*, or James Stewart and Margaret Sullavan. That is a war film? Of course not, but some lovers may battle all their life. Marriage knows no peace; it thrives on disagreement, like a boat fighting waves. So while working together in the same Budapest gift store Alfred and Klara are forever at odds, the least likely mates. Yet each of them, privately, is writing letters to a stranger they believe they do love. And the strangers are . . . ? Yes, those crossed purposes are a familiar trope in fiction. So the adroit direc-tor Ernst Lubitsch will bring them together at last with a lovely piece of cinema. That was 1941, and Alfred and Klara are still in love even if their players are dead.

Leave space in your minds for war films where, as the bombs burst in air and things get worse, friends and lovers fence with talk or kissing silences. Even combatants can be absent-minded. I speak as an egg scrambled around the moment of Dunkirk, when parents might have known better. But some of us can't say no to risk.

Early in the movie *Pierrot le Fou* (1965) we are at a listless Parisian party for a jaded smart set. There is an air of thunder and woe in the salon, as if the unease felt by our protagonist Ferdinand (Jean-Paul Belmondo) is spreading. He believes that things are over—his marriage, Paris, the principles of sentiment, his contemplation of Velázquez, and the idea of calm.

Again, you are growing anxious, saying this does not sound like a war film.

Wait and see. Anxiety is natural. War is there in dawn, the smell of flowers, or scenes from a marriage. Have you ever seen a baby being born—a soul escaped! The disruption! Have you been caught up in a quarrel over scrambled eggs and the contrary ways of making that subtle dish?

There is a woman at the Paris party holding her drink, propped against the wall, her dress pulled down so that her breasts and necklace are hanging there, challenging anyone to notice. This is not an orgy, just a disconsolate diagram from a children's book on what orgies might have been, once upon a time.

Then Ferdinand meets an older man, short, implacable, his iron hair in tight curls, his gaze taking aim through his dark glasses. He feels like a prisoner, yet he might be an unnoticed Gatsby at the party. Ferdinand gets in conversation with this man. A translator—another wan woman—says he is a film director, named Samuel Fuller.

There was a real Samuel Fuller. This is probably him.

Ferdinand asks, "What is movie?" in a general way, sniffing the thunder and the smoke from Fuller's cigar.

The director replies—he announces this, as a sphinx might utter—

"Film is like a battleground. . . . Love . . . Hate . . . Action . . . Violence . . . Death . . . In one word, Emotion."

Fuller was five feet six, but you felt he could be dangerous. He began as a journalist, and he served in Europe in the Second World War in the 1st Infantry Division. That prompted his string of war pictures: *The Steel Helmet* and *Fixed Bayonets!* (about Korea, made during that war, but shot in Griffith Park in Los Angeles); *Run of the Arrow* (starting with the last shot fired in the American Civil War, where Rod Steiger is passionately rebellious); *Merrill's Marauders* (the war in Burma); and *The Big Red One*, where Lee Marvin plays a sergeant with Fuller's career record.

In placing Samuel Fuller in *Pierrot le Fou*, director Jean-Luc Godard meant to signal that this love story could be a battleground. Ferdinand leaves his wife to go off with the babysitter, an old flame, Marianne (Anna Karina). This seems like a renewed amour yearning to depart from life's drab norms. But there is a warning: Ferdinand is a respectable name, but Marianne calls him Pierrot all the time in a way that starts to make him angry. "Pierrot le fou," she says early on, as if guessing their rapture will terminate.

So in love, she despairs of him and, in a muddled spree, amid fragments of unexplained criminal/political warfare, they both end up dead. (It's their way of being together.) Their voices still whisper of shared bliss (and Godard and Karina had ended their own marriage as the film was made), but conflict was their love bed. Very soon there will be weapons, a corpse here and there, and daubs of blood.

As Ferdinand and Marianne run away from Paris they go deep into the rapture of southern France. You feel the warmth, even if that's impossible. They reach a deserted shore and live there for a while, growing sunburned and disillusioned as they sing and dance. He reads and writes; she walks the beach lamenting, "What am I to do? I don't know what to do." They are running aground on his inwardness, while she is embittered and dangerous without things to do. He is a philosopher, she the assassin: so many marriages know this seesaw. In a perfect place, a kind of vengefulness builds. Eggs with misfit ends.

Don't minimize these roots of narrative battle. From the end of the nineteenth century onward the audience was exposed to a rush of film that sang of conflict as the way of getting us to keep watching, to see what would happen next, to see who wins. You can find that conflict in prior entertainments—the stage, an opera, a novel, a poem, or a joke. But only tiny minorities were exposed to those forms. Then appreciate the drastic transformation in a medium seen by "everyone" and as graphic as "photorealism." The sudden stress on attention in movies was ruthless and we called it suspense, or matters of life and death. Something like war.

With *The Birth of a Nation* (1915) audiences were agitated to see whether the white women would keep their virtue intact; would the little colonel carry the day on a battlefield; and could the Klan riders arrive in time to preserve the South? (Here is the slave trade again.) Audiences were seduced by the breathless action, the battle for survival, all as heightened as edited photographs. When so much seemed lifelike, it could be hard to recognize how life had been warped or omitted. For close to fifty years, in the name of suspense, enthusiasts ignored what *The Birth of a Nation* was about. We were keeping pace with the film's engine, not assessing its destination.

That empire began with movies in theaters, where they lasted in awe and dominance for about fifty years. That yielded to television, which inhaled so much more material. Moviegoers who had seen a couple of pictures a week could now accumulate that time in one night of TV. Couch time might not seem as well spent as being in a theater, though maybe *Gunsmoke*, *The Fugitive*, and *I Love Lucy* were not so different from classic cinema's dreams (just faster and more codified). Suspense was the consistency still (Could Lucy bamboozle Desi? Would Richard Kimble stay free?), so audiences took sides, picking the good guys from the baddies, and enlisting.

As if history is only sides. Did this concentration on oppositions smother a different tendency? One that wondered if conflict might be secondary as a rhythm in human discourse? One that saw how the shape of an egg came from the hen's labor? Wasn't there a level of existence where imitation, fusion, and pretending were as intriguing as the dance called "versus"? It's not easy to describe this sensibility quickly—it may grow on you in the course of the book. Keep faith with passages of uncontested existence, of being there instead of having to win while you are there. Recollect how during the Great War, Matisse painted enchanting impressions of the view through a window, and don't reproach him for being a lightweight. *The Shop Around the Corner* is not a war movie, though it was made during a world war, to remind us of the value of small follies. And it pretended to be in Budapest, a place closer to peril than Culver City.

We are coming up to a section on film and the Great War (the First World War), and while that war was too early for the newsreel coverage that might have stopped it, there have been many story films proud about uncovering the war as a huge and disastrous event. So this section can employ Chaplin's *Shoulder Arms*; King Vidor's *The Big Parade*; the movie of *All Quiet on the Western Front*; and even Kubrick's *Paths of Glory, Oh! What a Lovely War*, and Sam Mendes's *1917*.

But those films might not be sufficient. We should recall things written and observed under the influence of war—like some of the poetry, *Mrs. Dalloway*, Cocteau's *Thomas the Impostor*, Debussy and Ravel, and Louis Armstrong, the writing of Stefan Zweig and John Dos Passos, and even Henry Williamson. We should be interested in how the place of women altered as quickly as a gun being fired. And how attitudes changed with column after column of obituaries printed in the *Times*. How did that society (the most up-to-date there had ever been, it said) come to terms with loss? How could a rational sensibility accept that the encompassing war was inexplicable? Let me recommend a book that catches that dilemma.

Ford Madox Ford's *Parade's End* (a sequence of four novels) was published in the 1920s. He had served on the western front; he knew that war and fear had become staple subjects. So read this from *A Man Could Stand Up*, the third of the four novels in *Parade's End*. The book's leading character, Christopher Tietjens, is an unsettled man and an indecisive officer in the war, but a resolute observer. If you find Tietjens unheroic, recall that in the television adaptation of 2012 (scripted by Tom Stoppard and directed by Susanna White) he was played by Benedict Cumberbatch. There's a movie name to make you pay attention—not that this scene I'm talking about got into the TV version. Its ironic depth does not lend itself to urgent camera impact. But in being about opening fire, it helps disarm that romantic duck shoot from *Across the River and Into the Trees*:

> Nothing had much more impressed Tietjens in the course of even the whole war, than the demeanor of the soldier whom the other night he had seen firing engrossedly into invisibility. The man had fired with care, had come down to reload with exact drill movements—which are the quickest possible. He had muttered some words which showed that his mind was entirely on his job like a mathematician engrossed in an abstruse calculation. He had climbed back on to the parapet; continued to fire engrossedly into invisibility; had returned and reloaded and had again climbed back. He might have been firing off a tie at the butts!
>
> It was a very great achievement to have got men to fire at moments of such stress with such complete tranquility. For discipline works in two ways: in the first place it enables the soldier in action to get through his movements in the shortest possible time; and then the engrossment in the exact performance begets a great indifference to danger. When, with various-sized pieces of metal flying all round you, you go composedly through efficient bodily movements, you are not only wrapped up in your task, you have the knowledge that that exact performance is every minute decreasing your personal danger. In addition you have the feeling that Providence ought to—and very frequently does—specially protect you. It would not be right that a man exactly and scrupulously performing his duty to his sovereign, his native land and those it holds dear, should not be protected by a special Providence. And he is!

Not even a generous television adaptation would let that passage be read into the record, over shots of a pensive Cumberbatch and an empty-headed rifleman. To make "into invisibility" cinematic could crush it. That is a measure of the information automaton in movies where it is so hard to be casual. Everything we see seems chosen and approved. Still, Ford has grasped the numbing in war that can exist irrespective of declared "conflicts." This affects us all the time with movies. We may wonder whether Ilsa will go with Rick or Laszlo in *Casablanca*; we place our bets on the war game (the Allies to win in six?). But we get to care so little about the condition of North Africa, its sheltering sky, or its bemused indifference to a self-important "world war." No one with a speaking part in *Casablanca* is from that city. No one is of Morocco, or even on the road there.

This leads us to a film with a larger context of warfare, one that makes you think about the entire atmosphere of "Guadalcanal" instead of just the medals and the kill count. This is a film about battle, but it observes the field, too.

James Jones was seventeen when he enlisted in the army in 1939. He was posted to Fort Schofield on Oahu, in Hawaii, the setting for his novel *From Here to Eternity*, and after December 7 he was in the Pacific war, notably at Guadalcanal (an island in the Solomons), which turned into another novel, *The Thin Red Line*.

For the post-1945 generation, *From Here to Eternity* is a central experience, yet it has only a small flourish of battle when the Japanese planes descend on Pearl Harbor at the close of the story. The deeper struggle is between Private Robert E. Lee Prewitt and the US Army as he is hazed and victimized for not joining a regimental boxing team, the hobby of a lousy captain. This is the enlisted man against the system, with the Japanese as mere placeholders. There are thwarted love affairs between a sergeant and the rotten captain's wife (Burt Lancaster and Deborah Kerr), and Prew and a hostess/hooker in town (Montgomery Clift and Donna Reed). If you saw the film at the right age you are in its regiment forever, lined up for eternity. There is also Maggio, also known as Frank Sinatra, in the stockade, a rowdy scrap of doomed life force.

That stress on the love stories made a war picture more accessible for the female audience. Daniel Taradash's clever screenplay shifted the balance of the novel and handled many elements that had been thought unfilmable. What emerged in the film was the pattern of its love affairs and their prospect for a better society. We wanted those couples to be together.

Eternity the movie was a defining hit, establishing the war romance for guys nearly as much as for women. Jones was made forever, whether he liked it or not. He wrote *The Thin Red Line* eleven years later, and determined that it should be total combat. As such, in his mind, it was a completion of *Eternity*, and a vindication of the soldier's world. Prewitt becomes Private Witt, and Lancaster's Sergeant Warden is picked up as Sergeant Welsh. Still, I'm not sure that Jones (who died in 1977) would have been fully approving of Terrence Malick's film of *The Thin Red Line*, which opened in 1998.

The film begins in darkness with sounds of birds and insects in the jungle. We see a crocodile in the green scum on still water. A male voice wonders, "What is this war in the heart of nature?" The speaker is Witt, tanned and at ease on some Pacific island where he watches the natives play. He has gone away from the war—we never discover how—but he has been AWOL before in a gentle spirit of resistance. Then a patrol boat comes by and we realize that Witt will be arrested and restored to the army. We see him with Welsh, who is half-amused, half-despairing, over Witt. "In this world," the sergeant tells him, "a man himself is nothing. And there ain't no world but this one."

That warning is unanswerable, but the idea of a mysterious nature battling with human duty permeates the film. It also raises the point how in our society, a man—a good man—can be so poor or disadvantaged that the army may be his one chance in life. That is not the army's fault; it is a commentary on our larger aimlessness.

As played by Jim Caviezel, Witt is not so much a loner as a desert spirit, enlisted but aware how flimsy the schemes of war are beside the imperatives of nature. If this sounds fanciful, prepare for an uncannily pacific war film. Not that there won't be terror, gunfire, slaughter, and the moral exhaustion that comes with combat. But those spasms pass like rain.

Almost immediately, Witt is part of the amphibious landing in the Guadalcanal campaign, shot in Queensland in northern Australia. This war is self-important—isn't that the way of it?—but Malick insists on nature's indifference. There is a hill that has to be taken, long and steep, with Japanese bunkers embedded on its ridge. It is the reasonable opinion of Captain Staros (Elias Koteas) that it cannot be taken by frontal assault without the loss of too many of his men. "Sir, I must tell you that I refuse to obey your order," says Staros. This drives the insecure Colonel Tall to towering rage—and it permits Nick Nolte to give the most emphatic (and comic?) performance in the film, or even in his career. Tall is a humiliated buffalo, John Wayne without a regular script, confounded that reasoning disputes his orders. He is so fearful of being disobeyed.

Then there is the hill. In ravishing forward tracking shots we go up the slope like attackers, crouched in fear, and in that process we inhabit the lush grasses on the hillside, as if grass might become a subject of the film. Is this arty and botanical? I suspect some veterans have been uneasy with *The Thin Red Line*. War is not like that? Agreed, films are like films: that is their prison. But those skeptics will get their satisfaction. As the hill is duly taken (with a flanking movement), Malick gives us extended scenes of attack, with the Japanese being picked off and their bunkers turned into death traps. Good stuff.

We realize that the ridge was not just held by the Japanese; it was planted with them—but they are cadaverous, as if water has run out, leaving them crazed or stunned. They seem like distraught children with the American attackers. So they are wiped out. If you collect attack sequences in war films, this is one of the most sustained, beautifully photographed by Malick and John Toll, yet stricken with our wondering how such things get to be "beautiful." In all the frantic action, there are no heroes or villains. The battle is a storm in which individualism and motive come and go.

There is more than the hill and its grasses. It includes the blindingly colored parrots that watch the khaki soldiers; it is insects crawling across flat leaves; and even a disturbed snake that makes a Balanchine-like plié in the air as it goes AWOL. While the land and its wildness may be disturbed for a year or so, their kingdom will return. But the frenzied fighters, dead and alive, will depart, some in aircraft, some in long boxes. So "the thin red line" is not simply Kipling's ideal of infantry resilience and courage carrying the day against great odds. It sees man's war and the battle as fussy sparrows settling on the continental body of an elephant, or on nature itself.

Malick made another key decision. We know from *Eternity* that Jones was mindful of the women whom soldiers had left at home. The pathos in the first film was of two broken romantic relationships, with Kerr and Reed meeting for the first time, bittersweet, on the ship taking them back to the States after Pearl Harbor.

In *The Thin Red Line*, Private Bell (Ben Chaplin) will scout the last ascent up the hill and then be prominent in the winning assault. Not that the film attempts to raise him as a hero. Bell has a wife at home, somewhere in hinterland country where curtains stir in the breeze, but near the sea, too. It is as resonant a place as "home" when you are away from it. We see the couple together there in scenes of wordless rapture. Sexuality is at hand, but these are glimpses of love in which she fluctuates, like flame in the sunlight.

The wife is played by Miranda Otto, filmed with tender reverence. There is one shot of her at night where she looks at the space beside her in bed, and in the gunmetal gloom we are not sure if she is missing Bell. Or is she imagining another man asleep? There will be one of the most sensuous shots in cinema, of this woman in a swing, swaying across the wide screen, viewed from an upside-down camera. It sighs in ecstasy and downfall. So it is not entirely a surprise when Bell gets a letter: "Dear Jack, I've met an air force captain. I've fallen in love with him. . . . Forgive me, it just got too lonely."

Privates in the infantry know not to trust air force captains. And whereas war can seem like a fireplace for comradeship and us all being together, don't doubt the gravitation toward solitude. Bell wins and loses on Guadalcanal.

A war movie can uncover a degree of action, hand-to-hand, that never lets us forget our loneliness. In the finale, Witt is on a jungle patrol seeking to save his fellows by drawing off the Japanese. He is surrounded by silent enemies like accusing trees at a clearing. Instead of surrendering, he goes AWOL for the last time. His resignation ends the film. A thin red line may last a year in the jungle, but it's soon overgrown. The natural world is waiting for our indignant conflicts to subside, like the war in *Gulliver's Travels* between Lilliput and Blefuscu as to whether a boiled egg in its cup should be served with the small end up, or the big one.

Scholars say Jonathan Swift conceived his two egg islands in mockery of France and Britain and their humorless religious hostilities. So be it. But we should realize that in our history eggs have outlasted every fitful and pretentious religion that passed by.

Just make the best of life and hope for decent scrambled eggs, soft but firm, fluffy like clouds, to be eaten with a small spoon. The spoon is in your backpack, soldier, beside the bayonet.

II

HOSTILITIES

On how the sport of war turned into an industry,
and etiquette gave way to technology.

6

1914, SUMMER

Summer, the shared season, sprawled across Europe, sighing and shifting like someone asleep. Summer for the young when it seems to last forever, or when something deep in existence seems to hold us together, no matter what is threatening in the news. In both our world wars, there was a last season of peace, gloried in later as a time for picnics, taking out a punt, for cricket and caresses beneath the trees. If you are English—or French, or German, or Russian—your family probably lost some of its own in the years 1914–18, and your elders will have told you that the world had died, quietly then, or in a way that did not have to be noticed.

In August 1914, let us say, in some depth of rural France—in the Dordogne, within walking distance of the medieval marvel of Sarlat?—it is possible that a young farm laborer did not understand the looming state of war. He was planting winter vegetables and watching as the basic crop—the wheat, the corn—grew heavier and began to be promising. He was a citizen of the *campagne*, living in a hut on the farm; he had to pump water—so long as the drought stayed *normale*—and he existed without electricity. He cooked on a woodstove, and he ate the same every meal, except for Friday. He didn't know how to give a damn about any war, even if the French army had mobilized on August 1. That is what he had heard, from others who read a newspaper from time to time, reporting decisions and military impulses far away, in other countries that were like the stuff of legend. But the world was coming into being modeled by war.

We have to try to comprehend cultures and what they knew when. In the early 1970s, my wife and children and I had a few summers in the Dordogne in the stone house of a friend, a London doctor who had this getaway place. His house was next to a farm—the world of Farmer Cluzan, as we knew him. He was amiable and he was fond of our younger daughter. We would talk with him in our awkward French, and one night he had us to his farmhouse where his wife served a dinner for which every item had been grown or raised on his farm.

We got talking, and observed how in that area there were memorials to French resistance groups that had been rounded up and murdered by the Nazis. Oh yes, Cluzan said, the war. As English people we were sympathetic; we had had our war, too.

Ah, really, he wanted to know—out of curiosity, without any kind of superiority—"Was England in the war, too?"

This is not to fault Monsieur Cluzan or the attitudes in France. But in that August 1914, far closer to the heart of the nation than the Dordogne was to Paris, in Kennington at the Oval, people were watching cricket and in the way of small talk they might wonder if the season—the County Championship—could be played out in time before "hostilities" intervened, whatever they were. So spectators studied the nimble steps and decisive strokes of Jack Hobbs—the best batsman in the world—driving the red ball here and here, advancing on 2,697 runs for the season. Such a wonder. But the large outfield of the Oval was already being requisitioned for troop camps.

And as the players and the public tried to relax in the same summer, the thing called war was no more than an idea, caught between "Don't think it'll ever happen" and "Home before Christmas, mark my words."

"I mean, after all, Arthur, what's the ruddy war about? Can you tell me that?"

Arthur was at a loss then, but at Ypres he lost the right side of his face. Summer prevailed still, with its degrees of ignorance or unknowing.

But that sounds rather aggressively foreboding or superior, so full of later insight, when one thing to grasp about the Great War is that in the steady dullness of human society and intelligence, so little consequence was foreseen at the time.

One can't say "August 1914" now without the gravity of imminent tragedy. Barbara Tuchman and her book *The Guns of August* may be coming next, along with *Paths of Glory* and *Oh! What a Lovely War.* So take a few moments to appreciate how that August is just like your month now, wherever and whenever you are, with you trying to believe in the best, hoping for enough sunshine for a picnic after punting, with maybe a chance to swoon on the ground with that fellow you have been fancying.

The summer is a season of hoping more than knowing. If you look across the meadow, you may notice a line of horses and their harrows—Suffolk punches, I believe—turning over the ground for planting. Or are they the four horsemen of the apocalypse?

The most limiting trait in history and education is to deplore the stupidity of others. The trick is to see how stupidity works and to wonder whether any "error" exists, except in the minds of moralists.

By now, the absurdity that let the Great War happen is a model of mistake—and of the human race's weakness for disaster. Thus a series of airy treaties in Europe rested on the immense structure of armaments. Alliances are not in themselves pointless: we have lived decades now with the theoretical association of NATO to general advantage. And if it is not absurd, surely it is understandable that powerful industrial nations seeking respect from others should equip themselves with ships, aircraft, armies, and their human agents—whatever ingenuity can invent. It's reasonable (if far-fetched) to envisage a future world in which all the nations are united in a scheme of sharing and assistance. You can argue that August 1914 was an attempt to make that arrangement. But it turned into a lethal board game, the triggering of hostilities and causes that no general or prime minister understood better than their enlisted men.

Just leave enough space for this dangerous thought: the Great War happened because enough of us assented to it in our careless way.

An arcane scaffolding of consequences was poised in 1914 involving Serbia, Russia, Austria-Hungary, France, Germany, and Britain that would have them all at war in a matter of months. This booby-trap mechanism was set in motion by the nearly accidental assassination of the archduke and his wife in Sarajevo on June 28. This was a sign of how fringe souls may be as potent as emperors. What happened that summer was a weird assertion of the rights of the common man. I am not being facetious: 1914–18 is an experiment in regarding the unknown soldier as an illustrious or model figure. It was an experiment in liberty—a very risky enterprise—that became a prison.

It's natural for smart historians and writers to feel some satire in what happened in 1914, as an enactment of our studious foolishness. A. J. P. Taylor, a lively popular historian who seldom resisted the temptation to be surprising, proposed that the outbreak of the Great War had hinged on how the railway timetables of Europe had dictated the mobilization of armies. So many nations felt the urge to move first to avoid being caught lagging. Playfully, Taylor pointed to congestion in railway systems, but he was saying more profoundly, The bigger the army, the more natural mobilization becomes; so war draws closer.

If you're keeping big armies you have to give them something to do or they may plot against the state. At a smaller, poignant level, in his novel *Beware of Pity*, Stefan Zweig has a scene where a minor but serious failure to communicate (leading to the death of the story's agonized heroine) occurs because the telephone lines (quite new then) are jammed from the consternation over what had happened that day in Sarajevo.

Beware of Pity was published in 1939. Zweig had been an official pacifist during the war, though he served in the Austrian military archive. He was a famous author, seemingly settled. But then his world collapsed. Quitting Austria in 1939, he went to England, America, and finally Brazil, where he killed himself in 1942 in despair. His novel concerns a commonplace lieutenant who becomes involved with an appealing but partially paralyzed and neurotic young woman. The officer is never sure whether he loves the woman, or is simply sorry for her. The novel is a study of vacillation and our confusion over romantic urges. It leads to the woman's suicide, in part because the officer cannot reach her by phone.

Beware of Pity has been filmed twice: once badly, in Britain in 1946, with Albert Lieven as the officer and Lilli Palmer unduly lovely as the woman; and then in France, in 1979, far better, with Mathieu Carrière and Marie-Hélène Breillat. I hope others will try again, for the book resonates with our sentimental muddle: deciding you are in love (for keeps) can be as final and misguided as going to war. It is a large part of Zweig's talent or disposition that he reveled in human error. We deserve movies about people beset with doubt, for that is a respectable and humane condition. But, as you may have noted, the generality of movies is handicapped by characters sure they are doing the right thing. That is not simply their temperament. Chosen, scripted, directed, and posed, they are being aimed as if they were weapons. This is so often the energy that drives conflict.

7

ERROR AND HENRY RAWLINSON

Why pick on poor Rawlinson? I'm not sure if, even in Britain, a century after his role in military history, that many would have a ready answer—or lingering bitterness. Let's say he commanded what is still the worst day known to the British army. Not that there is any point in blaming him. He was a general in charge, but he was impelled by a command structure, a family tradition, a way of seeing war and the world, and the undeniable weight of his credentials. He was in the system, mobilized if not primed with foresight. The Great War is a landmark in modern history, but none of those who fought it was up-to-date.

Henry Seymour Rawlinson (1864–1925) was the son of Henry Raw-linson (1810–95). That father can be depicted as an eccentric stalwart of the British Empire, a mix of scholar and imperialist. By the age of seventeen, he had learned to speak Farsi well enough that the army sent him to Persia to drill and improve the troops. An English teenager running the show—you can feel Lawrence of Arabia ahead. But Henry Senior plunged ever deeper into the languages and the culture of what we would call the Middle East (that abiding label, loaded with blind imperial confidence). He was a soldier still, and he served honorably in the First Anglo-Afghan War (1839–42)—though I'm not sure how honor was defined there. To this day, the rules can be different and mysterious in Afghanistan.

Serving the East India Company and the army, he lived in Baghdad for years, pursuing his research. One of his papers was entitled "The Persian Cuneiform Inscription at Behistun, Deciphered and Translated, with a Memoir on Persian Cuneiform Inscriptions in General, and on That of Behistun in Particular." He was a president of the Royal Geographical Society, an occasional member of Parliament, and a steady foe to Russian aggrandizement in Afghanistan. In the portrait we have of him, he has an inquisitive, tender, humorous face. He seems like someone we would have enjoyed.

His son, the next Henry, does not have as endearing a look, but we should be cautious in such interpretations. In photographs, in middle age, he is losing his hair and adding a drooping mustache. He seems alert, and open to argument. It is not a stupid face, or blind. This is a thoughtful general with an air of caution.

He had been born on a country estate in Dorset. Educated at the military college at Sandhurst, he was a lieutenant in India at the age of twenty, and his father's influence then got him a plum job on the staff of General Lord Roberts, commander in chief in India. It was clear that young Rawlinson was set on a course of preferment, but that does not mean he lacked talent or good military instincts. He fought in the Omdurman campaign in the Sudan, and that's where he met Churchill—the two would become friends who went on painting holidays together.

It's hard to find traces of his character in the record, but there is no question about his proficiency. As well as in the war against the Mahdi (the tribal leader in the Sudan), he had distinguished service in the Boer War, and he was said to have acquired thorough and modern principles when he was engaged in military exercises. He was a colonel by 1901, plainly aimed at a responsible position if the gradual alignment of forces in Europe turned into war. Such officers were planning their careers. He was a major general by 1908, known for his enlightened policies with the army Staff College. More or less, that should have meant a thoughtful approach to the question of how a future war might be fought. In September 1914 (at fifty) he was appointed commanding general of the British 4th

Infantry Division in France. It was in that position that he would be field director for the Battle of the Somme.

This can be seen as an impressive record leading to an ideal appointment. Rawlinson had devoted his life to the army; he had served in action, and he had spent time considering the theory and practice of fighting. At the same time, against the Mahdi and the Boers, he had been involved in mobile skirmishing where boldness could carry the day. Not that he was simply given over to the role of cavalry and unexpected assaults. In 1915, at Neuve Chapelle, he had had success with a focused artillery bombardment clearing the way for infantry advances. That was the state of mind in which he approached the action on the Somme.

By that summer of 1916, the war on the western front had turned to stalemate. The uncertainty over its larger aims or purpose was caught up in the difficulty of finding a means of strategic conclusion. After the defeat of the initial German attack through Belgium at the Battle of the Marne in 1914, the threat of German victory in France had been alleviated. All across northern France strengthened battle lines had been set up, the basis of what we think of as trench warfare: secured lines, hard to penetrate, but not easily able to advance. It might even be that some cynics or enlightened observers could regard stalemate as a prelude to settlement. Especially if no one had a strong idea of what the war was about—unless it was the need to punish the hideous Germans for their cruel or ill-mannered treatment of the Belgians at the start of the war. There were stories that nuns had been raped and babies massacred. But there was already a public relations machine to create and broadcast those stories for their shock value. There were ugly events in Belgium: thousands of civilians were killed; the library at the university of Leuven was burned down; and there was lurid stress on sexual outrages. But beneath this reporting, there was a need to link the vast and mysterious war to Allied indignation at home. German nastiness was an establishing mood for a public who might be watching and thinking. So few earlier wars had been put to an electorate—or seen.

There should be a movie about young geniuses in PR caught up in that campaign. The Great War was beyond explanation, but it was the first war in which governments felt the need to justify the exercise to those who served.

The British army that Rawlinson was ready to lead was surprisingly new. In the summer of 1914, its strength had been not more than a hundred thousand. That is a sign of how British politicians doubted the likelihood or the gravity of war, let alone the need to deploy and fund enormous armies. There was hope and the expectation that a modest standing army could cope with whatever arose. But at the outbreak of war, the old warrior Lord Kitchener (the new secretary of state for war, aged sixty-four) became a beacon of advertising. There was a famous poster with the text "Britons Need You—Join Your Country's Army." But the words were minor next to the emphatic close-up image of Kitchener staring at us, or at the camera, with his hand and pointing finger seeming to reach us. It was a movie shot, or a type of graphic presentation that was being unleashed by the new medium.

The British government had called for volunteers. And in the next year about two million men signed up for the army, often lying about their age: recruits had to be nineteen, but a lot of youths sneaked in. Documentation was not strictly tested. You could leave school at twelve in 1914—so what were adolescents to do? For Britain—and for the other participants in the Great War—there had never been such a demonstration of popular faith or loyalty, and never anything so close to a raw mass army. For the most part, that volunteer force had not yet been tested in the spring of 1916. Of course, if those young men had had more experience, it is possible that they would not have turned up for the big day. There are times when armies need to be mindless, whatever the state of consciousness in their leaders.

It was not that General Rawlinson had decided: This is what we will do at 7:30 a.m. on July 1, 1916. He was part of a command hierarchy and subordinate to Field Marshal Douglas Haig, just as all officers served the Liberal government of Prime Minister H. H. Asquith, who had been in office since 1908. But such levels of government are not easily turned into movie drama. For the years 1915–16, cinema can offer Peter Weir's

Gallipoli, Neil Jordan's *Michael Collins*, and Sarah Gavron's *Suffragette* as melodramas on the deeper conflicts preoccupying Britain: Could the European war be galvanized by the old-fashioned adventurism of the Gallipoli campaign; what would happen with the Irish pressure for independence after the uprising at Easter 1916; and what was the new status of women?

That plan to attack in the Dardanelles had been motivated by Churchill (first lord of the admiralty); it was the kind of headstrong thrust that always appealed to him; and it was an innovative adventure by which politicians might pretend that the grind of war could be bypassed. It was a disaster, and demoralizing, with over 56,000 Allied dead and 120,000 wounded or sick. The Peter Weir movie (with Mel Gibson as a reckless young Australian) is compelling, and accurate in stressing the Australian participation in the venture. New Zealanders did as badly. The Turks did worse still: 56,000 dead and 97,000 wounded. But the British scenario of swift, drastic success had been trashed. *Gallipoli* is an important film, for 1915, and for 1981 when it was made. And I will return to it.

Failure in the Dardanelles and stagnation on the western front had only increased British need for a big victory to relieve pressure on the French at Verdun. The need to work in alliance was a load on Asquith, who was losing popular support, and on a cabinet that included his natural successor, David Lloyd George. Something new in the world was spreading alarm in the hearts of politicians, and it is crucial to the story in this book: war had become a big public show—it was a movie that needed to play. You can't drum up a volunteer army of two million, with half a dozen family members clinging to every man, without being on the brink of a performance to make the public feel justified in their sacrifice, or their investment. Or their hope. Especially if they still don't have a reliable idea of what the war is for. Let a standing army stand and it begins to see itself as a model for society, a kind of union.

But government can be too immense and complex for the wisest human beings. So very often those exhausted leaders must count on the momentum in the machine—or the beast—they are trying to ride. What could anyone do but let the beast thrive?

Everything in Rawlinson's life guided him in how to proceed. There would have to be an assault, and a breakthrough in the German lines. You couldn't have that many men waiting without telling them what to do. Not to do this, not to attack, was tantamount to saying, *Well, really, there is no point in being here. We could go home.*

That insight was beyond political understanding or courage. It usually is. So, instead, Rawlinson foresaw an immense artillery bombardment rained down on the German lines. The purpose of this was to beat the German trenches to rubble, to break up the lines of barbed wire and the other impediments to physical advance; to eliminate the machine-gun posts established by the Germans; and to reduce the German soldier to terror. Then, pause the bombardment, and send your own infantry over the top, advance across no-man's-land, and treat whatever is left of the woeful German soldiery to bullets and bayonets. Thus the German line would be broken, and their surrender and suing for peace could not be far behind.

"Isn't it pretty to think so?"—a line from 1926, said by a man damaged in war and about to represent its legacy for a generation, even if he seemed to have had his privates shot to bits. Not that Hemingway details the damage Jake Barnes has suffered in the war in *The Sun Also Rises*. Hemingway had served, though not in the American army. He was attached to the Italian forces, like his heroes in both *The Sun* and *A Farewell to Arms*. And while he took the money for the film rights on both books, he was savage about the travesties produced, with Gary Cooper (in 1932) and then Rock Hudson (1957) attempting to be Frederic Henry in *A Farewell*. Goodbye to much chance of emotional resonance with Helen Hayes and Jennifer Jones as Catherine Barkley (Jones was nearing forty at the time). So those movies tried to concentrate on battle scenes, preferring troop movements to views of lovemaking.

At the appointed hour on the Somme on Saturday, British infantry would go over the top, in uniform and Brodie steel hats, with loaded rifles, shovels, and rations to last a couple of days, including a backpack. That load could be close to fifty pounds, with no-man's-land often half a mile wide. In summer light and warmth. There is a cliché that the front was fought over in clinging mud. But on July 1, 1916, there were wildflowers in the firm ground. Then the cessation of the bombardment was a cue to the Germans for what to expect.

So on your feet and attack, my boys, on this summer morning.

I am describing an action that you feel you "know" already because it has become a routine way to dramatize combat in the Great War—it is the good show with the offhand but piercing instant of some young soldier from Shropshire or Somerset, a kid we have met and smiled over, being struck in the forehead in the first seconds and tumbling back into the trench, his summer over. Of course, no one on the Somme, July 1, had seen such films. The soldiers' sense of combat was based on famous paintings, folklore, and the wild tales told by the noncommissioned officers who had trained them. So it is necessary to understand that the volunteer army went over the top, scared but loyal, sometimes waiting patiently in single file for the narrow gaps in their own wire. They did not collapse or falter. Nor did Rawlinson see an alternative, though it is clear from his letters that he was not certain the bombardment would work.

There is a documentary film on YouTube about the July day on the Somme in which Rawlinson is depicted without blame or anything like complaint. In shirtsleeves, at his war table, he seems an honest, well-intentioned man, uncertain whether he is running a victory or a disaster, if only because communications then were so primitive. There was no way that harassed lieutenants could radio back to headquarters, "Tough going here, sir!" or "We've broken through the Boche line." In a literal and immediate sense, Rawlinson could not be sure what was happening, though it became ominously clear that the bombardment had only scratched the surface of the German lines. The trenches were largely intact. Much of the wire stood firm, as fresh as the wildflowers. And the machine guns were chattering away like crows.

8

THE MG 08

It was an enticing instrument, a marvel of engineering, a beauty, without a thought in its head. You can think of it as a star or a movie camera. You could hardly be taken aback if it killed you or a few hundred thousand of your comrades. This was the industrialization of death, what it did, so much more personal than artillery shells lobbed aimlessly a mile or two in the fine air. The machine gun wanted you, as surely as Kitchener's finger. You could hear that in its nagging voice and the intimacy of being accurate. With eyes and a mouth.

I am looking at the German heavy machine gun of choice on the Somme and elsewhere.

"If you want to make a pile of money," someone told Hiram Maxim, "invent something that will enable these Europeans to cut each other's throats with greater facility." America ready to save the world.

Maxim had been born in Maine in 1840, and his passion was for inventing things that might make the future for its honorable citizens as much as its cutthroats. He had this idea for a gun that fired automatically, and for passages of time. He was thinking of a blanket or a veil of fire; he had heard about the Gatling gun, invented in America in 1861, and used sparingly at the siege of Petersburg in 1864–65. That gun was clumsy, mounted on wheels, and subject to breakdown. It was in 1881 that Maxim moved to England and in a south London villa developed what would be the Maxim gun, using the recoil energy from one shot to fire the next. So it was, in West Norwood, that work went on that would lead to most of the machine guns in the Great War. Vickers took over the venture for Britain, but the German government made its own arrangement with Maxim, which led to the Maschinengewehr 08, or MG 08, as manufactured by the Deutsche Waffen und Munitionsfabriken in Berlin and at the Spandau arsenal. He was open-minded, sort of neutral.

I can imagine the 08 before me, a splendid plaything for a boy, but as instrumental in the culture as the telephone or the toilet—so much was still recent and unexamined at the turn of that century. So picture this poised beast, this dynamo. And warn yourself not to fall in love with it.

The 08 was a machine gun on a sturdy tripod, mounted on a base or a platform. It weighed over 150 pounds, which included the necessary eight pounds of cold water to cool the machine as its firing heated up. You see, the 08 felt alive and so much more than inert.

It was nearly four feet long, counting from the tip of its muzzle to the eyepiece that the gunner used. It required Mauser bullets, 7.92 millimeters by 57 millimeters, and these were held in a handsome fabric belt that was fed laterally into the weapon. The 08 could fire 450 rounds a minute and—please be ready with your awe—it was efficient at a range of 2,000 meters. But the fabric belt had only 250 cartridges, so the crew of four had to have a supply of belts along with a proficiency at loading them without mishap. While topping up the water to keep the 08 cool.

There's no need to be partisan: the Vickers machine gun adopted by the British was similar and equally worthy. It was water-cooled, too, and if the water boiled, then Tommies used it to make tea. You should understand that while the machine gun had been available by about 1890, it had had very little testing in action, though there was a mitrailleuse employed in the Franco-Prussian War. Nor did many experts guess that the western front was so ideal a proving ground that inventors might have been stunned by such providence. (I must not omit or disparage the French machine gun, the Chauchat, manufactured by Hotchkiss.) We have to recognize that the machine gun was latent, or predictable—which does nothing to mitigate its disruptive surprise.

But there's something else to stress. The 08 offered a field of fire, or a flow—it felt like a continuity, a wave. The bullets were separate, of course, no more than an extension or an industrialization of every single rifle bullet. But confronted by a line of 08s (or whatever), the advancing infantryman could feel he was pressing into a wave, like daring himself to go into the cold water at some seaside resort. And on the Somme, any section of the front had twenty or so machine guns, competent at 2,000 meters and firing 450 rounds a minute. They really did not need to be aimed, so much as pointed.

Here's another thing: as I examine the mechanics of the gun closely I see that it resembles the way film—so many still frames—was loaded into a camera or a projector and then animated by what we call persistence of vision. In both cases, the crucial or live element was "shot." I don't want to sentimentalize this process, but I think there is an affinity between the workings of film and the performing action of machine guns. They both mimic time, or take it over.

That's just a coincidence, you say. But I am not sure that coincidence adequately explains cultural mechanics. To be fired at by rifles was one thing: you had to believe luck would preserve you. But to be advancing against a battery of machine guns was to appreciate the nearly abstract force of modernity, a true tide of hostility, impersonal and uniform.

So we need to recognize the plight of the British infantry at 7:30 a.m. on July 1, 1916, carrying some fifty pounds of equipment, trudging across the dry ground, for a summer stroll, seeing the flowers, and realizing that a wave of hot fire was coming at them. With that macabre chattering noise. When you're making a war movie, it is important to get the right sound effects, for different weapons have their own voice. And the machine gun was like a mocking witch. You had to be there—and, of course, we weren't. You do see that imagining a war, or ten minutes of battle, is to take a huge, unwarranted leap of pretending. But we love to do it. And weapons systems free us, just as the crew of the 08 could fire away at 2,000 meters without ever thinking that they might be shooting out the eyes and the privates of some hopeful kid from Somerset or Shropshire. It was the first war in which so much damage could be administered without the killers seeing what they had done.

There are scholarly disputes, and one cannot trust the clerical accounting of death in 1916—some bodies were lost, as if at sea. Some were unaccounted for; you can't always have a roll call when slaughter is here and now. But it is accepted that the British had over 19,000 killed that July 1 in a total casualty count of over 57,000. (That number is so close to the total of US deaths in Vietnam—in that entire war.)

Moreover, the Germans had 21,000 casualties, and there were places where the British infantry did break through their lines. But the bare numbers tell the story. It was a disastrous day for the British army, graver than a defeat, and the signal of a new normality. In a defeat you can live to fight another day, but these losses promised so many more dire days. In the next fortnight telegrams and letters descended on the home front so that the civilian population at last understood the nature of this modern war.

And Rawlinson and Haig ordered the same thing next day, and well into October. I am not blaming the commanders. It would have required a flagrant genius, a rebel wizard (at risk of being called a traitor) to say stop, hold your ground, or sue for peace. There really was a destiny by the summer of 1916 that the whole appalling war had to be struggled through until the end, or until social and political exhaustion thought to alter the nature of society. The purpose of the war, its decency or humanity, was blocked by the command structure. That sounds preposterous for an organization of working men that was subservient to officers and gentlemen and had no notion of questioning them. But it is what happened in Russia, and prompted Germans to tell their British foes, "Look, *there* is the real enemy! The Bolshies."

After four months on the Somme, with the British and French making technical claims for a victory (they had advanced about six miles) the total casualties were in the region of 1.2 million. Not all fell from machine-gun fire. There were 77-millimeter field guns and howitzers; there was rifle fire, and hand-to-hand bayonet work in the trenches. There was illness, and the slow death of wounded who could not be reached by stretcher-bearers—that department of the army had been fearfully understaffed. (The future social historian R. H. Tawney, who had volunteered with the Manchester Regiment, lay wounded in no-man's-land for thirty hours after the morning of July 1. His *Religion and the Rise of Capitalism* was published in 1926.) But those types of contests were traditional. What was novel, and therefore most appreciated, was the torrential or riverlike imperative of machine-gun fire, and the pervasively automatic quality of its death.

IT HAPPENED, AS I WROTE THIS CHAPTER, THAT I KEPT A PHOTOGRAPH OF the machine gun on my desk, so I could look at it every now and then for inspiration or impetus. It was a kind of pinup picture, if you know what I mean. There was the MG 08, poised on its tripod at a revealing angle, showing itself off to the best advantage. It was like one of those shots of Marilyn Monroe where her open-mouthed abandonment does not look directly at the camera, so our scrutiny (rather cold-blooded) is permitted or invited. A kind of voyeurism. Yet it's more likely (I think) that I would have been ready to be interactive with MM than fire the MG. But pictures do sit there, wondering what we intend to do. They ask us to examine our intentions. The machine gun was lovely but menacing. As I looked at it I began to realize it could resemble the tiger I was worried about earlier. Sometimes I could see its face.

But then I started to appreciate the extraordinary rapture of photographed mechanics in the years just before and during the Great War. It's easy to surmise that 1914 was "the past," a precious summer on the brink of savage modernity—I ran that play. But we should realize how far depiction—as art or diagrams—was so thrilled by the new mechanics that were blooming everywhere. Cubism was very arty or avant-garde: one can imagine the common soldier laughing himself silly over its absurd departure from realism and the lifelike. But the world was catching fire in the implicit lessons in photography.

In Cubism there was the half-grasped intuition that a face (say) had so many different aspects or facets, and where did that knowledge come from but in looking at still photographs and that tentative way in which they edged into motion? In 1912, Marcel Duchamp startled spectators with one of the most beautiful and foreboding pictures ever painted: *Nude Descending a Staircase, No 2*. It is a collage or a frozen montage of a figure on a staircase, a way of absorbing a few seconds and steps. Because the title says "Nude" it has a distant erotic implication, but in truth it's hard to determine the gender of the figure. One is too excited by the brilliant, witty rendering of motion and the sense of a new emotion that comes with it.

You may be saying, *Please, this is not meant to be a book about art theory*, and *Nude Descending a Staircase* is not a movie—nor does it have a hint of war. That's only partly true: look at the picture again (you can find it easily) and see how, in a few seconds, Duchamp had captured the marching progress of a kind of soldier. You could call his painting "Men in War" (a title coming up ahead). What that means is the half-buried appreciation, in some of the most innovative art of this period, that automation and mechanics were invading human existence—that we were half in love with the allure of becoming machines. The new report of our ordinary movement was changing us. So you can look at a picture of the MG 08 and wonder if you are looking at a beloved. Or at a devil.

If this line of thinking begins to intrigue you, let me recommend *Man with a Movie Camera*, made in 1929 in the Soviet Union by Dziga Vertov. This *is* a movie, though its world seems not just at peace but exuberant over the love affair between a new mechanized reality and the faithful and symbiotic attention of a movie cameraman. It's a joyous film, and we have time for that. But surely its excitement contains hints of society and existence beginning to conform to the remorseless frame-by-frame passion and progression of movie. I dare you to look at the Duchamp and the

Dziga Vertov while rereading the account of Tietjens observing the automatic rifleman in *A Man Could Stand Up*. Opening fire was becoming not just natural and human.

But necessary.

For leaders, and society at large, it might be easier to think of wounded soldiers as broken toys, with sliced-up faces from Picasso.

9

SHOULDER ARMS/SHOULDER CAMERA

Never mind the chance to be heroic or self-sacrificing: most soldiers recognize on their first day in uniform that they are going to make fools of themselves. It may be a saving depth in our nature that we are inclined to overlook the shattered bodies and the absurd plans in favor of a good laugh. From Evelyn Waugh to Joseph Heller, some of the best war novels fly the flag of farce. We like the thought that laughter is a salvation and a tonic, another kind of victory for chumps. So in early 1918, Charlie Chaplin had the idea of making a comedy about the war.

He shared the thought with a few friends. They were wary because Charlie was being reproached in Britain for not enlisting in the war (he was twenty-five in 1914), and in America because he might be un-American. How easily Private Chaplin could have been lost to us in some fruitless assault. No less than Cecil B. DeMille warned him, "It's dangerous at this time to make fun of the war." He proved mistaken. *Shoulder Arms*, at just over forty minutes, was a big commercial success, which may reinforce my point that the soldiers of the war and the public beheld the disaster with a relative tranquility that we now find hard to grasp or forgive. The timing is crucial: looked at today, in the light of how we have placed the Great War in our history, *Shoulder Arms* is close to grotesque, a curiosity as much as a good laugh. But that tells us so much.

Chaplin had landed on his feet—that was always the key to his unique ballet. Born in London in 1889 in extreme poverty, he was the right age to join the volunteer army, and he was so unprivileged that he might have thought of taking that easy escape from the slums and being looked after. But by then, in the Fred Karno vaudeville company, he had started on a tour of the American circuit. That was the launch for Chaplin's prodigious success and celebrity. He became of two volatile minds: Was he his own private story; or could he fall back on the sentimentality of the common man, the Tramp, who was the trigger to his exploding wealth?

This is not an attack on Chaplin, but an attempt to balance his inner conflict between ego's glory and the pathos of failure. This is not just the personal story of a south London vagrant with the knack of coinciding with the universal movie show. Chaplin was, simply, a model of movie success. So he ignored DeMille (and others) and went ahead with *Shoulder Arms*. That could be seen as a risk, but only for those who failed to realize how Chaplin was already, by 1918, a phenomenon who could have landed on his feet with any challenge. In *Shoulder Arms*, he would capture the Kaiser. That seemed silly and cheeky, but if you paused a second you realized that Chaplin was by then so much more important than the idiot German emperor.

The Tramp would go to war. Charlie (or whatever name we give him) is a soldier (American, for sure) whose ineptness takes him behind German lines but lets him capture the German command structure. Then the doughboy wakes up. Why not? There must have been a dream for so many actual soldiers of winning the war, or settling it, being home for Christmas (without specifying the year). In one sequence, Charlie becomes a tree, and resists being chopped down by a blundering German soldier. I don't know if it's funny now, so much as a lesson in how ordinary people (soldiers included) thought about themselves in 1918.

Later in life, as a movie star, Chaplin visited a hospital in Brighton to see and be seen by "the incurable spastic cases who had been wounded during the war":

It was terribly sad to look into those young faces and to see the lost hope there. One young man was so paralyzed that he painted with a brush in his mouth, the only part of his body he could use. Another had fists so clenched that he had to be given an anesthetic in order to cut his fingernails to prevent them from growing into the palms of his hands. Some patients were in such a terrible state that I was not allowed to see them.

There's the rub. In 1918, audiences (especially ex-soldiers) knew that *Shoulder Arms* was fanciful, a comic act and a dream. But we need to realize what a very limited sense the public had of what the war had looked like, and how decently it could be portrayed. There is so much that could not be shown, or seen, and not just by the public and the parents, but by the commanding officers. Imagine a competent newsreel starting at 7:30 on July 1—but ask yourself how those cameras should have been used. And wonder how long the Battle of the Somme would have lasted if this newsreel reportage had played a day later in British movie shows. (Such a radical screening is coming—but it was a hundred years too late.)

Paintings were more impressive at conveying the moment of the war. In the summer of 1918, Britain's War Memorials Committee had asked the American painter John Singer Sargent to go to Arras and Ypres and make art of it. The result is beautiful (I think) and very moving. Whatever he actually saw on the battlefields, Sargent delivered a painting (90 inches by 240) of a line of soldiers who have been blinded or disabled by a gas attack. The picture is called *Gassed* (it is in the Imperial War Museum in London) and it shows a line of eleven khaki men, clinging to each other and standing in a sea of corpses or wounded men. It is naturalistic (it seems to respect a duty to be nearly photographic) yet it has the elegance that Sargent never abandoned and is so mysterious in this panorama.

He did the picture in his studio in Fulham in west London, and he was conscious of the Bruegel painting *The Parable of the Blind*. So the composition has an air of mythology, and the longer you look at it, the more it becomes a little too cold for comfort. But it is as brave as it is lovely, and it is an image that could reach the public only in a museum.

Of course, gas—mustard gas or phosgene—was another new wave, an atmosphere that might be more devastating than so many bullets. Its impact was more fully disclosed in poetry—here is Wilfred Owen so much more vivid than a photo in "Dulce et Decorum Est":

> *Gas! GAS! Quick, boys!—An ecstasy of fumbling*
> *Fitting the clumsy helmets just in time,*
> *But someone still was yelling out and stumbling*
> *And flound'ring like a man in fire or lime.—*
> *Dim through the misty panes and thick green light,*
> *As under a green sea, I saw him drowning.*

Owen would be killed on November 4, 1918, a fortnight after *Shoulder Arms* opened, a week before the Armistice. You only have to picture Charlie's "tree" somewhere in the line of eleven to feel the cultural stress and torment of the Great War.

10

THEY

The British soldier had too much to carry already, so he did not think to take a camera with him into no-man's-land. The Kodak box Brownie had been introduced in 1900, and there was a worldwide craze for it. But it had not penetrated the army, and if it had, the cameras would likely have been confiscated. The principle of war as a grim spectacle, or subject to freedom-of-information inquiries, would not have impressed military discipline or anxious thoughts of maintaining "security." Recruitment is not a sure sell when accompanied by a naked snap of body pieces blown apart by a howitzer shell, or a corpse in a forgotten trench, black from hardened rot so that the rats need to gnaw hard to get at the shreds of meat.

"So aren't you ready for some of this, my lad?" asks the sergeant.

The years of the Great War saw the first explosion in moviegoing, with Griffith, Chaplin, Mary Pickford, and Douglas Fairbanks carrying the medium forward, and serving up entertainment not just despite the truths of war, but to keep us all positive. Accordingly, there were moving picture cameras that might have been taken into the lines to record the action and the atmosphere of the war—official imprints of history, rousing propaganda, or even the casual footage for "home," shot by bored soldiers. "Hallo, Mum. Glad you're not here!" But the war was a touch too soon—soon enough for its own good if you care about the livelihood or longevity of wars. So, more or less, our film record of what happened is restricted, as if in accord with the horror and the shame that would be attached to the conflict once the participants shrugged off the first cheeriness of doing it as a good cause—for Britain, Germany, France, or even Serbia. Journalism was not catered to. By 1917, the authorities had appreciated that there should be censorship of letters sent home from the front. But it had taken that long for institutional innocence to wear off.

So the war was fought in cinematic oblivion on the home front. It took a hundred years before there was a concerted effort to round up the scraps of footage and make them presentable. The result, *They Shall Not Grow Old*, is one of the most arresting war movies ever attempted, an unassertive chronicle that makes *The Four Horsemen of the Apocalypse*, *The Big Parade*, *All Quiet on the Western Front*, et cetera seem befuddled posturings of archaic chivalry and a hopeless effort to re-create the texture of the Great War.

In Britain, especially, there was an urge to memorialize the Great War a hundred years after it had occurred. History could be ready for prime time—too ready, perhaps, for the public soon became jaded at all the memory, some of it contrived and unreliable. But an organization called 14–18 NOW came into being as a means of ensuring a "First World War Centenary Cultural Programme," led by the BBC and the Imperial War Museum.

That museum was first thought of in 1917, and there were early requirements that it do nothing to glorify war, except in remembering the suffering. It was a gathering place for memorabilia, but rapidly after 1970 it was taken over by a creative, theatrical approach. By the 1980s, under the directorship of Noble Frankland, there were large immersive presentations with extraordinary projection effects that reproduced the experience of the trenches in the Great War and of the Blitz in 1940. These shows, living movies, made the Imperial one of the most innovative and popular museums in Britain.

One of these NOW ventures called for some kind of documentary film, and it ended up in the hands of Peter Jackson. As you read this book, you may be compiling a list of the films you should see. *They Shall Not Grow Old* is high on that list, but be careful, for it has a candor that may eclipse or shame hundreds of other well-intentioned story pictures. As you likely know, Jackson was responsible for the *Lord of the Rings* pictures, and earlier he had made a small marvel, *Heavenly Creatures*. Still, this job for 14–18 NOW is his great work—and it is dedicated to his grandfather who had fought in the war.

Do not overlook the film's enigmatic title. You can settle for the rhetoric, the "never forget" that had always been part of our Armistice reverence. It reaches from the Cenotaph war memorial silence every November, to Prewitt playing "Taps" for Maggio in *From Here to Eternity*. It is a way of telling ourselves, "We understand, don't we?," when the wish can be stronger than the reality. That is a way of saying, *We humans are tender and mindful of what has happened—you can count on our sensitivity*. But Jackson's title has a harder edge to it, the awareness that, literally, so many million lives never got past youth. And in that clash of rhetoric and substance there may be a wondering whether we deserve anything better. Or is it just pretentious to believe we have spirit?

It was Jackson's idea to collect as much wartime footage as could be found, and much of this consisted of materials in the archive of the Imperial War Museum. Then as he looked at the black-and-white film, he began to consider colorizing it. As he said, the real soldiers had seen the war in color. In addition, the new film took footage that might have been shot at 16 frames a second and subtly double-printed some frames to acquire the extra fluency of 24 frames a second.

That was only part of his transformation of the footage, for as Jackson saw ways of organizing all the fragments, he thought of a soundtrack of voices—not a narration or a verdict, but the matter-of-fact recollections of men who had been there. Over the decades, the museum and the BBC had accumulated so many oral memoirs. Suppose a sampling of those voices could bind together the visuals. Suppose a simple arc of history could shape it all, so that the documentary went from outbreak and enlistment to the Armistice and the unnerving isolation of veterans by the larger community. As if "home" could not understand or tolerate their contained violence and grief.

The resultant film deserves to be called a documentary, but it is a fabrication, too, in a good sense, and Jackson has been candid about its creative inaccuracy. Some disapproved of the colorization because that alters so many emotional undertones. When we see the first British tanks, as much reptiles as machines, they are a green color; yet history says they were closer to brown. Some of the old footage has been gently doctored; all of it is subject to the revisionism in editing; and a lot of the sound recordings have been cleaned up, or clarified. It's even possible that some of the texts were rerecorded, using actors or nonprofessionals who had never been alive then to have such thoughts.

I don't think any of that matters, compared with the blunt question: Would you rather live in a world that does not have the innovative daring of *They Shall Not Grow Old*? Can you actually conceive of a film being an impeccable and factually faithful record (in two hours) of a war that lasted over four years? Had this film existed in 1914–18, could the war have lasted that long?

But the voices never sound like actors; they seem like fussy, gruff veterans who are not eloquent in themselves—except for what they say. Some are voices that most directors might reject because of their oddity. So you hear what they say, instead of the intent in acting: "I wouldn't have missed it"; "I have never been so excited in my life"; "I liked to be told what I had to do"; "Made the best of it"; "We didn't complain"; "It was just a job of work."

No one registers as articulate or acting up, but they quietly testify to my point that in the Great War men did not appreciate the full nature of the war they were fighting. Your local regiment might seem erased some days, but the surviving soldiers need not realize the enormity of all the losses. They were not informed how the war was faring. But they believed they were fighting that rascal Jerry, to send him home in disgrace, without grasping the reach of total war and the demise of martial chivalry or diplomatic strategy. The heart of it all was in the mud and the craters and the futility. No wonder some raw German soldiers conceived the notion of becoming supermen and taking hold of human society by brutal force. Ideas spread like illness in the ordeal of the trenches. It inspired the best as raw material, and every year the circumstances shifted: gas, aircraft, and tanks came along gradually, in company with an awareness that "great" meant not just size and significance, or how many people were affected, but the extent of the catastrophe and the horrors that people had taught themselves to endure. It's in the voices as much as the footage that one appreciates the atmosphere of those four years as a naive adventure turning into a prison from which the most likely exit was the one you would not be alive to remember.

As the voices register as commonplace, so we come to terms with the faces. A lot of the men are "having a good time," or they have made the effort to signal that in bravura grins and show-off boisterousness. But many more simply watch the camera, like animals in a zoo studying the passing faces on the other side of their bars. Some are cocky; far more are shy or suspicious of being seen. Humans were still in the early stages of getting familiar with cameras—and we are not finished with that education yet.

So many are scraps or wrecks. The intake of 1914 was full of thin bodies with gaunt faces and gaudy grins (this is colorizing), and the turmoil of unassisted teeth. These faces could be from the sixteenth century. In service—with physical training and modest set meals—the average recruit put on fourteen pounds and an inch in height. Once you mount a civilian army you are on the road to health care for all whether you meant to be or not. You want your people to be physically fit, with stamina and athleticism to wrestle with the vaunted German soldier—and Lord help you if your line faced Prussians, because they were not human, and are as daunting as the Scots. But what could that infant system do with mental health? Hard liquor was dispensed, for courage: rum and gin, cheap stuff watered down. For it was hard to ignore that men were trembling all day—had they been drinking too much? Or wasn't that a privilege reserved for officers? Was it easier to tell yourself that good soldiers needed to be fired up or just a little unhinged?

Not that being in the army was simply good for your health. As the trenches turned to mud and ponds of stagnant water, so the men got trench feet, with only crude remedies. That could develop into gangrene, with lice and rats as your medics. On the western front, the lines were ready to attack or be attacked, but there were no such things as dormitories or lavatories, and the recreation areas had not been thought of. There are hotels and bed-and-breakfasts now for tourists on the Somme—but not in 1916.

Men slept on the ground, in the mud, on the duckboards, or propped against the wooden supports to stop the trenches from collapsing. They would get a breakfast as a right—bread, butter, tins of plum and apple jam, a slice of bacon if you were lucky, and tea—and there was a stew later in the day, the recipe for which was a military secret. The piece of breakfast bacon had one stripe of lean in it, so the soldiers called it a lance corporal.

If you needed to take a piss or a shit you went to the latrine area where a row of bare bottoms sat on a thick pole, depositing their waste in a trench and hoping the pole didn't break. There were few facilities for washing or laundry, so the men tried ingenuity or they stank, or they waited for leave days when they could go to the nearby brothels and get sorted for sixpence. That reminds me, the common soldier's wage for this adventure was a shilling a day, from which you had to buy smokes and any extra food, and take your chance in the constant gambling. When your number can come up any minute, you become crazy for number games— like how many rats are there on that horse carcass over there?

Don't forget the horses when every gun being hauled, and every truck of ammunition or dead bodies, was likely to be horse-drawn. In the whole war, Britain used about six million horses, and few of them went home. That required stabling and blacksmiths, and more consideration than the men received, oats and bran to eat and all their dump to be dealt with. But men loved the horses, and the animals may have been their highest measure of affection, apart from being pals and negotiating that forbidden feeling when so many nursed a silent need for comfort and being touched.

So animals could be precious. In September 1918, a corporal in the

US Army Air Service found an abandoned litter of puppies in a German kennel and cared for them. He sneaked two of them on the boat back home in 1919. The corporal's name was Lee Duncan, and one of the German shepherds became Rin Tin Tin, a true star of silent cinema and a model for the two-legged.

Young men said they wanted combat, until they got it. Bravado is only a cut ahead of devastation. It was in exhausted hindsight and the crush of fear and being alive still that trench life picked up a fatuous glow of nostalgia. As if survival relied on character. Did these men believe in God? There were padres and services, but an immense collapse of faith began after the war.

They got used to fatalism with the smell of decay that came from human corpses. There were bodies that lingered everywhere: the funerary services were uncertain, so a vagueness spread about who had been killed and whom it was you simply hadn't seen for a week or so—few knew what day it was. Sentries fell asleep at their post occasionally, and that could mean court-martial and a firing squad. But sometimes there were simply the unknown dead. I had a father-in-law who tried to sleep one night in the trench mud and woke to find he was in the embrace of a corpse that had eased its way out of the slime. All you can do with that is make a joke of it and hope you live long enough to regain the habit of sleep.

Some men were straightforward: they would sooner be killed in one blast than wounded and rescued. They had observed the inept, harassed work of casualty services, even if there were some doctors and nurses who worked through their exhaustion and the wounded's screams. A new kind of surgery was opened up by the Great War, a way of sewing faces back together and patching up the loss of limbs. Such skills were learned on the run. But the surgeons were in short supply and it was hard to find a level, clean, well-lighted place in the squalor where the most ingenious manipulator of broken bodies might help a man walk again, or explain to anyone concerned how his privates were not on parade. "Isn't it pretty to think so."

They Shall Not Grow Old has no agenda; it doesn't need one. I'm sure that Peter Jackson guessed that showing the footage would be enough to set us in tears at hearing the terse, effacing dismissal from the voices about just doing the job. And this goes all the way to the Armistice, and the guns falling silent, of men being shipped home and demobilized—the fit and the invalids—and then realizing how they had become "a race apart."

It was not just that businesses were wary of employing them, as if they had gotten into bad habits, or not caring. The bereft confidence of all their gambling showed. They were scattered or unbelieving, not quite serious or dull enough now for steady jobs. So many were disabled physically or mentally. But their sacrifice was greeted with mistrust. In life itself few asked to hear the stories, from shame at having been safe at home, or anxiety over a kind of infectious nihilism that went with the empty eye socket and the palsied face. Some men said the "fear of fear" had been what kept them going—the distress at being seen as cowards—that unmentionable word, that constant condition. And that tension had lasted long after hostilities ended. It was as if men realized that war was the bitter air they had to breathe, and in parts of the battlefield it hastened communism, anarchy, and contempt for any sermons on purpose. The Hapsburgs, the Romanovs, and so many lofty families were done with.

One of the most pregnant scenes in *They Shall Not Grow Old* shows British troops and Germans mingling together once the war was over. The Germans are prisoners, but they are no more abashed or dismayed than their captors. There is no caption to tell us the time or place (Jackson chose not to do that), but what is so striking is that the men of two sides are chatting to each other in broken German or English. They smile sometimes; there might be awkward jokes and respect. The Germans are not the ogres of propaganda. The British seem friendly and shy. What can they all do now? There is not quite conviviality, but the mercy and the fatigue of "no more" eclipses winning and losing. The two groups of men are like actors or extras waiting for a crowd scene, and they exchange cigarettes and bemusement over why this was ever allowed to happen.

Such men were then poured out on their homelands, without much pension or rehabilitation. They had won and lost—wasn't that enough?

Now they were ready for the Spanish flu, for unemployment in the following years, for feeling misplaced in their family circumstances, and being incoherent or stunned from what had happened on the front. They could only listen to the wrangling at Versailles over the unenlightened peace terms. Of course, your widow got a pension, if she knew how to claim it and if she could prove she had been married to you, as opposed to merely cohabiting. The unhealed wound of the war was the indecency with which people were treated. In this mingling scene you may feel that mood dawning, at the loss of being told what to do, and getting on with it. It's as if, in an offhand way, the war had proved to be about human rights, even if not all the humans appreciated them at first.

To watch *They Shall Not Grow Old* a few times (it is habit-forming in its beautiful desolation) is to realize that you are observing the nature of British society in the years 1914–18. But the men seem from an earlier century, when politicians and generals trusted to the scum of the army carrying the day. The front was an infinite prison where millions served and over a million Britons died. It was the Great War (a term that was widespread by late 1914) because of vain, romantic ideas of history and glory, but the greatness was cultural and intellectual, for it had revealed the nature of war and the dumb, all-powerful industrial states that wanted it as play.

Few opted out of the murderous, irrational enterprise. That existential resignation was a while away yet. There were about three thousand British court-martials on the western front in four years, and only about a tenth of those were over desertion. But you didn't have to be a poet or an outlaw to feel the urge to disown the enterprise. Who knows all that happened in the education set free? The privileged social structures that had carelessly permitted the war are still trying to keep up with the changes it began.

In a book that gathers many war films, I hope it's useful to propose one that never got made. Imagine the story of a deserter, someone who despairs in the trenches of the human race, and who is too brave to insist on smothering his fears. So he slips away in the night, without a plan but with a revolver, and maybe on horseback. This was not so hard a thing in

the untidiness. The bureaucracy might be oppressive, but it was haphazard. He reinvents himself—that is an American model. Then years later,
this escapee reappears somewhere with a new grasp on life, calling himself
George Harvey Bone or Jimmy Gatz or James Allen or John Hume Ross.
You can look those names up. There are so many characters after the
war—in fiction and in life, mad or sad—who seem on the run from an
indescribable calamity. The deserter becomes a type, a haunted everyman.
So Jay Gatsby could be the richest man on his coast, but he's never going
to be at ease.

A TERRIBLE PLACE

The Four Horsemen of the Apocalypse (1921) is not a good film: a century later it seems content with inane high-mindedness; its gloom is gloss, really. But we cannot do justice to the bonds between war and the movies without being ready to sit through hours and years of poor stuff, and to imagine what those films meant on their first day. No other genre gets away with more pompous nonsense. Still, *Four Horsemen* closes with one of its few surviving characters looking at an awesome military cemetery, where rows of white crosses undulate across the folds of a hillside, and tells us, "Peace has come—but the Four Horsemen will still ravage humanity—stirring unrest in the world—until all hatred is dead and only love reigns in the heart of mankind."

That was the adaptation of a novel, by Vicente Blasco Ibáñez, published in Spanish in 1916 as a preemptive attempt to proclaim the waste and devastation of the war—never mind warnings about what might be to come. The film was epic (and labored): it ran over two and a half hours, and it made a small fortune. Audiences were impressed, even if the metaphor of the horsemen seemed fanciful. That word "apocalypse" does things for us, now and then. But from the outset, *Four Horsemen* would be known for a vivid sidebar: the scene, early on, where a young rake enters a cantina in Buenos Aires, in boots and spurs, swag pants, cummerbund, and an insolent flat-topped sombrero with chinstrap, and sweeps a ripe but coarse young woman into a tango.

That was Rudolph Valentino in his debut. His playboy character later finds himself in melancholy romance with an otherwise married woman (her husband is blind). This Julio succumbs in the war, along with many others. Valentino would be dead soon himself (in 1926), but his aliveness on-screen transcended the sententious lamentation for the losses of the war. There was a lesson in that: filmmakers understood the war had been a very bad thing, such as *should never happen again, so woe unto us* (to the extent of $9 million at the box office), but some small, riveting glimpse of human action might be more lasting than sermons, and it would help the $9 million.

Thirty-six years later, *Paths of Glory* is so much better a film, and still compelling, even if it's sixty-six years old now. In part that extra comes from being made by an arrogant creative ego (Stanley Kubrick) while *Four Horsemen* was a studio blockbuster arranged by a traditional pictorialist, Rex Ingram. But it's also because *Paths of Glory* nurses a bitter certainty that what happened in battle was minor compared with the machinations that had put men in the field.

It does feel like a Kirk Douglas film: when we first see him he is stripped to the waist; the film was made by his company, Bryna, and Kirk is vigorously tormented as Colonel Dax, a lawyer in civilian life, but a commander on the front who is the pivot of the action. It is his task to lead an assault on the Ant Hill, a minor ridge among many on the western front. This is the French sector, though the film that emerged would be banned in France until 1975 because it had no illusions about vanity and cruelty in the French command structure. General Broulard (Adolphe Menjou, aged sixty-seven) orders the attack as a dutiful gesture to French presence in the war. He pays lip service to the myth that the assault can be successful, but he does not bother to hide his cynicism. He assigns the mission to a more junior General Mireau (George Macready, fifty-eight), who is ambitious for personal glory.

Dax protests: he says the assault is doomed, and will produce many casualties. Mireau refuses to hear of this. He may be the most hideous Great War general we have on our screen. Macready is aquiline and super-cilious, with a long scar on his face; Menjou is more a dormouse, or a rat in obsequious disguise.

The more you watch the film, the clearer it is that Menjou and Mac-ready are its fascination. The assault does fail, at deadly cost, and to save face Mireau calls for court-martials and firing squads. Cowardice was to blame, he insists; this will be confirmed in a swift, rigged trial. Mireau is all for executing a lot of men, but the urbane Broulard says surely three will be sufficient. We meet those sacrificial victims and sit through their ordeal (Dax will be their hopeless defender), and the actors are very good—Ralph Meeker, Timothy Carey, and Joe Turkel. But as the decades pass I find myself overlooking their pathos. I want to have more of the two wicked generals: their ruthlessness, and the political web that has taught them what to do. Kubrick's urbane tracking shots show us the palatial headquarters Mireau has secured for himself, so that the clash between ordinary service and corrupt leadership is plain. But our urge to under-stand the Great War begs for more exploration of how corruption reached its decisions.

Not many films are as suggestive of a society's formalities undermin-ing its military intelligence as *An Officer and a Spy* (2019), a very care-ful and controlled account of the Dreyfus case (1894–1906). It has no illusions about the prejudice and iron stupidity in a French command structure that would soon need to be very alert. As you may know, this excellent film was made by Roman Polanski, which accounts for the like-lihood that you have not been able to see it. Though you are still free to revisit *Rosemary's Baby*, *Chinatown*, and *The Pianist*, which received Academy Awards for best actor and best director, some twenty-five years after the incident for which Polanski is now reckoned to be unforgivable.

The Ant Hill attack is a striking part of *Paths of Glory*, even if it owes a lot to films like *All Quiet on the Western Front*. Above all, Kubrick reveals a no-man's-land pockmarked with craters from constant artillery barrage. The men try to seek cover in these holes, but that lasts only so long. In time, in tatters, they crawl back to their own lines, leaving us to recognize the hellish upheaval of the ground. It is like a terrible sandpit, with scoops of water and mud, the tracery of wire, and old corpses here and there. Kirk Douglas does his best to be heroic and athletic, while the one proven coward gets away with nominating his enemy as one of the three accused.

There is something else, touching and curious. After the firing squad, after Mireau has been exposed to disgrace because he had wanted to have artillery fire on his own cowards, the film pauses at a French canteen where the war-weary troops are drowning their sorrows. A young German woman is dragged in to sing for them. There are cries of mockery and abuse until the woman—without special talent—silences them with a simple song, "The Faithful Hussar." She lets the mass of rough men admit the pathos of their service. Is this the sardonic Kubrick trying to tell himself the human race is going to be all right? That idea can be a besetting malady in antiwar films. Whatever he intended, he ended up marrying the woman (Christiane Harlan Kubrick), and they were a fond couple until his death, in 1999. Does that scene make us feel better? Is it the "love" alluded to at the end of *Four Horsemen of the Apocalypse*? Or was it just a way of getting off? We know that Colonel Dax is going back to the front. We guess that the two generals might prefer him dead. In a really bleak film, they could contrive his death—isn't that the measure of politics?

I HAD THOUGHT IN THIS PART OF THE BOOK TO DISCUSS HOW THE GREAT War was digested, how so many realities sank in with an honest accounting of what had happened. And what befell the solemn sensibility that this must never happen again. Or again and again. How does that show on the screen? I'm sure Kubrick had studied how Lewis Milestone had shot the battle scenes in *All Quiet on the Western Front* (1931), that landmark antiwar film, except that its combat scenes are not just spectacular (a good deal more detailed and costly than those in *Paths of Glory*). They became a model for future antiwar films that felt obliged to include a good battle scene so that we should be horrified, yet satisfied.

So what is a good battle scene? And how does it relate to actual battle? The attack scenes in *All Quiet on the Western Front* and *Paths of Glory* are alike in key ways: they are both black and white, with music in the air—thus the immediate confusion of "realism" and melodrama. They both opt for commanding high-angle points of view—that instills the possibility of control or order in a realm so many participants feel is chaotic. And they have the same tracking motion to animate or excite the attack. Beyond that they follow the common dynamic in their editing: soldier A does something—he fires or thrusts a bayonet—cut to soldier B who is shot and killed, or transfixed. That also means that both films balance shocking action and decisive result—so in killing a foe you will win—isn't it pretty to think so? And whether the film is pro-war, or antiwar (as it thinks), we are being shaped by this rhythm of cut and thrust. The pictures have something else in common, not to be mocked or forgotten: they want to make money. We are paying for battle.

Add one more thing: because this rhythm, or syntax, is so thoroughly organized, we can buy into the premise that battle is equally foreseen, or ordained. Or omniscient. In other words, you can think yourself antiwar and disillusioned and critical of the ruinous geopolitics that made the Great War. But you're buying it. And it's more than a small matter to wonder how far the charade has enabled the beast. The filmmakers are always looking for piquant anecdote, and that risks losing sight of the boredom in war.

Let's take an example from battlefield life that could easily catch the attention of the studio class that greenlights films—who let them be made. You'll recognize what I'm talking about because it is a story that transcends fact or history. If it didn't happen, we say, then it should have. It's legend.

It is December 24, 1914, on what was becoming known as the western front (as if it was a focus for Europe). It is a cold winter morning, but I think it is legitimate to have a little pale sunshine on the light snow that has fallen. Had snow really fallen? I don't know. But it's hardly a stretch to imagine, and if you're making a movie snow has emotional value. Still, let's settle for a hard frost, more or less certain in that country in December. Can you see a thin glass of ice on the puddles? Please don't be disconcerted; war deserves some art direction and prettiness.

An English soldier, a foolhardy private, has poked his head above the top (you can see the crosscut shots: his cheeky face and what he sees—his reaction). "What's that Jerry done now?" he asks aloud. This is an ordinary line and I'm not saying it couldn't be improved. A lieutenant hears him and considers it his duty to look more closely through the glasses (cut and cross cut: his binoculars and the blurred horizon).

"It's a damn Christmas tree," decides the lieutenant—he had wondered at first if it was a new, cunning instrument of war.

"That's nice," says the private—you should think of the likely kids you'd put in the part. I'd suggest the childish Dickie Attenborough, but he's dead, of course. Still, he'd have understood: just think of his war record as an actor. Or the early John Mills.

And as the twenty-fourth winds down, so a few of the Tommies start to sing carols for Christmas. They might have done it quietly for themselves, but I think they're encouraged by the notion that Fritz understands Christmas. No need to underline this or be heavy-handed, but we are at a point in the war where trench life is hardening into stalemate, when grown men likely to die are wondering what for. And it may occur to them that Jerry feels the same way.

The Tommies could sing "Away in a Manger" or "Once in Royal David's City," a mix of sentimentality and marching. There is a pause—shot and countershot, again—and then the lowing sound of German voices (not a regulated choir, but a tenor gathering) and they do "Stille Nacht" as twilight comes in.

That's a hell of a scene, don't you think?

And I am confident that something like it happened, even if without the crisp intercutting I have indulged in with a movie in mind. You see, I have sketched out the cessation of hostilities as if it was an attack. But that is the spirit of movie narrative, the way of taking charge of our attention. It closes down our minds to a deeper strain of thought, like Tietjens observing the rifleman in *A Man Could Stand Up* and grasping what had happened to soldiers in the routine of war.

That twenty-fourth and twenty-fifth of December, 1914, as many as 100,000 troops seemed to get out of their trenches, go over the top, walk across no-man's-land, unarmed and ill-equipped, and "fraternize" with the other side. And they did it without a script, or orders or understanding. Let's say they nodded and offered a few words, looking for translation. Perhaps smokes and a pastry served that function. Maybe plum and apple jam crossed plates with apple and plum. You hear that games of football were played, but I feel that's going too far, on such broken ground. Not that a ball or a puppy may not have been passed around. Not that photographs of wives and kids at home were not exchanged and ticked off as being essentially the same photographs. Not that I have ever seen actual photo records of the fraternization.

My guess is that this was a spontaneous gesture by ordinary soldiers. Officers may have been anxious not to break orders and the proper line of battle. But soldiers on both sides wrote home about the wonder of it all and how it came and went. Henry Williamson (nineteen on that day) described a trench scene to his mother with this surprise—he was in a German trench, visiting. And Williamson was one of so many who were not the same after the war. Was it because of that unofficial day?

As well as *Tarka the Otter* (1928), he wrote a series of fifteen novels, A Chronicle of Ancient Sunlight, about a man much like himself who goes from serving in the war, coming home to remake a life, feeling dismay over Britain in the Depression, then gravitating toward Oswald Mosley and the British fascists. When war broke out again in 1939 Williamson was briefly detained, but he was too thoughtful and too sad to be a serious threat. He had been wounded and gassed, in and out of military hospitals, but he had a high creative spirit that had been darkened by the war, and was deeply moved by the December truce.

Here's a problem with this parable of truce. The moral of the anecdote is too final and clear. For the sake of a tidy parable, mystery is removed. How did that many men put down their arms for a day—and then take them up again? The two sides, in their commonality, could have packed up and gone home. Didn't they know that was the decent response to all they shared and to the clash between the paraphernalia of this military expedition and its denial? How did the recognition grow that Fritz's wife looked like yours, and that Agathe and Daisy were too young to be joined in widows' mourning as soon as normal combat resumed? That Christmas Day of 1914 is so transparent it's stupid—because there was no mechanism or mutiny that would act on its spontaneity. The human race had achieved an automaton obedience enough to say, *Well, really, don't we deserve war, us idiots? In which case let's make a good show of it. Aren't we the guns ready to be fired?*

A RECKONING IS REQUIRED TO SHOW THE SCALE OF THE SILENT MAJORITY of death—one of the most significant union movements that has ever gone unnoticed. A little earlier in this book, we left the Battle of the Somme on its first day. So it's time to report how in that whole battle, lasting into October, the British lost about 420,000 men, the French another 200,000, and the Germans around 520,000. These numbers cannot be twisted into declaring a winner. Nor can one escape the caution of the rounded figures or the conclusion that in 1916 no up-to-date nation knew its exact losses.

The numbers are equally beyond imagination, if you think that *They Shall Not Grow Old* has some crowded frames where there might be three hundred or so good-natured soldiers waiting on the camera. But if we're thinking of movie deaths—Lew Ayres dying in *All Quiet on the Western Front*, or Valentino in *Four Horsemen of the Apocalypse*—and if we're supposing that you can't really kill a man in less than ten seconds of screen time (isn't that decent?), then here is a simple equation for the Somme losses:

1,140,000 men × 10 seconds each—then you'd need 132 days of continuous viewing to witness all the deaths from that battle strung together. As General Broulard might respond, with a fatalistic smile, "Well, surely, that's out of the question." He'd be right, of course, but the number is worth bearing in mind every time you see one of those terrific deaths in a movie, or when you count the scruffy, mousy faces in *They Shall Not Grow Old*, greedy for a few days more.

Moreover, the Somme was just one battle. If we try to assess the Great War as a long-running show, then the same principle of round numbers leads us to just over a million killed or missing from Austria-Hungary; 1.115 million from Great Britain; 1.398 million for France; and 1.8 million each for Germany and Russia. But the sense of accuracy is just a bureaucratic vanity. Take the world as a whole—the greatness being disputed in that war—and we estimate in our history books that about 18.3 million were killed or never found.

A blizzard of souls? I use that phrase because I've just seen mention of a 2021 movie of that name. It's a film from Latvia about a young man in the Great War, when Latvia, it is said, lost half its population. Did you know that? Could you find Latvia on a 1918 map? Can you grasp the numbers?

If you were a would-be moviemaker in the years after 1918, and if you yourself had been in some theater of war, then that was a lot to digest before you staged a vivid movie death. King Vidor had not served, but in one of his books he explains how in filming an artillery explosion, the earth that had to leap into the air was sieved free of rocks or stones so that the risk to extras spread-eagling themselves in the blast would be minimal.

From Texas originally, King Vidor learned the camera as a boy, and was in Hollywood raring to go by 1919. He quickly found his way, and at Metro-Goldwyn-Mayer became a favorite of the head of production, Irving Thalberg. One day this boss took him aside, and Vidor confessed how much he wanted to make a big, serious picture. This was 1924; Vidor was thirty and Thalberg twenty-five.

"What subject?" asked Thalberg.

Vidor pondered and then proposed a film about steel, wheat, or war. That gives you a taste of Vidor's youthful, pioneer vision. He looked at story as an American landscape begging to be developed.

Thalberg chose war. His was the kind of genius Hollywood needed.

So Vidor went away and started to think of Great War scenarios. There were veterans limping around with stories wherever you looked. He met Laurence Stallings, who had been in the Marines and was so wounded at Belleau Wood that later he had to have a leg amputated. Together, they came up with a script. It didn't exactly stretch anyone's imagination. Jim is your average American guy, not interested in enlisting for the war. But he's pushed into it by his parents. Soon enough, he and his new pals are shipped over to France, where they meet a nice country girl, Melisande. Jim and Melisande are sweet on each other. But then Jim goes to the front and life gets tough. His chums are killed in battle. Jim takes a bad leg wound. Back in the States after the war, his leg has to be amputated. Still, Mom tells him to go back to France for his girl. She knows story.

So there is Melisande plowing a field on her farm when one day she sees a figure coming down a hillside, limping toward her. The two of them end up in each other's arms. That is *The Big Parade* of 1925. It may be the most influential war movie ever made. Its mix of battle and romance (and box office) would be crucial. A genre was established.

The Big Parade ran two and a half hours; it cost $382,000; it earned rentals of about $20 million. As much as *Ben-Hur*, it was the project that established MGM as a studio, and it's of much more than historic interest. Vidor was a very adventurous director, with a practical but inspirational faith in people. Maybe the title sounds like a musical, but it really was a show grand enough to persuade audiences and theater owners that war "had legs."

Nothing was spared. In that farmland finale, the plow Melisande is pushing has handles that are bright in the sun. They are new wood, perfectly shaped, and not a plow that has been used for many years and grown dark in the process. This one was supplied by Props. Furthermore, Melisande is a lovely French actress, Renée Adorée, with bee-stung lips. In the same way, Jim is nothing like the coiled, wizened soldiers in *They Shall Not Grow Old*. He is John Gilbert, nearly six feet and regularly promoted as one of the most handsome men in pictures. The film has many scenes of doughboys on the march, and the timing of one march was so orchestrated by Vidor as to have a funerary pacing. But the coats the soldiers wear are brand-new, fresh out of Wardrobe and even laundered, instead of the bedraggled, stained, stinking clothes actual soldiers wore. Everything has been organized for effect.

At one point, with thousands of extras at his command, Vidor foresaw a striking scene of a column marching down a dead straight road. That geometry would be foreboding, he thought. But when he sent the extras off with assistant directors and clear instructions, those idiots used roads with bends and curves. So the footage lacked panache and fatalism.

What are you going to do? asked Thalberg, and he egged Vidor on to shoot the whole damned march again on a certifiable straight. That's how the title of the film is nothing like *Blizzard of Souls*, but a rousing come-on. In its wholesale public acceptance, *The Big Parade* was a landmark for a view of war that was easier to take if you hadn't served. It's spectacular. Gilbert is handsome. Adorée *is* adorable (her actual name was Jeanne de la Fonte).

THE WAR WAS SO RECENT IN 1925, NO WONDER MGM AND THE AUDIENCE were eager to think well of its sacrifice and the investment. After all, it had been the war to end all wars: that was the deal. Yet somehow the punitive terms of the Versailles peace conference of 1919 had set up the vengefulness and the damned pride that would need a second take sooner or later. Not that Versailles has ever become the subject of a movie, with diplomats and military people haggling over the misguided idea of punishment for a purposeless war and trying to persuade themselves about a braver new world. Most of us did not want to get into that infernal backstory—and how could you ask John Gilbert to play a manipulative diplomat or an aide to the high-minded racist Woodrow Wilson? Audiences wouldn't go for that. But if you want to know more about the Versailles process, you can go to John Dos Passos's novel *1919* (published in 1932), a dazzling marriage of fact and fiction, prose and cinema.

So the martial enthusiasm of *The Big Parade* suited 1925, and it exercised King Vidor's naive physical optimism. It's easy to see how the picture worked. But in that same 1925, a novel was published that starts with an educated, well-off woman walking in London. She is too busy preparing for a party she is giving to look for a cinema where *The Big Parade* is playing. Still, in writing *Mrs. Dalloway*, Virginia Woolf—who is not a Hemingwayesque figure, or someone we think of as exploring the darker corners of warfare—had described a character who is so shell-shocked that he will end up killing himself, casting a shadow on the exhilaration of Clarissa Dalloway's party. That man is Septimus Warren Smith, and I don't know of a mind so damaged by war so fully described at that time. Was that research, or plain imagination? Was Septimus subject to Woolf's own delusions? We may not have an answer, but *Mrs. Dalloway* remains one of the most discerning novels done under the influence of the Great War.

The literary foreboding emerged ahead of political dismay over appeasement and the likelihood of a second war coming almost automatically, or in a way that felt beyond restraint. The war poetry was being published. Robert Graves had been so badly wounded on the Somme that he was invalided out of action, and his memoir, *Good-Bye to All That*, was a valedictory on not just the war but British complacency and continued class privilege afterward. He recounts how the life expectancy of a young officer on the Somme was about three months. He was also unwavering in admitting the brutality—with prisoners being killed, and executions for desertion—that leaves *The Big Parade* seeming like holiday streamers dragged through the mud. *Good-Bye to All That* was published in 1929, the year that brought *All Quiet on the Western Front* into print.

Erich Paul Remark was born in Osnabrück in 1898 to working-class parents. Aged eighteen, he was drafted into the German army, and he was soon serving on the western front. But he was so badly wounded by shrapnel that he spent the rest of the war hospitalized, when he began to write. By 1927, he was at work on what would become *Im Westen Nichts Neue*. At first publishers declined it, perhaps because it was despondent about the war and too determined not to glorify it. But it was published in 1929 as

All Quiet on the Western Front and rapidly became an international best-seller. The author changed his name to Erich Maria Remarque, to honor his dead mother and as a gesture toward admiring the French.

Carl Laemmle Jr., the son of a man born in Germany, had just come to power at Universal, the studio founded by his father. He bought the film rights to Remarque's novel, got the playwright Maxwell Anderson to write a script, and hired Lewis Milestone to direct a film in which German soldiers would be played by American actors, speaking American. Born in the Russian Empire, Milestone had come to America in 1913 and served in the Signal Corps, making training films but not seeing combat. The hero of the film—another Paul—would be played by Lew Ayres.

So, if we choose, we can say that *All Quiet* is a rather phony war. But that hardly touches the plausibility of its realism and thus its pathos. The use of American actors is a subtle reminder of how similar all combatants were in their war experience. Paul has a professor who encourages the war, and enthusiastic service from his students. So Paul goes off to be trained, and to be killed. That's abridging a lot of story and detail, but we can note several improvements on *The Big Parade*: Paul does not find a girlfriend in France, he does not get out alive, and he has no feeling for the parade. The "quiet" introduced in the English title is poetic and ambivalent, and it leaves us wondering whether it can be achieved by peace, or mortality. (The German title says, simply, *No News on the Western Front*—I think the change was magic. And subversive.)

The combat scenes are still stunning. Milestone's big attack scene (clearly imitated by Kubrick in *Paths of Glory*) is superior to the later film. It may be too "exciting" in its tracking shots and its accumulation of detail. But the thrill of the master shots is undercut by the brutality of close-ups. There is an excellent account of how the MG 08 worked and of the damage it did. The film is unrelenting, and it does not shrink from the doom or futility of war. It is the landmark of Great War movies, and it's easy to understand how it is still seen and respected while Vidor's film has slipped into oblivion. *All Quiet* was a triumph for Laemmle. It won the Oscar for Best Picture and another for Milestone. It was acknowledged as an important film—but note that on a budget of just over $1 million, it earned only $3 million worldwide, a fraction of what *The Big Parade* pulled in.

Milestone had a long and distinguished career, with many routine pictures and some that are regrettable. His last job was trying to rescue a remake of *Mutiny on the Bounty* from Marlon Brando's petulant indecision. But he did direct *A Walk in the Sun*, a decent movie about the infantry in Italy; and *Pork Chop Hill*, with Gregory Peck holding on against great odds in Korea. He was always known as a war director, but he would never regain the occasion or the gravity of *All Quiet on the Western Front*. In our cultural history that film stands for a moment—the early thirties—when the world had a chance to act upon what I have called the pained reassessment of the Great War, and see how the deepening economic calamity was accelerating the standoff between communism and fascism that was likely to make further war.

The movie ends with Paul, disillusioned, wounded in no-man's-land, reaching out for a butterfly. That movement attracts a sniper, so Paul is killed. The butterfly (not in the book) is sentimental, to be sure, but that is a fair record of how entertainment had seen how we had become so bleak yet still preferred to limit our diet of hope. We may not be moved by the shot now, but there's no doubt about how it conveyed the dead reckoning of 1930. Here is a popular film that is not overwhelmed by the need to please the crowd.

The film's star, Lew Ayres, later acted on Paul's impulse. In the Second World War he was a conscientious objector and much abused because of it. But then he enlisted as a medic and served three dangerous years in the Pacific. It is a shock, but no surprise, that Hollywood has never dared make a movie of his story.

In the thirties, in Germany, Remarque began to be attacked by the Nazis for having written an unpatriotic book. Eventually, in 1938, he had to quit his country. He moved to Switzerland and to America. He became a celebrity, married to the actress Paulette Goddard (he had affairs, too, with Hedy Lamarr and Marlene Dietrich). He would write a fine novel,

Arch of Triumph, about Paris during the occupation. It was filmed in 1948, with Ingrid Bergman, Charles Boyer, and Charles Laughton, and it was well directed by Milestone again. But Remarque was not free. In the war years, still in Germany, his sister, Elfriede, had been arrested for undermining Nazi morale. At her trial it was said that while her brother had escaped, "You will not get away from us." And she was beheaded.

Remarque's story was remade in 1979 for American television, and then in 2022 a German version appeared, directed by Edward Berger. It was slow and grave, in an odd blue light, but it has some fine scenes, notably when Paul kills a French soldier and is then stricken with remorse. This new attempt, the first from Germany, impressed a world in agony over Ukraine. It won nine Oscar nominations. But what was being acclaimed? Was it simply the fact of Ukraine that urged us to "face the truth" about war and feel respectable? Or did the period detail from a century ago dip into nostalgia? Was it a new grown-up way of saying we hate war? Or was that such a dead cliché that it deserved deeper questioning or mockery?

The best thing in Berger's film was the least necessary, an angle Remarque had never used. So the 2022 film explores the labored protocols in how the Armistice was reached. This is ironic, or bitter, but it showed how the diplomatic history of warfare might be a better education than the endless spectacle of failed assaults.

IT WAS A SIGNIFICANT NARRATIVE ACHIEVEMENT TO LET PAUL DIE AT THE end of *All Quiet on the Western Front*. The immense totals of the dead had to be acknowledged somewhere. But suppose, in a commercial compromise, Paul had had no more than a life-threatening wound. Suppose, in surviving his physical ordeal, he had taken on the trauma of damage as well as the overlay of what had happened to German confidence. The attempt to resurrect that rueful nationality would be vital in the two decades of terrible peace. Suppose Paul had been put on morphine to endure in 1918–19. So he was never the same again. But maybe the wreck of the man could pull himself together enough to become Gereon Rath, a police inspector clinging to his drugs and the desperate hope that loss and damage could steer Germany home. Rath is the central figure in the television series *Babylon Berlin* (2017–22), an adventure epic and a love story, trying to find a compelling duty in the space between two wars, when the nature of the world is stunned by war.

Rath (played by Volker Bruch) has hopes still of being a good man, but he is an outlaw, too, as well as a policeman. An air of danger or unwholesomeness can attach itself to these honored outcasts. Travis Bickle in *Taxi Driver* seems to have been a hero in Vietnam—he did learn about guns somewhere. He has an urge to save the child whore, Iris, but he will destroy several others in that attempt. Even some classic military servants, injured in the process, can end up being told they were losers. Think of John McCain, and how his war was disowned by a disgraceful presidential sham. There are heroes who come to appreciate that their side may have been corrupted.

Heroes for Sale (1933) is not a big film, and not well known, but it has astonishing power in its 76 minutes. Thomas Holmes (Richard Barthelmess) is serving on the western front. There is a need to gain battlefield intelligence, and he volunteers for a reconnoitering mission with his friend, Roger. But Roger is too afraid, and Tom goes forward alone. He is wounded and taken prisoner by the Germans. Their field hospital cares for him and puts him on morphine. When he gets back to America, he finds that just as he is now addicted to the drug, so Roger is regarded as a winner.

Tom hauls himself up by his bootstraps, his true grit, and that Hollywood spirit. He advances in the laundry business (few films deal with that); he gets a sweet girl for himself (Loretta Young, no less). But the business is taken over by exploiters. There is a riot. His girl is killed. Tom goes to prison because he is deemed responsible. But he isn't down—not at all. He ends up delivering a rousing speech for FDR and the hopes for a new deal: "You know it takes more than one sock in the jaw to lick 120 million people." The film opened in 1933, that fraught year for misunderstood heroes. *Heroes for Sale* was written by Robert Lord and Wilson

Mizner and directed by William Wellman, who had flown with the La-fayette Escadrille, the French air force unit of mostly American volunteer pilots.

The haunted vet becomes a type. Sixteen years later, there is another modest, neglected film. Frank Enley is a hero in an idyllic Californian town, Santa Lisa. He is revered in the community because he was involved in an escape attempt from a German prisoner-of-war camp. He is Van Heflin, rugged, cheerful, a pillar of society; Janet Leigh is his happy wife, and they have a baby. This is 1949 and life feels swell, until a dark, limp-ing figure appears in their lives. He is Joe Parkson, gloomy; and a part for Robert Ryan, who seldom seemed happy-go-lucky or confident. (In the *New York Times*, Bosley Crowther said Ryan was "infernally taut.") Joe drags his injured leg (you can hear his menace coming), and he's looking for Frank. *Act of Violence* is a melodrama, but it's directed very well by Fred Zinnemann, who would go on to *From Here to Eternity*. It turns out that Frank betrayed the escape attempt to the Germans. He is a rat, de-spite that salesman smile, and Joe is the figure of retribution.

Or turn to San Antonio, Texas, in 1973. Charles Rane comes home; he is a major and he was seven years in a prisoner-of-war camp in Hanoi, where he was tortured and brutalized. An official hero, he will get a silver dollar from the city for every day of his captivity, plus one for luck—that's $2,556, and a red Cadillac to top off the package. Where are the movies about the PR scoundrels who concoct these deals?

But Rane finds that his wife is with another man, and his son hardly knows him. As he went away, life let its dark waters close over him. He becomes increasingly alienated until he turns to the violence he learned in Vietnam. The film is *Rolling Thunder*, directed by John Flynn from a story by Paul Schrader, who also wrote *Taxi Driver*. Rane is William Devane, and his best buddy is played by Tommy Lee Jones. They are bleak veterans who cannot be handled or treated lightly. Don't count on them for endorsements in those commercials about service, drawn swords, and being all that you can be.

Some hoodlums reckon to steal Rane's silver dollars. They capture him and stick his hand down a garbage disposal. They kill his wife and son. So Rane gets a hook for a new hand and sets out as a raider. It's a movie, another melodrama, and Rane is fiercer than most; but the civilization of those who did not serve, yet prospered in the victory, has a degree of guilt that prompts lurid tales of revenge. Travis Bickle may not have been in Vietnam. He may be a liar or a confidence man. But his ragged infection is part of the legend of our broken social contract. That's where the Great War is foundational, for introducing the theme of a young, willing guy who has been betrayed by the deal over going to war. The union movement that never came through has left addicts, cripples (that old word), and men every day at risk of shooting out their brains. Not that many, of course—don't let melodrama lead us into social exaggeration. The political meaning in the numbers is not encouraged.

But about twenty vets a day do kill themselves, which is twice the rate in the general population. Amid the drollery of *The Big Lebowski*, John Goodman looks like a huge lost child until his anger breaks out in a mad rant against Vietnam. So it's insufficient to say that *Heroes for Sale*, *Act of Violence*, or *Rolling Thunder* are not war films. The ethos and the hangover from cinematic conflict is everywhere. It's in the paranoia that clings to America being great. Or is it great again, as if we know our past is gone?

In hindsight, it's remarkable that Great War vets did not complain unduly, and did not know the language of post-traumatic stress. But in the new climate of war, we have become accustomed to the shocked mind seeking to disown the experience. So it's hard to offer a vet in a movie as halfway calm, reasonable, or the beneficiary of his service. Instead, war has left us caught between shame and neurosis. Nowhere is this dilemma plainer than in how we represent our police, the largest regiment in the land. The US has close to 700,000 law enforcement officers and an army of under 500,000.

The face of the veteran returned, but dismay is not a comfortable sight in the tradition of victory and calm. Tommy Lee Jones has one of the least assuring faces in modern cinema. There he was as the friend in *Rolling Thunder*, a damaged survivor at the end, utterly dispirited by the world that had sent him to war. Decades later, in 2007's *In the Valley of Elah*, Jones is the father, a Vietnam vet, who learns that his son, just home from service in Iraq, has been found dead under suspicious circumstances. So he sets out to ask why this happened. As written and directed by Paul Haggis, *Elah* is typical of a feeling that the service the country has called for may have been betrayed by corruption at large. To have a just war you need a culture that has some sense of living justice. To go to war without that may be to embark on mere murder.

FUNNY OLD WAR

In working out this book, I had reckoned that the Great War was a defining event. I suspected that two movies—bold departures—would deserve special attention. They were *Oh! What a Lovely War* and *1917*, films that surpassed regular models for war pictures. Then quite quickly I decided that *They Shall Not Grow Old* might be as significant; it was more real, or ordinary, and also more innovative. Maybe that is the great movie on 1914–18. But not having seen *Oh!* since it opened, in 1969, I was unprepared for how awful it had become. Was it always that bad?

It had begun life as a radio show, *The Long, Long Trail*, created and produced by Charles Chilton for the BBC in 1961. This was based on popular songs from the Great War era, but it included plenty of talk about what the war had been like. Two years later, Gerry Raffles and Joan Littlewood turned it into a stage musical that played at Littlewood's Theatre Workshop at Stratford in East London. It was a radical, satirical production, without uniforms or military equipment; a pantomime for adults, certain that the war had been a ruinous masquerade for simpleton soldiers and heartless leaders. The damage it had left was obvious, but it was the stupidity that seemed most offensive.

This was part of a general understanding that the Great War had been not just a disaster in a dazed society but a mishap inflicted on us by moribund leaders. That might have been acknowledged by most of the war's participants who were still alive in 1969, aged seventy or so. But like a lot of British satire of the 1960s, the show carried an air of superiority, as if to say, *Well,* we *wouldn't do that again.* As it was, the Labour government of the 1960s, led by Harold Wilson, had worked ingeniously to keep Britain out of the Vietnam War without offending President Lyndon Johnson too much. In that pious mood, *Oh!* was so acclaimed onstage it moved on from Stratford to the West End and Broadway.

The film rights were in the hands of John Mills and the thriller writer Len Deighton. It was Mills who approached Richard Attenborough about making the picture—the popular actor had not directed before. Deighton had done a screenplay that adapted the stage show quite freely: its premise had a family (the Smiths) visiting a show on Brighton Pier called the *First World War.* It started with a kind of chessboard setup staged on a carpet map of Europe where various dignitaries enacted the origins of the war: there was Ralph Richardson as Foreign Secretary Sir Edward Grey, Kenneth More as the Kaiser, John Gielgud as Count Berchtold of Austria, Ian Holm as President Poincaré of France, Jack Hawkins as Emperor Franz Joseph, Paul Daneman as the Czar of Russia. These potentates were all in a macabre dance they couldn't give up.

That plan had won financial support from Paramount: several star appearances would compensate for the uninteresting, if not tedious, Smiths. There was panache in the opening: at the Sarajevo assassinations, the victims toppled over like bowling pins. But there was too little humor or edge—the mood needed a mocking danse macabre. And then the pier show framework gave way to realistic-looking but routine re-creations of the battlefields. Joan Littlewood, who had directed the stage version, would complain that this flat realism erased the surrealism and killed the show. When the film turned to the generals, they were treated as vain buffoons, instead of solemn men acting in woeful error. That sad group included Sir Laurence Olivier as Field Marshal Sir John French, Sir Michael Redgrave as Field Marshal Sir Henry Wilson, and John Mills as Field Marshal Sir Douglas Haig.

That dismissive tone was misleading. Haig had been esteemed as a hero and the victor at the end of the war. There was a large equestrian statue in Whitehall commissioned at his death in 1928 and unveiled in 1937. The view of him as a "butcher" grew slowly. The statue has been criticized, for its size and for its choice of a hero. But it's still there, inadequate as a reminder of what that war meant to common people, and misguided in its assertion of Haig's success. The subject of the leadership required a radical intelligence that was not in Attenborough's soul. It was as if he wanted to keep the picture reassuring for the new age of satire. So the complex failure of wartime command has not been treated in a movie, and likely never will be.

There is one vivid star turn, to show how the epic satire might have worked. It has Maggie Smith as a music-hall singer encouraging young men to enlist in the army so she can make a man of them. Smith is gaudy edging into grotesque; she understands the scurrilous sexual allure, and the etched caricature. But most of the musical numbers seldom reach a level of pain; and the mise-en-scène, with picnics and poppies on the South Downs, becomes glum and predictable. There are some war scenes, or attempts at them, but they do not make the film urgent or dramatic. It needs the acid verve of the Kit Kat Klub scenes in *Cabaret*. At 144 minutes, *Oh!* is fifty minutes too long, granted that what remains could have felt like a Lubitsch musical laced with Buñuel's savagery. What happened in fact was so frightening, yet this film feels resigned. It's as complacent over the mistakes of Haig as it is with the pain of the Smiths—characters who should have been dropped at the outset.

Is that asking too much? Or is it part of the risk in going back to old movies? *Oh! What a Lovely War* was well enough received in 1969. It had no Oscar nomination, but the New York Film Critics Circle voted it runner-up (to *Z*) in the best picture category. Even so, Vincent Canby in the *Times* felt its "elephantine physical proportions and often brilliant all-star cast simply overwhelm the material with a surfeit of good intentions." I think it's the concept and the script that are wrongheaded and plain dull. The cruel farce had been tamed by a conventional reverence for the war. No one is angry or insightful about how or why it occurred. The film could have taken hints from Jean-Luc Godard's *Les Carabiniers*, from 1963, a breathtakingly cheap but deadpan analysis of the reckless urge to go to war, especially in young louts.

Yet the film did not seem absurdly mistaken in 1969; instead it looked like the natural exploitation of a stage hit and an attempt to tell us our culture had become more grown-up since 1914. Nearly fifty years later, *Oh!* seems clumsy and trivial beside *They Shall Not Grow Old*. But will even that documentary fade in time? Or are we facing the mystery in which something as drastic and fatal as a war can turn into a fossil of itself? I could tell you that the Thirty Years' War was a series of catastrophes for humankind, and with the most sympathetic will in the world you would be comfortable with that. (Historians estimate its deaths at around five million.) The War of Jenkins's Ear may sound like a sketch from *Monty Python*, but it lasted from 1739 to 1748 after an English sea captain had had his ear cut off by Spanish sailors. It came in at about 25,000 dead or missing. One deep cause of that war was Britain's wish to sell slaves in Spanish America.

So will every war pass away just as the buried bodies enrich the soil? Is it in our nature to fix on the stories, the grief, and the slogans? (The phrase "Jenkins's ear" was coined sardonically by Thomas Carlyle.) Or are the politics of warfare an affectation in which professional history is a tenure track more than a way of speaking to society? We like to say the Great War is notable and shocking for its absence of motivation, but perhaps that was a new and challenging verdict on how limited humans really are.

SAM MENDES'S *1917* OPENED IN DECEMBER 2019, A YEAR AFTER THE PROlonged anniversary of the Great War had concluded in Britain. By then, some of the nation felt it had had enough remembrance—the war could seem ancient or removed for people born after the Beatles. (Sergeant Pepper was a quaint relic, not a real soldier.) So Mendes had reason to go for a spectacular novelty to scatter indigestion after the banquet of poppies. He was also intent on paying homage to his grandfather Alfred, who had been a lance corporal two years on the western front. Born in Trinidad, Alfred had sometimes been a brave messenger on the dangerous front, and *1917* is a film about a message. Mendes wrote the script for the picture with Krysty Wilson-Cairns, and it is insanely ingenious.

In the spring of 1917, the Germans, depleted and exhausted after so many battles, reckoned to withdraw to stronger and more secure lines, known as the Hindenburg front. Perhaps this looked like the start of retreat and even concession; but could it be a trap?

The British are planning a major assault on the new line, confident (yet again) that victory is within grasp. But intelligence has reached General Erinmore (a fictitious figure, played by Colin Firth) that this is a German ruse; any big push against the new line will be destroyed. It's not clear how this information has been obtained, or why it can't be conveyed to the troops about to attack. Erinmore says only that Jerry cut the telephone lines. So he assigns two men to walk the nine miles to the forward British positions to call off the attack. He picks two chums, Blake and Schofield (Charles Chapman and George MacKay), raw lance corporals.

We meet them reclining against trees, looking out over a meadow of wildflowers. They get the word to report to Erinmore and walk back across the field and into a trench system of increasing density. By my calculation, they walk at least three hundred yards. All in one tracking shot backing away from their advance, past camp and kitchen, chatting as soldiers will. This transition is far-fetched, but it is wonderful, too, and there we have the enigma of *1917* and the fear that moviemaking can be taking over history.

Different histories overlap. So that innovative tracking shot in *1917* owed a lot to earlier, and later, films. That includes one of the more misguided historical interpretations of 1939–40, Christopher Nolan's picturesque *Dunkirk* (2017), a test case for movie splendor becoming vacant and decadent. *Dunkirk* is a panorama of what happened when the British Expeditionary Force was pushed onto the beaches by the German attack in the spring of 1940, and then rescued by an impromptu flotilla of small and large boats so that about three-quarters of that British army (over 300,000 men) was rescued instead of being annihilated or captured on the beaches. It is a film of extended takes and large vistas, where the coherence of actual war yields to the atmosphere of the place. It is spectacular, but curiously vague.

If you share Tolstoy's respect for tactics and terrain, you might wonder if the firm sandy beaches at Dunkirk would have assisted a continuation of the tank attacks, as well as being a begging target for German air superiority. (Britain had resolved not to lose planes and pilots over France, foreseeing the imminent crisis of a battle for Britain.) In other words, are we passive enough to watch *Dunkirk* without asking the child in ourselves, "Why do the Germans pause? Why do they not make a decisive attack on the Tommies?" Or have we been trained not to wonder whether some appeasing talks were going on, a fortnight after Churchill had become prime minister? But neither *Dunkirk* nor Joe Wright's *The Darkest Hour* (Gary Oldman as Churchill) was prepared to investigate that background, or disturb the Dunkirk legend eighty years later.

Dunkirk was a forerunner for the "total cinema" illusion of *1917*—though I think it had been surpassed in the single-shot five-minute Dunkirk sequence in Wright's *Atonement* (2007, one of the spellbinding moments in modern cinema). But neither film addresses this possibility—that Germany elected to let the Brits go at Dunkirk because Hitler did not have the will or the strategic resolve to crush them or to invade the sceptered isle. Because he felt already that he was in the wrong place? He should have been pushing into the Soviet Union. That pragmatism is at odds with the sentimentalization of the campaign that still pervades Britain and which has Winston Churchill as its figurehead, an opportunist who became a savior. That's not to sneer at Winston, or the long line of actors who have served in his regiment. But it does urge a historical interpretation consistent with what really happened, instead of just the legend of public relations. Dunkirk and Britain were a sideshow in what was to come. But "Dunkirk spirit" was still a battle cry in the ruinous Brexit decision.

In *1917*, we are facing an industrious attempt to make us believe this is 1917: that trick can be helped in authentic uniforms and rifles; the diligent reconstruction of trenches as an insane, battered hotel; the array of abandoned artillery on the ground; the nearly casual or random placing of corpses on the barbed wire, of severed bodies in craters, of hands and faces peering out of the mud, and of the rats eating any flesh to be found—the "bastard rats" in a world of lost parenting. The panorama is studiously arranged (it is a monument of art direction, from Dennis Gassner and his associates) so that it can verge on the picturesque or the significant. And don't knock beauty in a movie. If you want to know what the front could be like in 1917, then Mendes and his regiment have done so much to satisfy you while these two lance corporals take a walk. But the film also planted a fanciful number of black soldiers in its army to gratify modern hopes. (It would have been no more fanciful to add females to the regiment.)

That said, the military strategy of the situation is fatuous. A major attack is out of reach of its commanders? Severed phone lines could be repaired and need not impede visual signal systems over flat land, or prevent the several aircraft on view from dropping a message. Never mind, this is an adventure film, among many other things, so we are on the side of these two brave men and their attempt to get through. It is their task to deliver the precious orders—inscribed on paper—to Colonel Mackenzie with 1,600 men of the 2nd Devons, to tell him to call off the assault. There's a little extra story point in this, for Blake has a brother who is a lieutenant with the Devons.

Mission impossible, or very difficult—there's nothing wrong in that in a movie where action and heroics are legitimate ways of life and thought. But the boldness of Mendes's decisions on style compel us to feel the risk of artificiality or contrivance. And will. Why does the camera never cut? Because Sam Mendes has told it not to. So is he higher in the chain of authority than Erinmore?

In no genre is authority more compromising than in the war picture. After all, the strategy of creating a ruined battlefield for movie sport is a weird contrast with the desperate efforts of an army to achieve victory. So the more *1917* tries to tell us, *Look, you are there, and all of this is happening,* the more clearly we are led to admire the vision and the film-craft that have set it up. Sooner or later that opens a gulf of taste between slaughter and composure. *1917* is a symphony of disaster and loss, but it accumulates its music with pride in every foot of film, and every second of apparent continuity. Early on, we guess that this effort is going to win medals.

To trace just a part of *1917*, April 6, we start with Will Schofield and Tom Blake dozing under their trees. Then it's those three hundred yards back through trench systems to a bivouac where General Erinmore gives them their orders. Then they're wending their way through other trenches, heading to the British front, clambering fearfully into no-man's-land and beginning to thread their way across its upheaval. They come to a crater that is a small lake and something intriguing happens: the two soldiers have to circuit round its edge but the camera moves across the water itself, as if it is floating. As if we're watching a romance.

And it's all one shot.

Nothing daunting, no battlefield too testing for this camera, beyond the abandoned German lines; and in the warren of underground passages it contains, they come to a farmhouse. It is deserted, but recently—there is a pail of fresh milk just taken from a cow—and they watch bi-planes in the distance, three of them, in a dogfight. One plane is hit and it starts to billow dark smoke before it swoops down in its dying fall and comes directly toward our boys and into the camera. It crashes and brings fire. They drag a German pilot out of the plane. They smother his burning uniform but then he tries to attack them. All so sudden, but complete. He stabs Blake in the stomach before Schofield shoots him dead.

"Am I dying?" Blake asks. Gravitas descends in an instant.

"Yes, I think you are," says Schofield, and we are bound to agree in what is still the same shot from the beginning of the film. Blake's face is now turning deathly pale. We see the change. He dies.

Still the same shot.

We feel the loss of Blake (he was a good, amusing fellow) and the aloneness of Schofield. And we are stunned by the illusion of a single, unrelenting shot—or gobsmacked, for there is something childish or gleeful about the trick. Of course, a hundred years after 1917, we know we are being tricked. We have lived through the glory of real tracking shots in actual space—we have reveled in Max Ophüls, Jean Renoir, Anthony Mann, and Kenji Mizoguchi—but we know now that the computer and its digitizing of imagery can do anything. So the camera does not need to sink into darkness to hide a necessary cut. The stream can be doctored without a ruffle of discord. The continuity is transfixing still, but cold-blooded and helplessly artificial. And Mendes and his people can say, with justice, *Didn't you know the movies are fake?* Isn't their own aplomb a part of the fun? *1917* says it's a panorama of ruin, but it's very pleased with itself.

The stream of movie, its roller-coaster, needs to go somewhere, and in the second half of *1917* momentum runs up against question marks that begin as "plot" but take us deeper than that.

The 2nd Devons are nine miles away (we remember that) and no one could make rapid progress in this ripped terrain, not while carrying equipment, or when you'd rather not step on corpses. As it is—we may notice later—the journey takes part of one day, through a night, and into the next day, so the apparent continuation of the camera coverage is actually cramming twenty hours into two. The trick is in not noticing what has been left out.

That means those things included need to be more pressing, or dramatic. With the aid of another officer, Schofield gets directions, but he has to negotiate a town that is being fought over. By nightfall, it is burning, in imagery that comes close to a dream state. But Schofield finds a place to hole up, a shattered building, and that's where he meets a French woman with her baby girl. This is not a Melisande (as in *The Big Parade*). But she does keep faith with the movie ideal that a man in war may meet a woman. And when the baby cries in hunger, Will remembers that canteen of milk he took from the bucket at the farm (you do recall?) so the baby is fed and quiet. The couple exchange a few words but no embrace. Still, you feel the film sighing with relief at this respite from headlong, blind advance, and we make a note of the insurance proviso—that under such stress people are kind at heart.

Schofield plunges on. In daylight he comes to an enchanted forest, thick with waiting British troops who are listening to an a cappella voice singing "The Wayfaring Stranger," about home and mother. The sound is as pure as the echo in a cathedral, but the film's mood is swinging back toward the emotions of silent cinema, or the sentiments of 1917.

These men are the Devons. But Schofield has a river and a waterfall to negotiate. And then there is the crush of time. What hour is set for the imminent assault, for which the men are preparing? Will comes to a trench cut in chalk; the brightness seems hallowed or extra perilous, and the same driving shot carries him in search of Mackenzie. But a D. W. Griffith–like suspense exists now. Isn't the attack beginning? In desperation, Schofield climbs out of the packed trench, onto the green bank beyond it, the new no-man's-land where any German sniper could pick him off. Officers tell him to stop, but no, he starts running toward where he believes Mackenzie is waiting. He is as valiant as Roger Bannister breaking four minutes for a mile at Oxford in 1954 as shells burst around him. It is crazy, hysterical. He cannot survive—unless the camera carries him along in safety, in a halo.

All in one shot—the same shot? He gets there. Did you doubt it? Did you ever think he would be blown to smithereens? Or will he manage to present himself and his piece of paper to Colonel Mackenzie? Surely he must—isn't that why Mackenzie is Benedict Cumberbatch?

I suppose there could be a *1917* story line where Mackenzie says, *Alas and damnation, lad, but it's too late, the assault has begun,* or where the piece of paper is too torn or bloodstained to read, or where the colonel decides this late information is unreliable—Schofield might be a spy, an enemy agent. But Sam Mendes—as noble as Bannister—is not quite that brave, not with a $95 million budget in his backpack. You can't do the western front in one shot for less these days.

Mackenzie does call a halt. The front subsides. The day is saved, though the war has another nineteen months to go. And Cumberbatch has some good lines, like telling Will not to trust miracles. The war will go on, he says, to be won by "the last man standing." Then he sends Will away—"Now fuck off, lance corporal." If I'm ever in such a pickle myself, I hope I have a Cumberbatch as my colonel.

The film was a triumph, and it stirred up war buffs. Worldwide it earned just under $400 million (so maybe they could do a one-shot routine again for Passchendaele, Verdun, or even the Somme?). It received ten Oscar nominations, including Best Picture. It won for visual effects, sound mixing, and cinematography (for the excellent Roger Deakins). It lost Best Picture to *Parasite*.

I hope you and Sam Mendes can understand how much I admire the film. It is a ravishing, virtuoso experience. But in those last moments, war gives up its ghost to be a show; 1917 turns into *1917*. As you follow on in the tracking shot as Schofield goes through hell without any promise of getting back, you cannot shrug off the feeling of being sucked in by the ooze of forward motion in a video war game. The battlefield has been reduced to decor by technology. And you want to keep your finger warm and supple on the trigger. The re-creation is not much short of divine, but the reality of the Great War is fading in the dawn light, like our recollection of Jenkins and his ear.

13

THE GALLIPOLI ADVENTURE

Something in *1917* made me think of imagery I seemed to have seen before. Like waking from a dream. Why not? I have tried to suggest how filmed combat is often a set routine, like solitaire, with red jacks going up on black queens. It may be a silly illusion to say we keep these fragments in order, a chronology of death, instead of admitting the confusing rapture in which films overlap—as if one screen held them all. So we have digested the repeated shots and crosscuts—the heads tossed in pain, the bloom of fire from a gun, the slumped body—and have forgotten where they began. But I had seen another noble boy before, running frantically in danger, as if history depended on him.

In the expanse of Western Australia in 1915, Archy Hamilton and Frank Dunne are eighteen-year-olds who become friends in their passion for sprinting—just running as fast as they can in that empty quarter. They are played by Mark Lee and Mel Gibson. You may have forgotten Lee, but Gibson is world-famous, not always liked, but a force on the screen. He was twenty-four in 1980, born in Peekskill, New York, Irish American, the son of an Australian who shipped the family back to his homeland when Mel was twelve. He had done a few films before *Gallipoli*, notably the original *Mad Max* with its first hint of truculent outlawry. But this war film established Gibson as an athletic, brave hero, a lurking rebel, and as good-looking as a silent-movie star. He seemed fresh still, hopeful and cheeky.

The project meant a great deal to Peter Weir, its director. He had had success with *Picnic at Hanging Rock* and *The Last Wave*, but a serious war film was an expensive departure, and one where he felt resistance in the Australian picture business (it would cost five times the budget of *Picnic at Hanging Rock*). He had thought of setting his film in Flanders, but then he had taken a hiking holiday in the eastern Mediterranean. One night he slept out in the open. "Something woke me up about 1 a.m. I was instantly awake, instantly afraid. That kind of animal fear, the cold sweat, the special alertness you can feel in a moment of profound danger. But why? There was no one about. I hadn't been dreaming and yet I knew instinctively I had to get out of there."

The next day he told a local about this odd feeling, and the Greek said, *Of course*. Weir had been sleeping on a battleground—from before the time of Christ. A few days later, Weir reached Gallipoli itself and found the old trenches preserved as a museum. That felt like a signal. He had discovered his subject, the legacy of battlefields, and he knew, like every Australian, that Gallipoli had been a landmark in his national history. As he told an interviewer, that campaign had triggered "the birth of a nation . . . Not just the battle and our part in it, but most importantly the referendums on conscription."

After the shock of the Dardanelles campaign, and the shocking Australian losses, the prime minister, Billy Hughes, had felt compelled to put compulsory conscription to the vote in 1916. The measure lost, narrowly, and then it lost again in a second-thoughts referendum. This was a crucial step in Australian separation from the mother country and any assumption that the members of the empire would always do what London told them. Empires only work for so long.

Moreover, Weir's *Gallipoli* came just a few years after the Vietnam War, in which Australia had been involved beyond its wishes. Over seven thousand Australians served in Vietnam, and five hundred were killed. (From the West, it may have been easy to think that Australia and Vietnam were in the same theater. Get out the maps: Australia is nearly 3,500 miles from Taiwan, and that gap could come into consideration again.)

Gallipoli was still only a movie, made for a big crowd, but it had a political point of view, whereas *1917* is curiously locked in the hopeful opinion that brave boys will carry the day, that the message will get through in defiance of the lethal meaning of bullets. So Schofield plunges into glory in his sprint. At the end of *Gallipoli*, Frank (Gibson) undertakes another desperate run to carry a message that an attack should be stopped. But he gets through too late, and the very ending is a freeze-frame of his pal Archy being cut down.

It's not that Sam Mendes "copied" this effect. It's as likely that the treasury of war screens had passed into his bloodstream. But then he took a creative way out so that the message was conveyed . . . and combat films might not be the same. This helps us see that *1917* has less interest in political history than *Gallipoli*. And it leaves Mel Gibson desperate in anguish, a warrior who has come back to us many times over.

The benefit of *Gallipoli* is in its study of a friendship, and of the spirit in which young men in 1914 and briefly thereafter existed in such innocence about what a Great War would be. These boys feel the world— spacious Australia, Egypt, the Dardanelles—is their playing field. Until the rules become grimmer. As time passes, it is easier to appreciate the cultural correction that came from that war. Another consequence of this, a lesson we may prefer not to heed, is in guessing at the calamities that lie ahead. You may sleep on an ancient battlefield and find fresh hostility in the morning. "World war" is not just a caption in history. It's a wounding lesson in the fragility of "world."

14

APRÈS LA GUERRE

What was it for, the whole thing? Where is history's omniscient tracking shot going? For so vast and damaging an event, we feel there must have been some purpose, or excuse. Aren't we obliged to wonder if we hope to deserve history or destiny? Can we really keep up with this mad race of ours if we lack goals or explanation? Is war just one of our fretful ways of giving ourselves a role? Or is its terminal meaning that there is no significance beyond the tidal changes of evolution? One lesson of *1917* is how far we have moved on from the Great War. Very soon we could be as much its onlookers as we are with Waterloo or the Battle of Lepanto (1571).

War reorders life under the guise of drastic severity. But its promoted "causes" and "consequences" can mean less than the unexpected forces turned loose. The American Civil War, schoolbooks say, "preserved the Union and emancipated slaves" (as if those were the intentions). It also undermined national identity and put a curse on black people. Those consequences have not ended. The Great War rearranged the board game of European principalities, and hoped that the game would never be replayed. A hundred years later, there are still borders fringed with hostility. The Crimea is active again.

Yet so many of us prefer to forget. Bertrand Tavernier remembered how difficult it was to raise the funding for *La Vie et Rien d'Autre* in the late 1980s. Who wanted to know? His prospects could seem as grim as those facing France in the years after the Great War when the story was set. Moviemakers can get so caught up in their creative venture that they use it as a metaphor for every other struggle in life. Tavernier wished to tell the story of a major, a despairing man who had made it his calling to identify the remains left in the topsoil and in the anecdotes of recent battlefields. So *Life and Nothing But* is a film about obsessive pursuit for a man who counts the dead while yearning for life.

"You mean this is just the story of a charmless officer and so many corpses?" the money people must have asked. You can't fool those idiots. Nothing seemed easy or promising. The film would be done largely on location, in unpicturesque country in Aude and Haute-Marne. In unfolding several stories, it would need to take its time. The two stars, Philippe Noiret and Sabine Azéma, were so moved by the venture they put half their salary back into the budget. They must have guessed the rare opportunity the film offered actors; maybe in rehearsal they saw a prospect of affection. So the unlikely and ambiguous script was made. It would be a war film without obvious combat. But then the predicted disaster won respectability,

Life and Nothing But earned eleven nominations for the César, the national film award of France, including for best film, best director, best actress, and best screenplay. Noiret won as best actor. He had been intrigued that his character had a damaged arm that was never explained or offered as a cue for our sympathy. But if you watched carefully you realized that this soldier lacked the full use of his saluting arm. Or was that a mark of his withered emotions? It was that kind of a mystery film—*Life and Nothing But*, among the greatest and most original war movies, and one that understands how a war persists long after its proud peace documents have been signed.

As part of that pomp, two years after the Armistice, the archaic code of French glory had determined to celebrate "the unknown soldier," a mythic ghost to uphold the supposed romance of the war. This lofty scheme was invented in France in 1919. But Major Delaplane in *Life* is disgusted by its frivolous evasion. He knows that for a self-important, modern country it is a disgrace that no one really knew what happened in the confusion of those four years. Officially the French dead numbered 1.5 million. Those bodies were retrieved, decorated, and given impressive funerals. But an extra 350,000 were blown apart in jigsaw fragments beyond careful "doing." They were termed "missing in action," clerically unaccounted for. Delaplane hates war, but he clings to the idea of a nation staying faithful to its memories. He tries to be aloof but he sings dirty songs with the men. His blue serge coat is a way of masking his radical self. He has become regimented, but he despises his own bargain. Bristling with anger, he waits for his crisis.

Delaplane serves under an odious general who is set on identifying an appealing "unknown" soldier, but the major resists that sham effort, and spends his days gathering evidence from the battleground—rings, bones, and buttons—trying to measure the remains against the recollection of relatives who want to know the truth, but who live in dread of hearing it. By the end of the film, when the general has found his unknown candidate and a portentous ceremony, Delaplane has identified and confirmed over 51,000 of the lost dead.

But life has another way of testing him. Two women appear as searchers in his area: Irène de Courtil (Azéma), wealthy and Parisian; she has lost her husband—he was part of an aristocratic family that helped run the war for France; and Alice (Pascale Vignal), a country girl and an out-of-work teacher, looking for a boyfriend. Delaplane notices Alice's prettiness, and tries to help her; he also makes a blunt pass at her that she rebuffs. He is one more common soldier, made harsh by loneliness. From the outset Delaplane and Irène seem at odds: he strikes her as brusque and unmannerly; he assumes she is spoiled by privilege. They quarrel, without quite knowing why. She is a fashion plate out in the fields: she wears fur stoles; her long hair is coiled beneath designer hats and a heavy gray veil. She stands apart out of class austerity and apprehension. There is a crushed longing in her stance and it reaches out for more than a lost husband.

Delaplane wears his fading blue coat every day, his boots, and his military cap. He is in charge and short-tempered because of it. He falls into a kind of contest with Irène that is not far from screwball attraction. Can a war movie be that playful and still be somber? Yes, so long as neither character yields to any hint of coyness. They are tough spirits who watch each other warily as a lonely respect sets in. He gives her a permit and then a plate of canteen food with a prized piece of lean meat. She begins to assess his dedication, and listens to his outbursts at the disaster of war and the official vanity in tidying it away. He is a kind of revolutionary but he is attracted to her class; she is a society figure tempted by his rough candor.

We realize that, until Irène appeared, he had no one to talk to. He can turn coarse and garrulous, as if ashamed of his loneliness. Tavernier shows the two of them as fellow isolates who somehow run downhill toward each other in this harrowing place. It is dangerous ground: plow a field and you may set off an old bomb; there is a tunnel nearby, a death trap, because a munitions train was caught there by the Germans and is still likely to have its explosions.

Without having seen the film, you might decide that I am preparing you for a love story. You would not be wrong, but mark how unexpected a love this is. So many war films have a romance in which frightened or displaced characters cling together—so long as they are heterosexual; the natural inclination of gay affection reaches all too few films. The impact of endangered straight love takes all the oxygen. So love makes a war go round. *From Here to Eternity* deplores the Japanese treachery on December 7, but it aches over its frustrated love stories, and the way its two women must go back to America alone.

Our culture likes to assert that women cannot understand war—because they are not fighters. Apart from the withering nonsense of that, it leaves naked in the cold air the absurd supposition that men do understand it.

Life and Nothing But takes all of its first half (over an hour) in teaching us the condition on a front once the war has passed away. Patience is required in the viewer, just as the broken nation needs time to heal or believe in the homily that things are very well now. But we learn a little more. The major was married, but that is over; and against first impressions it becomes clearer that Irène did not quite love her husband, despite her duty in seeking proof of his death. It is as if Delaplane's commitment to the facts of death begins to impress Irène and her buried sensibility. She makes friends with Alice, and when they share a sleeping partition (Alice was being pursued by a lovelorn soldier), their dark hair comes down and we see how alike they are. In another way, Delaplane has noted how the women's stories are versions of the same pattern. As Irène befriends Alice she endears herself to Delaplane—until the major has to tell the girl that his research knows her boyfriend was already married. Irène scolds him for that honesty—as if it had not moved her.

Irène and the major are growing into mutual understanding. Filmgoers sense what is coming. One night the couple are driving in her plush rented car. She orders him to stop and abandons care or discretion. If you like, she goes over the top, that Great War tradition monopolized by men. She tells him how much she feels for him and how he needs to say only three words for her to be his. This is not just a sexual overture, or a proposal; it amounts to an assertion that life can surpass death and bury the past. He is astonished but alarmed. He does not have the courage or the revolutionary energy to say the three movie words. So they part: she goes off to America, as in giving up France. Retired from his army, he lives alone on his farm. But then he writes to tell her what hope she has unearthed in him. This is a movie about burial and resurrection.

It has no shots fired in action, no combat. The bravery is of an intimate sort hidden to onlookers. It is also a lengthy, gradual picture that comes to a rapt climax—that exchange in the car is as tense or embattled a love scene as you will find, without a kiss or any note of happily ever after. One can decide that it is a tribute to French sadness after the Great War, and Tavernier was more of a historian than most film directors. But it is a war story on the consequences of the game such as every general and private, every elected prime minister and authorized thug, should see once a year.

We witness the disordered rural life, with poverty and unemployment and high-level corruption. Delaplane describes deals made during the war. The Germans would leave factories intact so business could thrive afterward. There are bombs and mines in the ground still, ready to be touched off. And, of course, if not yet in 1920, then by 1989, Tavernier and his audience knew that the peace was only a gesture, waiting on so much more. That large war had not ended so much as paused. There has been no true peace or stillness since 1914. Tavernier would be born in 1941 into a France occupied by Germans. His sense of war was far-reaching. He died as I was writing (March 2021).

The deepest mystery is the love between Delaplane and Irène, and it rests on how we read the film's ending. In that taut confrontation, in the car stopped at night, she has challenged him to admit to his feelings. And he is taken aback; she is so much stronger or more desperate than what she calls the foolish men's club of war. (War can be a final fortification in the fortress of hollow male superiority.) So we hear Delaplane's voice-over in a letter he has written to Irène saying of course he loves her—so she must come back to France to be with him.

It's a pretty ending, but too suave or complacent. Was Tavernier pushed to resolve this difficult picture with a comforting close? Or did the two players beg for a chance of reunion? How are we to read the later Irène seen in a well-appointed salon somewhere in Wisconsin? She wears a twenties flapper dress and has her hair bobbed. She's as cute as Daisy Buchanan or some other Scott Fitzgerald woman. She seems to smile as she reads Delaplane's letter so we can think *Happy ever after*, if we're chumps enough. But is that smile alive, or detached? Would she really give up Milwaukee (or wherever) for that rural life where he is solitary in the landscape and his vineyard mimics a field of crosses for the wartime dead? Or does she have a cocktail party to attend?

Could a damaged nation be healed by the marriage of an old officer and this liberated woman? Can they be contented, or has conflict forever undermined their emotional landscape? Did we see the future in that café scene, with live music from a young black soldier playing a soprano sax?

Irène asked the major to dance, but he was too shy or old regime, as if the malady in his arm had spread to his whole body. Perhaps Irène is too modern, too willful, too insistent that a challenge be accepted on the spot. Women can be braver; some veteran soldiers stay scared forever. Perhaps Delaplane is too lonely and locked in to chance a new marriage. War shakes up the ground but it is just as upsetting for fixed romantic clichés. *Life and Nothing But* can seem warming and sentimental—we can regard the film as an affirmation. But it is too intelligent for that. It is a challenge to us, too, and Delaplane may not be quite brave enough to live with it.

LIFE AND NOTHING BUT HAD BEEN COWRITTEN WITH JEAN COSMOS, A NOV-elist, a screenwriter, and a songwriter. Always a writer himself, Tavernier had enjoyed collaborations: his wife, Colo Tavernier, had worked with him on *Une Semaine de Vacances*, *Sunday in the Country*, and *Beatrice*. Cosmos was eighteen years older than Tavernier so he had had a closer experience of the Second World War. But the two men would make a team that meant as much to Tavernier as his partnership with Philippe Noiret. Cosmos was specially good at dialogue, and some people noted how Noiret and Tavernier could sound like twins in the dark.

The success of *Life and Nothing But* urged Cosmos and Tavernier into another project: in 1996, they delivered *Captain Conan*, adapted from the prizewinning novel by Roger Vercel. Despite bad eyesight, in the Great War Vercel had served as a stretcher-bearer and then as an officer on the eastern front, where France and Russia opposed the Germans and the Turks. That front was far longer than the western front so, often in mountainous regions, it made for a fluid war with bold troop raids and a premium on initiative. That begins to explain Captain Conan, the charismatic leader of a group of volunteer fighters famous for their reckless night assaults, their taking no prisoners, and their panache. This is the Great War without the depression acquired in trench warfare. It is battle fit for old-fashioned heroes and new wolves. That touches on an important theme in military movies: the accomplished warrior initially true to his code, but so independent or rogue that he inspires our rebellious allegiance. This contradictory figure reaches from *Patton* to Colonel Kurtz in *Apocalypse Now*.

As the film opens, Tavernier presents us with a last great battle in which the French defeat the Bulgarians. Tavernier was never a Samuel Fuller or an Anthony Mann (though he admired those action-driven Americans), but this is a thrilling fight sequence, roaming over steep hillsides with adventurous camera movements and a feeling for rapid skirmishing. We share in the audacity and brilliance of Conan, the use of cutthroat knives, and the esprit de corps that he has aroused. In the form of actor Philippe Torreton, Conan is dark, belligerent, irascible, and always agitated—a demon for action drives him. He has a ruthlessness that makes its own code without second thoughts or guilt. If you intend to kill the enemy, killing has to become your nature. His men adore his commitment, while his army has to smother its reservations.

There was an armistice with Bulgaria in September 1918 that led to the Armistice that ended the whole war in November. But the war did not go away or resolve local enmities. Conan and his men are next assigned to Romania, and soon they are engaged against contingents of the new Red Army. The Great War ended in tribal confusion on the eastern front among small nations with histories of hostility enflamed by the new Soviet Union presenting threats (and hopes) not thought of on the staid western front.

Conan makes an unlikely friendship with Norbert (Samuel Le Bihan), an academic fellow as restrained as Conan is uninhibited. Norbert realizes that Conan is a kind of legitimized murderer, and he wants to resist Conan's conviction that nothing else will suffice in war. But the orderly observer is drawn to the wild man. At the same time, we feel a mounting loathing of it all in Conan, as the extrovert sinks into a brutal depression.

This opposition is not as fully explored as it might have been. By contrast, the struggle between Irène and Delaplane is more compelling and complex. But in the deteriorating conditions on the eastern front, as official war turns into a kind of gang warfare, and as Conan becomes increasingly reckless, Norbert is assigned as a defender in courts-martial. Conan may have committed crimes. There is one case where a young man seems wrongfully accused and Norbert and Conan join forces to have him exonerated. This is like a last stand for decency. The peace turns increasingly toxic as war degenerates into piracy. Conan is an officer in a vast army, but he carries himself like an outlaw. So many peace arrangements let us turn our backs so the dirty business can go to its limit. At the end in Vietnam, the United States just wanted to get out and stop having to see what was happening. And then Afghanistan . . .

Time passes in *Captain Conan* and there is a coda where Norbert— a success now—goes to a dejected village in France hoping to see Conan again. The hero is heavier and seems much older. His earlier attacking crouch is sunken now. He may be dying, and wishing the end to come quickly. There are so many dead ends for war's heroes. The old friends part, and we are left with a feeling for the many kinds of damage done by the war.

Captain Conan won Césars for Torreton as actor and Tavernier as director. But the film was too unsettling to do well commercially. War films are invariably expensive, and to get that funding back the project may need to feed the public a few tasty white lies. Even an antiwar crowd enjoys a thrilling battle, and *Captain Conan* starts with its most exciting scene. It is not as rich a film as *Life and Nothing But*. The relationship between the two men is not as developed as the love affair. But a seed is there, the example of a rogue warrior. You have to go to Werner Herzog's ecstatic, terrifying, but pretentious *Aguirre, the Wrath of God* (1972) to see that sort of insane leader in full flight.

Tavernier and Cosmos did one more picture together, *Laissez-Passer*, or *Safe Conduct*, made in 2002. It sprang from the historian in Tavernier being intrigued by the uneasy circumstances of French filmmaking under Vichy control. There was an orthodox way of looking at that period and condemning all forms of collaboration, without sorrow or pity. But France was not simply a nation committed to resistance. Life is often more complicated; the clenched fist keeps its fingers crossed. So Tavernier wanted to do a film that was a tribute to the screenwriter Jean Aurenche (1903–92), who had lived through the Nazi years, often in a writing partnership with Pierre Bost, trying to work but not wanting to collaborate. (Picasso and Cocteau had similar wars and buried compromises.)

In fact, after a period of neglect—the pair had been attacked by the New Wave generation—Aurenche had worked with Tavernier as the director began his career. They combined to make *The Clockmaker*, *The Judge and the Assassin*, and the brilliant *Coup de Torchon*, which transposed the Jim Thompson pulp novel *Pop. 1280* from the American South to French West Africa.

Safe Conduct traces the 1940s relationship between Aurenche and an assistant director who was in the Resistance, Jean Devaivre. The film is long and the narrative drifts. Its good intentions end up compromised, and Devaivre sued Tavernier for giving him inadequate credit. This is all the sadder because Tavernier was better equipped and more willing to explore the life of occupied France than most directors. He lived and worked in the tradition of the French master Jean Renoir.

15

A BRIEF ILLUSION

Any Great War connoisseur will agree: this survey has to include Jean Renoir's *La Grande Illusion*, made in 1937. Isn't that the classic, a film for the duke?

We are with French prisoners of war in a German castle. These fellows get along more or less, but one Frenchman, an aristocrat (Pierre Fresnay), used to know the German commandant (Erich von Stroheim). They were both "in society" in the old days, when Europe was their playground; they lived by the same rules of privilege and they speak English together. They exist in a brotherhood not offered to the lower-class prisoners, like the characters played by Jean Gabin and Marcel Dalio. But a plot crisis comes when the commandant has to shoot and kill his French friend, who is trying to stage a diversion: it is the German's duty to open fire, and a mark of fatalism protecting the bogus regime of honor. But as the Frenchman intended, in the distraction of this shooting, two prisoners get away.

La Grande Illusion is more than very good. At its end, as the two Frenchmen escape, a gentile and a Jew, and after Gabin has fallen in love with the German woman (Dita Parlo) who shelters them, they trudge through the snow to cross the Swiss border. German guards see them and prepare to shoot. But their officer tells them to stop because the Frenchmen may be over a frontier that is hard to discern in the snow.

This was hailed as a humanist masterpiece and actually nominated for best picture at the Academy Awards, recognition that had never before been given to a foreign-language movie. It did not win (Frank Capra's fluffy *You Can't Take It With You* got the Oscar), but the nomination was seen as a measure of intelligence and maturity, as if in 1937 fine irony might still save the day. Goebbels ordered that all prints of the film in Germany be destroyed. As Renoir put it, the reasonable world was reassured in acclaiming a great antiwar film; and then two years later war broke out, or escaped.

If it pleases you, you can say *La Grande Illusion* is "antiwar," but I think Renoir had realized how war made a showcase for his natural, and benevolent, irony. Before he made movies, Jean had served in the French cavalry and been wounded in the Vosges. He limped the rest of his life because of that. But it was in recovery from the damage that he started watching films, and wondered about a future beyond being just a famous painter's son.

He was rueful, by 1939, for part of his own illusion was that a worldly antiwar attitude might redeem him, and us. Another part was in hoping movies could save the world. We've all held on to that romance. But I'm not so sure. I doubt there is any such thing as an antiwar film. That has to do with our duplicitous nature, and with the bursting firepower of movie itself. In the dark, whatever the official motive or the orders, we go to war for excitement. In 1937, Renoir could think he had made his finest film. Tacitly he was sentimental over the officer class that umpired the battle. (Years later, he would write a fond novel, *The Notebooks of Captain Georges*, about a young man coming of age in the cavalry.) When von Stroheim's commandant points his pistol at the French officer, we know he has to shoot. The fatalism in film's machine cannot resist fatality. Some movies are more sophisticated than others, but every gun offered will be fired.

III

THE JUST WAR

Because a war had to be fought so it lay in the
sunshine of being "just." But there was an overcast,
too, that understood it was just war.

16

HORSE FEATHERS

By 1938, there were those in Britain and in the world at large who believed fresh war was certain. Many assured themselves that they regarded this prospect with dread or foreboding. Most saw the resumption of war as a shaming thing in history. But a few nursed shy eagerness, as if by 1938–39 one way of feeling the resonance of the "world," and disputes in a mass society, was to join in the test of universal war. Was the failing of the Great War just an inability at making hostility work? Then there was the faithful generality of humans, those who would follow orders as a way of avoiding doubt or the testing possibility of critical intelligence. Sometimes that protective habit can seem as daunting as air raid sirens. But doing as you are told—and waiting to be told—is a way of clinging to your leaders, and the theory of their wisdom.

In *The Lady Vanishes* (1938), under the guise of an amusing adventure, Alfred Hitchcock had a trainload of English people caught up in a fascist Europe. The characters made light of it, but Hitch knew the ugliness that was building. As a student of German cinema, he had felt the coming peril. And he himself always suspected the worst in people.

In September 1938, Prime Minister Neville Chamberlain had returned from meeting Hitler and Mussolini in Munich waving a piece of paper whereby Britain, France, and Italy had signed off on allowing Germany to occupy the Sudetenland region of western Czechoslovakia as the last claim the Third Reich would make on more living room. "Peace for our time," he said, but he was in pain. Chamberlain was welcomed back to Britain, and to Buckingham Palace, as a savior, in nervous glory. He was dying, but the piece of paper perished first.

So many had been afraid of war, and eager to give appeasement every chance. On the other hand, Clement Attlee and the British Labour Party disapproved of the Munich settlement. Winston Churchill believed real war was only a matter of time. As a leading Tory without official position, he recognized that war could be his chance to come in out of the wilderness of neglect. He had called for opposition to the Hitler who had barely masked his contempt for Chamberlain. In the British armed forces there was a mounting sense of imminent hostilities, and a muffled attempt to get ready for the war. British military investment had declined by 500 percent after the Great War in a spirit of exhaustion and ill-judged relief, but by the late thirties new ships were being built, and plans were laid down for the development of Hurricane and Spitfire aircraft.

The Spitfire (a single-man fighter plane) had been test-flown in 1936, whereupon the Royal Air Force ordered three hundred copies. Its inventor, R. J. Mitchell, died in 1937, but in 1942 he would be the subject of a heroic biopic, *The First of the Few*, directed by and starring Leslie Howard. By then, the Spitfire was a proven force in the skies over Britain, and a testament to the efficacy of brilliant, fast machines and inexorable technology. Howard was a hero of the moment, the pale, soft-spoken Englishman, but in June 1943 the plane flying him home from neutral Lisbon dropped into the Bay of Biscay and he was dead, shot down by German aircraft. Had they simply picked off a passing flight or reckoned to eliminate the hero? Had they thought Churchill might be on the plane? Amid secrecy and security, stories go wild.

Armorers were thriving everywhere. Far away, in the Marin headlands, north of San Francisco, as early as 1938, mighty guns were set up on the cliffs, batteries that could fire twenty miles out to sea, in case of some gesture at invasion. That was not coming from Germany, but the chessboard of strategy regarded Japan as the likely enemy. And the "shock" of Pearl Harbor was nearly four years away.

Amid all of this, in the same 1938, the enterprise known as Korda, or London Films, prepared to make a spectacular movie from the adventure novel *The Four Feathers*, as if to say machines are all very well, but don't forget legend or horse feathers.

There were three Korda brothers, Hungarian: Alexander, the visionary businessman but a director, too; Vincent, who was a master of production design and decor; and Zoltan, who was a director and the force behind *The Four Feathers*. By way of Budapest, Berlin, Paris, and Hollywood, they had come to London and recognized the foolish diffidence with which the British picture business was mishandling History, Gentlemen, Posh Houses, and Honour. Why did it take Hungarians to feel the promise of *Masterpiece Theatre* and the empire that would be known as *Downton Abbey*? With charm, no shame, and borrowed cash, they became showmen patriots. A friendship sprang up between Alex Korda and Churchill. The brothers had had an international success with *The Private Life of Henry VIII* (for which Charles Laughton won the best-actor Oscar). They had another prestigious hit with the H. G. Wells novel *Things to Come*. But they had an urgent sense of a martial dawn by 1936.

It was in that year that A. E. W. Mason, a gentleman author with a good record in the Great War, published a novel, *Fire Over England*, which employed the history of the Spanish Armada (1588) as a pointed warning to what the late thirties might face as a new authoritarian threat from Germany. It was a book that stirred Churchill and Korda, so a movie was set up with Laurence Olivier and Vivien Leigh as the young couple who bear the load of the story. That casting was astute, for Larry and Viv were a romantic couple in life—and Korda was personally enchanted by Leigh. The adventure ends with Queen Elizabeth I (Flora Robson) speaking to the naval forces at Tilbury that await the Armada. This was actually the first big movie presentation of Elizabeth. It had taken Korda to understand the melodramatic resonance in the queen and the monarchy.

And as that film was made, maybe Mason urged Korda to look at some of his backlist. *The Four Feathers* had been a bestseller for Mason in 1902. Set in the 1880s, in the England of country houses, it concerns fellow officers in the Royal North Surrey regiment. There is excited talk of the need for Britain to restore order and authority in the Sudan, where the Mahdi had recently killed General Gordon and his occupying forces at Khartoum.

At this point (I mean in 2023), you may want to consult an atlas just to be sure where Sudan is—and what its potential may be. What I mean by that is a deeper understanding of what the Sudanese wanted and awareness of the Mahdi as a serious man and respected leader, instead of just the exotic villain in our adventure. This loss of Gordon was a terrible thing in British eyes, in which a savage heathen (or the Islamic leader in the Sudan) had failed to grasp the benefits of being a British colony. His real name was Muhammad Ahmad and he desired freedom from Egyptian and British control. Years later, this was spelled out in the film *Khartoum* (1966), where Charlton Heston played Gordon and Laurence Olivier—in the blackface he had just popularized as *Othello* onstage—was a saturnine Mahdi.

In the England of *The Four Feathers*, young officers and gentlemen are ready to ship out to the Sudan for British order and imperium. One of these is Harry Faversham (John Clements), the latest in a long military line, but so much more thoughtful than his fellows that he has doubts about this new war. Harry's father has been worried about the boy ever since he started reading poetry—Shelley—and flinching at bloody tales of victory. But now Harry resigns his commission and retires from the regiment. This horrifies his old chums, notably Willoughby, Burroughs, and John Durrance (Ralph Richardson). Gravest of all, it raises confusion in his fiancée, Ethne (June Duprez). Suddenly Harry is an outcast, reduced from dress red uniform to a plain suit, and the recipient of four white feathers, the brand of cowardice.

Thus the title for the movie and its rigged setup. "There's no place in England for a coward!" Harry is told by his commanding officer and by Ethne's disappointed gaze. But is he a coward? What does that term mean? Is he shamefully afraid—is it shaming and damning to admit fear, that mainstream of life? Or could it be wisdom? At one point, Harry speaks of "the futility of this Egyptian venture," but he is not permitted to expand on a political explanation, that Britain might withdraw from the lordly rationale of empire and the folly of foreign ventures. He does not make a case that Egypt and the Sudan are the playthings of business interests that indirectly sustain the privileged country house life he and the others enjoy. The motion picture—the Korda venture for 1939—is not prepared to say that its hero might be a coward, or that there could be courage and sense in opposing the cast iron of regimental thinking.

In 1902, and then for 1939, *The Four Feathers* disowned its warning message all too swiftly. No, Harry is not going to write or publish poetry; he is not headed for socialist thinking, or a romance with a suffragette (Wendy Hiller, maybe?). Instead, he immediately reappraises the glimmer of his own reformed wits and decides that, Yes, he *was* a coward, letting down the side and the chaps. So he takes himself off to the Sudan as a lone operator. The film does not bother to ask how he can afford this trip, or admit that his turnaround is nonsensical and demeaning, and a convenience of the scriptwriting. He puts on brownface and Arab clothing; he consents to be branded on his forehead to indicate his belonging to a mute tribe—to accommodate his lack of local languages. He goes very tastefully native. And why? In time he manages to rescue Durrance, who has been blinded by the sun and is generally discombobulated, as can happen to a good chap in a land of heat and dust and savages (one intertitle calls them fuzzy-wuzzies), where you can't get a good cup of tea. Harry Faversham now behaves like a glorious but effacing hero: Clements is generally subdued in his performance, while Richardson's overacting carries Durrance over all the tops a blinded man can't see.

Harry rescues his three chums, after being beaten and tortured by the savages. No matter, he has helped turn the tide for the valiant British army and the Royal North Surreys. The tactics are rather vague, until at last we get a movie battlefield we can understand as if it was a tabletop demonstration. On a semidesert plain, twin lines of unshakable British riflemen mow down waves of attack from dervishes on horseback or camels. The thin line is khaki, not red, but its resolve is as emphatic as a textbook. This is a satisfying show for those who like battles to make sense. Later on, Faversham returns to Britain and all is forgiven and reconciled. Durrance was about to marry Ethne (he is reading poetry himself by then, in Braille!) but he makes a tactful withdrawal so Harry and Ethne can be wed. They deserve each other in linked simplicity, but I fear we can assume that Harry will return to the regiment: he could be a colonel by 1914.

There had been a silent *Four Feathers* in 1929, produced by David O. Selznick, an imperialist at heart, with Richard Arlen as Harry, Clive Brook as Durrance, and Fay Wray as Ethne. It had gone to Africa for second-unit work, but without the lead actors. A decade later Korda scorned that half measure. He went wholeheartedly to the Sudan, with Technicolor cameras. The result was often called "splendid" though one may need heatstroke to take it in properly. It has stuff to impress the eye, and uncritical nonchalance in its adoption of the heroic code.

The Kordas spared nothing. Zoltan was allowed to shoot immense amounts of desert footage and battle details. It stretches credulity but some of this color material was adapted for CinemaScope for a remake of *The Four Feathers*. This was called *Storm over the Nile*, with Anthony Steel as Harry and Laurence Harvey as Durrance. The name Ethne was dropped (it was way out of fashion). The female lead was now named Mary to suit the actress Mary Ure. Those names may signal more amazement, for the remake opened in 1955, by which time the real storm over the Nile was that of Egyptian independence as led by Neguib and Nasser. But the Kordas chose not to notice.

None of this would have been judicious preparation for young soldiery in April 1939, when the Korda *Four Feathers* opened as Britain and Poland signed a military pact against the threat of German invasion.

Nothing raised any questions about imperialism. The white man's burden in putting up with savages was intact. The movie had no interest in or recognition of Sudanese feelings. But it had the same disdain for the experience of the common English soldier. This was a story about the officer class, no matter that by 1939 it was obvious that wars would be fought by the great mass of anonymous people—even the civilians. Harry and his pals are not the sharpest minds in the desert, or at home, but the movie does not think it possible to be critical of them.

Korda liked to be called lavish, but he did impose one large economy on his picture by not insisting on the cavalry charge that settled the Sudan. The Royal North Surreys were part of the British decision to send General Kitchener to restore order in the Sudan and defeat the army of infidels. The crucial action centered on the city of Omdurman. It was there that a celebrated battle was won (1898), after the British had cleared the way with the superiority of artillery and crude machine guns. It was the climax of that battle when the 21st Lancers mounted a cavalry charge that would be acted out in many paintings and movies. That was British gentlemen on fine horses, sabers and lances drawn, and clearing the field. It would become known as the last great cavalry charge by the British army—the tactic would not have worked on the Somme. A young officer in that charge was Winston Churchill, who also had a journalistic assignment with the *Morning Post* where he described the battle. Ambitious soldiers guess the story will be crucial, so they take charge of it themselves.

I am not doubting that Winston was active at Omdurman. He wrote a letter, on September 29, 1898, to "Sunny" (the Duke of Marlborough and his cousin), in which he says:

I had the good luck to ride through the charge unhurt—indeed untouched—which very few can say. I used a pistol and did not draw my sword. I had no difficulties and felt confident that I should get through if neither my horse fell nor I was shot—for I must tell you the ground was execrable and there was the wildest shooting in all directions. . . . I shot—three I think I killed. It is difficult to miss at under a foot's range. The whole thing was a matter of seconds—for as you may have gathered—we burst through their line and formed up the other side. The loss was most severe—1 officer and 21 men killed—9 officers and 66 men wounded and 119 horses out of only 320. Such a proportion and such a loss has been sustained by no regiment since the Light Brigade—forty years ago.

The severity, the horror: 1 officer dead and 21 men, with 119 horses—or does Churchill mean that there were just 119 horses left standing out of 320? The official figures for Omdurman say that 47 or 48 British were killed, and 382 wounded in a force that included Egyptian and Sudanese soldiers. Rounder figures are left for the enemy—12,000 killed and 13,000 wounded. Horses? There do not seem to be reliable numbers. But cavalry charges are tricky events to film.

This is the difference between real combat and the game. There is a running situation in *The Four Feathers* where General Burroughs (played by C. Aubrey Smith, who was seventy-six) takes over every dinner party by recalling his exploits in the Crimean War. He clears the table to be Balaclava and enlists walnuts, fruit, and a palace-sized pineapple to diagram the battle. This is clearly a bore for most onlookers, but it proves humbug, too. The final test of bravery for Harry Faversham is to remind Burroughs that his eternal story is wrong, because the alleged call to charge was forestalled by his unruly horse, which simply took off without any magic word. Horses are not as obedient as soldiers.

But in the days we are talking about, the dream of a beautiful cavalry charge on-screen faced problems. It would require several hundred horses, grooms, and wranglers to organize, actors who could really ride, and some respect for the animal lovers who said you should not injure or upset the horses. For you had to have a real charge in which horses and riders might break their necks. And it was hard to call the whole mob back for more takes. Rather, you needed a lot of camera setups in order to cover as much of the action as possible in one mad rush.

In 1936, for Warner Bros., Michael Curtiz (another Hungarian) had directed *The Charge of the Light Brigade*, a blithely imaginary version of the real charge at Balaclava on October 25, 1854. History was reorganized for the picture so that a young British major would be a fit role for Errol Flynn. As Curtiz's biographer, Alan K. Rode, puts it, the script was "apple sauce." But the production was at pains to get the charge right—which is not so much the pursuit of accuracy as the wish to be a crowd-pleaser. Out at the Lasky Mesa location, under the second unit director, Breezy Eason, 280 extras and 340 horses were assembled. Flynn seems to have worried about cruelty to the horses. But the stunt crew was skilled in the running W harness whereby a rider could bring his horse down without injury. The spectacle is still vivid, a romantic epic that deserves to be in the pantheon of combat scenes on-screen, accompanied by music (by Max Steiner) and the sound of hooves, to say nothing of the dynamic of the editing (by George Amy). It seems that four horses were killed, or put down. The Warners film was black and white, but it was so accomplished that *The Four Feathers* may have been timid about competing with it.

In the real charge by the light cavalry at Balaclava in October 1854, there was a misdirection of command that aimed the charge at the wrong artillery positions. It may not have been ordered, even. But 110 of the regiment were killed, with another 261 wounded. It was a disaster, but legend resurrected it as a noble defeat. Disputes arose over which British commander—Lords Raglan or Cardigan—had been more at fault. The French marshal Pierre Bosquet said, "*C'est magnifique mais ce n'est pas la guerre. C'est de la folie.*" Within weeks, Tennyson wrote a chanting poem about it:

> *Half a league, half a league,*
> *Half a league onward,*
> *All in the valley of Death*
> >   *Rode the six hundred.*
>
> . . . .
> *'Forward, the Light Brigade!*

'Take the guns,' Nolan said:
Into the valley of Death
    Rode the six hundred.

. . . .

Theirs not to make reply,
Theirs not to reason why,
Into the valley of Death
    Rode the six hundred.

There is a wax cylinder recording of Tennyson reading his poem in 1890. If you care to play it over the scenes from the Warner Bros. movie you may feel how the surge of storytelling is so often in conflict with any careful process in pinning down the reasons why.

Errol Flynn dies in that Lasky Mesa charge, but not before he has exemplified the proper valor by killing a villainous enemy leader, Surat Khan. Korda had another such hero up his sleeve. In 1940, encouraged by Churchill, the producer seized upon the idea of Horatio Nelson, who had crushed the French navy at Trafalgar in 1805 in a way that was exemplary for a Britain just at war—and for the United States as it considered its options. So it was that *That Hamilton Woman* aimed to be both a splashy costume romance, and an instrument of propaganda.

In the way of the Korda empire, this did not happen smoothly. At first Alex sent Vincent to research "that bloody general." His brother reported back with volumes on Wellington, at which point Alex realized he had meant "that bloody admiral."

A Hollywood veteran, Walter Reisch, was called to London, and amid falling bombs he wrote the first script. It described how a courtesan, Emma (real name Amy Lyon), frequently painted by George Romney, had risen to be wife to Sir William Hamilton, the British ambassador to Naples. When Nelson came to that city to rest, he and Emma fell into a notorious love affair. It was Korda's plan to cast Laurence Olivier and Vivien Leigh again as the couple. They were both in California, and thinking about getting married. Even so, the Breen office (named after the manager of the Hays Code) examined the script with a view to censorship and was concerned over its celebration of adultery.

Plans moved swiftly, but with Korda-like pitfalls. Olivier rigged himself out in costume, and looked dashing, but the actor had a problem: "Which arm and which eye was Nelson missing?" No one knew the answer until a Hungarian opera singer was unearthed, a man who had sung Nelson in a forgotten operetta. But he could not be sure; he thought he had varied the mishaps from night to night. If you go to the movie itself, you may discover the final decision—but is it consistent from scene to scene?

Korda meant to make the film quickly, in Los Angeles. He would direct it himself, and his brother Vincent would design the airy sets. At the same time, Korda opened offices in New York and Los Angeles that were cover for British secret service operations in that period (September 1939 until December 1941) when it was uncertain how or whether America would get into the war. This prompted isolationist protests in America and charges that the film was a mask for devious political pressures. Korda was attacked by the forces determined to keep America out of the war. Congressional investigation was in the air. But the picture proved a great success, with obligatory tableaux of Trafalgar and a hero who perished in the moment of his great victory. The picture cannot be blamed for failing to mention Nelson's complete support for the slave trade—but that omission helps us appreciate the blithe ignorance in patriotic cinema and the influence it exerted.

At Churchill's instigation, Korda was knighted in 1942, the first person from the movie business to receive that honor. This was part of a habit of gift-giving: when Winston had been short of money, Alex paid him for a film script about the life of the Duke of Marlborough—a project that did not get made. As Alex's nephew, Michael Korda, would observe, "Churchill liked and respected Alex, and was grateful to him for many favors large and small. They shared a common distaste for exercise (Churchill went so far as to have his valet pull on his trousers and tie his shoes), and a fondness for brandy, cigars, good conversation, and first-class food.

Each of them, in his own way, was an adventurer." In the one's leadership of a nation and the other's command of London Films, there was the same boyish thrill—and a corresponding escape from humdrum experience. Therein lay the huge appeal of movies and their capacity for making war vivid but distant, arousing yet free from damage and death.

For the common audience member—soon to be soldiers, nurses, mechanics, steadfast assistants, and helpless victims—*Fire over England, The Four Feathers*, and *That Hamilton Woman* were filled with throwback romance and the assumption that war was a field for officer-class heroes and movie stars, not drab or fearful civilians. Even in the Great War the home front had been a notional entity. Paris was under threat—the Germans came within almost twenty miles of the city—but it did not fall. London had occasional zeppelin bombing raids from Germany (there were about five hundred casualties). Berlin was intact. Most of the capital cities were innocent of war's reality. When Picasso's *Guernica* appeared in Paris in 1937, most people thought it was an insane mess—and did not register its accuracy. Were they terrified by the face of fear, and a new way of seeing?

Of course, Petrograd had collapsed: there had been that unexpected transformation in which civilian protest had overthrown aristocratic commanders and centuries of unquestioned privilege. Spasms of revolution afflicted Europe at the close of that war, along with the Spanish flu and intemperate peace arrangements in which Germany was cast as a future enemy. But the public had only read about the terrible conflict in the newspapers. And those reports had toed the line of discretion and looking on the bright side.

That ancient stability and its confidence were over. In 1937 *Fire Over England* could be the promise of entertainment, but by 1940 real fires were started.

17

MASSES

World war is itself a mass medium. Think of it as a uniting spasm or an expansive tremor.

It is also a story and the several technologies that convey it, taking charge of the airwaves, our hopes and fears. It cannot occur without profound and unexpected ways in which people—all of them, of us—respond to it and reassess our status in creation. So those potentates who lead us into war should think carefully: the history of the twentieth century is that radical, uncontrollable change comes with war. For all the destruction, this habit may see liberty at the end of its tunnel. Unless the tunnel caves in. The mute obedience of troops cannot be relied on, for they are citizens, first.

This realization was not simply British. Russia had split apart because of the Great War. Germany was so wounded that it slid into fascism. France was twice demoralized; its self-importance had been betrayed. By 1945 America felt it had found its greatness. But in Britain, there were such stirrings of regret, criticism, and conscience that the culture improved itself. As if a self-effacing outrage had arisen. One sign of that is the way the nation developed a line of documentary filmmaking that deserves to rank with the way fliers handled the Battle of Britain, sailors kept the North Atlantic convoys going, and foot soldiers allowed British xenophobia to get a taste of life in Europe, Africa, and Asia. This may sound flippant but world war promotes tourism, even if few are having a grand time fit for cheery postcards. The two wars helped to break down British insularity, or so the country thought before Brexit.

Britain had immense casualties in the Great War, though they were not greater than those suffered in other combatant nations. It would be said that an officer class had been so decimated that the British class system would never be the same again. Wishful thinking or self-pity? There was a generation of war poetry, not just rueful but convinced of failed leadership and sacrificial casualties. Wilfred Owen's "Anthem for Doomed Youth" was characteristic and a marked departure from Tennyson's view of Balaclava:

> *What passing-bells for those who die as cattle?*
> *Only the monstrous anger of the guns.*
> *Only the stuttering rifles' rapid rattle*
> *Can patter out their hasty orisons.*

That poem appeared in 1920, after Owen had been killed in action a week before the Armistice. But his mood has lived on, notably in *The Donkeys* (1961), the book by Alan Clark that regards the war experience for Britain as lions led by donkeys—in other words, a failure of character and intelligence in the officer class. There is a similar conclusion in Woolf's *Mrs. Dalloway* where the exhilaration of a society party is offset by the difficulties Septimus Smith has in having his shell shock appreciated, let alone treated. Indeed, he commits suicide. (He is played by Rupert Graves in the 1997 movie, directed by Marleen Gorris.)

In the novel, Clarissa Dalloway is sensitive to the death of Smith as reported casually at her party: "He had killed himself—but how? . . . He had thrown himself from a window. Up had flashed the ground; through him, blundering, bruising, went the rusty spikes. There he lay with a thud, thud, thud in his brain, and then a suffocation of blackness. So she saw it."

That was published in 1925, the year before Hemingway's *The Sun*

Also Rises, when it was widely reckoned that lady authors would not understand violence.

Britain had its first Labour government in 1924 and then again in 1929–31, as the country suffered from the Depression, unemployment, hunger marches, and mounting anger in the trade union movement. Socialism had mixed fortunes in Westminster but it was active and idealistic in the intellectual culture. Among other things, it helped promote the idea that movies be about ordinary people, and not just fantasies offered up to keep them happy. Film might adhere to its documentary potential. And if commercial companies were unmoved by that feeling, then maybe the government should produce the films.

No one played a larger part in that merging of interests than John Grierson. Born in Scotland in 1898, and a graduate of Glasgow University, he traveled in America in the mid-1920s on a Rockefeller grant. He visited Hollywood and met leading figures, and he became concerned about the impact of movie dreams on modern thought. In 1927, he joined the Empire Marketing Board's film unit in Britain, and two years later he directed a film himself, *Drifters*, about the fishing industry. But that was his only directing credit, as he became a producer figure, first at Empire and then at the General Post Office film unit. There was a preacher-like intensity in the man, as well as a talent for organization, and thus he led the move to short documentary films about how Britain functioned and how it depended on ordinary and unknown people. Remarkably, by our standards, several of these shorts played at regular cinemas along with feature films, a cartoon, and a newsreel. These films were meant to be useful and inspiring, and Grierson ignored or overrode objections that this was not the purpose of cinemas.

The most memorable of his productions is *Night Mail* (1936), a twenty-five-minute tribute to the overnight train service carrying mail to Scotland and back. It was officially directed by Basil Wright and Harry Watt, though Grierson was a scriptwriter on the project. As well as the documentary voice-over, the film commissioned a verse section from W. H. Auden, and Grierson was one of the voices on the soundtrack—

itself organized and mixed by a talented Brazilian, Alberto Cavalcanti (it also had a score by Benjamin Britten). *Night Mail* is still a treat that makes you feel good about its subject, though the film was prompted by poor wages in the Post Office and a loss of confidence in its workforce. So it was an advertisement for the service, as well as a lyrical film poem, with surging locomotives and soaring hopes. Of course, it's not a war film, but it is part of a way of thinking that met the test of the Second World War.

Similarly, Mass-Observation was a current in a crowded sea, hoping to become a tide. It began as a colloquy of Cambridge friends, a sweeping hope and a secret society, founded by Tom Harrison, an anthropologist; Charles Madge, a poet; and Humphrey Jennings, who was ready for anything—poetry, painting, and even filmmaking. They were motivated by the implicit but unexplored relationships between the mass of people and the emerging media. Quite simply, in enlightenment and lofty idealism, they proposed to observe how people really lived and felt—as opposed to the recommended public policies of "team spirit." During the Blitz at the start of the war, Mass-Observation asked citizens to keep diaries of what was happening.

The public understood, with degrees of comedy and anger, that for so long governments had treated expanding populations with the pompous policy of issued orders. No one had bothered to study or respect the private psychologies that the mass contained. The impulse to do that was humane, academic, and socialist, and in general the movement thought it absurd to expect mass society to be treated in any other way. Granted that authoritarianism, or fascism, was not recommended.

But within the study of life on a city block or in the farmlands, there was always the apprehension that a mass could turn into a negative force. Even in the best democracies, governors have a tendency to be afraid of the people not behaving "sensibly." The inner confrontation of the next war was at hand, and it turned on profound questions of how a society should function, and what it should expect of its numbers, if only to insist on individual membership and responsibility. In the twentieth century, the clash of liberty and required behavior would grow sharper. In this century it will have to be resolved. Mass-Observation was often local, incidental, and as sharp as a still photograph, but it was mindful of civilization and its destiny. So it was a kind of rearming for an enormous battle.

Consider Humphrey Jennings. He had been born in a rural Suffolk town, Walberswick, in 1907, and he would get a degree in English at Cambridge. He designed sets for student theater; he wrote poetry; he helped organize a groundbreaking exhibition on surrealism in London in 1936; and he began to assemble an anthology—of anything that interested him—which was the basis for a project he called "Pandemonium: The Coming of the Machine as Seen by Contemporary Observers." (It would be published eventually in 1985.) You can see or feel in that his delighted but apprehensive appreciation of order and disorder at the same time. To that end, he was drawn to the beauty in the montage possibilities of cinema. It was as much his vital medium as it was for Jean Renoir, Luis Buñuel, and Alfred Hitchcock. But instead of going Hollywood, or Pinewood, he became a part of the Post Office film unit, as a documentarian but a poet, too. Gradually he realized that the war was his opportunity and his subject. He was as alert to peril as Hemingway.

From the midthirties, he was designing sets for documentaries, he was working as an editor, and by 1938 he was directing. In 1940, with Harry Watt, he made the ten-minute *London Can Take It!*, which was simply an assertion that in the damage of the Blitz, the city had found beauty and resolution in "the greatest civilian army ever assembled" (narration by American journalist Quentin Reynolds). The genius of Jennings was to see that the sudden exposure of bombed buildings might be lovely and arresting—there is a shot of a double-decker bus tipped up against a shattered building like a Magritte.

The bomb-damaged city was a new landscape in our history, just as civilians in their warm beds might be targets. Picasso's *Guernica* (1937) was a pioneering depiction of that new danger. But there were subtler visions of the damage. Sometimes it was a feeling writers noticed, like sudden wildflowers on bomb sites. In her novel *The Heat of the Day* (1949), Elizabeth Bowen (who was there during the Blitz) writes about 1940: "Never had any season been more felt; one bought the poetic sense of it with the sense of death. Out of mists of morning charred by the smoke from ruins each day rose to a height of unmisty glitter. . . . From the moment of waking you tasted the sweet autumn not less because of an acridity on the tongue and nostrils; and as the singed dust settled and smoke diluted you felt more and more called upon to observe the daytime as a pure and curious holiday from fear."

The shock could be more immediate, yet more lasting. One evening in 1944, a writer, Maurice Bendrix, is making adulterous love with Sarah Miles when they hear the noise of V-1 bombs—"doodlebugs," the English called them. They were long-range rockets that came droning overhead. Once they cut out, you knew the bomb was falling. That night of theirs in south London has one of the great bombs of literature in *The End of the Affair*, by Graham Greene (published in 1951).

When the bomb falls, thinking Maurice may be dead, Sarah makes a deal with God that she will give up her lover if he is kept alive. This sense of God and prayerful bargains seems startling now, but that was a war in which some people clung to belief and the idea that divinity and civil virtue were under threat together.

There was a poor film of the novel, in 1955, with Van Johnson and Deborah Kerr as the lovers. Far better, in 1999, Neil Jordan remade it, with Ralph Fiennes and Julianne Moore. In that film, the destruction of the house—the sudden, ragged window on sky—is a revelation of spiritual repercussions.

In 1942, in a similar poetic impulse, Jennings delivered *Listen to Britain*, a twenty-minute montage of the sounds of the nation. This was abstraction at the height of the conflict. If the scheme seems precious, the film opens up the essentially peaceful tenor of the country.

Then in 1943, for the Crown film unit, he made *Fires Were Started*, one of the great British films. It was typical of Mass-Observation that it might acknowledge that the Blitz was a famous conflict between German bombers and brave British fighter pilots. It could observe how the initial German plan in the summer of 1940 had been to destroy fighter command and its airfields, and how Hitler and Goering had then moved on to the idea of night raids against British cities to cause fear and demoralization. But then the moment went deeper: it said, Just think of the life of the ordinary firemen who did their desperate best to put out the fires started in the London docklands area and in the dense population centers. Those firemen are on the front lines every night. Isn't that an obvious subject for a documentary?

Fires Were Started is eighty minutes, feature-length, and it has the bones of a story in which an educated man is posted to a working-class firefighting unit in East London. Ten years later, this might have been a mainstream picture at the cinema, with Dirk Bogarde as the outsider—a doctor in regular life, let's say—getting along with the blokes and having a polite crush on one of the girls in the operations room (Virginia McKenna?). That is not to sneer at Bogarde, who had a very busy war in intelligence and air reconnaissance and was one of the first Allied soldiers into Bergen-Belsen. But I hope the possibility shows up the clash between wartime realism and the fictional gloss of those films in which Britain later tried to clean up the war and have it fit for stars.

Nothing was more important in *Fires* than Jennings's decision to use real firemen as the figures in the film. They would not bother to move in glamour, and they would talk together in their own way. There was no script to learn and recite, just the minimal rehearsal that gave the men a lead and a way of discarding awkwardness. So we are seeing men playing themselves with ease yet shyness. Improvisation melds into actuality and the simple structure of an outsider joining an existing group and mixing in. Accordingly, the firefighting stuff was shot in the docklands during German incendiary raids. Not that German planes are shown, or German airmen abused in the way the firemen talk. It is as if fire is a kind of inclement weather, a curse that these men must try to deal with. In the process, one of the group is killed: the danger of the job is not laughed off, and the death scene is brief but compelling, vivid but not overly dramatized, and confident of the natural, unstressed pathos in the close-up face of fireman Johnny "Jacko" Houghton.

The film never bothers to say, *Look, these firemen are brave and noble and essential*. That meaning is simply there, latent, for us to absorb and respect. Made a couple of years after the Blitz, *Fires* does not trade on the melodrama of bombing raids. It just says, *This happened*, and it was dependent on the regular but generally unconsidered service of these common, unofficered men. The newcomer is Barrett, played by William Sansom a fiction writer who worked in advertising. He's a dandy, but the shape of the film lets him be integrated with the group. There is an inspiring sequence as the men hang out in their mess room and Barrett discovers the piano. He can play quite well, with flourishes for the guys, so a singalong develops, run-of-the-mill yet as arranged as something from an Astaire movie, composed and shot with true awareness of an implicit musical, yet without glamorizing the humdrum fellows.

You realize that, within the intent of documentary, you are seeing a filmed vision made by an artist. It was also part of the war effort that Fred Astaire did *You'll Never Get Rich* (1941) and *You Were Never Lovelier* (1942), both with Rita Hayworth, titles to make ironic fighting mottoes for grim soldiering. Indeed, "You'll Never Get Rich" came from an old army song—"You'll never get rich by digging a ditch; you're in the army now!" In that picture, Fred is drafted into the army to put on a show for the GIs.

As if artistry can thrive in a terrible war. That is the comfort of *Fires Were Started*, and it is as powerful as the line of men at Houghton's funeral dissolved with a munitions ship sailing out to sea and its delivery. It's not that that will win the war. It's rather that the service is what common men and women can do in the crisis, without feeling the warm spotlight of being A Hero in a War Picture. These lives are hectic and poised for an alarm bell, but they have the rare tranquility of men hanging around for the charged cry for action. They are chatting, joking, having a cup of tea, idling and waiting, or joining in the song "One Man Went to Mow." It is a matter of wistful elegance, this waiting for danger. There is a similar scene in *Saving Private Ryan*, beautifully judged as a record of comradeship without choice.

Beauty is a tricky thing in a movie. If it hits you over the head from the start it may separate you from the action being shown. Jennings is never so vulgar or Hollywoodesque. But he always saw calm in damage, and grace under pressure: that was the influence of surrealism. As you watch *Fires Were Started*, you feel its buried hint that fire was organic and eternal, and let loose by impersonal actions. He had a more subtle and gentle eye than those that made spectacular entertainment movies. He was unimpressed by excitement. The long shots in which he covers the firefighting are so poignant. His feeling for the trunk-like hosepipes made of rawhide, for the gush of white water in the night, and for the beast that is fire—those elements are serenely graphic, and they grant fire an agency or oxygen that is not dependent on bad people or good guys dealing with it. Fire is light and a way of animating the crisis of war. Fire is deadly but it is life. That is how *Fires Were Started* has endured, and still feels mysterious.

You can think for a moment that Jennings should have made proper war films. But that misjudges the nature of his creative personality. He would have flinched from actors. He never stoops to a "love interest" in this firehouse, though there are fifteen seconds or so of a radiant, untidy young woman serving tea as dawn breaks that fits with the shots of men and teaches us how romantic montage or editing can be. The film is like a poem married to an essay, or like a piece of music, on the varieties of war against which most story lines would seem trite and demeaning. The result is very English, and London even, but it would work for Dresden or Hiroshima. Fires were started there, too, fires like infernos, and fire may be our destiny. In London throughout the war of bombing raids, it is reckoned that 30,000 died—firemen, police, and civilians—but in Dresden, in three days of February 1945, the death total was 245,000.

The Fire Service had given Jennings access and they must have been pleased with the result. But how much deeper into the war effort could this patient, objective process reach? Would a frontline battle unit let a Jennings be embedded? The official filming of the war was cautious, strident, often inept and dishonest, and without the wit or the humanism of Humphrey Jennings. The newsreels played in cinemas were vivid, but dominated by the need for high morale (a kind of ratings system). They were propaganda, not so different from similar reportage offered in Germany or the Soviet Union. So what could Jennings do more?

In all of that indecision, it was said that Jennings could be aloof, overly intellectual, and difficult. Those qualities are apparent in the film with which he concluded his observation of the war. *A Diary for Timothy* (1944–45) is an uneasy work, spurred by a good, sentimental idea. So you can feel Jennings trying to ride the public mood but coming under strain. The film is directed at Timothy Jenkins, born September 3, 1944, to a demure madonna and a father who is serving overseas. At first, this happy baby is an emblem of optimism: the war is being won; there is talk of it being over before Christmas. But while no one doubts eventual victory, the winter provides a series of setbacks: the failed parachute attempt on Arnhem (late September); the German offensive in the Ardennes (December–January); the plain fact of another winter.

As that reality sinks in, so the film's commentary becomes more anxious and high-minded. This was not a conventional narrative text. It was a rumination, written by E. M. Forster and read by Michael Redgrave. So Tim is a character in a story that will not be finished. As it builds, larger if vague questions loom about how the peace is going to be determined. We are reminded of the poverty in Britain that preceded the war and carried on afterward. How can that be resolved? Jennings was going out on a limb, but he was prescient. Less than a year away was the election of July 1945, in which the accumulation of grievance, hardship, and the feeling that the officer class took the people for granted would break in the landslide victory that pushed Churchill out of office (393 seats won by Labour over 197 for the Conservatives).

Still, *Diary for Timothy* is often awkward or tendentious in its attitudes. There are uncomplaining examples in the film: a miner, a farmer, and an RAF flier going through rehab after a bad injury. But we don't feel they are being blunt or honest. There are ecstatic things, too: the cinema of a winter morning, with trees crisp and bright in the frost, accompanied by the carol "Oh, Come All Ye Faithful," is one of the most moving passages in all of British film. Jennings's eye is piercing still, but the commentary is sometimes nagging, yet reluctant to break out as a political campaign speech. It begs the question: What are we to expect of committed leadership, and where was Mass-Observation going? Was it only possible to sustain this rhetoric in a time of war? But hadn't war exposed so many of the disconnects in British society?

In Europe, the artistic urgency of Jennings's wartime films can be felt in the work of Alain Resnais, whose *Night and Fog* (1955) was one of the first widely seen reflections on the concentration camps; and Chris Marker, whose *Description d'un Combat* (1960) was an essay on modern Israel and its battles. By then, Jennings was dead: he fell while climbing cliffs in Greece in 1950. He was only forty-three, but it was hard to see his career expanding. Minus the pressure of war and its interest in home-front morale, how could a Jennings find subject matter or funding? He made *Family Portrait* (1950), as part of the Festival of Britain celebration, but he was not a natural celebrant. It was hardly conceivable that he could be an ideal director for *The Cruel Sea*, *The Dam Busters*, or *The Bridge on the River Kwai*. The documentary spirit would have a second wind on British television, but that was still years away.

Pressures were complicated, and confounding. In 1945, as led by Sidney Bernstein at the Ministry of Information, wartime camera crews filmed the concentration camps just relieved. This was gruesome material, but necessary, as the crews felt. There had to be a record of the infamy. Alfred Hitchcock was called in to help organize the film, and the academic and new MP Richard Crossman wrote a commentary. The result was entitled *German Concentration Camps Factual Survey*. It was finished and ready to go, but then politics intervened—the new Labour government felt the film's revelations could be unsettling or damaging in the postwar attempt at reconciliation. So it was shelved. The material, or some of it, only surfaced in 2014, in *Night Will Fall*, directed by Andre Singer.

As for Mass-Observation, its energies dwindled. But the research data that had been accumulated over the years, on what people wanted and how their minds worked against every cliché of duty, found a new home.

By 1960, the movement had been incorporated into the advertising agency J. Walter Thompson. They were eager to understand how private minds worked in the crowd. The stress on individual need and desire could be monetized in the attempted thought control of marketing. Humanism, or human thought processes, would make so many compromises in the inescapable mass society.

THERE COULD BE NO QUESTION ABOUT IT: FOR EVERY PARTICIPANT IN THE Second World War, film was a weapon of war, communication, and white lies. Sometimes the result might rise to the level of art, but along that way it had to be propaganda. The United States War Department was swiftly persuaded to make a series of movies—documentaries that they hoped would explain to the public and the troops why the war had to be fought. Similar ventures preoccupied the enemy nations, too, but "we" learned to believe that our pictures were honest or fair, while theirs were not. Some of those delicate issues are only resolved by who wins the war on the ground and is then able to fill archives and libraries with series like *Why We Fight*.

Those films were funded and executed under military orders, and for the most part the War Department relied on pros, preferably those with starry names. So Frank Capra was put "in charge" of the series and "we" were soon telling ourselves that the product had the "Capra touch." Frank became a colonel; he had a swank uniform, drivers, and secretaries, and he was in command of a small studio setup with jobs for plenty of Hollywood pals. I think that's the way to look at the films. Unable and unwilling to be at the heart of real combat, the unit was an editing machine, mastering an array of newsreels, foreign footage, and endless, all-purpose scenes of explosion, founded on the dynamic of cutting and crosscutting, with emphatic voice-over commentaries to tell us what we were seeing, and how to feel about it.

That is not to disparage the *Why We Fight* film series, or the conviction with which they were made. The films were as predictable and sustaining as military rations and ammunition. But a lot of the "action" was restaged—like Robert Capa's famous photograph from Spain of a soldier in the instant of being killed—because the end triumphed over the means. Roosevelt loved the results and he wanted the public to see the films—in movie theaters showing unashamed fictional versions of the war, pictures made in the same airy style. It would be said that fifty million Americans had seen some of the series, and we are still unsure how valuable the experience was or how far it introduced the dilemma we have never solved: of not knowing what to trust. Truly, film was a weapon system that could never be pushed back into the bottle.

Another director involved in those documentaries was John Ford. He made short films on the Battle of Midway and the resonance of December 7—and one on sex hygiene that fought the war on syphilis. But his great war picture was not released until after the peace. *They Were Expendable* tells the story of motor torpedo boats in the Pacific as America and General MacArthur were in retreat. It starred Robert Montgomery (who had served in the navy); and John Wayne (who stayed in pictures), whose character has a romance with a nurse played by Donna Reed. It is quieter and more somber than many Ford pictures, and it looks better with the years. In its title alone it admitted truths often pushed aside.

But an issue was exposed, true for 1945 and then for Matthew Heineman's vision of the abandoned Kabul in *Retrograde*—can we really digest the truth of war, or do we settle for its show?

18

BLIMP

Imagine a *Fires Were Started* in which Barrett screws up. It's not that he loses his nerve in a crisis; it's more that he might be as inept or clumsy as anyone trying to subdue conflagrations at night with little experience or training. That prospect is out of the question in the movie—we know it. The Fire Service did not want to advertise itself in incompetence. The Crown film unit, the Home Office, and the Ministry of Home Security (the other supporters of the project) did not care to admit any cause for dismay. The restrained but implacable energy of "the war effort" was behind the film and our seeing it. Humphrey Jennings was singularly short on bellicose instincts, but he couldn't let the side down. One might as well ask Goebbels, in 1943, to greenlight a picture in which an ordinary farmer conscripted into the army has doubts about the oath of loyalty to the führer. (That is the basic situation in Terrence Malick's *A Hidden Life*, made in 2019.)

But there was such a film made in Britain in 1943, 163 minutes long, and not cheap or secretive, and incurring the disapproval and then the wrath of Prime Minister Winston Churchill. *The Life and Death of Colonel Blimp* could seem opposed to the necessary positivism of going to war. Many felt it was letting the side down. Yet it is one of the most remarkable and least expected of war films. If it is not quite a great, or tidy film, still it is one of the most audacious and endearing. Every time I see it, I marvel that it got made.

It was produced by a company known as the Archers (they believed in aiming and accuracy) headed by Michael Powell, born in Canterbury, in southern England; and Emeric Pressburger, born in what had been the Austro-Hungarian Empire. So they were unlikely collaborators in the era of official hostilities, but that was the creative inspiration for this study of friendship.

The story stretches from 1904 to 1943. Clive Wynne-Candy has been a young officer in the Boer War, where he won the Victoria Cross, the highest medal for valor (though his exploit is not spelled out in the film). On leave in England, he gets a letter from Edith, a young English woman in Berlin who says the anti-British feeling there is out of control because of dire stories about the Boer War. Without official permission, on a whim, Candy goes to Berlin to help allay these sentiments. He meets Edith, takes her out, and gets into a silly confrontation with Prussian officers. Satisfaction is required. A duel has to be fought (with sabers) and Candy's opponent—drawn by lot—is Theo Kretschmar-Schuldorff. So these two men meet for the first time, in order to do their best at killing each other. Surrealism is alive and well.

Candy's upper lip is wounded; Theo has a laceration on his forehead. Then they convalesce in the same hospital, becoming friends, and as Theo learns English, so they both fall in love with the visiting Edith. Candy stays silent about his own feelings for her as Theo and Edith become engaged. Friendship is too important for another duel. Deep feelings stay buried for the sake of honor. So far, the film's story line is very odd, but we go with it because it comes from a culture where "good form" could battle true feeling.

Now, here comes the Great War, with desolate scenes of the western front managed on a sound stage—the Archers loved theatrical decor. Candy believes this terrible war has been won as proof of right overcoming might—he is certain that his side fought with honor while the Germans often played dirty. But this insecure perspective does nothing to interfere with the ethos of friendship. The two men have corresponded intermittently, but then after the Armistice Candy discovers that Theo is in a prisoner-of-war camp in the English countryside. Old enemies resume their friendship, and Theo tells Clive that Edith is well in Germany, the mother of their sons. But in the course of November 1918, Clive spends a night in a church with a group of British nurses. That's when he sees a young woman, Barbara, who reminds him of Edith. So he falls in love with her. They are twenty years apart in age, but they will marry.

More time passes, and Barbara dies. Clive learns that Theo has come to Britain in 1934, a widower, too, and a refugee, but a father rejected by his sons, who have become Nazis. (Emeric Pressburger, too, had been forced out of Europe by the Nazis.) Thus Theo is not just older, but sadder, shabbier, and beaten down as he tells Clive that war is no longer a field for gentlemen. Blunt savagery has taken over. War has become so grave, its consequences so ruinous, that it is not a game to be played according to old rules of chivalry.

By 1939, Clive is a veteran, overweight, a bit of a buffoon, but steadfast in his allegiance to the old code and to his friendship with Theo. He is a brigadier general, but out of touch. He is ready to give a talk on the radio after Dunkirk, to say that perhaps the war is not worth winning if decency has to be abandoned. On reading his script, the BBC drops him from the broadcast; he is obliged to retire from the army. But he is unbowed, and he elects to become a leading figure in the home guard—that assemblage of old men and grown children who present a last barrier against possible invasion.

As such, Candy has a uniform and a loyal girl driver, Angela (also called "Johnny"), to take him here and there. Inadvertently, she alerts her boyfriend, an ambitious lieutenant, about Clive's plans for an approaching exercise. So the boyfriend breaks the rules: the exercise is meant to start at midnight, but the lieutenant steals a march (he jokes about Pearl Harbor), and Candy is captured and humiliated. It is not a war now for old men, much less gentlemen.

This is a long synopsis, and it may indicate awkwardness in your author. But it is a wayward, rambling film, too, and that is part of one's affection for its lofty amateur air. Michael Powell knew from the start that this venture was a test: "To make a hard-hitting film which lampooned the military mind and said we must pull our socks up if we were going to win the war at a time when we were losing it hand-over-fist, was a bold enterprise. We went to see David Low."

Low was a New Zealander and the best known cartoonist in Europe. The Nazis had reviled his brilliant, mocking cartoons about dictators. Britain and its army had had mixed feelings over his character, Colonel Blimp, the epitome of the old guard, inclined to be a pineapple in endless, inaccurate replays of past battles. The Archers wanted Low's permission to use the Blimp name, though truly Clive Wynne-Candy is subtler, warmer, funnier, and more thoughtful than the famous caricature. But Low agreed, so we have the strange title of the Archers film. It's not just that Candy is so much more appealing. It's also that he doesn't die. The film closes on a close-up of him valiantly saluting the very regiment that had outsmarted (and cheated on) his home guard. In truth, the story of Candy doesn't require any reference to Blimp.

But *Blimp* is a complicated movie, ambiguous and emotional. It's almost a love letter to the military from the Powell and Pressburger who had never seen service but who were drawn to the quirky human story beating beneath a uniform, even one that bore a Victoria Cross. In addition, Micky and Emeric were cheeky outsiders, less deterred by opposition from the government than stimulated by it. Official interests did not like their screenplay, or understand the value of an abiding friendship between an Englishman and a German when a lethal, uncompromising duel was under way. So they blocked the Archers' first wish, to have Laurence Olivier play Candy, and did their best to forbid the film from using any real military equipment or hardware. Churchill let it be known that he did not want the film to be made. He may have sighed sometimes at not having the authority of Goebbels.

The Archers exulted in just the unexpected adventuring that Churchill loved, and which gave him the feeling that he might be a figure in a movie. The Archers ignored obstacles. They stole military vehicles and other items of uniform and gallantry not well looked after by inefficient regiments. They forgot Olivier, and instead cast Roger Livesey and his uniquely hoarse but ardent voice. This became one of Olivier's gifts to film history. He could not have matched the impetuous warmth, the dogged honesty, or the romanticism of Livesey.

There are three reasons why this misguided film works, above and beyond the wit of the two Archers. One is Livesey's heartfelt portrait of a decent chump. The second is Anton Walbrook as Theo, in what becomes an unrivaled portrait of how a good man has been crushed by Nazi control. There is a speech in which he quietly explains himself to a British immigration officer—seeking refuge—that should be in any montage of the fearsome twentieth century.

The third is Deborah Kerr playing the three women in the story. The first plan was to cast Wendy Hiller in the parts. She would have been grand, for she was an expert actress, as witness her Eliza and an Oscar nomination in *Pygmalion*. But she was pregnant at the wrong moment, so the boys turned to the twenty-one-year-old Kerr, who was just beginning to be noticed. One day in London, she walked over to meet Powell in his office. "She was bare-headed," he wrote years later, "and I remember her hair shining in the sun like burnished copper. . . . We looked at the bulky script together and I watched the subtle transformations that passed over her face as I made suggestions about the script. Again, I felt that mysterious affinity, as between an artist and his model, which is one of the most inexplicable of the sensual sensations. I made up my mind. I said that frankly we had no time to lose. So long as her agent agreed to our terms, she had the part. She stopped breathing and looked at me. She has told me since that I was already thinking of something else."

I don't think that sensation is so inexplicable, and I lived to realize that Micky or Michael was not just uncommonly fond of redheaded women. He lived in hope of finding them. So the tripartite Kerr was like a recurring song. She is the warm spirit and alertness that links up the many anticipatory scenes. She is the flawless lady who knows something else is being thought about. As filmed by Georges Périnal, in adolescent, horny Technicolor, she is the glowing face that transcends gaps in structural narrative. Two of her roles die, but we only see her alive and breathing.

With Kerr, Livesey, and Walbrook together, this may be the best burning love story in a war film, and enough to say that whatever the outrages on battlefields or in torture chambers, the marriage of a sad smile and its latent blush can be as important.

Of course, none of us exactly believes that as being more profound than Auschwitz or Stalingrad, but as we watch *The Life and Death of Colonel Blimp*, we want it to be so.

So much is left out of the film: there are no battle scenes—there is no glimpse of Dunkirk, the Battle of Britain, or the Somme. The film begins its Berlin saber duel, but then soars out of the gymnasium to observe snow falling outside. There is not really much impish satire leveled at British military habits. The picture does not pause to consider that there may have been ugly, racist incidents during the Boer War; it does not cross-examine Candy's assumption that the Huns behaved badly (or like Huns) in 1914–18. There is no apology offered for the trophy room Wynne-Candy fills with rows of the wild animal heads he has shot, including a German helmet from 1918, and a lush portrait of his wife, Barbara.

The film knows Clive Candy is a relic and a liability; it understands he is not suited to total war; and it has no doubts about the extremism that totality insists on. But it does not care to show us the shocking brutality. The movie cherishes and protects Candy; it has a sweet tooth for the sturdy way in which he takes on the world, including glory and need, but utterly aware that respect and loss are in the diet of a warrior. Men need not bother with war, we realize, if friendship and feminine intuition may be available as alternatives. Still, Clive Wynne-Candy could be a dangerous commander in a desperate situation. He takes those who follow him for granted, and may not notice or appreciate their anxiety. It is a very Tory film, masquerading as modern and subversive. Would you hope to serve under Wynne-Candy? Or to avoid him?

But *Blimp* has sidebar blessings, the gifts of time and chance. In the

Great War scenes, Candy has a driver, Murdoch, a wintry observer of it all, played by John Laurie, a distinct and gloomy Scottish actor. (He had played the cruel Khalifa in *The Four Feathers*.) Murdoch is so devoted to his officer that he becomes his manservant for decades. When Murdoch dies, Candy puts a tribute obituary to him in the *Times*. And the gift of chance came gradually, for decades hence Laurie would be cast as Private Frazer in the BBC television comedy show *Dad's Army*. Created and written by Jimmy Perry and David Croft, *Dad's Army* was a steady hit from 1968 to 1977; it had audiences over fifteen million for eighty thirty-minute episodes. It was an ongoing story, a comedy of errors and dainty disaster, amid the whimsy of a home guard contingent defending the sedate torpor of the fictional Walmington-on-Sea. Its leader, Captain Mainwaring (Arthur Lowe), is a bank manager in the resort and a small statue of fussy pomp. Frazer is said to have fought at Jutland and to have served with Shackleton. He is a survivor, crying out, "We're doomed! Doomed!" at every sign of panic. Laurie was eighty when the show ended.

Dad's Army should be remembered in any chronicle of entertainments about war, and it was an enduring comfort for anyone who had put on a uniform but made a mess of the show. Total war, its ruthlessness, is often the reappraisal of inept calamity.

WE CAN STILL LAUGH AT CAPTAIN MAINWARING AND THE REST OF *DAD'S Army* while marveling at the way nostalgia kept its hold into the allegedly daring seventies. Decades later we can amuse ourselves with home guard folklore. But Britain had felt in peril, and it was not much more than twenty miles from ports and airfields in France. There were even silent, waiting elements in Britain that might have welcomed a German presence, just for the sake of reliable order. The moments of Dunkirk were not as clearcut as history has chosen to make them.

There was one movie, made as entertainment and propaganda (that wartime double act), that is still disturbing. *Went the Day Well?* opened on December 7, 1942 (the anniversary of Pearl Harbor). By then, the threat of invasion for Britain was reduced, but it had not gone away. All over the country, in newspapers and on radio, there were warnings to trust no one, to stifle loose talk, and to be ready. This was an ideal theater for British reticence and suspicion.

Went the Day Well? is set in the fictitious country village of Bramley End. The exteriors were shot at Turville, a village in Buckinghamshire, but the place feels as if it could have been only ten miles or so inland from Walmington-on-Sea. The idea is piercingly simple. The calm of country life, its network of associations, are nagged at by the arrival of British soldiers who will prove to be German paratroopers preparing for an invasion. The locals work out this truth and then, as home guard and plain civilians, they do all they can to resist the threat. The film has the air of a mystery thriller in part. But there is no doubt about the threat or the total commitment of the Germans.

This was the work of the Ealing Studios, produced under the leadership of Michael Balcon, directed by Alberto Cavalcanti, and with a script taken from a Graham Greene short story. Not the least originality in the project was that the local squire (played by Leslie Banks) will be revealed as a leading collaborator, ready to be the boss installed by German command. While the conventional warning of the time was to watch out for fifth columnists, or spies, this film alerts the audience to being equally nervous over conservative pillars of the community.

Indignant villagers are rounded up in the pretty church. Some of them are executed. It's the sort of thing that happened in France. When the home guard comes to the rescue, they are mowed down on their bicycles. The gentle rural atmosphere is violently shaken up. It is an effective suspense film, with music by William Walton, misleading summer charm, and nasty Germans impersonated by actors Basil Sidney, David Farrar, John Slater, and James Donald. There is a host of British character actors, too, and an amiable sense of rural community. With this result: the picture is a textbook study of British resilience—but it could be a model for takeover by Germans, or anyone else with a thought of subverting the settled order. You never know when some local disturbance is going to get out of hand, or when a state of war needs to be recognized. There are so many ways the day can go.

19

DAMN FINE SHOW

Went the Day Well? could have given Britain the chills in 1942, and made rural life a little less secure. Churchill's dark promise of June 1940—"We shall fight on the beaches, we shall fight on the landing grounds. We shall fight in the fields and in the streets; we shall fight in the hills"—had never come to pass. But bombs had been dropped; parts of great cities had been burned down; British troops had fought all over the world, and died there.

Then there was the peace. Some sour wits in Britain reckoned they might have been better off if they had lost the war. They heard stories of investment being lavished on Germany and Japan, to rebuild those societies and to kill off any resurgence in fascist ideas. Britons compared that legend with food rationing at home that would last until the 1950s, with bomb sites that were not rebuilt or made safe. With beaches still dangerous and unusable because of anti-invasion defenses, including mines. The country was broke, and while the Labour government had ambitious plans and hopes (especially the National Health Service) they were hard-pressed to make Great Britain feel great. There were power cuts, especially depressing in the unusually severe winter of 1947. There was good reason to feel anxious about the world a Timothy might inherit. It was hard to be warm and relaxed, and housewives might have to flirt with butchers to get an extra cut of meat. I recall a cinema newsreel where Sir Stafford Cripps (Dickensian in name and bearing), the president of the Board of Trade, warned that bread might have to be rationed. A wag in the dark shouted out, "Take a couple of slices off the loaf, mate!"

Somehow, British cinema had never been better, more vigorous or inventive. These were the years of David Lean (*Brief Encounter, Oliver Twist, Great Expectations*), of Carol Reed (*The Fallen Idol, Odd Man Out, The Third Man*), and of Powell and Pressburger (*I Know Where I'm Going, A Matter of Life and Death, Colonel Blimp*, and *The Red Shoes*). At a markedly less inspired level were the British war films—boisterous, cocksure, often foolish, but loaded with syrup to pour over the suet pudding of abashed morale. Sometimes bad films tell you more about the country that made them than the masterpieces.

In the war years, most British films had shied away from combat. It was too expensive and difficult to mount, and there were worries that it might come across as too tame, or too frightening. So the British cinema had done little to match the gusto, the aggression, and the racism of films made in Hollywood, like *Dive Bomber, Bataan, Air Force, Pride of the Marines*, and *Objective, Burma!* And don't forget *Cry Havoc*, in which Margaret Sullavan leads a band of nurses and other women during the Battle of Bataan. These films did very well at the box office, especially in Britain at a time when many natives were encountering "Yanks" for the first time as they gathered in England in preparation for D-Day. Young men were thrilled by combat films and guns for toys, and Hollywood rejoiced in the success of the genre. *Objective, Burma!* earned close to $4 million—though that was without British box office. The Warner Bros. film, directed by Raoul Walsh, had cast Errol Flynn as a US paratrooper working to lick "the Japs" in the jungles of Burma (all filmed in the Los Angeles Arboretum). There were many in Britain offended by the assumption that what had been largely a British theater of operations was assigned to American heroes. Churchill protested, and the film did not open in Britain until several years after its American premiere in early 1945.

The lesson of rousing combat films was not lost on the British picture business. It was as if original fears were now smothered in the reckless parade of a "damn fine show"—that line is blurted out by the commanding officer (John Mills), in *Above Us the Waves* (1955), a fabrication about underwater mini-submarines trying to destroy the German battleship *Tirpitz* in a Norwegian fjord. Invariably, the armed services were fully collaborative on these pictures, for the sake of recruitment and intensified funding during the Cold War.

There had been a turning point in British war films, and it was so unexpected as to fulfill every rueful feeling that there was never much planning in war, just the chaos of one damn thing after the other. Early in 1943, Laurence Olivier had been summoned to the Ministry of Information. They had a two-picture deal in mind for him: one was a story to make Britain love Russia; the other was *Henry V.* Olivier did the first, *The Demi-Paradise*, with a spiffy Russian accent, but his head was full of the second project, not just King Henry V (1386–1422), but the Shakespeare of it.

Anyone could see that, in 1944, as D-Day went forward, the story of Harfleur and Agincourt might be a radiant opportunity for positivism, martial decisiveness, and glory. Admittedly, the enemy in the Shakespeare play was the French, but British xenophobia was extensive and indiscriminate, so an audience could be trusted to feel for the king's resolve. And the stirring reminder that this was the feast of Saint Crispin (the patron saint of cobblers and tanners):

> *This day is called the Feast of Crispian.*
> *He that outlives this day, and comes safe home*
> *Will stand a-tip toe when this day is named*
> *And rouse him at the name of Crispian.*
> *He that shall live this day and see old age,*
> *Will yearly on the vigil feast his neighbours*
> *And say "Tomorrow is Saint Crispian."*
> *Then will he strip his sleeve and show his scars,*
> *And say, "These wounds I had on Crispin's Day."*

Old men forget; yet all shall be forgot,
But he'll remember, with advantages
What feats he did that day.

Dallas Bower at the BBC had had the idea first, and then Churchill
became hot for the project. They guessed that a fine *Henry V* might capture the spirit of "glorious and victorious" service, the sacrifice and the
flags, the dead and the decorations. Crispin's Day was October 25, and
Agincourt had been fought in bad weather and clogging mud. Never
mind, a movie could doctor the reality. And Crispin's Day did not have
to be underlined: it stood for Dunkirk, the Battle of Britain, the dam
busters, and D-Day. It would be the official history, with a rush of English
arrows falling on the vain French cavalry. Olivier had not directed a film
before. He had half an idea of asking William Wyler to do it. But why not
an Englishman, and why not Larry, who was on the point of picking up
the sacred sword of English acting?

As he did his duty with *The Demi-Paradise*, he was meeting with
Bower, Paul Sherriff, Carmen Dillon, and Roger Furse to work out what
the damn picture would look like while requiring no more than a British
budget. The idea arose (it was inspired) to start at the Globe Theatre itself just before a performance. That would let them begin with primitive,
cheap sets for the early fifteenth century. In turn that could move into the
style of Giotto paintings, or the illustrations from the *Très Riches Heures
du Duc de Berry* (an illuminated manuscript created around 1415). And
then . . . a battle fit for the camera, and for dreamers who had never suffered an hour of combat or terror in their lives?

So it came together as one movie: the Globe in London with a nervous actor impatient in the wings, waiting to walk into the glow of king-
ship; and then the Chorus (Leslie Banks) striding toward the audience
and asking, "O for a muse of fire that would ascend the brightest heaven of
invention." How had Shakespeare understood what movies would be like?
Yet even he would have been astounded how at the crucial moment, the
wooden stage gave way to the rolling meadows of Wicklow on a summer

day, so that the men in armor on horseback could carry out the magnificent exercises of a Technicolor Agincourt.

At the age of four (in 1945) I felt this was the greatest English movie I had ever seen—it had to be, for it was the only one I had seen so far. I did not follow all the language, but in the battle when the appalling French set fire to the English camp so that page boys were burned alive, I was so distressed I had to be carried out of the packed cinema in tears. My father did the carrying, and complaining. I had interrupted the passion—but he had had the reckless instinct to take me to see the film. He said it was a matter of duty. So every Englishman of a certain age was locked into the legend of Crispin's Day, and of the cinema itself.

Then four-year-olds grew up to inhabit a mythic world of British war films, climaxing in the annus mirabilis that gave us not just *Above Us the Waves*, but *The Dam Busters* and *The Colditz Story*. All of which did better at the box office than *Henry V*. It was not only infants who had trouble keeping up with the poetry, or the dynamic shift from decor to location.

The essence of *Henry V* may have been that passage where the king, under a cloak of disguise, walks through the English camp the eve before battle—"A little touch of Harry in the night." The play revels in the disputatious comedy of soldiers from rivalrous parts of the country: it is a flag of Welsh independence. But in the larger view there is a benign regard for team spirit, the leadership of good officers, and the silent desire in subalterns and common soldiers to be patted on the head for a damn fine show.

You can see that in *Scott of the Antarctic* (1948), a movie that celebrates the second-place finish of the British expedition to the South Pole (1910–13) under Captain Robert Falcon Scott (John Mills). Directed by Charles Frend, shooting in Norway with Jack Cardiff as one of the cinematographers and with a fine score by Vaughan Williams, *Scott* is terrific hero-mongering, astute enough to ignore Scott's many shortcomings as a planner—and the complete social separation on the expedition. In the long polar winter, when officers and scientist gentlemen had to live with ordinary seamen, there was a blanket wall put up to divide the hut and to keep the social groups apart. Is that how the Second World War had been fought? Was that a reason why Churchill was put out of office in the summer of 1945?

There may have been some feeling that these films were lopsidedly patriotic. So *The Cruel Sea* (1953) was embarked on in a spirit of tough realism. It came from a 1951 novel by Nicholas Monsarrat, who had served on frigates in convoy protection in the North Atlantic. This was a war of attrition fought in bad weather, and with steady casualties: the British had lost 36,200 regular sailors and more than 32,000 merchant seamen. Over 3,500 ships were sunk. On the German side, the losses were as bad: the dreaded U-boats did great damage, but over 750 of them were lost and over 34,000 men were killed. If you were hit and overboard in those circumstances, the chances of survival were bad.

The movie opened in March 1953, written by Eric Ambler and directed by Charles Frend. Its mainmast is Captain Ericson (Jack Hawkins), who commands the corvette *Compass Rose* in its convoy protection duties. As the film opens, a young Lieutenant Lockhart (Donald Sinden) joins the ship and he rises to "number one" status once the thoroughly nasty (and less than top class) officer played by Stanley Baker has succumbed to a duodenal ulcer. So Ericson and Lockhart begin to make a team. Lockhart will be allowed a sketch of private life, but it is notable that we learn nothing in the film about Ericson's home existence. It is as if, for him, service has meant abdicating from that burden.

Ericson's voice-over stresses the cruelty of the sea itself, and there is some good footage of moderately bad weather. But far more scenes are shot on a millpond—filming at sea is one of the toughest assignments in the dreamy process. There could be much more of the sea and its variety of lights; there should be some observation of the claustrophobic lives of the ordinary sailors, but they hardly speak. The action is in distinct acts. The *Compass Rose* is involved in a situation where Ericson believes sailors floundering in the sea are exactly above a lurking U-boat. So he determines to drop depth charges in the ocean (killing many of the men—they are British sailors) in a need to get the U-boat.

Someone calls out, "Bloody murderer!," and Jack Hawkins is required to weep. He has a famous speech: "It's the war. The whole bloody war. We've just got to do these things and say our prayers at the end." The playwright David Hare has written about the schoolboy derision he and friends expressed at hearing such sentiments. But maybe that mood came later in revival screenings for a more cynical or educated age. At the time, *The Cruel Sea* worked for British audiences. It was the most successful film in the country for 1953 (the Coronation year for Elizabeth II) and it broke a barrier that had existed for British war films in America. It earned over $500,000 in that country, and Jack Hawkins rose from being a supporting actor to an international star.

Apart from weeping once, Ericson has to let some of his own men below decks perish when the *Compass Rose* is struck by a torpedo and sinks in minutes. He gets a new command, the *Saltash Castle*, and is touched when Lockhart agrees to stick with him as number one instead of moving on to his own ship. They remain on a surname basis, but they have nights together on the bridge, in duffel coats, drinking cocoa, and content with the small talk of authority and its marriage. But a bond develops, and decades beyond 1953 it leads us to wonder what men did on ships apart from reading their lines and waiting for torpedoes.

There are women in *The Cruel Sea*. One wife (June Thorburn) is seen briefly at a party; another (Moira Lister) is cheating on her husband, Lieutenant Morell (Denholm Elliott, as thoughtful and fatalistic as you might expect from that actor). But these are minor ties, compared with Lockhart getting entangled with Petty Officer Julie Hallam, the "glamour pants in Ops," played by Virginia McKenna. No, we do not get to see her pants, and that reference does not fit the impeccably handsome and adorable McKenna, one of the last actresses who would represent lovely virtue on-screen without seeming daft or coy, or curling up in smothered irony. Hallam and Lockhart fall for each other, and they seem perfectly matched at a superficial level. They go for a picnic, on a studio set, and there they are stretched out on the grass. Julie has not a hair or a garment out of place. The realism in which two such people in 1943 might have been ready for more is passed by. (In the novel it is clear that they spend a leave together in bed.) It might be enough to have us thinking that Lockhart's heart is really locked in with the lonesome Ericson.

There's more: like a faulty valve, the sexual suppression in *The Cruel Sea* leaked over into real life. A year after the filming, Virginia McKenna and Denholm Elliott were married. There must have been intense innocence on both sides. A few months later, the marriage collapsed because Elliott was seeing too many male lovers. Those domestic events overlapped with the film, and in hindsight one wishes that they might have seeped into the picture's staid relationships. Thus, on shore, Morell could see a suitable mate in Julie, but out on patrol he can't help bunking with able seamen. That may seem far-fetched, or tasteless, but the men on the *Compass Rose* need inner lives that go beyond "Aye, aye, sir." They might try to draw the ocean, or study seabirds; they might play chess or read Sherlock Holmes stories; meditate and masturbate; gather over a windup record player or an illegal kitten; they might put on little plays—suppose they are a team of eccentrics, all clinging to a private world to keep from being afraid. We should be seeing real, odd, normal men.

So much was changing as wartime codes gave up the ghost. But we should recollect the way the films felt for their time. If McKenna had shed her blouse in that picnic scene it might have killed the picture, as easily as if the *Compass Rose* had become a paddleboat. David Hare was only six in 1953, so he may be remembering a revived *Cruel Sea* ten years later, in the sixties, when so many attitudes to duty were shifting. But the widespread adoption of duffel coats (they were nearly uniforms on the Campaign for Nuclear Disarmament marches to the Atomic Weapons headquarters at Aldermaston) says something about how much *The Cruel Sea* meant. We can be stupid when we want and maintain the right to be suckers for bad movies. At the same time, a lot of what Hare learned growing up led to his great play *Plenty* (1978), about the postwar torment of a young woman who was shaped but led astray by dangerous espionage in the war. (She's Meryl Streep in the 1985 movie.)

The Cruel Sea inspired imitation and led to several flimsier films. So we come to *The Dam Busters*, the most commercially successful British film of 1955.

Its reason for existence was that on the night of May 16–17, 1943, 617 Squadron of the Royal Air Force bomber command attacked the Mohne and Edersee Dams in the Ruhr area of Germany, and interrupted industrial production to an uncertain yet heavily promoted extent. Two dams were breached; over a thousand civilians died in the extensive flooding, including Soviet prisoners doing forced labor. The 617 lost eight Lancaster bombers and fifty-three crew members.

The raid depended on the work of Dr. Barnes Wallis (Michael Redgrave), who had developed the idea of bouncing bombs dropped at low level, so timed that the series of bounces across the reservoir lodged the explosives against the dam wall. It was a scheme that only a cricketing country could have conceived. Wallis was an engineer at Vickers, dedicated to inventive bomb delivery. In 1939 he had written a paper, "A Note on a Method of Attacking the Axis Powers." Thanks to the movie, he became a pioneer in the "boffin" archetype, the unworldly genius who might put his finger on the magic button. One can see his successors on the Manhattan Project and in Q, the gadget wizard who assists James Bond (and the British car business).

The more vivid element in the raid was Guy Penrose Gibson, squadron leader at the age of twenty-five. In the movie, this flamboyant leader was played by Richard Todd, who was close to Gibson's age but not quite as good-looking. Gibson's parents had separated, and the mother who cared for him became an alcoholic. We know very little of the real Gibson from the film, and nothing of his marriage to a showgirl seven years his senior. Gibson had joined the RAF in order to learn to fly. He was reckoned just an average flier, and a hard, superior man, known as "a bumptious bastard" or "the boy emperor." That was not quite hero material, but 1955 was as eager to make a statue of the man as public relations had been to acclaim him after the raid. In life, and in the movie, he had a black Labrador he named "Ni**er."

Gibson had led the flight on the dams, and as the other members of the squadron lined up to drop their bombs he acted as a decoy for anti-aircraft fire. (There seem to have been no German fighters in the air that night.) He behaved well and bravely, and in the euphoria that greeted the raid he was awarded the Victoria Cross. Meanwhile, Albert Speer, the German minister of armaments, could not understand why the raid was not followed up with concentrated attacks on the industrial area. It had turned out to be a bit of a self-contained show, and an example of military strategy being calculated to boost public morale—to be like a movie. Whatever; Gibson had done his job well, and I am happy to think he was brave, even if the VC was a gesture.

The Dam Busters had a rousing piece of music, a march written by Eric Coates, and it made schoolboys out of men of all ages. The raid was lucidly explained and well shot, even if the absence of fighters seemed unsporting. The film has been enjoyed and laughed at in the decades since, and the name of that Labrador is one of the howlers of history. But what happened to Guy Gibson? That is another kind of movie.

He was made into a celebrity by air force organization and government funding. He and his wife were sent to the United States on a promotional tour. This was awkward because Gibson was affected by his own legend: he went after other women in an automatic way; he started drinking—which is not uncommon in men afraid of being afraid; and he gave up on the discipline of being a bomber pilot. It was said, in fighters and bombers, that the men had to be ready to do it every night as habit. Draw back and you suddenly understood the terror and the gamble. Your nerve might be shot.

Gibson was still in service, and his reputation led him to command positions with new ventures. But he did not know the new planes he was given, and he seems to have done a poor job of mastering them. He was about to get a divorce. He was too full of himself to listen to advice. This character deserves a real film, written by Terence Rattigan, maybe, whose service in bombers made him very good on pilots with broken spirit, as witness his plays *Flare Path* (1942) and *The Deep Blue Sea* (1952). After D-Day Gibson felt left out of the fun, and he nagged his way back into action. On September 19, 1944, he was made controller on a bombing raid on Bremen. This provoked disbelief in many of the other men, who felt Gibson was out of his depth. The raid was a series of mistakes, or bad luck. He crashed at Steenbergen, in Holland, and was reported "missing" though it was known that he was dead. He was burned beyond recognition in his Mosquito, an aircraft on which he had had only a few hours flying. Churchill called him "the glorious Dam-buster."

The other movie event of the year was *The Colditz Story*, a romance about British, Dutch, and Polish prisoners cooped up in the gaunt Colditz Castle (in Saxony) because they had tried to escape before. This was based on a book by P. R. Reid, who had been an inmate at the castle and who had escaped. His role was another uniform for John Mills to wear in a cast that included Eric Portman, Bryan Forbes, and Lionel Jeffries. The film was directed by Guy Hamilton, who was only years away from James Bond and *Goldfinger*. Frederick Valk was the German camp commandant, and so much less interesting than von Stroheim's character in Renoir's *La Grande Illusion*. By contrast *The Colditz Story* is a shameless board game, and another version of naughty boys in school, with not a woman in sight yet without any concession to British military hormones.

It's easy to attribute *The Colditz Story* to 1950s team spirit, but then realize that in the decades since it has been the model for two television series, in 1972–74 and even 2005, both entitled, with unerring imagination, *Colditz*. There is still an officer class in Britain that likes to think it went to a prep school, a public school, and the castle.

The pressure to be in that military club could be unkind. So many real men failed the class test. In *Separate Tables* (a play by Terence Rattigan in 1954, and then a film in 1958), there is a Major Pollock, living at a hotel in Bournemouth. David Niven does him as a brittle pillar of some forlorn social order. Pollock's war record is trumped up, a mess of lies and hope, and his standing at the Hotel Beauregard is humiliated when the local paper reports that he has been harassing young women—in a cinema. *Separate Tables* is excruciating, but it is one of the few works that give the game away: there was an enormous regiment that had let the side down.

20

KWAI

In 1945, the British armed forces numbered 4.69 million men and women. That number dropped fast with peace, but it was still not much less than a million into the early 1950s. Many of those personnel were stationed in Germany or in other parts of the world that might be vulnerable during the Cold War. National service was required of young men—two years starting at the age of eighteen, not relaxed until 1960.

The million or so were also ready for the Korean War (1950–53), in which the British had about 15,000 fighting under the United Nations flag, with losses of just over a thousand. Many of those deaths were suffered by "the Glorious Glosters": 650 men of the Gloucestershire Regiment were opposed by about ten thousand Chinese. These odds were not fair, the press concluded in their generally dejected view of that war. Conventional strategy was horrified by the idea of pouring Chinese "hordes" into attack until an objective was overwhelmed. Could the thin red line resist the yellow peril? That racist language was taken for granted. Why were we all there in Korea? How many of us still know what that war was about, or how little it settled? There was a British film, *A Hill in Korea*, but not until 1956. The cast of *A Hill* included Michael Caine in a small part, but not because he had served in Korea. Indeed, his advice on what that country had been like was ignored, and his assurance that the film's

Portuguese location was unlike Korea in every detail, especially weather, was shelved. Caine didn't mind; he preferred Portugal.

Such ironies were modern, I think. Though the rhetoric of glory was coming under suspicion. The patriotic bluster of war films was being noted and regretted. And actual British military operations were queried. It was reported in Britain that "our" emergency efforts to prevent communist insurgence in Malaya had succeeded. But an independent Malaysia emerged from that crisis. British soldiers were sent to Kenya to protect white settlers against the raids of "Mau Mau" terrorists. That term referred to an African nationalist movement, but it rapidly became a slogan for the hateful Other. In *Simba* (1955), Dirk Bogarde and the ubiquitous Virginia McKenna try to uphold standards of decency in Kenya. That film was shot at Pinewood studio because it was reckoned unsafe to send the stars to Kenya. The outrages there were deemed savage, inhuman, and typical of uneducated natives, not so far from fuzzy-wuzzies. There was local slaughter in the war, but it led to independence for Kenya and established some "terrorist" leaders as respectable politicians.

Then there was the Suez War of 1956, in which it became clear that Israel, France, and Britain had colluded in a coup attempt against Egypt, which wanted to take over the Suez Canal and discover its independence. Britain lost around a hundred lives in this war, and it was recognized as a shabby disgrace. The theory of British military prowess was getting harder to sustain in practice. There has still not been a good movie about this combat in Suez, though it is background in John Osborne's *The Entertainer*, where Archie Rice's son (Albert Finney on-screen) is killed in the desert, but not seen there.

Was Britain's martial temperature cooling? In 1957, there was more than ever testing of hydrogen bombs in the atmosphere. That did seem out of the league of the Colditz kids. Did it help explain the ironies in *The Bridge on the River Kwai*? Or was that famous picture just an occasion for a new kind of wartime blockbuster, made in the old exuberance of the Kordas? It seems unlikely now, but as producer Sam Spiegel first dreamed of the venture, Alex and Zoltan Korda were leading candidates to do it.

The project had begun with a French novel by Pierre Boulle, *The Bridge on the River Kwai*, published in 1952 and translated into English two years later. The French director Henri-Georges Clouzot (*The Wages of Fear*), had wanted to try its subversive tone, but when the project seemed too large for French money it was bought up by Spiegel, an Austrian who had established himself in Hollywood, where he had produced *The African Queen* and *On the Waterfront*. Carl Foreman (the writer of *Champion*, *The Men*, and *High Noon*, who was now blacklisted and living in London), had been intrigued by the book and he had been talking to the Kordas about a partnership to make the film. But as the Kordas ran out of money, Spiegel stepped in with funding from Columbia, and said of course Foreman should write the picture. Then, after considering many possible directors—notably Howard Hawks—Spiegel offered the script to David Lean. Lean had read the novel and been impressed: "One feels almost at once that the stage is set for a tremendous clash of wills, and that the situation can only be resolved by a mighty climax in which some of the leading characters are bound to die."

The situation was 1943, in the jungle of Burma. A contingent of British prisoners of war, led by Colonel Nicholson, are required by the Japanese camp commandant, Colonel Saito, to build a bridge over the River Kwai that will carry locomotives and troops. Saito declares that officers should work; Nicholson says that's not on—officers are privileged. The two colonels become caught up in a battle of wills from which Nicholson emerges victorious. The Japanese agrees: officers may rest. So the lower-class British prisoners begin to build the bridge. But back in serene Ceylon, the British headquarters has heard this news and is putting together a small commando party to destroy the bridge.

Lean disliked Foreman's script; he thought it had too little sympathy for Nicholson. Director and producer were at odds, but Lean holed up in a hotel and started to rewrite. He began to see the picture he wanted. Spiegel hired Michael Wilson (a second blacklisted writer) to do another draft. All the while, Lean was pushing himself into the picture—and the film owes so much to the passionate wrongheadedness of Nicholson, a state of mind that depended on Lean's confused urgings to be in charge while doing his duty.

Born in 1908, in south London, Lean was raised as Quaker. He was not allowed to go to the cinema—and he never did military service. But he dreamed of making movies, and without a university education he got into the British film industry, making tea, sweeping up, and then gradually learning the craft of editing. It was as he edited the Powell-Pressburger *One of Our Aircraft is Missing* that he had made a casual remark, about old age changing so much, that led to *The Life and Death of Colonel Blimp*. But he was thirty-four when he became the protégé of Noel Coward, who wanted to make the film that became *In Which We Serve*. Coward wrote it and played the lead, the sea captain whose ship ends up being sunk. This figure was based on Lord Louis Mountbatten, whose ship had been lost at the Battle of Crete.

The title of the film indicates its reverence for wartime service, and the picture is a survey of all ranks: the captain is central, but so is an ordinary seaman, played by John Mills. Lean served, too, for Coward asked him to share the directing load. Coward handled the actors while Lean concentrated on the camera and the editing. It worked, and led to a partnership between the two men that had its highlight in Lean directing Coward's screenplay for *Brief Encounter*, a classic of repressed emotion.

For the next ten years, Lean pursued modest yet brilliant films, though his two Dickens adaptations grasp the entirety of very rich novels. But he was eager, close to fifty, to establish his importance as a director, and Spiegel decided to give him the opportunity on *Kwai*. This was never going to be a modest picture. Those classic British films, from *The Cruel Sea* to *Colditz*, had been in black and white, made economically, as if war had to look grim. But Spiegel resolved early on that his *Kwai* would be shot on location, in Ceylon (which is Sri Lanka now). It deserved color and a CinemaScope screen; it is made of money and ambition. From the opening, with a large bird floating over the prison camp, Lean took on the epic nature of the terrain. The bridge is handsome and endearing, but Lean loved the river, too.

A make-believe bridge would be built and then pulled down in Ceylon. The cast of prisoners would be large (if at a distance) and the story needed stars. Neither Lean nor Alec Guinness believed at first that the actor was right for the part. It is not easy: Nicholson is authoritarian and stubborn, yet strangely dreamy and detached. Ronald Colman, Charles Laughton, and Ralph Richardson were all considered. But it was Spiegel who kept coming back to Guinness, telling the actor this project would give him a necessary size in the business. Disputes over casting are not uncommon in pictures, but they are part of the conflict that can consume so many production relationships. To make a movie can be to go to war, so the gulf between Lean and Spiegel was formative and valuable. Lean and Guinness had this in common: *Kwai* would make them major figures.

Kwai was often seen as a height of respectability in war epics, in part because it has that dash of antiwar feeling. But it was loaded up with old-fashioned American compromises. For wider audience involvement, one of the commandos was made American, and William Holden became its marquee name. Then his character was given a silly sequence with a willing English blonde. Lean hated this addition, and it marked a gap between British and American sensibilities. But while Holden got $250,000 and 10 percent of the gross, Guinness made $150,000.

Holden was a natural choice. He was established as an easygoing commanding figure in war stories, and he had won his Oscar as the cynical prisoner in Billy Wilder's *Stalag 17* (1953), a picture that many Americans adore for its artful thriller story line and for a smart, acerbic loner being a reliable member of the team. In hindsight, one wishes that his character, Sefton, could have been kept as a calculating black-market operator who was using the camp as a site for a criminal operation. That is how American prisons function.

In time, *Stalag 17* was accepted (without much reason) as a model for the TV show *Hogan's Heroes* (1965), though by then the prison camp was a proof of American cheek making fools of the stupid Germans (Colonel Klink was not a standard German camp commander, or a credible human being). *Hogan's Heroes* lasted into 1971 and its camp (Stalag 13) was almost a holiday place for its guys.

The condition of the prisoners in *Kwai* seemed harrowing in 1957, but it was less than the reality in Burma. The Japanese were not meant to be unduly offended by the picture; they were part of its business. Colonel Saito (played by Sessue Hayakawa, once a romantic star in silent pictures) is not just understandable—he has a backstory that lets him speak movie-friendly English. And even if the war in Burma had been murderously harsh, nothing would be spared in the production. The film ended up costing just under $3 million, which meant it had to earn $10 million.

Despite the natural spectacle and the bridge built for the picture, it is also a small story about honor. Nicholson is a stickler for the rules, one of which is naked class advantage. He quotes the Geneva Conventions to Saito and the rule that officers do not have to do physical labor. This fits the code of British war movies whereby the officers have the best parts, the memorable lines, and the close-ups. Moreover, Nicholson does not protest other sections of the Geneva code—on torture, beatings, starvation conditions, et cetera—that are being overridden every day in the camp. Nicholson wins in his struggle of egos with Saito, but the British soldiers have to labor in the heat, with poor food, illness, and beatings from the Japanese guards.

Saito had been furious at Nicholson's refusal to accept orders. He shuts the officers up in a compound and he imprisons Nicholson in a small metal hut that becomes an oven in the sun. This is torture, and Guinness plays it to the hilt, emaciated, very weak, and with a staggering walk copied from his young son as he was recovering from polio. It makes the viewer angry, for the scenes reek of torture and racial loathing of the Japanese. This was a delicate issue in Western culture. There had been torture, privation, and many deaths under Japanese control. We have still not quite come to terms with that cruelty in the war. An Australian, Russell Braddon, had written a bestselling book, *The Naked Island* (1950), about wartime conditions in Changi Prison in Singapore. "It was written to tell the world what sort of people the Japanese could be," said Braddon. And just two years before *Kwai*, there had been a film, *A Town Like Alice*, in which Virginia McKenna is in a group of women captured by the Japanese. She has a very hard time and the Australian she meets and falls for (Peter Finch) is crucified by the vengeful Japanese for giving the women extra food.

Saito is humiliated, and defeated by Nicholson's iron politeness. He agrees that the officers need not work, only to be further demoralized by Nicholson concluding that the British attempts to sabotage the bridge are unworthy of national honesty or duty. He also determines that the Japanese plan for the bridge is inept. Its scheme of engineering needs to be corrected and the very siting of the bridge must be changed. Nicholson takes it over and runs it as a sensible British venture, just to teach the Japanese the cultural handicaps of not being British. (This was the element in the picture that most offended Japanese audiences.)

Other British prisoners are bemused by Nicholson's conscientious approach. The medical officer, Major Clipton (James Donald), begins to see that he is serving under a composed madman. In production, Donald and Alec Guinness were both troubled that the project was coming off as anti-British. Which leads one to wonder what is wrong or right with Nicholson. He is a slave to being under orders; he does not seem impressed by the deeper necessity of the war with Japan; he is aiding the enemy's war interests without being aware of it. What allows this is that he is a strict, unimaginative man. I'm not sure Alec Guinness delivers that person (he said later that he never quite believed in the part), because Lean cannot help admiring the forlorn heroism. It is hard for any star actor to feel dull, or boring.

But a crisis is coming as the commando party draws near the bridge: this is not just Holden, but its commander (played by Jack Hawkins), and a younger lieutenant (Geoffrey Horne). The commandos place dynamite charges on the bridge at night. The next day they plan to detonate the structure just as the first train is crossing it.

Then overnight the river level drops, and the punctilious Nicholson notices the wires that will make an explosion. He walks down the riverbank to discover what has been done, and tries to cut the wires to protect his bridge. This causes a skirmish in which Holden and Horne are killed. Only then does Nicholson appreciate his predicament. "What have I done?" he cries out, wounded, letting his dying body fall on the detonator plunger and bringing down the bridge.

What had he done? "Madness! Madness!" says Clipton in the last words of the film.

There was no doubting the impact of *Kwai*. It became an international event, and many reviews endorsed the opinion that it was a critique of the follies of war. Or was the real target the eccentricity of the blind British? Opening in late 1957, it had rentals of $30 million. It was nominated for eight Oscars, and statuettes went to Spiegel for best picture, to Lean for directing, to Guinness, to Jack Hildyard for cinematography, to Peter Taylor for editing, and to Malcolm Arnold for the score that made use of the song "Colonel Bogey." The script got an Oscar, too, though that was received by Pierre Boulle (who spoke no English) because Foreman and Wilson were too black-red to be acknowledged. The two writers were "rehabilitated" as late as 1984. Sessue Hayakawa was nominated as supporting actor, but he was the one loser.

Is Guinness that good in the film? Is Colonel Nicholson plausible? Near the end, on a beautiful evening, he is on the bridge surveying the countryside when Colonel Saito comes by. Nicholson tells his foe that tomorrow will mark his twenty-eight years in the army. He says he wonders if it has been worthwhile. That time span means he served in the Great War. He says he has spent fond years stationed in India. We do not hear whether he has a family. It's possible that he hardly has an English home.

Has he believed in making the best bridge possible for the Japanese? Is he a real officer, or a part to be acted? In the real war on the ground, about 16,000 Allied prisoners died from illness, malnutrition, and the brutal labor system. Has Nicholson failed to notice this? Is he really so stupid (or insane) that he cannot grasp the perversity of his duty? In which case, how does he discover the error of his ways in his final moments?

It was said at the time that *Bridge on the River Kwai* indicated a new attitude to war, a skeptical offset, while still delivering exciting combat at the end. But were Lean and Spiegel really trying to say that the war in Burma, in Asia, or in the whole wide world, should be reappraised in this new fatalism? The shallow exhilaration of those earlier British films might be becoming dated, though there would be more all-star military epics ahead, like *The Longest Day* (1962) and *The Battle of Britain* (1969), that had no time for doubts over the war effort. But in the end, *Kwai* was just a cute way of repeating an old story without coming to terms with its actuality. Nicholson is fascinating, but hollow—the same could be said for Lean's next hero at war, *Lawrence of Arabia*, and its rather sentimental vision of a poet, loner, warrior. The "madness" verdict in Kwai is a sly boast more than a diagnosis.

So many class realities were overlooked. One of the supporting actors in the film is Percy Herbert, a familiar face in cheeky working-class roles in seventy British films. He makes snide jokes in *Kwai* but has little useful to say. We never get the ordinary soldier's thinking. Alas. Herbert had served in the Royal Army Ordnance Corps, and he was captured and imprisoned at Changi for four years. He would have seen so much that is not allowed into the picture—even though he had been signed on as a consultant as well as an actor.

IF YOU HAD RETAINED QUALMS OVER *THE BRIDGE ON THE RIVER KWAI* FOR SO many years, you could have felt rewarded by *The Railway Man*, which opened fifty-six years later, in 2013, and quickly closed.

This film claims allegiance to a "real story." Eric Lomax was a British soldier taken prisoner at the fall of Singapore in 1942. He was sent north to work on the railway, under the severe conditions Colonel Nicholson's men endured in *Kwai*. Yet they are harsher this time. Lomax is one of a group of prisoners who build a secret radio. They do this to hear voices from London with news of the war. But the Japanese decide that the radio was part of an espionage plot to liaise with the Chinese army. So Lomax is brutalized and tortured. His repeated waterboarding is uglier and more cinematic than anything in *Kwai*. It would not have been permitted in a 1957 picture. Lomax is especially the target of a Japanese interrogator, Nagase.

In time, that war ended; Lomax was rescued and restored to Britain. But the emotional damage of the experience never left him, despite the comfort of a good marriage. After years of mental suffering, he went back to Asia to find Nagase (who was by then leading tours of the prison-camp site). Some kind of reconciliation was achieved between them. Lomax wrote a book about this, published in 1995. Nearly twenty years later the film was made, scripted by Frank Cottrell Boyce and directed by Jonathan Teplitzky. Colin Firth plays Lomax as the older man, and Jeremy Irvine is very credible as the younger man. Nicole Kidman is the wife Lomax finds after the war—he meets her on a train, which means a lot to him because since childhood he has loved railways. (The film does not admit this, but she was his second wife.)

The Railway Man is not a great film. It's more testing than that, and more disconcerting if "Colonel Bogey" still plays in your head. The later film is graver on the suffering of prisoners in the jungle, and much more detailed on the Japanese torture. It leaves us angry, so that we want Lomax to find Nagase (Hiroyuki Sanada) and deliver a just vengeance—or movie comeuppance?

But enough time has passed. Nagase says he realizes he was lied to by the Japanese command. He has suffered from guilt for decades. He is even ready to submit to Lomax's revenge; he puts his arm on blocks, ready to be broken. But when Lomax cannot carry out this punishment, Nagase collapses and apologizes. The two men embrace, and the titles at the end of the film say they became friends.

There is too much convenience in this tidiness; it raises more questions than it solves, including the cultural differences between the two sides in that war—and whether they were resolved. In fact, there was an abyss of racism at work: Churchill was astonished that nonwhite forces could have taken Singapore so swiftly; a similar distancing aided the dropping of atom bombs on "other" populations. None of which softens the cruelty in the Japanese response to defeated and captured enemies. Or helps us absorb the waterboarding carried out by Americans in a film like *Zero Dark Thirty* (2012). Which side was most cruel, and does that question insist on being answered? Nearly eighty years later, has the pious sense of German and Japanese "misbehavior" gone away? Or have the movies accustomed us to vivid scenes of people behaving badly? Does the presentation of brutality perpetuate its darkness? Or serve as an instructional manual? Are there war crimes, still, or is war a culture of criminality?

Hideous criminal acts at the Abu Ghraib prison in Iraq led to relatively minor sentences for a number of American soldiers, men and women. A commander was demoted. Secretary of Defense Donald Rumsfeld said that he had offered his resignation, only to be disappointed by President George W. Bush. There is a terrifying re-creation of Abu Ghraib in Paul Schrader's *The Card Counter* (2021), a frenzy of wide-angle tracking shots in an intestinal maze, as if the prison and its horror had been devised by a scholar of mise-en-scène. I'm sure Schrader has shown this hell as a warning, but he cannot help feeling entranced.

The "based on a true story" imprimatur of *The Railway Man* comes apart, because particular incidents are easily lost in the historical perspective and the way victors tell the best stories. Are we prepared to live with the way, over time, anger can fall away in our ingenious search for a healing benevolence? Terrible things were done in that Burma, as in every other theater of war. Peace treaties and movie homilies may say the criminals are forgiven. But how much evil can civilization digest before the range of human nature itself has altered? Do these films leave us asking ourselves what unsettled burden remains in war bringing out the worst in us? Or have we become complacent about that worst and the user-friendly glorification of what happened?

The Railway Man works, as an anecdote about anguish. Firth and Irvine are very touching. Kidman makes a lot out of her adjunct role. I only found the film several years after it opened because I was careless; it had been condescended to in reviews, and then did badly at the box office. *The Railway Man* does not say enough about the war with Japan or the building of that railway. Movies are rarely adequate as history. On the other hand, if anyone reminisces about the glory of *Kwai* I recommend this rueful picture. The attempt to describe our guilty past is a duty cinema has neglected: such scrutiny doesn't sell, and its dismay is at odds with the glamour of battle and our mad longing to be aroused.

A FEW MONTHS BEFORE *KWAI* OPENED (DECEMBER 1957), NICHOLAS RAY'S *Bitter Victory* was presented at the Venice Film Festival, and began to be forgotten in the aftermath of failure. But it's the better film, and deserving of rescue. It comes from a novel by Rene Hardy that concentrates on two officers in the British army fighting the Germans in the North African desert. Major Brand (Curd Jürgens) is an insecure careerist while Captain Leith (Richard Burton) is a romantic intellectual and an archaeologist by training. They are assigned to a dangerous mission, to steal plans from a desert outpost behind the German lines. They have something else in common: Brand has just married a woman who was once in an unhappy love affair with Leith.

This is one of the best things Burton ever did. Leith has his head in the past; he speaks Arabic and understands the ruined buildings they find on the mission. By contrast, Jürgens seems hunched and nervous, in part because he is miscast, but also because Brand is self-serving and fearful, while Leith embraces violence as a test of manhood. There was talk of having Montgomery Clift play Brand, and that would have been better, for Clift could show us the neurotic in the part. As for the wife, played by Ruth Roman, she needs to come alive, and feel torn between the two men—it could have been Deborah Kerr, or why not Virginia McKenna tempted into infidelity?

With two parts wrong, how can the picture work? It succeeds while limping because of Ray's taut handling of the desperate action, because of Burton's rapt, forlorn gaze, and because these men in war are much as they might be in life: petty, passionate, jealous, in love, and making mistakes. In black and white and CinemaScope, *Bitter Victory* is a wounded plan for a great picture. That could have been enough. But its distributor—the same Columbia as did *Kwai*—hated it; they cut it and let it loose on the world without promotion. But in the passage where, stranded in the desert, Leith has to shoot one man and then fail to carry another to safety—in a scene with superb pained music, by Maurice le Roux—there is a delivered tragedy that surpasses all of *Kwai*. The madness in the bigger film is observed from a safe distance and patronized; in *Bitter Victory* it is inhabited.

21

THE BASTARDS AND THEIR DEMON

You could conclude from *Kwai* and *Bitter Victory* that war might be manageable if one didn't have to have madmen or cowards in charge. But how can a nation get along without those types? Won't the circumstances of war and the crises of battle drive a lot of us out of our minds? Once iniquity is admitted as part of warfare, so honored leaders may put on the malevolence that signals strength and indifference. They become leaders of the gang we have hired. It will be sentimental to dispute this. And we hate to seem like softies in a crisis.

George Smith Patton was always picking for a fight, so some of his own men wondered if he was crazy. He is the exemplary American commander, a throwback it seems at first, but maybe a prediction of the unhindered force that may be coming soon. Suppose we find ourselves on a field where "they" and their system have gone away, but then some astonishing master appears to run the show, like a leader out of Wardrobe.

Born in 1885, Patton entered the Virginia Military Institute and went on to West Point. He had a hobby, designing swords and cutting edges. He fenced, and in 1912 he represented the United States at the Stockholm Olympics and came fifth in modern pentathlon. That event involves fencing, swimming, equestrian show-jumping, pistol shooting, and cross-country running. It is the epitome of military preparedness as a sporting contest, and it goes back to ancient Greece. Whenever war raises its sleepy head—as it would two years after those games—there could be a case for setting aside costly mobilization and a few million deaths and opting instead for a prime-time weekend of modern pentathlon, five-man teams, with the winning nation receiving a gold medal, the Balkans, and all the stallions on the steppes.

In 1916, Lieutenant Patton was part of the military expedition sent to rebuke Pancho Villa's incursion into New Mexico. There was an incident in which three Mexicans were killed, and possibly this was down to Patton's ivory-handled Colt revolver. He cherished that gun. Whatever; he picked up the name of "bandit killer," an attitude that has had a lasting influence on US military policy toward impudent freedom fighters.

In the Great War, Patton was instrumental in the development of tanks. That made him a pioneer in the war that transformed warfare: those years saw the annunciation of the machine gun and long-range artillery; it introduced the submarine and aircraft, poison gas and the home front, not to mention a scheme of armies as the embodiment of conscription, uniformity, and bureaucracy, to the point of genocide. We could now kill people at such a distance we need not know it had happened. Does this resemble battle cinema, where strangers in another realm, the screen, are shot down for our fun as we sit in safety?

This book begins in earnest at 1914, which means it neglects centuries of spectacular local conflicts from Hannibal to Napoleon. But after 1914, and the idea of "world war," those historical engagements became picturesque, like paintings of cavalry charges where the horses had all four legs splayed out. That stance was disproved by Eadweard Muybridge's series of advancing still photographs that taught us how horses moved in a different way. That was 1872.

But if real horses cannot live up to their pose in romantic paintings, then humans have a similar shortfall. So maybe the flourish and the glory of Jacques-Louis David's flamboyant equestrian painting, *Napoleon Crossing the Alps*—eight feet high—needs to be measured against the scuttling crouch we adopt in running for cover.

By the Second World War, Patton was a brigadier general, a wayward genius in his army and a law unto himself. Inspired by the German blitzkrieg of 1940, he had revolutionized training exercises in the desert southeast of Palm Springs, and then carried that approach onto the real battlefield. He was a spectacular winner in North Africa and Sicily. It was Patton who took Casablanca. He and that city would be flags signaling war and success. And then, despite Eisenhower's feeling that George's intensity made him a public relations liability, Patton became central in the Allied thrusts that followed D-Day and reckoned to ram the Nazis back into their dark hole, Berlin. He was already so splendid, slapping his soldiers for cowardice, standing erect to watch bullets pass by, that he was like a man in a movie.

This winning Patton did *not* take Berlin; he would have said he was not allowed to because of fussy political compromising. But in the video game *Legends of War: Patton's Campaign* this failure is corrected. A skilled player can get George into Berlin *ahead* of the Soviets, with good, hectic illustration of how it would be done. This revisionism comes from Enigma Software Productions and it is in the bold spirit of George's desert exercises. How long before our history accepts that version?

We say we know this general, we hear his voice, even if George C. Scott's Patton had a rasping baritone while George spoke in a high-pitched tone not ideal for what he wanted to say:

> Now, I want you to remember that no bastard ever won a war by dying for his country. He won it by making the other poor dumb bastard die for *his* country. Men, all the stuff you've heard about America not wanting to fight, wanting to stay out of the war, is a lot of horsedump. Americans traditionally love to fight. All real Americans love the sting of battle. . . . That's why Americans have never lost, and will never lose, a war.

That is the celebrated opening speech from *Patton* where Scott appears in riding breeches, helmet, and boots, with decorations and regalia. He seems dressed for Christmas, an operetta, or a state funeral. He tells his bastards what is going to happen in war and why he is proud to lead them. As he speaks, he stands before a huge Stars and Stripes that has taken over the sky. If you feel Scott carries himself well, with truculence toward all, you may thank his four years in the marines. Or was it just that he was an actor?

Patton played in 1970, two years after the Tet Offensive, deep into the dismay and the fog of Vietnam. Yet it won best picture, best director, best actor, and nearly everything else you could think of. Scott declined his Oscar, and the statuette ended up at the Virginia Military Institute. It's still there. Franklin Schaffner directed the movie and it was written by Francis Coppola and Edmund H. North, just two years before *The Godfather*. Scott was on the short list to play Vito Corleone.

As late as 1970, America cherished *Patton* and few objected to its fascist thrill. Today, the idea of a Patton in military leadership is unthinkable—and will be, until our decorous scheme of military order gets closer to panic. Command codes may then be up for grabs as survivalism takes power. In American glory, one has to be very flexible, ready to raise—and then take down—an equestrian statue of Robert E. Lee nine times life size. That reappraisal happened September 8, 2021, in Richmond, Virginia. A dozen or so other actors have played Patton on the screen by now (including Kirk Douglas, Ed Asner, and Ed Harris), but history knows he acted like George C. Scott. That legacy is harder to dismantle than a statue.

Patton felt lost in the European peace. He wanted to be assigned to the Pacific, but that was blocked. He was appointed military governor of Bavaria and then fired by Eisenhower. George would boast about his sexual prowess. He talked of being in an affair with his niece. When out shooting pheasant near Heidelberg, he had a driving accident and broke his neck. Twelve days later he died, December 1945, at the age of sixty. He seems like someone out of Hemingway's head.

He was human and vulnerable, a broken, restless victor. There's a second film, *The Last Days of Patton* (1986), with Scott again, that treats its hero very lightly. But a few years after his death, the army named a tank for him.

22

FURY

Don't you love tanks, and sometimes wish when in traffic gridlock on the 405 that you had the armor and the force to drive the still shit of dead vehicles out of your way? Driving can make one angry and violent.

You can say that the tank is the central character in *Fury* (2014), the film, but that's kidding ourselves and being kind to the romantic American tradition that idealizes vehicles and our prowess in locomotion. With such a vast naked land expanse to come to terms with, Americans had to believe they could conquer and digest space and get from A to B.

This is an M4 Sherman tank, a line brought into service in 1942, about nineteen feet by nine, with a top height of just over nine feet six inches. With armor and a 75-millimeter gun it weighed about 75,000 pounds, with a five-man crew and a speed of over 20 miles per hour. Put like that, it sounds as archaic yet as noble as a cavalry horse. But, named after William Tecumseh Sherman, who directed the most devastating campaign fought on American ground, the Sherman was one of "the weapons that won the war," as well as being a death trap. Over 20,000 Shermans were supplied to the US Army and the marine corps during the war. Thousands more were leased to Britain and the Soviet Union.

About 10,000 of those Sherman tanks under American command were lost in the years 1942–45. Their armor could not resist antitank fire, and a serious hit might turn the cozy American camp on tracks into an inferno from which the five occupants were desperate to escape. In *Fury*, there are scenes of men totally on fire screaming as they get free. One of them takes out his own gun and shoots himself in the head. The movies now can do these effects and make them brilliant and terrifying. A man on fire can be as pretty as a firework.

Why are these aggressive engines called "tanks"? During the Great War, the British devised machines that could move over uneven country—like the battlefields of the Somme—and so might break the attrition and stagnation of trench warfare. If men were endlessly cut down in infantry attacks, why not mechanize the advance, give it some armored protection and a gun equivalent to light artillery? But to fool German intelligence, these new vehicles were called "tanks"—with a British nudge and a wink—as if to say the odd-shaped carriers were simply supplying water or fuel. Of course, this ruse didn't work.

But for the Second World War, in North Africa, in Russia, and then in western Europe after the Normandy landings, the Sherman became central as an attacking spearhead. It was instrumental in winning battle after battle; and it was certain in all those conflicts to sustain heavy losses, in part because it was vulnerable to the greater firepower, speed, and range of some German tanks—Germany does machines, too. The panzer tank had been vital in the blitzkrieg attack on Belgium and the Netherlands and the taking of France in 1940. Those tanks were vulnerable, too, but the German command of panzer attacks was based on shock and speed, all of which became contributing factors in German overconfidence in its own military glamour. By 1943, the Germans had evolved to the Panther tank (it was used in the enormous battles on the Russian front) and it was arguably the best tank in the war. Not that vehicle supremacy meant more than availability, supply and repair, crew training, and rational direction in a war that was frequently chaotic. On all sides, tank crews suffered heavy casualties. The Soviets lost over 80,000 tanks in the war, more than were deployed by both sides on the western front. But the war was different in Russia; it was total and uncompromised, and in turning a blind eye to that the West helped set up another conflict, the Cold War. The Russian front was regularly minimized or neglected in reporting, and so people in the West never quite registered the astonishing sacrifices made in the Soviet Union.

This particular Sherman, our tank, rolling across broken ground, is named "Fury" by its crew. That word is hand-inscribed in white paint on the barrel of its gun, like a flag. But if you think about it you must appreciate that the paint would be eroded by the heat of firing, the weather, and the mud. The people in set decoration would have to keep touching it up, to have the name fly bravely. But it looks good all through the film. There is cheating going on. We don't wage wars without lying to ourselves and our armies, and without taking possession of the story. Controlling the narrative in war can be more determining than capturing cities and executing enemies.

What does "Fury" stand for? Well, it is chest-beating, a way of warning the enemy that this fucking tank and its five Americans are so angry it would be folly to stand in their way. What is the source of the anger? Is it a thorough philosophical disdain for National Socialism? Or a response to anecdotes about how badly the SS behaved? Or is it simply rage that these American country boys have been ripped away from their plain lives back home and exposed to remorseless risk and danger? Are they furious because they are afraid of dying? Is their resentment ultimately directed at the condition of humanity in the modern age?

Do we go to war as a distraction from more complete failure?

Yet in the crisis for this crew, in what seems like their last stand, the hard men sigh and tell themselves that to be together in their cockpit is a kind of bliss, the thing they feel happiest doing. Is that a white lie to fend off imminent incineration, or is it the idea of a male liberty, a response to danger that may not be far from the thinking of the dread SS? Is there even a glimpse of the ineluctable madness in war that is driven to justify and rationalize itself? What is *Fury* the film getting at? Is this hell, or something stunned survivors may one day call the best years of their lives?

The good tank "Fury" is a hero of April 1945. *Fury* the film opened nearly seventy-five years later, obsessed with a certain level of period verisimilitude—and it was a big success. On a cost of about $70 million it earned nearly $212 million. And it deserved every bit of it as a thoroughly entertaining film, with endearing rough-hewn characters and a lucid command of action. Its keynote is how easily you can follow the action—and that may be its biggest lie. Real battle doesn't conform to storyboards or scripts. As written and directed by David Ayer, *Fury* offers a way we might like to have our wars run. The toughness of the show does not conceal the wishful thinking.

As the picture begins, we meet a tank and a crew that has been through it all. They fought in Africa before they came to Europe, and we are led to believe that the same tank got through all those campaigns, with a solid crew. This is a film that adores its team and the idea of persistence. That is a stretch: so many Shermans were destroyed in those years, so many crewmen were lost. But here we are with "Fury" in April 1945, under the leadership of Sgt. Don "Wardaddy" Collier, as presented by Brad Pitt. His gunner is Boyd "Bible" Swan (Shia LaBeouf); his driver is Trini "Gordo" Garcia (Michael Pena); and his loader is Grady "Coon Ass" Travis (Jon Bernthal). That only makes four. "Fury" is also carrying the corpse of its fifth crew member—referred to as "Red." So they need a replacement. Call him Ishmael?

A kid, Private Norman Ellison (Logan Lerman), is assigned to "Fury." He has been in the army eight weeks, and his declared job is that of typist. (I told you, typing can be a step toward battle.) But Norman has been deployed under orders and, from Wardaddy down, there is no arguing over the matter. So four seasoned veterans, bound up in comradeship, take in this meek youth as their number five, aware that his ignorance and innocence could get them killed.

Pause a moment. A few things are astray. It is possible that an untrained kid might have been pushed into a tank crew that April. But it is less likely that a sergeant of Pitt's age (fifty-one) would still have been in charge of the tank. The rest of the crew are twenty-eight and thirty-eight. That seems acceptable, even if it's out of line. The average age of a soldier then was twenty-six, and the draft did not go past forty-five. Thirty was old for tank commanders; and at thirty Pitt had been the wild Montana boy who lives to fish and get into trouble in *A River Runs Through It*. Only two years earlier (1991) he had been that sly rascal in *Thelma & Louise*. In shaping the drama that throws Norman into the firing line we have to make some allowances, ones we hardly notice if we're going with the flow.

So the setup of *Fury* is at pains to make Wardaddy not just a father figure, but a veteran guide to life. He is tough on Norman, but the film does nothing to rebuke his severity. Instead, there is the assumption that the kid must make a bargain with it, getting a war daddy in return. There are barely buried elements of a recruiting film.

There are greater disparities still.

The compelling story arc of *Fury* proposes that a trusty tank can be in great and critical danger in April 1945. Whereas the war by then was over in the eyes of most participants. Hitler had moved into his bunker (January 16!). German forces were in retreat or surrender. Berlin itself was close to surrounded by Soviet forces. In the west, Patton had crossed the Rhine on March 22. Churchill met Eisenhower on the field and told him, "The German is whipped. We've got him. He is all through."

In the first week of April the German army was defeated at Kassel (northeast of Frankfurt) in one of its last concerted stands. There was isolated German resistance still, but it was demoralized, undermanned, and exposed to total Allied command of the air. *Fury* will pitch its noble tank into desperate battles where mere survival turns into astonishing victory, as "Fury" overcomes German tanks and antitank guns, and a fighting force of German soldiers that comes marching down a country road as if it's 1941 still, at least two hundred strong, chipper, mean, and from another era.

That makes a thrilling fight for the movie and a far-fetched sacrificial American victory, but it is not true to what was happening in Germany that month as the Allies advanced. Their aircraft could have been called in to pick off enemy tanks. And German forces were nowhere near as focused and deadly as those seen in *Fury*. This is not to say that Americans and their tanks were not being destroyed here and there. But something has been rigged: the deployment of forces that suggests "Fury" is fighting a crucial action. Why not? Isn't this a movie, and aren't we prepared to enlist in this crew from our dark if it means having Brad Pitt as our sergeant? How could such a build-up turn out boring or incidental? But how is this old history made new, in 2014?

Without knowing the history of this tank, we take it for granted that it has a tough, smart crew and we feel that Wardaddy is a bleak master at his bitter task—because he's Brad Pitt. At the very least, Brad is going to be there with his guys until the end. Pitt is a believable actor: he grasps the weary, ingrained realism of his role—but he cannot shed the assurance of the Mr. Pitt who is close to a guarantee on pictures and is getting at least $10 million for *Fury*. Like proper recognition for getting this picture made. Credible as he is, this boss-like Brad Pitt is squeamish about being uneasy. So we trust his presence, just as his crew have learned to follow him to hell—and back, they hope.

The cast did boot camp for a week. They were encouraged to get into fights, like boys on a team. So much of *Fury* feels authentic: the tanks, the uniforms, the firearms and the sound of their firing—even if the setting is the English countryside because that country has good tank museums as well as lanes and trees that can stand in for Germany (though they are unduly lush for April). But the movie is also an advertisement for military order, the discipline of teamwork, and what you have to call doing the right thing, even if sometimes it looks grim. So many of our soldiers trained at acting school.

There's a simple urge in the film, enough to marry period accuracy and eternal wishful thinking, that it needs to tell a human story in the context of combat. This assumes that we want to see battle (as if participating in a video war game) while hoping for some exploration of character and even philosophy. We want to get our aggressive rocks off while feeling good. So there is to be a relationship between Wardaddy and Norman that is akin to father and son.

The sergeant knows this novice is a risk. On their first patrol, Norman sees kid German soldiers in the woods but fails to call an alert—aren't they just boys like him, as well as Hitler Youth? (These were very fierce fighters, sometimes as young as twelve.) But those kids wipe out one of the other Shermans, and Norman is to blame. Whereupon, at a halt, Wardaddy drags Norman into hell. There is a German prisoner pleading for mercy. Wardaddy insists that Norman kill this man. He pushes his own pistol into Norman's hand. Norman is desperate and aghast. His sergeant hauls him into a position to shoot, clamps Norman's arm until together they pull the trigger. Norman has to learn quickly how to kill krauts—which means kill them, and then move on fully equipped, without a qualm. This is the realist education of war, but it appalls Norman. For a few minutes.

I do not doubt that incidents like this occurred (violations of the Geneva Code) and I recognize the brutal melodrama of the action. It is a bigger step to see how quickly Norman will handle his light machine gun from the tank, shoot down several Germans, and admit that he almost enjoyed it. Of course, that is a kindness to us, for in the dark we are counting off the kills with the relish picked up watching combat films. We have done our basic training. If asked, could we execute unnamed strangers in battle, without horror? But in the passion of watching a movie we fire away imaginatively, and Norman's education helps us come to terms with ourselves.

The writer-director David Ayer has a record in this tricky bargain: he wrote *Training Day* and *The Fast and the Furious* (both from 2001) and in addition to *Fury* he has directed several violent action films including *End of Watch* and *Suicide Squad*. He is now embarked on a remake of *The Dirty Dozen* (1967), one of the first films that turned military murder into a game. He also served in the navy as a submarine sonar technician, so he has had experience of men crammed together in a tight steel home.

The most unexpected part of *Fury* involves Wardaddy's education of Norman. The sergeant seems impressed with the progress the kid has made in a day or so. Their tank becomes part of the taking of a small German town. As the soldiers relax after that victory, Wardaddy leads

Norman inside a building where he has seen a woman looking out of the window. Together they find two women in the wreck of the house: one of about thirty and her younger cousin (Anamaria Marinca and Alicia von Rittberg). They are both attractive by the hardship standards of 1945. What I mean by that is they are good-looking enough to be in a movie even without makeup or glamorization. In truth, they are not as "attractive" as Wardaddy. When the sergeant takes off his shirt to wash himself he proves to have Brad Pitt's enviable torso, which is passed on to the audience in the way, once upon a time, Marilyn Monroe's breasts might have been alluded to. This Brad has been at the gym in ways that seem beyond a sergeant's reach.

The women make a simple meal for the two men. Norman plays the creaky piano and the younger woman, Irma, does her best to sing along with him. There is a spark between the two kids, and the sergeant gruffly tells Norman that if he doesn't take the girl into the bedroom then he will. This is duly accomplished in a sudden swoop of sweet lust. The older woman wonders maybe if the sergeant is saving her for himself.

Whereupon the other three crew members blunder into the home and eye the food and the women. There is a prospect of rape and the exploitation that goes with winning in war and overcoming yet hating one's fear. But Wardaddy makes it clear that no one beyond Norman is going to get any satisfaction, as if suddenly the kid's innocent feelings have become precious. Gloomily, and in resentment, the rough men abide by this. It is a perilous moment in terms of story and a weird gesture toward delicacy in hell. But the sequence is very well shot and acted, and I find its surprise intriguing even if I can guess how an audience of hardened tank crews might laugh it off the screen. But we do like to think that we have gone to war for the sake of tender liberties and decent reactions to life. As well as "Fury" on our gun barrel, we like to think that "Virtue" can be read there if you look closely.

Norman's initiation rankles with the others as unfair privilege. Then, as the men prepare to move on, a stray shell hits the apartment and Norman finds Irma blasted and dead, her body lately warm and now cold forever. That is putting it bluntly, but there is a rough awareness in *Fury* that quickly carries the guys past its sentimentalities. Let's face it: military service is rather like college—it's a means for young people getting laid and coming closer to death and, generally speaking, if you're going to war, it's preferable to have officers and companions who have had some of that.

The stage is now set for "Fury's" glory and the movie's climax. The kid is accepted in the crew—the other guys call him "Machine." So the tank goes back to battle, and there is a spectacular sequence in which it outmaneuvers a German tank that is hamburger for combat pros (I mean accomplices like you and me who have never been to war). And then "Fury" moves forward, a lone tank in empty countryside, the evident hero.

They see a crossroads ahead with a farmhouse that seems deserted. But as they move toward it, the tank hits a land mine. No one is hurt, but one of the tank tracks has been blown away. All of a sudden they are stranded. As they try to repair the vehicle, Norman is sent up the road ahead to scout for any enemy. Be careful now: I am going to tell you how the story works out, and that may be a spoiler if you're thinking of watching *Fury* tonight.

The scout sees a contingent of spick-and-span Germans. There are two hundred or so, but they have no tanks. The kid hurries back to report, and the five have little doubt about their peril. Wardaddy tries to order the others to get away as best they can while he stays with the tank. But they will not leave him. This is a group of practical, realist survivors who know the war's end is near. Do they take this emotional plunge? Does Wardaddy need to stay with the tank? Never mind, esprit de corps holds firm—or you can call it American greatness if you feel inclined. So the sergeant makes a plan. They will disguise their own tank to let it seem disabled and abandoned. But the five of them will hide inside the shell and then take out as many of the Germans as they can.

Night is falling, so the gunfire will be prettier—that really is the word to use if you don't feel the bullets could hit you. The plan works. The Germans are deceived. Our guys are steadfast, heroic, and entirely skilled. The wounded tank is its best, defiant machine. Many Germans are cut down. A small victory has been accomplished. But our crew members are picked off and at last just two are left—you know who they are. Then Wardaddy is hit by a sniper's shot; as the Germans make their final advance, he tells Norman to escape through the bottom of the tank.

He does this and tries to bury himself in the ground beneath the tank. But one young German soldier with a flashlight sees him. Those two kids stare at each other in silence. And the German elects to do and say nothing. He moves on with his contingent. Next morning, American troops come upon "Fury," and tell Norman he is a hero. "And I only am escaped alone to tell thee"—as the Book of Job declares.

And so are we, in our dreamy way, for having come through a very compelling picture. I have made the claim already that so epic and critical an engagement does not fit with the military situation of April 1945. We can live with that, for we have known all along that this show is put on for our fun. The coming of age of Norman is too tidy, maybe, but I can live with that even while being aware of all the cultural traps in the theory and practice of how young Americans will do their duty.

In military history, I suspect Norman would win a decoration— a serious one. The crew might get the Medal of Honor (if the authorities could persuade themselves that the stand at the crossroads served enough purpose). There could be a film on how the shattered Norman goes home—wherever he is from—but cannot live up to the adulation that accompanies his medals. To say nothing of the trauma that followed his war. He is haunted by how afraid he was, and how callous he became. That is a delicate part of team spirit. No matter his education, he was emotionally ruined. In this other film, he might make an effort to trace the family of Wardaddy—Brad Pitt was born in Shawnee, Oklahoma, and then he lived in rural Missouri—and I can imagine a scenario where he discovers the Collier family broken apart by poverty. Suppose they only vaguely recall Don or his two failed marriages. But he left a wayward daughter who reminds Norman of Irma. . . . You're grown-up, you can do the rest of the story. You can do story; that right goes deeper than the permission to bear arms. You sing.

There's another movie that might have been. In the Battle of the Bulge (December 1944–January 1945), the last serious attempt by Germany to win the war, the German Panther tank performed too well against the Sherman. So it was that a struggle evolved in American military thinking between the Sherman and the Pershing tank, which some serving soldiers thought was more effective. Today there could be a movie in which a bespectacled engineer, still mocked by the men, campaigns to persuade the army to opt for a better tank (she might be Jessie Buckley?). No, dense arguments over armor and traction are not as winning as Brad Pitt without his shirt, and the fraternity of supporting actors he commands.

But decisions over equipment are vital in war, and they are bound up in economics and politics and the profitability of making and selling armaments. As well as the ego of the arguers. By 2020, the US had 6,000 M1 Abrams tanks with not too many ideas about where and how they might be used. Launched in the 1970s, every Abrams now costs close to $9 million as manufactured by the Lima Army and Detroit Arsenal plants. With a 105-millimeter gun, it moves about twice as fast as the old Sherman. It has been used extensively in the Middle East, a war theater we keep telling ourselves we'd like to quit. It gets an outing in movies still, though a good deal of scenario energy is more thrilled by the buzzing agility of helicopters. Ukraine wants that tank.

Russia has a lot more tanks than the US, but America has vast air superiority, and *Fury* fails to disclose how readily aircraft or drones can pick off tanks like shooting duck in the marshes. These days, one has to wonder whether tanks need to be manned. Truly, weapons have acquired a life of their own.

David Ayer said that in making *Fury* he had been influenced by the book *Death Traps* (1998) by Belton Y. Cooper, a bestselling memoir on service in tanks that argues the case against the Sherman. This matter is still controversial in military circles. But to this day, to keep the country great, prodigious sums of money are spent on weapons systems the actual use of which is often called unthinkable ($770 billion for 2022). So citizens should not overlook such issues, or the fortunes made by corporations, like Alco, the American Locomotive Company, that have manufactured many of our tanks. War is too lethal and rewarding to be trusted to the movies' boyish scheme of glory.

Yet the success of *Fury* is undeniable. For what it is, it is a very good film—I think a proper description is "enjoyable"—and I have watched people come out of it in what appears to be a jaunty spirit—like German soldiers marching down a country road without having read the film's script. We are going to have to test the word "enjoyable," along with "battling," and so many others.

23

THE BEST YEARS OF OUR LIVES

In the structure of this book, I was not convinced by a straightforward "chronological" approach. It's a lesson of war that sometimes a lot of things are happening at once. History is some kind of crab forever scuttling off in different directions. Some are having breakdowns, others are being at their best. But which is which?

So it could easily be that Fred Derry, Homer Parrish, and Al Stephenson get back to their Boone City (a fictional place, though Cincinnati was used in aerial shots) only days after the atom bomb was exploded above Hiroshima, August 5, 1945. I wouldn't mind a scene where the three men hear that news and try to assess it. Or they might read over reports of the Potsdam Conference or the signing of the United Nations Charter. All of that was happening in August. It's unlikely that the guys would have heard about the organizing of opposition to French rule in Indochina. That was announced on August 14 and it involved a man named Ho Chi Minh (not always spelled correctly). It would have been useful if Americans had grasped that small event early and foreseen its consequences.

So I'm edging aside to go forward. And we know a lot about Derry, Parrish, and Stephenson in *The Best Years of Our Lives*. Captain Fred Derry was a bombardier flying raids in Europe and he is coming home to his wife—they are Dana Andrews and Virginia Mayo. Al Stephenson was an infantry sergeant in the Pacific (he is forty-eight) and he returns to a wife and children. Fredric March is Al, Myrna Loy is his wife, and Teresa Wright is their grown daughter. The youngest of the three men, Homer, lost both his hands in the navy when his ship was sunk. He is played by Harold Russell, and the movie is conscientiously playing fair with life in that Russell had lost his hands, too. This realism was an event and a selling point in 1946 when the film was released. Russell had been an army instructor teaching demolition in North Carolina when an explosive went off in his hands. He was given replacement prosthetic hooks. Homer wears them in the way Wardaddy had to have Brad Pitt's pectoral muscles.

In 1946, *The Best Years of Our Lives* was unmistakably a war film, without one scene of combat. The closest it comes to that is when a disenchanted Fred—his marriage is over; his demeaning job is shot—wanders into a graveyard for surplus aircraft, including B-17 bombers, the plane he flew in. He climbs up into the shell he occupied as a bombardier and then he hears a soundtrack montage of the war in the air. The scene is well done, tactful and imaginative, and it does suppose a kind of war that women left at home could be comfortable with. It's nothing like the horror Captain John Yossarian feels in *Catch-22* at the memory of a friend's insides spilling out in the aircraft. *The Best Years* is never that messy or disturbing.

But it was the movie event of 1946, an experience devoutly entered into by the world that had survived. Running its patient 172 minutes and having cost between $2 and $3 million, it earned over $23 million in America and was admired all over the Allied world. As a child of five in south London I was not allowed to see it—it was said to be too grown-up—but I was in no doubt about the respect my elders had for it. Only one detail troubled me: that word, the "best" years of our lives. In a house hit three times by bombs (or it could have been stray British fire—you kept an open mind), I trusted that the war had been a bad thing. I had an uncle who was in a prisoner-of-war camp somewhere over there; the father of my best friend was in France; my own father was "away"—that could have been because he was engaged in war work, making radios, but

I suspect he just preferred to be away (you kept an open mind). My family bemoaned the blackout, the obligatory gas masks, the lack of certain foods, and the bomb sites all around us. So what was "best" about that?

The war as felt in south London was not good: so many families had had losses. There was no football or cricket. Still, this was far from the suffering that had devastated the Soviet Union, most of eastern Europe, and the revenge that would be taken on Germany. Britain and America, domestically, had a pretty good war—so many things might have worked out differently if they had had just a touch of occupation with its extras of betrayal, informing, torture, and fascist policing—to say nothing of the wholesale bomb damage. Britain had been bombed, but in a modest way compared with the razing in other countries.

But that "best" was an inspirational concept, and it was allied to the key word "our." *We* had come through, it said; our every sacrifice had paid off; and hadn't we felt the kind of comradeship and unity that fills the heads of the crew in *Fury*—or which is pumped into their heads by the movie process? The "our" of it was really much more suspect. The truths of the war also involved black markets, corruption, unfairness, infidelity, lies, exploitation, and the general systemic called getting yours before it got you. The noblest wartime Englishman (Winston Churchill) had reason to sneer at the sentimentality of "our" in the summer of 1945 when the Great Wartime Leader (the caps of legend were set) and his Conservative Party were voted out of office, largely because the men and women who had served and the people who had endured at home considered that the social and economic organization of Britain (and its level of competence) was "fucking atrocious"—that is a direct quote, and the first time I heard the wicked word.

Samuel Goldwyn was a rich American in Beverly Hills who survived the war and thanked fate and gods for how narrowly he had escaped. He had been born Szmuel Gelbfisz in Warsaw in 1879. How many times he might have been erased, but at the age of twenty he had made it by boat to Philadelphia. He became an expert seller of gloves and after that he was in the picture business, a mogul and a showman. He had produced many worthy films and a regulation quantity of something far less. But he produced *Dodsworth*, *Wuthering Heights*, *Ball of Fire*, and *The Little Foxes*. And he was looking for the big one, the coup, a picture that might surpass *Gone With the Wind*, the landmark made by his friend and rival, David O. Selznick. Goldwyn wanted a best-picture Oscar, and he had the instinct to be up-to-date with it.

When *Gone With the Wind* opened in December 1939, audiences were in love with Scarlett O'Hara and Rhett Butler, but they were deeply concerned at the film's depiction of the ravages of war because they felt that storm was about to be released in Europe, and then even on America. In an attempt to keep abreast of team spirit, in 1944 Selznick had made a dark romance, *Since You Went Away*, about women left at home as men went to war. It was not a commercial success, but something in it helped Goldwyn see the appeal of a story that focused not on war directly but on its social and familial repercussions. By 1944, he had the idea of a picture about the domestic impact of war.

Goldwyn was not a cultivated man; his education was in the garment business, in how a Yiddish speaker could be in charge of talking pictures, and in the naked test of survival. But he was high-minded or lofty, too, and one of a generation that converted survivor's luck into the great cause of opportunism. He wanted to make a picture about the uneasy moment in which three veterans come home from the war. It was all vague and wonderful in his reckless head. But he felt it could be a picture unlike others—it had to be.

So he commissioned MacKinlay Kantor, a journalist in London during the war, to write a blank-verse novella, *Glory for Me*, about the 1945 predicament. He had the notion for a panorama of characters. He then passed the novella over to playwright Robert Sherwood to manufacture a screenplay. Sherwood had had stage successes with *Waterloo Bridge*, *The Petrified Forest*, and *Idiot's Delight*, and he had contributed to the movie *Rebecca*. Opposed to the war once, he had shifted to support the cause; he had also helped on speeches for FDR. Goldwyn loved his literary reputation, and Sherwood produced a good working script for what is a leisurely, reassuring, and expert congratulation to America. There was never a hint that *Best Years* might get too close to tragedy or awkwardness. But the man who kept positive control of Sherwood's writing was the film's director, William Wyler.

Wyler was another lucky survivor. He had been born in Mulhausen in Alsace-Lorraine in 1902, German and Jewish. So he had been too young for the Great War though he was there as it was fought. He had begun his working life in the garment business—this was a bond of understanding with Goldwyn—but he had grown bored with that, and so he had gone to America and to the West Coast. I don't think it's unfair to say that his training and his instinct for perfected style; reliable seams; and efficient, tasteful, but unassertive clothes would be translated into an ability to deliver American movies to the satisfaction of just about everyone. He had directed *Dodsworth* and *Wuthering Heights* for Goldwyn; he had handled Bette Davis in *Jezebel* and *The Letter*. By the end of the war he was the ideal controlling director for Goldwyn's big project. Beyond that, he had been seconded to the War Department to make *Memphis Belle: A Story of a Flying Fortress*, a documentary with dramatic touches, that had meant that Wyler himself flew several bombing missions—far more than Dana Andrews, who did not serve in the war but was the actor the film placed in a haunted B-17 cockpit.

So Wyler had personal experience and he had been in uniform. More important, he had a proven record with actresses and respect for the female point of view. But he had been considering a biopic of Eisenhower before the experience of common soldiers and their families captured his interest. So *Best Years* may offer itself as the story of three male veterans, but it reaches its heart in the treatment of their women. As the three boisterous guys (sudden pals confronting another scary crisis in their war) share a cab into town from the airport, we begin to register their mixed feelings about reunion.

Al has been hardened by the war. We never hear that he may have found female company overseas, apart from one drunken scene with his wife where he half pretends to be another man picking up a woman at a dance. But as he arrives home at his pleasant apartment, he stifles his son and his daughter at the door so as to surprise his wife—or is it to deflect the huge tension in being with her again? That pressure permits one of the gems of the film. Al is at the head of the hallway that leads into the apartment. His wife, Milly, is in a room at the end of the corridor. She hears the front door and then the silence, and she half guesses what it means. You have to watch this moment, so settled now but so touching and alive, as husband and wife advance from opposite ends of the corridor into an embrace. The shot plays on Milly.

There are awkward things about this great scene. Hugo Friedhofer's music feels horribly overdone now—yet it won an Oscar in 1946. Censorship would not allow the married couple to get into their bedroom, to liberate its potential. Not even Sherwood or Wyler can reach for the dramatic potential of two desperately aroused people held back by strangeness, years of enforced abstinence, and the fear over whether they can be in love again. But for 1946 enough of those fraught moods was conveyed. And the children are there to safeguard Hays Code decency. So Milly is placed as the abiding and obliging woman who will fit in with Al's mixed feelings and his rush to get drunk so that he cannot serve her. Myrna Loy was forty then, ladylike and attractive. And the film never explains what she did in the war. She had no job, except to wait for Al—in Kantor's novella she had been a model; Wyler resisted that pretty solution, but never solved the matter. As the Stephensons make their postwar way, Milly seems reconciled to being whatever he wants. Friedhofer's strident music has so many emotional cavities to obscure.

It can be unfair to challenge a movie for being old-fashioned, but sometimes it is necessary to point out the white lies that lurk in an original version. The film draws its smooth coverlet over any possibility that Al, in the Pacific, had whores or nurses or even male tenderness. But hasn't he learned to drink?—there is a plot line, not developed, that he may be alcoholic. Fredric March plays him as a sergeant, whose business it is to laugh off issues of tenderness or intimacy. This is not underlined, but he is a man who has been raised in Boone City to disdain the details of a sentimental education. He has no inner life—but that is a besetting omission of so many films.

Fred Derry's situation is more complex. Dana Andrews was thirty-six when the film opened, and he looked a little older. We learn that just four years earlier Fred had been a soda jerk in the town's favorite eating place. That's when he married Marie, only twelve days before he went off to war. These are hints of delayed maturity. Marie is very blonde and rather loud, and she works hard to live up to a project of being sexy. She has moved out of the house where Fred's parents live. She has a home elsewhere and she works as an entertainer in nightclubs. As Fred returns to Boone City, he doesn't know where she lives. Marie is happy to see him back home. She wants to take him out in his uniform and his decorations to impress her friends. But in the actors' discordant performances we absorb unmistakable limits. Marie is a gaudy woman, unsuited to the quiet, thoughtful Fred. You have to wonder how they ever got married, and you put it down to sexual urgency and how unsettled Fred was in his early thirties.

Virginia Mayo does a routine job as Marie as a woman hoping to be pretty, but lacking substance. Years later it is possible to feel directions her character has not been allowed. Maybe Marie wants to sing or dance in the club. She might even have talent, a show business flair that will not be domesticated. Maybe she only wants a job situation that makes it easier to sleep around. Does she like sex for its own sake? Why not? Does our society really require respectable standards of female subservience that restrain instincts for life, energy, and expression? Go a few steps down that line and you appreciate that the film's script was a setup for "polite" behavior. It waited for Fred to see through Marie and fall in love with Peggy, Al's daughter. As played by Teresa Wright, Peggy is perfect without being prim or pious. She and Fred are a natural couple for happily ever after, and the triteness of that plan is offset by the skill Andrews and Wright brought to the job. So in less than three hours Fred is able to discard a bad wife and find an ideal mate. Never forget how far *The Best Years of Our Lives* is a commercial for American can-do compromise.

And leave a window open in which Marie might become a Doris Day. Or Marilyn Monroe.

The most vexed of the three men is Homer. He has had his hooks long enough so he can light a match and smoke a cigarette. He can handle a cup of coffee; he can drive—he says; and he can open most doors. But he has learned the dismay in others when they realize his predicament. When he gets home, his childhood sweetheart, Wilma, comes out to greet him—she has lived all their lives in the next-door house. As Cathy O'Donnell, she takes slow, awed steps toward Homer. When they embrace, her hands caress the back of his head. But he does not put his hands up to feel her hair or her skin. Rehabilitation has not covered this and other intimacies.

Not that Wilma is going to be impatient, critical, or a person in her own right. It has always been understood that she and Homer would be married, but now back home he does nothing to act on this. It's easy to feel for his anxiety, though it is noticeable that the movie cannot spell this out. This tension leads to a rapt night scene, where Wilma comes over to Homer's house to tell him that her parents feel she should move away because the marriage is not going to happen.

Homer asks her to come up to his bedroom to see what is involved in his routine. He takes off the strapping for his prostheses and lays the hooks down on the bed. He can work his way into his pajama jacket, and then have Wilma do up its buttons. Russell does a loyal, serviceable job as an actor; he does not feel like a nonprofessional. And O'Donnell (who was falling in love with Wyler's brother during the production) is a vessel of cautious loveliness that lifted several other films of the period (like *They Live By Night*). But as we watch the scene now, in all respect and longing, we want her hands to move on from securing his pajama jacket to undoing one of her own blouse buttons. No kind of "sex scene" would have been wanted here in 1946—but that only fostered dreams of appropriate erotic contact in audiences. The pioneering respect for how a handicapped man gets on with life deserves something more than Wilma going downstairs and leaving Homer alone in bed, beatific in the moonlight. Wilma needs her body made active, but that fond instrument is actually more circumscribed than Homer's.

HOW PEOPLE WATCHED THIS PICTURE IN 1946 IS ONE THING, AND IT IS NOT disqualified by how we respond to it now. Old films can only grow older, with defects appearing like the problems of age. But *Best Years* was a major event and a stirring attempt to sum up a critical moment in history, so it has earned our retrospective point of view. Why was the war fought if not to enhance the life of citizens? Is "best" humbug, or can it be a way to reform and improvement?

Apart from its box-office glory, *The Best Years of Our Lives* took so many prizes. It won Oscars for Wyler's direction, for Robert Sherwood's screenplay, for Daniel Mandell's editing, for Friedhofer's music. Fredric March won for best actor and Harold Russell held the Oscar for supporting actor. The Academy was so tender toward Russell that in case he might lose as supporting actor, they had awarded him an honorary Oscar in advance.

Teresa Wright was not nominated for the most thoroughly felt performance in the film and the clearest sign of how this male club needs female clarity, criticism, and direction.

Myrna Loy and Dana Andrews were not nominated.

But Samuel Goldwyn won the Irving Thalberg Award for career achievement and—of course—the movie took best picture. It "defeated" *Henry V*, *It's a Wonderful Life*, *The Razor's Edge*, and *The Yearling*. As all soldiers know, some guys get the medals and some don't, which is OK and acceptable so long as you understand that it's an incomplete history.

There is more to be said, much of which sustains the idea that this really is a film about our attitudes to peace as well as war. Maybe the best years will begin with August 1945.

When Al comes back, his teenage son (a neglected character in the film), looks at the gifts his dad has brought home—a "Jap" military scarf and a samurai sword—and instead wants to hear about Hiroshima. The film says that Al had been there in the aftermath of the Bomb, but he does not seem to have noticed much, let alone the questionable future that now hangs on his son's shoulders. It's a buried but striking moment, fit to shake the easy identification of audiences. While Fred has his nightmare of the war in the air, Al feels no anxiety over the nuclear debut. Perhaps Goldwyn did not want to go that far in testing his audience's comfort and allegiance. Perhaps he was determined not to be political.

But how far could a film this long really keep that shelter? Or is there a level of realism in the picture that still nags at us? Wyler had wanted the film to feel naturalistic. He asked the actresses to buy their own clothes at regular stores. He sought out suitable suburban locations in the Los Angeles area. And he ordered that the rooms in the story should be kept as small as real middle-class rooms and without the extra spaciousness that made filming easier and which gradually contributed to the mythology of an America that had so much living room to enjoy.

In that spatial requirement, Wyler had requested Gregg Toland as his cinematographer. The two men had worked together before on *Wuthering Heights* and *The Little Foxes*, and Toland had shot *Citizen Kane*. He was renowned for his creation of deep focus in which a room or several rooms could be seen at the same time. This went with a taste for shots that held the screen and ignored the chances for rapid editing. So Toland made the world of *The Best Years* palpable, and this contributes to the feeling of the film as much as the quality of the acting. The wedding scene between Homer and Wilma, in a crowded room, with the dawning of a future for Fred and Peggy, is a classic and very tidy example. That style also made Boone City a place of wealth and splendor in the eyes of most European filmgoers. America really did look like the place to be—and that was inseparable from postwar politics.

Then there is the matter of money. It may be hard to believe that Fred, in his early thirties, was still a soda jerk, without any higher ambition. But as he comes home, he finds the neighborhood diner where he worked has been bought up by a larger chain and expanded. The creep who was once his assistant is now a floor manager, and it is all Fred can do to regain his job making delectable sundaes. He and Marie are pained that he is doing this for $32.50 a week when he was making $400 a month as a captain in B-17s.

But Al was an assistant manager in a bank, and now the president of the bank (an unctuous Ray Collins) is eager to have the prestige of the veteran on his staff. He wants to make Al vice president in charge of small loans on a salary of $12,000 a year (about $170,000 in purchasing power now). But very soon, Al is at odds with the bank. He faces an applicant for a loan, a man named Novak (Dean White) who served in the war—he was one of those who went ahead to Pacific islands to clear away wire and mines so that landings could be easier. This is not labored over, but it was plainly a hellish job. Novak has survived, and now he hopes to buy some land for a farm. Al has to ask him about "collateral," a word Novak does not understand. The bank policy is to award half of the $6,000 Novak is seeking. But Al overrides this and signs the bank on for the full amount. The president is not happy with this, and he tells Al to be more guarded in future.

This standoff is not settled. But there is a bank dinner where a half-drunk Al gives an untidy speech about being on Okinawa and ordered to take a hill. But that's difficult and dangerous, Al tells the officer—where is the collateral? No collateral, says the officer, just take the hill. Al gets away with this speech, but it's easy to guess the conflicts he will have with his own bank when the principle of rebuilding a great America with fair jobs for heroes is knocking against self-interest and corporate profit.

Goldwyn's economic rule was unshakable: fifty cents from you, and $23 million for the picture. He was a survivor who turned very conservative. But *Best Years* does spell out sums of money (an uncommon trait in movies still), and the panorama of Boone City is more complex than we might expect.

Toward the end of the film, Fred is a server at the diner. Homer is at the counter, and then a stranger comes in to ask for a sandwich. He gets in conversation with Homer. He admires his service and his suffering, and then he starts on a rant about how people like Homer were suckers in the great cause, how America was drawn into fighting the wrong enemy by "radical" interests instead of backing "old-fashioned Americanism."

Looking at the picture anew, I was startled at how this echoed some of the recent stress on making America great again at the expense of any responsibility to the world. This stranger is very well played by Ray Teal, a reliable cameo heavy. Fred gets into a fight with the man and punches him out. So he loses his job.

That's when he reckons to quit Boone City for good. He goes to the airport and waits for a plane, going anywhere. Then he wanders out to the graveyard of aircraft—this was shot for real at the Ontario Army Air Field. He climbs into a B-17 and has his reverie. But then he's ordered out by the foreman in charge. They talk, and the man thinks maybe Fred might find a job there, turning the scrap metal from aircraft into prefabricated housing. Not much, but a start. He kids Fred, too, as one of those "romantic" flyboys living on the legend of glory. *What did you do in the war?* Fred asks. The guy tells him he was in tanks.

Has *The Best Years of Our Lives* become dated? For sure. Is it still possible to understand what it meant in 1946? Without a doubt, because the feeling remains and because the whole project intuits a sense of America being an untidy agglomeration of competing instincts. (Though the film has no one of color.) One delusion or romance of war is to persuade us that we were all in it together, uniform and faithful.

The cinema of 1946 and Wyler's tasteful discretion were not prepared to get into the real sexual doubt of veterans coming home—which is not so far from the same turmoil in those who have always been home. But the film's attempt to contain so much of the country teaches us that there might be a new model of the story dealing with three veterans from the 2020 election, exhausted, demoralized, or elated, but coming home in the awareness that a country in dissension has to be appreciated as a ragged whole. Peace descended in August 1945, but only simpletons relaxed. World war had uncovered a disturbing truth—that some conflict will never stop.

EARLIER IN THIS CHAPTER, I COMPARED TWO BOMBARDIERS, FRED DERRY and John Yossarian, the central character in Joseph Heller's novel *Catch-22*, published in 1961, and in the 1970 movie where Alan Arkin plays Yossarian. Heller had been a bombardier himself for two years; he had flown some sixty missions, not that he made much fuss about it personally. But Yossarian has lived with horror that includes a fellow airman's shattered body and his entrails slipping free in the bomber cockpit. *The Best Years*, to be best, has to say the war was routine, and its organization benign. And if it was not, then we'll agree not to speak about it so that those who were at home or in charge will not be driven mad. But the ghost of *Catch-22* is its sense of an undead body struggling to escape premature burial. This has to do with unspeakable thoughts that must be uttered.

In the mid-1960s, I was reading the book on the Tube journey I took, from Hounslow in west London to the center of the city and a job in publishing. It was a difficult book to read on those crammed trains because I felt an antic need to laugh out loud at nearly every page. The book is hilarious, most of all in its satire on the managerial structures of the army. The deepest abyss of the novel is that the military is no place for a sane person. *The Best Years of Our Lives* does not want to hear about that. And I understand why. We have told ourselves we must not panic.

But on the Tube, the Piccadilly line, I felt a startling nausea, amid rows of silent travelers—no one spoke to anyone, as if we were all dead already. I needed to burst out, like those entrails, and tell implacable strangers, "*You have to read this book! Don't you see where we are going?*" And that pressure woke my dread of claustrophobia on those trains when they had to halt and wait in winding London tunnels furred with regret and decay. I gave up traveling on the Tube. Disturbance will not stay sleeping.

24

SAVING *SAVING PRIVATE RYAN*

D-Day. June 6, 1944, though it would have been June 5 but for weather that was deemed too problematic. A Tuesday, when the moon rose at 1:19 a.m. over the beaches of Normandy. The sun came in at 5:57 a.m. and the tide was at its lowest point at 6:30 a.m.

It was going to happen.

I am trying to write about this in the restrained but awed voice of some latter-day Virgil, or a Hemingway desperate not to yield to sentiment—or be left out of the story. A part of us imagines being there and rising on the song: arms and the man. Or manliness. As if women did not know about it?

I want to be blunt and factual, yet I know you understand and expect this to be the big one. Not just the greatest seaborne invasion there has ever been, but the long-awaited turning point in the Second World War. You were probably not alive that June; even so, you may look back on it as a venture that enabled and clarified your future. You may even ask yourself whether you have deserved it, or whether your life has matched up to the sacrifice of that morning and the ten months that followed it.

If you were on the winning side in 1939–45, if you were sympathetically attuned to the Western alliance, and if you were close to the southern half of England where the invasion forces gathered—then you take it for granted that this was a momentous occasion. And if you have seen Steven Spielberg's *Saving Private Ryan* (1998) and its Omaha Beach sequence you have an idea of the damage, the death, and the outrages to the body that took place there. You would be shocked if the film and its historic event were not part of this book.

In that predisposition, what would be your estimate of the Allied casualties on that June 6, and in the Omaha Beach fighting? In a way, I'm asking you how big the big one was, and urging you to measure the best known facts against the drama of *Saving Private Ryan* and many other films that touch on D-Day, even the tedious *The Longest Day* (1962).

Cases are made that the combat on Omaha Beach was the fiercest on D-Day, and it is true that American forces carried the bulk of the action there that day—in exiting the landing craft, struggling through the waves, encountering anti-invasion wire and obstacles, withstanding German fire from the bluffs above the beach including machine-gun fire and light artillery, and mounting those bluffs to take the bunkers and buildings, while killing or capturing the German opposition—the Allied losses were around 3,500 and the German losses were close to 1,500.

You must not be disappointed. In your imaginative reckoning, you have saved thousands of lives. Nor is anyone disdaining the 3,500 Allied deaths—American, British, and Canadian. Nor are we disputing the magnificent fabricated imagery in *Saving Private Ryan* of human entrails scattered on the pebbled beach, of blood changing the color of the sea, of a man retrieving his blown-off arm, of the suddenness with which a head scatters in pink puff and membrane. And the ordeal that Captain Miller of the Rangers endures as he seems to lose his hearing, several of his men, his courage, and his wits. Let's say his purpose. History tells us what was won on June 6, but so much was lost.

I was surprised to find the D-Day casualty figures "so low," though every death matters—that is what we tell ourselves, until, as time passes, we have to admit that that sensitivity is not really the point.

What is more the point is to remind you that on the first day of the Battle of the Somme (July 1, 1916), British deaths topped 19,000 in total casualties of over 50,000. In the Battle of the Atlantic (not much filmed and largely out of sight) that lasted the course of the second war, the British navy lost 36,000 men along with the same number of merchant seamen. The German navy—mostly in U-boats—lost another 30,000.

Are you saying to yourself, *That's more like it or more appropriate to the legend of our wars*? Let me carry you a little further. In what is known as the Battle of Stalingrad, lasting from August 1942 to February 1943, German casualties were around 800,000 and Soviet losses were over 1.2 million, which includes over 470,000 deaths. Especially in these numbers from the Russian front, the counting is uncertain. Bodies were buried in the mud. Men ran away. Thousands were executed or "lost." And the clerical organization of the armies was never so secure that it knew accurately how many lives it had to lose. So in the prolonged siege of Leningrad, a season of death and horror, the Soviets had over a million killed or missing and nearly two and a half million wounded or sick. How many then for the war as a whole? I wonder. Do you begin to feel the size that is coming in thinking about Russia? Why am I holding it back? Because I am affected by suspense, and because the numbers are hard to believe.

As someone British first and then American, I am astonished by these numbers and how they are still just a footnote in the West. It's like wondering if I had ever understood the war that is central to my life, if only because I realize how my country might have been occupied by a fascist regime that could have driven my parents to a test of courage or compromise, the sort that most people reading this book will have managed to avoid. And as the author of this book, I realize that *Saving Private Ryan* is as strange and tendentious as it is riveting. It can't be filed away. It has to be reopened.

WE ARE AT A CEMETERY, ONE OF THOSE IN THE FIELDS OF NORMANDY looking out over La Manche, or the English Channel. The grass is very green and the crosses are bone white, less from the stone used, I think, than because the cemetery attendants have been careful to keep the memorial clean and bright.

We are watching an elderly man. He wears slacks, a white sports shirt, and a pale blue windbreaker. He is not the sort of person you often see in movies, much less in the close examination of his face we have here. He is Harrison Young, and he was sixty-eight when the film was made. He might have been older, for he is unsteady on his feet and close to tears. I can't say how far that was acting or because Mr. Young was moved because of his assignment. He is walking across the green, trailed by a small crowd that includes his wife (Kathleen Byron), children, and grandchildren. There must be a dozen of them, and they are anxious on his behalf, mindful of the stress. He is looking for one cross and he falls to his knees in front of it. It is the headstone marker for Captain John Miller, and Mr. Young is playing the man who was Private James Ryan in June 1944.

That episode fades away and then we are in a landing craft at dawn heading into the prickly Normandy shore, reaching east from the Cotentin Peninsula toward Le Havre, where several beaches have the new labels of combat zones—Utah, Omaha, Gold, Juno, and Sword. This is the famous sequence of the film, and it surely was tense and purposeful in telling us, the audience, "You have not seen or felt war before, but here it is, the real and shattering thing."

Of course, there is an essential undertone that is not addressed, but it is the cover under which we shelter. It says, approximately, Don't worry. You are safe. The man next to you in the landing craft is throwing up—you can smell his undigested breakfast. The spray of sea is mixed in the droplets of blood from men who were shot dead as soon as the port on the landing craft fell! Great God, don't you see that you are in the first assault of D-Day, the big one, with slaughter at hand. But you, my dears, are safe—so long as the movie theater stays intact.

This is not whimsy talking, though there is an inherent marriage of panic and comedy. Rather, I am doing my best to address an essential conundrum in war movies—that you are at the brink of death and obliteration, but watching from a lovely faraway. Omaha Beach in *Saving Private Ryan* is desperate. The portrayal of human damage had not been attempted before with the same cinematic intensity. This is a knockout sequence. But it touches madness, too, because we will not be harmed or put at risk. Do we become domestic connoisseurs of damage, like commanders in a dream? Nothing else about the war and movies is so important.

The Omaha sequence (just over twenty minutes) is spectacular still, but I have to say "still" because it is so predicated on changing cinematic technology that it could be overtaken one day by the kinds of camera mobility put on show in *1917*. I am talking about the re-creation of a moment in terms of equipment, weaponry, uniforms, the sound of firing, and the heartfelt dedication to the degree of chaos that operated at the beach.

But chaos on film is a tricky matter: Steven Spielberg and his crew do so many things to make us feel disordered—the camera wavers as if it is driven by the fear and the danger; compositions are as "wrong" and even as out of focus as those in the still pictures Robert Capa took on the same day at Omaha Beach; the editing is deranged; we do not really know what we are meant to understand is happening—even if Tom Hanks's captain is a familiar and stable face, prominent from the start and viewed as intently (with big close-ups sinking into the faces) as Mr. Ryan is stared at in the cemetery. This early in the picture Hanks is not going to have his face blown apart. There is the turmoil of the soundtrack. There is the plain sense of men in terror, too stricken to move until they grasp the terrible vulnerability of chance. All of this is rendered with amazing respect so that it is impossible to watch without being excited and inspired by the order and control of these filmmakers.

There's the rub, if you like, and the uncanny mechanics, that let us behold terrible things with the calm of experts and engineers. Indeed, on streaming services now, we are able to isolate and revel in just the Omaha sequence, as if we might be filmmakers or generals contemplating some new invasion. This is not an attack on Spielberg or his craftsmen—Janusz Kaminski the cinematographer; Michael Kahn the editor; Thomas Sanders and Phill Zagajewski on production design; the sound team, et cetera, et cetera. The picture won Oscars for photography, sound, editing, and special effects. I do not want to omit people who did crucial work—who were there on the great adventure. But notice that even in the beach sequence, we are fixing on Tom Hanks, Tom Sizemore, Barry Pepper, and a few others, as if there were not thousands of other people—soldiers and actors—who were there, too. We find it hard to do or comprehend war on-screen—or in our thoughts in general—without picking out a few. But you cannot have a war without the power to order up the unknown masses.

And of course, there is Steven Spielberg, the begetter of the film and, in his way, as beloved or trusted a filmmaker as Dwight Eisenhower was esteemed as a military leader and the director of D-Day. I don't mean to accuse Eisenhower or Spielberg of vainglory or self-importance, though it is obvious that Ike was cast into an inescapable role, whereas Steven elected to make this film. Further, it is apparent from the outset that Spielberg's intent is more important in the project than any wish to be true or realistic in the depiction of combat. But what does Steven want? Why are we getting this immense and shattering Omaha sequence? How is it going to fit with that cemetery scene?

Spielberg never did military service, but it's reasonable to regard him as a commanding, exemplary figure in the film business, and even as a presidential aspirant. No, he has never admitted to what are called political ambitions. But steadily, for decades, he has worked in film with a need to shape and improve the way his nation and the world thinks. He does not make too many casual pictures for fun. Instead he functions in a mood that believes American movies are central to the well-being and proper deliberations of the country. That is a pretty idea and an uplifting hope, but it needs careful analysis and humbug alerts. Not least, we may detect Spielberg's knack in taking a vast and "impossible" subject and finding a small and far-fetched narrative way into it. So the unlikelihood of a blockbuster film on the Holocaust was overcome by discovering Oskar Schindler. And the size of D-Day and its ordinariness are relieved by the anecdote of Private Ryan.

There was a lightness in the young Spielberg. I think he knew that the conflict between a guy in his Plymouth Valiant and a monstrous truck in *Duel* (1971) was a pretext for a road epic (for only $450,000) and our amused thrills. I don't think he believed in extraterrestrial presences on Earth, but *Close Encounters of the Third Kind* and *E.T.* were thorough entertainments, in love with the wonder of movie. *Raiders of the Lost Ark* was a hoot, as were pictures like *Jurassic Park*—again Steven did not believe in or fear the regeneration of dinosaurs, but he understood the fun and the box office in the venture, and he was an enthusiast for the computer technology that permitted it.

There was one early film that went much deeper, and I think *Empire of the Sun* (1987) is the best work he has ever done. It is a war film, too, derived from J. G. Ballard's book about being an English kid, Jim, in Shanghai, caught up in the Japanese invasion in 1941–42, separated from family and having to survive in a prison camp. The most telling thing about the picture was how Jim (Christian Bale, aged twelve) could not distinguish the justice of the war and his own plight from the bizarre game he became part of and his mixed feelings over Japanese martial spirit.

Steven observed that boy; he did not quite identify with him. But the process of identification overtook him on *Schindler's List*, which is obviously a movie about the culture of war. It was a trick of convenience, too, for the hitherto unthinkable topic of the Holocaust was turned into a popular film. How could a large audience behold the Kraków ghetto and the camps in such detail? It might be possible if the story had an Oskar Schindler who went out of his way to rescue and save a number of Jews. A modest number to be sure—maybe 1,200. What can one man do? Still, this narrative thrust helped make *Schindler's List* an international cultural event, and the unmistakable proof that Steven was serious.

Saving Private Ryan came five years after *Schindler's List*, and it was an easier or more conventional prospect than the Holocaust film because it was founded on the humane idea that at least one Ryan boy should be saved from the war, and that a modest officer played by Tom Hanks could be the savior. More than that, spectators could see how their willing energy would be activated.

But the film is thirty minutes old before that narrative structure is revealed. There is a portentousness at work, not fully disguised by the

Omaha spectacle and its unprecedented war show. The impact of that sequence may be judged its best defense, and I think Spielberg was excited to harness some of the most recent advances in special effects to make it clear that the movies had always been as genteel over combat as they had been with sex. Still, it's worth noting that this new pitch of realism has very little to do with the film's narrative construct. Yes, that day and that war were bloody and terrifying beyond the belief of people who have never fought. And there may be some virtue in making this texture clear, instead of glossing over it. Not that Spielberg is ever bloodthirsty.

But then note the dilemma I have described: that there is a tension in all war films between the vivid peril on-screen and our demure safety in the dark. That discord encourages a perverse difficulty in coming to terms with war's horror (think of that as a kind of cowardice). So it is relevant to wonder how the fury at Omaha works in with the unease of the cemetery scene. There is a showiness in the Omaha sequence—a way of saying, *Look, we can do this, and this is what it was really like.* The sequence establishes the warrior experience of Captain Miller and his men, as well as their heroism in climbing the bluffs to take out the German presence there. So the suffering that Miller feels—the loss of hearing, the closeness of insanity—does not detract from his valor and his success. In the same way, his prowess is not offset by the plain truth: that those beaches were going to be taken because of Allied superiority in focused numbers, equipment, and air dominance. Eisenhower "went" because he knew he was favored to succeed. The "uncertainty" is an affect of our victorious storytelling. There were mistakes on the day, but the beachheads were secured.

So the strategic chronology of Omaha and of D-Day as a whole is not spelled out. It would be too laborious in a story film. The control of the air is hardly mentioned. The fact that the German forces were not of the best is set aside: in war films the enemy are invariably implacable—it's a kind of casting. But on that June 6 a lot went wrong: many paratroopers were dropped too far away; most of the American tanks floundered in the sea. In truth, the D-Day onslaught did not achieve its immediate goals. That is downplayed, yet it's not worth complaining. On-screen, the twenty-minute frenzy requires success. How can it be denied in the triumphant ethos of cinema? This is a story film, a kind of entertainment, and not a thorough account of the war.

But notice, just in passing, that a complete version would have to say how by D-Day the military resolution had taken shape. The war was being won. Sooner or later that process wonders why it had to be fought— yes, I am talking about political history—and why the colossal losses on the eastern front were waited out before a D-Day could occur. The Soviets did ask about that. None of this is Spielberg's responsibility. But perhaps it falls on us: we should not collapse in the habit of being sentimentally gratified onlookers. Even the twenty minutes of aghast suspense, or vicarious exhilaration, deserves some historical assessment of why and how it happened. It may be nice to save Private Ryan, but if salvation is touching, then there are so many other deserving cases. And extricating the last Ryan feels like a gimmick in a game, the opportunistic invention of no trumps or offside.

There is a planted close-up in the Omaha sequence: a dead soldier with the name "Ryan S." stenciled on his backpack. And then we go to a magical, nearly Dickensian passage, in which we see the clerical structure of war in a room full of middle-aged female clerks and typists who are in charge of accounting. The scene is filled with Spielberg's confidence about order. One woman clerk ascertains by cross-reference that the Ryan family is doing poorly. Daniel Ryan is dead in New Guinea; Peter Ryan was killed at Utah Beach; and we have encountered Sean Ryan's corpse at Omaha. She takes the matter to a higher level—to men. We see the officer staff registering this calamitous luck. There is a heartbreaking Wyeth-like scene of an isolated house on a prairie with the mother who notices the military car bringing news, and a priest with it, so that she subsides on the verandah in a faint that cannot quite lose consciousness. Then it is revealed that a fourth brother, James Francis Ryan, is a paratrooper somewhere behind the beach lines in Normandy.

Going up the chain of command (by way of Bryan Cranston as a colonel who has lost an arm), we come to General George Marshall, the army chief of staff. Confronted with the news, he quotes Abraham Lincoln's Mrs. Bixby letter of 1864, written to the mother of five sons all killed in the Civil War. Marshall is played faultlessly by Harve Presnell, a singer and an actor often hired for baritone bombast. But he is hushed and grave with the superb letter, and a credit to Spielberg's faith in virtuous leaders:

> I feel how weak and fruitless must be any words of mine which should attempt to beguile you from the grief of a loss so overwhelming. But I cannot refrain from tendering to you the consolation that may be found in the thanks of the Republic they died to save.

This is so overpowering a moment, I have to remind myself that the Ryan family are fictitious. Not that families did not sometimes suffer multiple losses. As he read about D-Day, the writer Robert Rodat had been struck by families that lost more than one person. In his book *D-Day: June 6 1944: The Climactic Battle of World War II*, Stephen Ambrose noted a family that had lost two sons. And he began to work this up as a possible movie idea. It was that script that found its way to Spielberg.

George Marshall did exist—and after the war his famous Plan for aid support may have saved more lives than any other general managed. But he is the godlike supervisor in this movie, so distressed over the Ryan news that he says the last brother left, the paratrooper somewhere out there, must be saved. It's a setup that blithely soars above the unlikelihood of any commanding officer making such a decision, or of having a clerical staff that could even ascertain the facts. For Marshall determines that a group of men must find James Francis Ryan and deliver him to safety. Whereas what Marshall and Ike and Patton took for granted was that some of their men would have to die.

Should any commander feel redeemed by such a sympathetic decision? Don't think of asking how many siblings have to be killed before you qualify for merciful relief. Don't begin to probe the sentimentality until you reach the insight that in heaven everyone should be saved. Most movies need a little warm oil to get the machinery turning over.

Thus it transpires that Captain Miller and seven men from the Rangers are charged with extricating Private Ryan from the war. The other soldiers are not happy with this. They feel they may be placed in extra jeopardy on behalf of a man who is not one of their group. They complain, and there is some hint of a reality omitted from many war films—that the grunt believed the command system was incompetent, unfair, and even the gravest peril he faced. Isn't that where officers like the dire Colonel Cathcart from *Catch-22* lived? Moreover, Miller is not seen as a faultless leader; he makes mistakes and he seems aware that no man can carry all the burden of command.

But dispute is stopped by the bonding between Captain Miller and his sergeant Mike Horvath (Tom Sizemore). Miller speaks reasonably, while the sergeant is much blunter. But they run the group; like good cop and bad cop, they have worked out a routine. Still, we get to know some of the men: Barry Pepper as a cool, cross-kissing, left-handed sharpshooter; Edward Burns as the rude lefty from Brooklyn; Vin Diesel; Adam Goldberg; Giovanni Ribisi; and Jeremy Davies as Upham, the translator they are going to need, a man as unaccustomed to combat as Norman in *Fury*.

They have adventures out in open country. But at last they find their Ryan, and we realize he is Matt Damon. (This means that the Ryan at the cemetery should be over eighty.) There is natural relief or pleasure in finding Damon, though we might have deserved an unknown. But that is followed by seeing just how exemplary or sanctified Ryan has become. A similar aura hovers over Captain John Miller—and the two of them will talk at night as saints in fraught survival. We learned in the landing craft that Miller has the shakes, or traumatic stress. Periodically, he trembles violently, something only Sergeant Horvath knows, and he watches over Miller like an older brother. Should this captain be withdrawn from war, too?

Miller plays a game with his men: he will not tell them anything about his civilian life, and so the men have made a guessing pool over him. What does he do, and where? This only adds to Miller's hallowed quality: he is the kind of noble, common man that Tom Hanks's career has turned toward, a tendency that has imprisoned or nullified the actor. We are in no doubt about his decency, his fairness, and his troubled wisdom: he may not know what he is doing all the time, but he will do his best. Whatever his stress—and perhaps it is disabling—Miller's men can count on him in the way we anticipate nothing less than self-effacing integrity in a Tom Hanks officer.

One may glimpse a subtler film, in which Miller claims he is a family man and a high school English teacher in Pennsylvania just to still a crisis in his group. But suppose that story line might be fabricated, like an actor sketching out the role of a perfect American of the kind Spielberg wants to believe in. Instead, Miller might be a mess, a failed family man, a Fred Derry; he might drink too much—is that part of his stress? He might even be a wrecked loser who is clinging to the only status or attention he has ever possessed in life. The everyman figure Spielberg is determined on could be more complicated, and braver—enough to help us feel that every soldier in sight is in similar confusion and desperate for orders that will absolve him.

Perhaps Spielberg would answer, *Well, yes, but there isn't time.* We have to have another major combat scene and we have to get Ryan back to his future. James Francis is reluctant to be separated from his unit and to be given unfair advantage. Damon the actor has to digest the loss of three brothers, without slowing the action of the film. Before they can shepherd Ryan home, the platoon pauses at a shattered French town named Ramelle (fictitious), to which a substantial German contingent with a few tanks is headed to take possession of a bridge in the town. This will be the lucid, measured combat we deserve as armchair veterans after the ordeal we suffered through on the beach. It is one of the most masterly scenes of warfare ever done. You may know it by heart.

Miller and Horvath plan a rearguard action, falling back on the bridge in the town and reckoning to blow it up before the Germans can use it. They manage to disable one of the German tanks with a homemade bomb. The sharpshooter picks off so many Germans from a church bell tower before he is himself blown away. This is all done with magnificent clarity, as if to say, yes, good soldiers can fight a clean battle successfully just as every boy dreams with his toy soldiers on the carpet. This may be the more pleasing in that the maneuver is essentially defensive. That is not to minimize the sequence. I have watched it over and over with unflawed satisfaction. But I worry over this pleasure.

Of course, our men are picked off one by one. Horvath will die and Miller, too. Only three are left alive at the end. At a key moment, American planes streak overhead to eliminate the Germans—at last, air superiority is admitted to when it might have avoided the Ramelle crisis. But the song of the film is at its climax. In a last piece of italic drama, the dying Miller whispers to Ryan, "Earn it." That is the creepiest thing Miller does in the entire film, sententious, preachy, and drunk on an adolescent scheme of destiny. But this is the Spielberg too ready to weigh the fate of mankind in his hands, without beginning to face the complex issues that confront that destiny.

With grinding tidiness, *Saving Private Ryan* now returns to the modern day and its Normandy cemetery. Whereupon Ryan asks Mrs. Ryan whether he has indeed earned it. This labored congratulation counters every report that Spielberg is skilled. Poor woman, what is she to say except, "Of course, dear"? And so the infinite question of just what has been earned is cast away in a picture where—we may realize—we know so little about Miller or Ryan.

None of this mattered. The film was and remains a box-office success. Having cost $70 million, it earned over $480 million. Spielberg won his second Oscar for best director. *Saving Private Ryan* is still rated as a combat landmark. It is widely regarded as a touchstone of American greatness, and magnanimity, and an emblem in the legend of the special generation that fought that war. Among the topics in the film that are also specious or shaming, there is not being good at combat, or succumbing to that rare movie disease—being afraid.

I am thinking of Corporal Upham, who is shuddering with a fear that leaves him helpless. This man is so true to life and terror; he deserves a medal. Or a whole movie about how he made his way in peace and back to solemn American umpiring. Perhaps he becomes a teacher to honor Captain Miller? Or a movie director.

25

ON BEING OCCUPIED

In *Saving Private Ryan*, the battleground of Normandy is a place of fields, lanes, suitable picnic spots, and bathing beaches, where the French have nearly disappeared for the season—there's nothing like the gesture of having Laurence Olivier and Liv Ullmann in *A Bridge Too Far* as Dutch citizens who do their best to help the Allied effort.

But in one of the great filmmaking nations in history, and in its dealing with the cultural ordeal of being occupied, there are so many French films about Resistance, and acceptance, honor, and betrayal. I think no country was more demoralized by the twentieth century.

One can turn to Jean-Pierre Melville's *Army of Shadows* (1969) to find a heroic version of the Resistance. It's a memorable film, where melodrama is like adrenaline for the hunted members of the underground. We meet a group of Resistance fighters—Lino Ventura, Paul Meurisse, Jean-Pierre Cassel, Claude Mann, Simone Signoret. They are comrades in secret arms but they cannot own up to this bonding because the fear of betrayal lurks in their enterprise. This is an experience, a repression of conventional heroics, unknown in countries that avoided occupation. So a moment comes in Melville's dry adventure when the others assassinate Signoret on the street—she expects nothing less—to avoid the risk of her breaking under interrogation. When interrogation can mean peeling off your skin, or threatening the life of a beloved child. Torturers are shrinks who think of everything, so it may seem. It may be best to live without children or skin.

Army of Shadows knows that opposing the Nazis could be nightmarish, demanding exceptional courage to a point of madness. Melville had been in the Resistance himself. But I also admire the strain of French cinema that appreciates doubt or something less than certainty. Imagine Jean Renoir's character Octave from *La Règle du Jeu* (1939), a man who was always most alive as a connection and a friend, but someone who didn't get out of France in time and now lives on the edge of Resistance circles, never sure about trusting others, yet drawn there through some feeling for a woman (or a man), and trapped because of that—trapped fatally and taken in for torture, a man who cannot escape.

In imagining that, I am crosscutting to Robert Bresson's masterpiece from 1956—*Un Condamné à Mort s'est Échappé*, or *A Man Escaped*, in which a resistance fighter, Fontaine, is captured and imprisoned in the Montluc Prison in Lyon under sentence of death. Then with homemade tools and ropes, in infinite patience and fraught suspense, he prepares to break for freedom. On the brink of escape, another young man is pushed into his cell, and Fontaine has to decide whether this is a plant, an informant, a betrayer, or just a dumb kid he needs to trust. It is a film about process: quivering faces, the details of a cell, prison sounds, the ritual of confinement, and the impulse to get away, a claustrophobia of fear and valor.

Or think of *Army of Shadows* on a double bill with Melville's first film, *Le Silence de la Mer* (1949), made from a novel published secretly in Paris in 1942 under the pseudonym Vercors. It is the story of a young woman and her elderly uncle who are forced to have a German officer billeted in their country house in 1941. At first they register their protest by declining to speak to him, but as time passes a degree of respect emerges from this cast-iron negation. The officer starts to talk, as if ignoring or forgiving their silence, and in that monologue his unwilling hosts discern a human being, a civilized man. He goes to Paris on leave and is shocked by the vulgar brutalism of Nazi control. Then he is posted to what he knows will be the hell of the eastern front.

I recall the Nevers passages in Alain Resnais's *Hiroshima Mon Amour*, where a German soldier stationed in France has a love affair with a French girl (Emmanuelle Riva). He is shot dead by the Resistance, and then her head is shaved and tarred by vengeful, righteous women. Resnais had his own resistance career, but in *Hiroshima* he seemed to understand that war was a wind that never blew just one way.

Were Resnais and his cowriter, Marguerite Duras, thinking of Arletty in creating Riva's character? Arletty was a miraculously understated actress in the thirties and forties: she was bittersweet in *Hôtel du Nord* and *Le Jour Se Leve*, and she is forever Garance, the easygoing courtesan in *Les Enfants du Paradis* (1945)—all films by Marcel Carné. But as she shot that film, she was having an affair with a German officer. After the war, she was rebuked for this collaboration, and charged with treason. She answered that while her heart was French other parts of her were international. The "other side" is someone else's home side. Arletty was confined for several months in a country house, but emerged to play Blanche in the French stage premiere of *A Streetcar Named Desire*. She died in 1992 at the age of ninety-four, and in history she has become a wry heroine. Bittersweet can be the safest place under occupation.

Indelicate behavior carries on, its own kind of betrayal. *Army of Shadows* was released in France in 1969, and the masterpiece was more or less disowned. The fashion for the Resistance had passed. The film languished—that is often a good place for searching out honorable prisoners. After ten years it opened in Britain and was critically admired. But it was into the next century before America realized that such a picture existed. Being thirty years late is a kind of betrayal, and sooner or later that disconnect could prove consequential. The inescapable need for a Resistance in the United States has not yet arrived. But we are patient.

Occupation doesn't mean being busy or fulfilled—like enjoying a good movie, and being taken out of yourself. It's a matter of living in your own country as provisional residents, knowing that there is a malign authority ready to call you in for questioning or much more. It's like coming out of that pleasant movie to find dark-coated figures waiting in the lobby (and not just familiar supporting actors), ready to interrogate you about the film's mise-en-scène and whether you identify with its moral.

Suppose the film is *Flame & Citron*. That's 2008, from Denmark, written and directed by Ole Christian Madsen. Do you know what happened to Denmark in the Second World War? Yes, it was a long time ago and in subtitles. But the Nazis invaded Denmark and used the local fascist movement to co-opt the country. That began on April 9, 1940. At first, the regular government was allowed to persist. But then some Danes resisted. By 1943, that mood had turned to violence, at which point the Germans took over the government.

There really had been these two young men, Flammen and Citronen, and Madsen thought the time had come to remember them as heroes. The couple had regular names, but they were elevated to the status of a daring, lethal gang. Without shame or any strain, *Flame & Citron* is an ampersand gangster film, with sedan cars ambushed on the open highway and perforated with bullets.

We never learn how these flamboyant desperadoes came together, but by the time the film starts they are lead assassins for the Resistance: some people in that movement gather intelligence and carry messages; but Flame and Citron have their vocation—tracking and murdering Nazis or Danish collaborators. You might think they would be furtive, trying to stay undercover. But they are louche, limelight characters. Citron wears a slouch fedora, spectacles, and goes unshaven, while Flame has glaring red hair that no attempt at a hat can conceal. The two guys swagger in this fame and attention. They are as vividly in a movie—that projection of their imagination—as Bonnie and Clyde. They aren't lovers, but they play to each other like a two-man trapeze act.

In addition, they seem ready to give up on ordinary life. Citron has a wife and a child, and he loves them in a rather disbelieving way, but he is prepared to abandon them as if his existence can only put them in jeopardy. We realize the grief this has given him when, accidentally, in one of their operations, a young boy is killed and Citron is devastated.

Flame's life is like his hair, the most unsuitable way he can manage. So he falls for a woman who has "femme fatale" posted on her movie marquee. She has brown hair but often sports a blonde wig. It is impossible to be sure of her allegiance: she works as a courier but gives off hints of double agency. She has an affair with Flame but seems to be mistress to the Gestapo chief; she sometimes seems part of the Resistance, but nothing contributes more to her noir attractiveness than the uncertainty and risk she brings to Flame.

All of this is assisted by vibrant performances: Thure Lindhardt as Flame and Mads Mikkelsen as Citron. It's easy to believe that young actors might relish gangster roles, but these men are Danish, so maybe their stylish daring comes from an understanding of what their country suffered before they were born. The set pieces, the murders, are shot with astonishing speed and gravity: there is no end to how we anticipate and delight in screen killings. But the film lets us feel how this suspense was in the Danish identity—the violent rapture of a hitherto peaceable society. These overgrown kids are falling in love with the melodrama of their task. They hardly know whom they are killing. The film's lyrical peril conveys the feeling of Copenhagen in the early 1940s and not knowing how its fraught situation is going to turn out. Beside Melville's *Army of Shadows*, this is a model Resistance film, and enough to leave one shamefaced at the team-spirit bluster of many American movies.

Still, if you entertain the conceit of coming out of *Flame & Citron* to be confronted by faceless men hunched up in dark coats, their hands thrust into their pockets, the questions they are going to ask are, "So how did you appreciate that movie?" and "What would you have done in Copenhagen in 1943?"

Or in Holland, under occupation. I find a lot of movie fans don't know about *Black Book* (2006), no matter that it is the film Paul Verhoeven made on returning to Holland after his very productive time in Hollywood, with the frisson of Catherine Tramell or Sharon Stone crossing her legs. You know about that.

Verhoeven was born in Amsterdam in 1938, and he was a child in The Hague, witness to bombings, resistance, and reprisals, if too young to understand the vectors of that conflict. But the thing about Verhoeven is how readily he loves those frantic vectors, and how fleetingly he trusts meaning. He made *Soldier of Orange* in 1977, a "true story" about the Dutch Resistance, starring Rutger Hauer, his regular actor and his muse. Then he was off to America, where no one bothered to restrain his lust for melodramatic incident, emotional violence, and lust itself.

But he came back to the Netherlands for *Black Book*, which is an inflamed dream about those war years, too impatient to stay "based in fact," convinced that fiction is supreme. It is a relentless glorying in a history of depravity and madness—as if Verhoeven reckons that only wild storytelling can contain our nature. To be brief, it concerns a young woman (played with fierce courage by Carice van Houten), a cabaret singer, Jewish, as chronically practical as any survivor, who becomes attached to the Resistance. She agrees with her comrades to offer herself sexually to a commanding officer in the Gestapo. There are vague reasons referred to on how this may benefit the Resistance, but the greater imperative is the window it provides us for sexual expression, betrayal, and endless secretive action. Plus, every moviegoer guesses she is going to fall in love with the Gestapo man.

It's pointless to synopsize the plot when you can gorge on the packed film for 145 minutes. It is a gallery of war movie memories, funnier, faster, and more rueful than Tarantino's *Inglourious Basterds* (2009). In the fermenting intrigue of Holland in those last years of the war, no one could be trusted, so every life was a performance. *Black Book* is giddy with abandoned decency and the bitter comedy Verhoeven loves. The picture may be a disgrace, but it is essential, and it has no superior in the insolent warning—if you're going to be occupied, keep your wits sharp, be ready to play any role on the spur of the moment, and carry a tactful gun.

If you ever wonder why so many Americans are armed, see *Black*

Book, and realize that we have given up the ghost of getting back to the best years of our lives. One lesson of the movies is in behaving badly without remembering.

OR IN PARIS. OR CLERMONT-FERRAND.

The most celebrated movie about the ordeal of occupation, the one Alvy Singer wanted to get Annie Hall to see, is *The Sorrow and the Pity*, conceived and directed by Marcel Ophüls, and released in 1969. As the son of the great Max, Marcel had had to hide out in southern France for much of the war before escaping to America. They were Jewish, and far too romantic for the Vichy regime. Though Max Ophüls might have understood and sympathized with the tremors in France after the swiftness with which Hitler's blitzkrieg had taken Paris and humbled French honor in a month. "We'll always have Paris," Rick had promised Ilsa in *Casablanca*, but that was one more shit-eating lie.

The Sorrow is 251 minutes; and its daunting honesty is in being prepared to be banal. Who would blame Annie Hall if she preferred to see *The Shop Around the Corner* or *My Man Godfrey*? To be sure, there are momentous events reported in the documentary, the spasms of cruelty and indifference, the newsreel of German troops on the Champs-Élyseés, the glimpse of naked French women being defiled because they had slept with Germans, and the patient faces of French people lying about what had happened and how occupation, plain fear, collaboration, and the abasement of France as a proud arbiter of civilization had been among the outrages of the Second World War.

"What would you have done?" After that thrill of fighting them on the beaches and the et cetera had worn off. After the unfortunate event of Winston being shot and strung up in Whitehall, upside down (in the way Mussolini and his mistress ended up in Milan in April 1945 at the hands of partisans).

The Sorrow and the Pity is relentless in stopping us in the lobby and quenching our fantasy enthusiasm by whispering to us, Isn't it more likely that instead of being on fire with an assassin's lyricism, you will teach yourself to be occupied by ignoring the worst intrusions on decency, by turning so many blind eyes to the iniquity of betrayal, that your very face disappears?

Marcel Ophüls's documentary had widespread influence. One can feel its urging in Louis Malle's disturbing *Lacombe Lucien* (1974). In 1944, in southwest France, we meet a kid, a handsome, impassive thug who shoots rabbits in the field for the sake of it. Little about him is appealing, save for his intense presence and the way the actor, Pierre Blaise, reminds us of a young Brando, sensual but not "acting." He tries to get into the Resistance, but they tell him he's too young. So casually he presents himself to the German police in Vichy as willing material. This was part of Malle's awareness that not everyone joined the Resistance (maybe 300,000 through the whole war, or less than 1 percent) while many more had gotten along as best they could. *Lacombe Lucien* is still unsettling (it was cowritten with Patrick Modiano, who would win the Nobel Prize for Literature one day). As for Blaise, the arresting young actor, a kid without any prior experience, a year after *Lacombe* he was killed in a car crash when he had been driving. His bursting blank stare hovers in the history of acting, and in our awkward relationship with collaboration.

OCCUPATION IS NOT SIMPLY AN OBJECTIVE FACT; IT'S A STATE OF MIND. Without always noticing their own trick, so many English-language war films are loyal to assumptions of how the proper, sensible world should be organized. *Black Hawk Down* is based on a notion that Somalia can't take care of itself. This is the geopolitical structure that fits with the social hierarchy of command to comfort the most conservative element in our society. Its heartbeat is order, and orders that must be obeyed. It is a matter of occupation and ownership in which politics is set aside as being too much for our weak heads to contain.

Pretend we are in 1879 in what we can call South Africa, or even Zululand. By the good graces of the gods of moviemaking, a small company of Welsh soldiers has been brought over the ocean to stand pointless guard in this beautiful country. They wear bright red tunics, with white cross-strapping (in case the Zulus are shortsighted). They have the most up-to-date Martini-Henry rifles to shoot with. They have two officers from different classes, but the rough, unsaved fellow, John Chard, has seniority over the suavely aristocratic Gonville Bromhead, who does not bother to be Welsh. He is Michael Caine and Chard is Stanley Baker, born in Wales and prescient enough to be a producer on this venture.

So the Zulus, who seem to have lived in this land for as long as anyone knows, are offended at the presence of a red-jacketed force and the intent of the British government to occupy and administer their country. The British had demanded that the Zulu army be disbanded.

The Zulus challenged this intrusion and had a great victory (the Battle of Isandlwana, January 1879, where a thousand British soldiers died), and now they will attack the occupiers at a small trading post named Rorke's Drift. Of course, the expense of sending the Welshmen this far, and the discipline of training them to be a fine Welsh choir, is not insignificant. So why are the Welsh and the British there? What this comes down to is that the Zulus have felt so irked at being occupied they have behaved badly, like naughty kids. They have no respect for the burden of empire, just as the film has no time to describe their grievance or their experience.

There is a terrific battle, and I say "terrific" without reserve. *Zulu* (1964), directed by Cy Endfield, is a classic of combat for what was regarded as an epic occasion in the history of British heroism. In January 1879, the game was on, and the records say that 17 of the Welsh soldiers were killed against 351 of the Zulus. The game is played out on-screen in repeated assaults and the undoubted valor of the thin red line. It concludes with the Zulus withdrawing after they have chanted a song of tribute to their opponents. Eleven Victoria Crosses were awarded for the skirmish (the most ever for one battle; 628 were given in the entire Great War). There would have been a twelfth, but Private Joseph Coy had been killed in valiant action, and you had to be alive to get that gong. The film earned $8 million at the American box office. Chances are, if you've come this far, you know and treasure *Zulu*, even if you wonder whether the Welsh were there so there could be a movie with its final tableau of a red line and a sea of lifeless brown bodies.

But there is something missing from *Zulu*. The officers and the soldiers talk about their plight at Rorke's Drift and the likelihood of death, but one doesn't feel that danger or the suspense. The order of battle is so self-evident, and so much a plan waiting to be executed. This is not blaming the filmmakers, or the actors, but the missing element is the climate of complete participation. I want to know what the Zulus are thinking, and how they relate this movie and the Rorke's Drift episode to their ongoing history. Two hundred forty actual Zulus were bused to the film's location; they seem to have been chosen for their physical splendor; and they were paid their per diems. But they are like stooges, because the film is being made in a context without their experience. Today there are about ten million Zulus within South Africa. They were forcibly relocated under apartheid, a system that applied when the film was made.

Why was this film called *Zulu*, when that people were a small part of any audience? With no interest in exploring the quality of Zulu life, was the title summoning up voodoo fears? Wasn't there some lurking sense of our innocent Welshmen being attacked by this awesome ethnic nation? Is that what happened? The Zulus hadn't invaded Swansea.

Now picture the exo-moon LV-426 at some vague time in the future. As far as the eye can see it is a pitiless and useless place, but a corporation has built a settlement there with colonists. Then that community stops returning messages. Truly, there are up-the-rivers where no sane enterprise should go, but the corporation wants to search out the reason for silence, and so the great heroine Ripley (Sigourney Weaver), survivor from an earlier combat with the alien (delivered by that master of battle, Ridley Scott), will accompany the mission.

Do you doubt what is going to happen? Why have we been assembled in the dark but for a timeless battle of the bitch mothers, with glamorous high-tech weaponry opposing the worst slavering jaws since the great shark of 1975? Ripley against the most dreamy, exotic, and cruel monster H. R.

Giger can create? The result is *Aliens* (1986), directed by James Cameron, a series of unremitting battles. I suspect you love it as much as I do. And there's not really any reason for guilt or regret, because if the Zulus deserve sympathy, the aliens are uncompromisingly sui generis. They can look after themselves. One appeal in zombies and other digital enemies is that we do not have to feel remorse over them. The more virtual creatures there are in sight, the less we have to notice them or take responsibility.

Now make a bigger leap yet and one so tricky it can defy safe landing. Propose that Americans in the era of their independence, and their access to the finest idea ever, a new principle of enlightenment, shipped quantities of Africans into their land and their economy. It's not sufficient to admit that was wrong when the guilt has been so hard to inhabit, not least by concepts like "the just war" when black soldiers were largely omitted from a conflict set on protecting the threatened existence of persecuted peoples. The guilt has not gone away, which suggests that Americans have not yet adequately described it to themselves. The "just war," which has sometimes seemed a term of honor, is also publicity—that authentic American talent and the fuel for the movies.

Why was this done, this transportation of souls which depended on their abasement? Well, the land was large and largely empty, so maybe Americans felt an urge to make it more populous. Then they saw the profit in a slave labor force to pick the cotton, plant the fields, mine for minerals, chop down the trees, shovel the shit, et cetera. Not least in that et cetera was the wish to have powerless bodies that they could rape, abuse, trade, and sometimes murder. Owning people is the ultimate occupation.

But there was more. The whites in what they had decided was the greatest land of all needed someone to hate and fear and take vengeance on. How could they have integrity without that paranoia? Does that seem far-fetched? Consider: they were a godly people, so they felt an undercurrent of guilt and shame and self-loathing, and it was that unease that necessitated the passion of *revenge*. A kind of genocide.

This was a providential setup for the most influential film ever made in America—because it established the picture business—*The Birth of a*

Nation (1915), the essential national melodrama, and the picture we are advised not to see now. That title is not kidding, or exaggerated. For it described the necessary courage and determination in the Ku Klux Klan to punish those Africans for being there, for occupying white space and trapping us good guys into being so ghastly.

The inescapable message in 1945 was not just a possible end for the world. It was the model of being occupied by an evil and controlling force of implacable intent, so the citizen had to decide whether to resist or collaborate. That was the wondering in the new fear.

26

RUSSIA

"Looks like there's a *War and Peace* coming on."

I've not heard that long-suffering line uttered, but I recognized its sentiment when, for the *Guardian*, in 2016, the patient Clive James thought to say a few words about the latest iteration of Tolstoy on our screens. James was then seventy-seven and not well, already living on borrowed chips like a Vegas gambler who found himself in the big room, playing for time. Still, he managed to be wry and cheerful about a television adaptation of a book he had been going in and out of for most of his life:

> The BBC's lavish, sexy, heart-rending, head-spinning and generally not-half-bad adaptation of Tolstoy's vast novel *War and Peace* finished last weekend, so this weekend there is nothing to do except discuss whether Natasha was credible when she fell so suddenly for the odious Anatole Kuragin, and to start waiting until someone adapts it again. At my age, I doubt that I'll live to see the next attempt, but I'm definitely thinking about reading the book one more time. It really is that good: good enough to get involved with again even if it's the last thing you do.

James had been through the *Wars*. As a teenager, he had faced the "original" movie from 1956, the one with Audrey Hepburn and Henry Fonda, mounted by Dino de Laurentiis and directed by King Vidor, a work disdained on account of its effrontery and vulgarity. A few years later, like kids who had always guessed our city was going to be bombed, we found a solid table to shelter beneath as we received the culturally stupefying Soviet response—directed by Sergei Bondarchuk, with Sergei himself as Pierre, a very big venture, as if to tell Hollywood and its imitators to stay off Russian ground.

That 1966–67 version ran seven hours and eleven minutes, as if to scorn the frivolous 208 minutes of the Dino-Vidor attempt. It did feel sincere and authentic—or was it just ponderous?

No one took notice of the Soviet warning. *War and Peace* was becoming an institution. So we braced ourselves for the first BBC television version (children, you may never have heard of this one). In 1972, this most complete adaptation was set off like an artillery barrage. Scripted by Jack Pulman, directed by John Davies, it had Anthony Hopkins as Pierre, Morag Hood as Natasha, Alan Dobie as Andrei, and so on, all the way to David Swift as Napoleon. Its twenty episodes stretched into 1973, with a total running time of nearly fifteen hours.

Britain could take it—and the world, and Clive James, who did not die until 2019. He might have feared that new versions would only get longer, until they came closer to being pure readings of the book—and honestly, if you were ready to give up fifteen hours to the show perhaps you were at a point of deciding to go the whole hog, and simply read the book (albeit skimming some of the self-interruptions that are so characteristic in Tolstoy).

As it was, the 2016 version—with Lily James as Natasha, James Norton as Andrei, and (a bold stroke) Paul Dano as Pierre—was no more than six episodes and a meager running time of eight hours. In hindsight, we can appreciate how lean or cursory this was, and—although I don't expect to live to see it—I wonder if a punchy 85-minute version does not lie ahead as war and peace have to conform to the convulsions of attention deficit disorder, or our mounting ping-pong of panic and ennui. It's conceivable that *Monty Python* once did a 7-minute *War and Peace*, and it's likely that it was meant as a joke.

Wars are educational; world wars promote geographical awareness; for years we study the maps, and the context of an outer world sinks in. We may even realize that *we* are on the outer reaches. But to this day, on a plain, undifferentiated outline of Europe and Asia, would you be confident about placing Volgograd, the Aral Sea, Nova Zembla, the chief regions of permafrost, let alone the old socialist republics? Or is Russia, somehow still a wild bear, as it was in the nineteenth-century heyday of political caricature? Is it that becalming vastness Chekhov's characters are in awe of? Should we begin with the Napoleonic War, or the Great Patriotic War (which is the Russian name for the Second World War)? Can any sketch of war omit *War and Peace*? You see, I feel the essence of our obsession with war (and our failure to understand it, or to improve on our relationship with it) centers on the Russian experience.

It's easy to turn solemn or pretentious over this. And it's remarkable now to consider how thoroughly the West tried to ignore Russian experience in thinking the world was our territory and game. Not that that failure can be remedied, or made up for. Already, history has moved on so that we need to do all we can to comprehend how China defines the world. Or is there a tougher task still: in coming to terms with the culture of artificial intelligence (at last, a true global scheme) whereby there will be less need or point in reading or writing a *War and Peace*?

"I just wanted to have a look," says Pierre in the novel, having reached the site that will soon be the Battle of Borodino. He arrives as a tourist or a sightseer in a hat that soldiers laugh at, but then he recognizes "the strange notion that among those thousands of men, alive, healthy, young and old, who had stared with merry surprise at his hat, there were probably twenty thousand destined for wounds and death (maybe the same ones he had seen). . . ."

Of course, twenty thousand will not cover it. Tourists don't easily grasp the numbers.

Was it legitimate (or inescapable) that the Italian American "they" would make a film of *War and Peace* in 1956 so inadequate there would be no need to say more about it? Is it a measure of our reckless liberty that such a folly was attempted?

So director King Vidor, producer Dino de Laurentiis, and a few hundred others might have introduced themselves shyly on camera: "We do apologize, but as we thought about doing *War and Peace*, this is how the hell of it turned out. It's rubbish, but since it ended up costing $6 million and lasting 208 minutes, we feel obligated to show it to you." In 1956, $6 million was colossal and absurd, but now the real folly is in not realizing how paltry a sum it was (a mere $60 million in modern money). Rembrandt might have painted over *The Night Watch* because he felt it wasn't good enough, but Dino and King were tied like prisoners to their *War and Peace*. Movies become battles that have to be fought. The picture "Comes Alive on the Screen!," its posters warned us in 1956.

What is telling about that film is that while it's lacking to a point of absurdity it is full of striking cinematic moments. The retreat from Moscow is very well done—but the film never dares get close to the muddled introspection of Pierre. That's how movies can creep up on us with their specious élan. So one of the finest elements in this *War and Peace* is Oscar Homolka as General Kutuzov, commander of the Russian army. I'm not sure how military historians rate him, but for me in this book he became an ideal general in his reluctance to permit a battle. Let me try to put him in a nutshell.

In June 1812, with maybe half a million men in his Grande Armée Napoleon invaded Russia. His motives are not clear now or sensible, beyond the pressing burden of Bonaparte being expected to do something drastic or imperial after his unsatisfying campaign in Spain. Did he believe he would conquer Russia, as he had done smaller parts of Europe? Was he even mindful of being in a book like *War and Peace* one day? Does that sound silly, or is it key to the lust for glory in great leaders? The more we contemplate such movies, the clearer it is that generals and nations are like inane movie corporations intent on clarifying history and their self-importance for all us idiots. They have to do something—so they run the risk of doing something stupid.

Just imagine if, in 1939–40, instead of taking over Poland, Norway, Denmark, Holland, Belgium, and France, Hitler had invaded the Soviet Union. Imagine he's playing Risk. That was the solid move to make, because no country on earth then would have thought of intervening. If he'd succeeded, if Germany had established a frontier a thousand miles east of Moscow, it's a different world, and just about every other government would have felt the relief and security of communism having its hat knocked off. Such dreaming is crazy? Of course, but is it wilder than what happened, and isn't it consistent with the new energy of scenario offered by the movies?

In 1812, Napoleon may have anticipated that Russia would oppose him in some decisive, pitched battle, after which Czar Alexander would have to sue for peace. Instead, under the direction of the recently appointed Kutuzov, the Russians fell back ahead of the French, yielding cities but doing all they could to deprive the land of the supplies that Napoleon had counted on—wheat, vegetables, cattle, and fresh horses. This has been called a "scorched earth" policy, and it put pressure on France's lengthening supply lines. It is not a strategy that lends itself to movie excitement, but it has a good record at avoiding defeat.

By September, Kutuzov felt pressure to prove himself and boost the morale of his army. So he did fight a battle, if at a disadvantage—at Borodino—less than a hundred miles from Moscow. This is the massive confusion described by Tolstoy, in which no one knew what was happening. He declined to follow the conventional idea that great men determined wars. This was not abstract conjecture. Tolstoy had fought in the Crimean War and been present at Sevastopol, shocked by the indiscriminate slaughter. But if you read *War and Peace*, you know that he was as fascinated by battle as he was disapproving of it. Wouldn't he have had the same mixed feelings about movies? If you read the book you feel his excitement at imminent battle as much as you know he adored Anna Karenina.

But he straddled the age in which battles shifted as spectacles. Till recently, armed conflict had attracted sightseers. Crowds came out to inspect the battlefield at Waterloo the day after the fight. They were upset by the stench of death. Pierre goes out to witness the Battle of Borodino like an inquiring mind, or someone who understands that war is a performance that society can observe and patronize with relative safety. But on the field he is caught up in the action, tending to the wounded, until he is in danger himself.

The French had it better at Borodino, by a touch, though the losses there were shared evenly and ran to 70,000 men. Archaic Russia felt it had achieved a moral victory, whereas the revolutionary Napoleon knew no such pious state existed. Again, Bonaparte thought there would be envoys seeking terms. But Kutuzov stayed silent and backed off once more. Meanwhile the French were suffering increasingly from illness, hunger, and some desertion. The confidence of the French army—the feeling that the war was *their* story—was faltering.

The emperor Napoleon had his problems at Borodino, and so did King Vidor. The director had found a pretty valley which he planned to fill with six thousand uniformed extras as seen from a distance. The blue and the red would make a lucid diagram. But Laurentiis changed that plan, and said they had to shoot the film at a military training ground near Rome, so his friends could come to watch. Vidor actually wept at this change—he had had a vision, he said—but Laurentiis had made a deal with a local general whereby that man's mistress would get a small part in the picture in exchange for use of the military ground.

So Vidor had to compromise, but he had a law for movie battles that said nuts to Tolstoy's ruminations over the sway of a limitless conflict. "Most people think you have to pay all kinds of attention to uniforms and all that, but really all the audience recognizes is motion. You have to have the men moving in the right direction. That way you can tell immediately which group is the French Army and which group is the Russian Army. I insisted that all of Napoleon's directions and movements were from left to right. The Russians all moved from right to left."

Can you remember that? Can you see how battles can be designed for simpletons seeking fun?

In 1812, the Russians fell back toward Moscow itself, pursued by the indignant but perplexed French. And then they gave up their great city. They quit—and still sent no messengers asking for an end to hostilities. It was October by then and the weather was turning. Vidor does very well with the sight of a hunched Bonaparte (Herbert Lom) looking at the darkening sky and appreciating his dilemma. Movie thrives on that kind of self-captioning image.

The French could hardly forage because of the thorough way the Russians had cleared the land. They were beginning to be badly supplied. There was typhus and cholera thinning the ranks. They were short of winter clothing and boots in the snow. And the Russians declined to play the game in the continental way Napoleon had employed with set battles. The armies were as large as armies had ever been in 1812, but Kutuzov was pioneering a brand of guerrilla warfare well suited to a nation being invaded. He created a system that has seldom been overwhelmed. This is the beginning of one of the great military defeats in history, as Bonaparte had no alternative but to retreat. The plan worked again in 1942–43.

At this point in the film, with winter and disillusion combined, the French morale crumbling, Vidor shows us General Kutuzov in his home. He is often sleeping, or praying, or merely waiting, hunched like a beast. There is nothing much else in the man but the hushed expectancy of a prisoner. But then as he is told the retreat is underway, that the tattered French column is prey for raiding Cossack horsemen, then Kutuzov comes out of his crouch. His body reaches up like an invalid being cured and transformed in an inspirational film. His creased face glows with satisfaction and apotheosis. He has won the great war by not losing. That is the surest way. His Oscar Homolka as Kutuzov is worthier of Tolstoy than Henry Fonda or Audrey Hepburn.

Homolka had been born in Vienna in 1898. That meant he served in the Austro-Hungarian army during the Great War. I don't know much about the nature of his service, but don't forget that he had been defeated, that his kingdom was broken up in the peace, and that he likely felt a citizen of a demeaned and occupied land. He moved on to Berlin and then to London, and proved himself a fine actor—his Verloc in Alfred Hitchcock's *Sabotage* is masterly. But I am surmising that in Kutuzov, Homolka could feel the regret of losing a war and the fear of succumbing.

This is of significance in the history I am describing. Russia or the Soviet Union have often felt on the brink of external jeopardy and humiliation. Whereas battle has not been fought on US ground since 1865. That may be taken as part of our country's status or prosperity. But it amounts to a terrible inexperience, too. To this day, the American martial spirit—which is not simply a military mind-set, but drunk on the dream of greatness—is vulnerable because it has not lived in the adult dismay of being occupied. That is how all modern war finds its pathos and its fatal knowledge in Russia.

Let me ask you a question, not unlike wondering whether you could find the Aral Sea (which is disappearing). Would you care to guess the deaths suffered by the Soviet Union in the Second World War?

If it helps you with context, I can tell you that the French losses 1939–45—dead and missing—were about 210,000, with nearly twice that number of dead civilians.

Yet the French had lost about 1.4 million in the Great War.

For Great Britain, the losses in the Second World War were 383,000 with 12,000 dead civilians. The British deaths in the Great War had been 1.1 million.

Is this helping?

The American losses in the Second World War were just over 400,000. With 12,000 civilian deaths.

Of course, I have given you the figures for what we think of as the "winning" countries.

The Germans lost five million, and two million civilians. In the Great War, Germany and Austria-Hungary had lost about three million.

You should understand that these numbers are approximate, and they cover uncertainty over how many had been there and were then not there.

There may be human vestiges still, sketches of DNA in the humus, that were never identified or counted. And in some cases, governments were less than kind to their own people or reliable in counting them.

So in the Second World War the Soviet Union believed it had lost eight million soldiers, and more than double that number of civilians.

IT'S EASY TO MAKE A CULTURAL MAP IN WHICH THE GENIUS OF LEO Tolstoy looms over the vain pandemonium of Hollywood moviemaking. But be aware of the near misses in history. Just think of an irascible and hardly stable Leo, being maybe ten years younger. Suppose he's only eighty in 1920. Dissatisfied, impulsive, unpredictable—true to life in every detail—he quits Russia in a post-Bolshevik huff and heeds some casual advice to go West. Suppose he then meets Louis B. Mayer in Culver City, and Louis bursts out in his unique, alarming enthusiasm—"Leo, you are our guy!" And Tolstoy feels he is home among mad Russians.

So many had left their home country in parts of what would soon be the Soviet Union at the end of the nineteenth century and in the first years of the twentieth, and ended up as celebrated figures in what became the film business. Louis B. Mayer had come from Dyme, near Kyiv; the Selznick family had its origins in Vilnius, in Lithuania; the Warners were from territory that was Russia before it became Poland; Al Jolson was from Srednik in Lithuania; Lewis Milestone was from Ukraine; the actress Alla Nazimova had been born in Yalta; Rouben Mamoulian was from Tiflis in Georgia; Gregory Ratoff came from Saint Petersburg itself. To say nothing of supporting actors, decorators and designers, and even the army of extras.

Many of those people had quit the shadow of Russia because the great bear was too cruel, too accustomed to subjugating lesser peoples (notably Jews), and because they wanted more of what they dreamed of as liberty. They came out of hunger and pogrom with no more intention than Scarlett O'Hara had of going back to poverty and hunger and fear. And Scarlett on-screen was a spirit created by David Selznick, as Russian as she was Irish. These escapees learned a certain amount of subterfuge and lying, and the need for charm to carry it off. The self-styled Michael Romanoff (easily misspelled as Romanov) was probably from Lithuania. But he was in the United States by 1901, when he was ten, and in a checkered career, crossing many lines, ended up as a restaurateur in Los Angeles—at Romanoff's, on South Rodeo Drive, a place where picture people felt they had to be, like Pierre at Borodino. Yes, they guessed "Mike" was a faker, but he was droll, a chronic insider, and charming. He greased the wheels.

This is a test case in the theorizing that after 1917, at least, a Russian in Los Angeles was likely to be a con man, a charmer, and very likely a spy or an actor. There are movies in this tradition that show too well how the brave new Russia struggled with fantastic interpretations. *The Last Command*, directed by Josef von Sternberg for Paramount, is an entertaining picture for 1928, yet a travesty. In Hollywood we meet a Russian exile who is now a successful director, Leo Andreyev (played by William Powell). He is casting a new picture from a file of photographs of begging faces, and he chooses one, "Sergius Alexander" (Emil Jannings, the German star), as if thinking he might have known this man once. Sergius arrives for work, elderly and unwell, close to destitute, and he is sent to Wardrobe to dress as a general in the Russian army.

What would you guess but that this humble Sergius was once Grand Duke Sergius Alexander, commander of the Russian army in the last days of the czar? That's when he encountered a captive revolutionary (our Leo Andreyev) and slapped his face for impudence. He might have executed the future director, but both men were hot for the same woman, the enigmatic Natalie (Evelyn Brent), so charm or honor or movie nonsense intervened, and Leo was set free so that one day down the line he could hire Sergius.

There's great stuff on a train where Sergius and Natalie fall in love and she lets him escape after a Bolshevik group has taken over the train. A civil war is going on, but it's made to seem like a thundery summer night. And in his mix of pomp and pathos, Jannings won what was the first Oscar for best actor. It wasn't real war any more than it was authentic Russia, but it was the make-believe that looked like life and in taking over the world would prove more influential than communism.

I said *The Last Command* is entertaining, but that only works so long as you keep it in the category of *The Prisoner of Zenda*, or even *The Four Feathers*. In that atmosphere romance assumes it can explain history. But suppose you wanted to make a film about the war and the turmoil in Russia in 1917, a film that really conveyed that astonishing tumult and its bloody mix of idealism and cynicism—and if you had a spare locomotive to play with, then you might try this story:

Since 1914, Germany and Russia have been at war, so the German army has an eastern front as well as the western one we know far better. The eastern front is as deadly and horrific, and both countries have been worn down by it. One theme of the Great War is the revelation of futility and fatigue as monstrous armies lose their momentum and script. It is in the grudging realization that war accomplishes nothing that it begins to be climatic. But this prospect is tougher to bear in Russia because the nation is cracking apart under economic strain.

In February 1917 there is a small revolution in Russia. It is not the big one yet, but it is enough to force the czar to abdicate in favor of a provisional government. Thus, consider the vexation of a prominent Russian revolutionist who is in exile from his homeland. He wants to get back home so he can lead the big one. He is a socialist desperate to be a star. I am putting this crudely because I am trying to get you excited. So, festering in Swiss exile, V. I. Lenin goes to the German authorities and charms them with a scenario. He suggests they put him on a train that can carry him, his wife, and an entourage into Russia. They will go, secretly, to the Finland Station in Petrograd (the wartime name for Saint Petersburg). Doesn't this feel like an adventure? With Leonardo DiCaprio as Lenin? Would he be willing to do it bald? Would he play Lenin as the insufferable man from history?

A fresh, virulent seed of turmoil is thereby planted in Russian ground by German cunning. This Lenin may undermine the Russian government and its war effort. On a muffled train, with more than twenty in the viral group, men and women, with German supervision and some fear of betrayal, or czarist intervention. Is that a movie or what? Strangers on a Train! Yet it has never been done, by American or English-language moviemakers, and the several Soviet versions are bogged down in propaganda at the expense of the human vivacity that a von Sternberg or a Hawks could have delivered.

What Lenin wrought would have a profound effect on history, but our "To the Finland Station" project ought to feel as if it is trying to keep its balance on a narrow brink of possibility or survival. How easily the adventure could go wrong; how quickly the Germans might have given it up as too far-fetched a sidebar; how much it depends on our normal human pettiness, oblivious to destiny. So Tolstoy might have relished this inadvertent proximity of the momentous and the momentary, which is not the worst recipe for movies. (He died in fact in 1910, as the medium was taking early steps—in time for a camera to record his shaky stride—but in a modestly revised 1920 it might have been "Story by L. Tolstoy.")

The closest we have come to this may be Warren Beatty's *Reds* (1981), a valiant attempt to interweave the stories of John Reed and his lover Louise Bryant with the Russian Revolution and the civil war that followed it. Jack Reed was a Harvard communist, a writer who went to Russia in its crisis, and wrote a book, *Ten Days That Shook the World* (1919), that popularized the revolution. It deserved a picture, and Sergei Eisenstein gave it a try in 1928.

Reed was dead from tuberculosis by 1920 and he earned nowhere near the place in history that fell to Lenin, but both lives have trains, war scenes, and fumbled romance (Lenin had a wife and a mistress). Maybe the two projects could have worked in unison: Lenin does appear briefly in *Reds* (played by Roger Sloman), along with Trotsky and Zinoviev. Beatty had the idea of interleaving the drama of *Reds* with interviews with people who had been alive in 1917—from Henry Miller to Rebecca West, from Hamilton Fish to Oleg Kerensky. Those halting, glowing faces may be as good as anything Beatty ever did.

Reds is too long for what it is, and my "To the Finland Station" doesn't even exist. Those handicaps say a lot about the difficulties we face in approaching Russian war and movies. Is it possible that the claims of love stories, plain heroism, and patriotic wars pale beside the confounding intellectual ordeal of such battle? *War and Peace* has given us Pierre, Andrei, and Natasha, the retreat from Moscow and the Battle of Borodino, but those narrative coups seem so slight when put next to Tolstoy's icy perplexity:

> In offering and accepting battle at Borodino, Kutuzov and Napoleon acted involuntarily and senselessly. And only later did historians furnish the already accomplished facts with ingenious arguments for the foresight and genius of the commanders, who, of all the involuntary instruments of world events, were the most enslaved and involuntary agents.

IF TOLSTOY'S RECKONING SEEMS A TOUCH PIOUS OR SPOILSPORT, TAKE A moment to track the insanity he was observing. Thus before, during, and after the Second World War, the Allies did not fully comprehend that this was a struggle between two types of authoritarianism, fascism and communism. Instead, the plan of democracy against tyranny was introduced. The rhetoric over days of infamy and fighting in the fields and on the beaches clung to threatened sovereignty or security, but did not always grasp the ideological substance of the war.

In seeing action (the movie principle), we can find it hard to understand structures of belief. That conundrum is steadily ignored in the study of film. Consider another film, with "battle" in its title. The Sergei Eisenstein who took on *Ten Days* had joined the Red Army at twenty in 1918. He did some service but he was quickly identified by his commanders as a precocious graphic artist with skills that might do more with posters and propaganda than he could accomplish with a rifle. In a few years, he was one of the pioneer generation of directors in the new Soviet cinema. Thus, in 1925, he made *Battleship Potemkin*, a silent film of 75 minutes, self-evident propaganda, but one of the most discussed films of the 1920s, and still a puzzle.

The *Potemkin* is a battleship of the Russian Imperial Navy on which the crew serve in a kind of slavery. The conditions are so grim that the mutiny is a semiformal action of class warfare. This is done in the vivid agitprop style that Eisenstein had laid down in his earlier film, *Strike*. But the *Potemkin* lies offshore from Odessa in the Black Sea and so news of the mutiny reaches the citizens. As the script puts it, "In those memorable days the town lived at one with the rebellious battleship." Small boats carried food and fuel to the crew. There are exuberant scenes of fellowship. But they ask us to overlook a large detail in the movie: the crew are working-class, beyond dispute, but the people of Odessa are bourgeois, nicely dressed; a polished, privileged society sympathetic to a mutiny so long as their servants don't hear about it.

Then "suddenly," as red flags fly from the ship and the Odessa Steps are thronged with well-wishers, "a rank of soldiers appear at the head of the steps." They are in uniform: white tunics and caps, dark breeches and riding boots, with fixed bayonets. We are never going to approve of them, or admit to being impressed, but they are one of the most superb units in screen history. They might have been filmed by Leni Riefenstahl for *Triumph of the Will*, which came only ten years later.

You may flinch at that comparison. You grew up in the orthodoxy that *Battleship Potemkin* is a cry against injustice as well as a monument to dynamic montage. But those two messages do not fit together tidily. So I'd ask you to see that the shocking ways in which the demonstrators are attacked and cut down—with that baby carriage bumping down the steps, and the slash cut with which a saber lacerates a woman's face— cannot be separated from the precision performance of the soldiers. Here it is again, the conundrum of cut and slash, action and reaction, the trigger mechanism in film, so that we feel for the civilians and for the troops. Isn't there something exhilarating in seeing how a troop of well-trained soldiers (a thin white line?) can clear the steps of demonstrators? Isn't that what we longed for at the Washington Capitol in January 2021?

Oh dear, this is very awkward—I hear the cry. And so it is as complicated as the imperious reasoning against war in Tolstoy's novel and the ceaseless interest he had in describing battle.

Potemkin bears little relationship to the events of 1905. It was as much a fabrication as my "To the Finland Station" (which doesn't even get the italic of a title). But the film moved everyone attached to the art of pictures. Selznick thought of remaking it in Hollywood! Eisenstein actually came to America for a few eventful months and speculated over making an American picture. Nothing worked out: he did not have the knack for compromise that carried a Milestone or a Jolson along on the new stream. So he went back to the Soviet Union in some ignominy and tried to rehabilitate himself by making *Alexander Nevsky* (1938), which is one of the most austere, mannered, and militaristic films ever made. A line of soldiers stirred Eisenstein in the way an insolent young woman aroused Howard Hawks.

Nevsky reached back in Russian history to celebrate a native stand against threats from Germany and Scandinavia in the thirteenth century. But it was plainly aimed at Russian anxiety over attack from Germany in 1939. The Russia of Stalin was well aware of the risk in sight. In a Kutuzovian gesture of improvisation, the Soviet Union even made a nonaggression pact with Germany as war was breaking (signed in August 1939). It couldn't last; it was a play for time, but it carved up Poland in a deal and allowed the Soviets into Finland. It is clear that Hitler and Stalin both reckoned that the Second World War was just another Patriotic War in which the two beasts of Europe would be engaged in the central conflict, leaving France, Britain, and even America as not much more than retrievers sniffing at the edges of the field.

Once war had been declared, and then when the United States had to reappraise the Soviet Union as an ally, the delicate scheme of a movie marriage came into play. The results are not pretty. In Hollywood, in the years after 1917, there was little sympathy for the revolution. The business was intensely capitalist and indifferent to a great deal of fact. The Russians in Hollywood were especially hostile to any hint of socialism. The culture that cherished Chaplin's "little man" was extra pleased that Charlie had become so rich. The picture business loved the rhetoric of "we the people"; it called it audience. But Hollywood did not like its own people stepping over the line closer to socialism. As a junior at Dartmouth, in 1934, Maurice Rapf had gone on a lengthy trip to the Soviet Union, during which his radical idealism fell in love with the new Russian program. Many thoughtful people were drawn to that Soviet alternative in the 1930s, and even if Russia let them down in the end, that doesn't disprove the quality of the ideas.

Maurice was the son of Harry Rapf, a leading executive at Metro-Goldwyn-Mayer, and he was cross-examined by his father about his dangerous views. Harry stood up for him as best he could in public but his fellow business leaders were unamused by any sign of socialism. Making American pictures then and now was cast-iron capitalism, terrified at thoughts of revisionism. All too soon, this paranoia would break out in panic attacks fearful that some Hollywood pictures had been red, instead of Technicolor.

But only a few years earlier, just as Stalin had made a pact with Germany in 1939, so Hollywood accepted that it should be generous to its new ally. How could that be managed? From 1936–38, Joseph E. Davies had been American ambassador to Russia, a Roosevelt appointment. Davies was not red, but he maintained a steady view of the Russian experiment, and kept quiet about such things as the trials and execution of dissidents, the genocidal treatment of kulaks (maybe five million disappeared), and the miserable life of many Russians. Those forgiving feelings were expressed in his memoir, *Mission to Moscow*, published in 1941 and such a bestseller that Roosevelt and Davies together prevailed on Warner Bros. to convert it into a movie.

You can say this is not a war movie, but it would become a test case in the Cold War. And it was a full-blooded Warners picture, released in 1943, written by Howard Koch and directed by Michael Curtiz, who would both be involved that same year on a picture called *Casablanca*, which has as much respect for the experience of North Africa as *Mission to*

Moscow has for Soviet life. Later on, as the movie became a target of loathing for the House Committee on Un-American Activities, its producer would admit it had been "an expedient lie for political purposes."

It's less clear how many of its participants were in on the lie. Curtiz was a trimmer and a survivor, accustomed to laying a veneer of stylishness and narrative momentum on any subject. He was wary of the project, but Jack Warner told him he "would come through with flying colors." *Mission to Moscow* is not smooth or in flight; it's clumsy with so much voice-over from Davies—played by Walter Huston with his regular, rugged decency. Ann Harding is the ambassador's wife, Marjorie Merriweather Post, the richest woman in the US, let alone the USSR. Mannart Kippen does Stalin, Gene Lockhart is Molotov, and in the carousel of show business Oscar Homolka was there to play Litvinoff. They all speak with accessible Russian accents that would have been acceptable in *Casablanca*. To top it all, the great Russian ballerina, Ulanova, is impersonated by a young Cyd Charisse. It's not just that the movie is a compromise; it's part of the new American faith that movies could do anything, so long as the trick blinded us to the lies. Nineteen forty-three was not a moment for satire, but in hindsight *Mission* needed Preston Sturges's merry disbelief.

There was more earnestness. In the same 1943, Samuel Goldwyn was eager to get in on the Soviet show. He hired Lillian Hellman to write the script for what would be *The North Star*, and none other than Lewis Milestone was the director. Aaron Copland wrote the score. This *is* a war film. As it begins, Dana Andrews and Anne Baxter are Kolya and Marina, Ukrainian peasants, happy for a moment and then shocked to learn that Operation Barbarossa has begun (Barbarossa was a twelfth-century German hero, a sign of Nazi passion for destiny). So the country kids become partisans or guerrillas opposed to Nazi invasion. The story hinges on a wicked German doctor who wants, literally, to drain off young Ukrainian blood (he is played by Erich von Stroheim). There is Walter Huston again as the Soviet doctor who uncovers his plot. The film is comical now, but it was a great success then, nominated for six Oscars, including one for Hellman.

In some ideal crosscutting panorama of the time (and in the persistent spirit that couldn't get "To the Finland Station" made), I'd like to propose an exercise in simultaneity in which a Preston Sturges comedy about the making of *Mission to Moscow*—"Some Like it Red"?—would go back and forth with authentic newsreel footage from Stalingrad. There's a name you know vaguely in history, without having a sure grasp of the detail of the greatest battle ever fought. I'm not proud of that caption, or excited, but I know we have mixed feelings over battle.

Stalingrad can be cast as a replay of Napoleon's ill-fated invasion of Russia. With the launching of Barbarossa, Hitler made three thrusts against the Soviet Union. They were obvious enough, you could have picked them yourself, granted you were rash enough to believe that the Soviet Union could be defeated—and nothing else would do.

The first attack centered on Leningrad in the north and led to a siege that lasted several years with hideous privations, including some cannibalism. That practice can seem like an ultimate in evil or degradation, but Leningrad commanded so many other sins against civilization.

There was also a thrust in the center of the country, and there was the attempt to take Stalingrad. That city is called Volgograd now, since it has always been on the banks of the Volga River in southwest Russia. The name was amended in the de-Stalinization programs put into effect by Nikita Khrushchev in 1961.

Axis forces attacked in late August 1942 after German bombing raids had devastated great parts of the city and made the essential condition of the battle: house-by-house fighting in streets that were no longer identifiable on maps. In the Great War, and in most other wars, there had been a weird gentlemen's agreement to hold our battles in stretches of open country where it was easier to manage tactics. In the Great War, those fronts had been largely rural terrain where trench cities could be built. But at Stalingrad an unavoidable truth existed: that the world was all one unruly trench, that housing and public buildings were like rocks, ridges, and forests where troops might shelter and seek advantage. There was a modern assumption in this: that the civilian population was an army, vulnerable to slaughter and demoralization. A battle was no longer an out-of-town venue arranged so as not to disturb the urban bourgeoisie.

The conflict in Stalingrad lasted five months (so that much of it took place in winter), but in that time many parts of the city were taken and retaken over and over again. Piled corpses became landmarks as evident as the shell of an old movie theater, or a municipal swimming pool where spoiled statues had sunk in stagnant water. It followed from the nature of this fighting that groups of soldiers easily became lost or isolated, functioning on their own or out of reach of reliable command structures. And once the battle had gone on several weeks, without clear conclusion, then the possibility arose that it might last forever, that the rubble of the city, endlessly rearranged by further bombardments and fires, was not so much a city in disrepair or breakdown as an attempt at urbanization that had sunk into an eternal state of brokenness. Stalingrad is our first postapocalyptic ruin.

The Germans nearly drove the Soviets out of the city. The Russians were clinging. The war might have shifted badly. (That might have hastened D-Day.) But then the tide turned—enabled by winter and German exhaustion—until the German Sixth Army was surrounded and cut off from resupply. Thus, at the end of January 1943—just as our cheery *Casablanca* was opening—Field Marshal Paulus surrendered, despite Hitler's insistence that he fight on to the last man standing. We believe that a million and a half men died in Stalingrad. Historians say that it was the effective beginning of the end of the war. But it was a start, too, in a hardening of the Russian spirit.

Truly, it does not exactly fit our classic sense of a battle. It was a way of death within the city limits that became the way of life. It is completely unfilmable (if we think of the total experience); it would be unbearable for an audience to sit still for it. And yet in the degraded nature of the place, we can get crazed snipers at shattered windows, and flamethrowers scouring underground tunnels, and the cut and thrust that prowls from room to room in what may have been an office building. This is the meat and drink of combat, ambush, disaster, and the small victory of plunging a knife in and out of an opponent until he gives up the ghost. So the nature of Stalingrad would cover the rearguard action in *Saving Private Ryan*, the no-holds-barred street pursuit of *Black Hawk Down*, and the tank's last stand in *Fury*. And it has been an inspiration for video war games—there is one called *Stalingrad*, a DTF Games product for Windows, a two-player game. You can be the German Sixth Army or the Red Army—only the helmets differentiate. And they are rather too alike for comfort (friendly fire can be a hazard).

If you like combat movies, Stalingrad is your training ground, your school. But nearly every place of official education in the actual city was blown to bits. The real teaching was in the gutted streets and the endless ingenuity of those trying to survive and clinging to that attenuated urge.

There is a movie, *Stalingrad*, German, made in 1993, written and directed by Joseph Vilsmaier. It is not very good, or exciting, or a must-see. It didn't really play in English-speaking territories. But it doesn't need to be all those glamorous things because it is unremitting, plain and crushing.

It begins with a group of German soldiers resting on Italian beaches, sunbathing and swimming. They have campaigned in Italy and North Africa, and they mention El Alamein as if it had been a good battle for the Germans. But the British think of it as one of their great victories. Let it be said that both sides together, in wide-ranging tank engagements in the North African desert, lost about 70,000 men. That's surely respectable, but trivial in the Stalingrad compression.

We meet some of these Germans in the way war films like to show us a few "characters": there's an inexperienced lieutenant, a rather ugly fellow who gets a job done, and a wry observer with large ears, a potential comedian. Then they board trains to visit the Soviet Union. It seems a pretty journey from northern Italy to the mouth of the Volga and they admire endless green prairies, without appreciating how far resupply will have to travel.

Then they are at Stalingrad, without much preparation for them or us. A conflict emerges between the young lieutenant and an older, cynical captain—there seem to be different ways of doing things. But there is something else wrong or disconcerting if you are used to those American films where a mixed unit is a model for diversity pulling together. Quite soon, there is a mood of despair over the action, and a realization that the war in Stalingrad is vague yet infinite, out of control. The action becomes fiercer and crueler and more incoherent. There are local conflicts but they're hard to follow. I don't think that's a shortcoming. It's more the sinking sense of formal battle being overwhelmed by hostility and chaos. Purposeful action is lost in the seething cellular interaction. When a city is destroyed, how can it be won?

The human damage is sickening, and the medical resources are perfunctory. The old questions of courage or tactics are smothered by technology: Do you have a flamethrower? Can we call in artillery? Is this old knife enough to do the job? Is that a cyanide candy? Please send more morphine. There is a specially upsetting scene where the harsh captain calls on the lieutenant and his men to make a firing squad to execute a bunch of inconvenient civilians. As they line up they see that one of the targets is a boy of about ten, a kid who had helped them, and who has an unusually wide, open gaze. So he stares at his executioners, as blank or impersonal as a mirror. He shows no fear, he does not plead for mercy; he only faces them, as if dead already.

And they say the death toll at Stalingrad, the collection, may have been a million and a half. Somehow you suspect it was more. The survivors gather the dog tags of fallen comrades, but who will be left holding the kitty at the end? As winter freezes limbs and glances, so we begin to comprehend that all "our guys" will be lost. There is no kind of positive resolution. The young woman partisan (played by Dana Vavrova, the director's wife) will not survive and she has only a fleeting "romance" with a German soldier. It's as if life has come to a halt. And this battle lasted five months. The Germans lost at Stalingrad—that was the official verdict. But any question of winning had come to seem absurd.

The great population of the Allied countries did not know what was happening in the Soviet Union. And I fear that we still do not know because we have not come to terms with how far Russia was an ally, just as much as Germany. What's that? How was Germany an ally? Simply in the way any war game requires two sides. Don't romanticize the competitive differences of it all, or the idea of justice in winning. On the tracery of severed streets in Stalingrad—a tortured nervous system—everyone was alike. At last the mythic bonhomie of Christmas Day 1914 is exposed to the light. All that in forty years. There is so much less difference between the two sides than we have been told.

But if I give my estimate that *Stalingrad* is not a very striking movie, it has a dullness, a spreading normality that is not simply upsetting. It is a portent of a totality in war that is more than a turn of phrase, or a telling title. It is a kind of winter that may not be relieved.

After Paulus's surrender, some 90,000 captured German troops were ordered to march to Siberia. With useless boots. That can be over 1,500 miles, which accounts for how only 6,000 survived the trip. Of course, there are risks in losing when the rules have been set aside for the remorseless attrition of a video game.

A contradiction arises: the apparatus of a film is reassuring, whatever is being shown. The projector keeps turning over, no matter that it is unwinding hell. Infinite destruction requires studious preparation and construction. Yet the facts of Stalingrad and the texture of this film allude to a prospect that is terrifying for those raised on battle movies. It is that the situation can go rogue, or out of control, a dread that gripped Europe in the years of the just war, and began to gnaw away at composed schemes of justice.

I know, all of this may be tough to take, and we still like to think of the movies as a bit of fun, so here is a more palatable Stalingrad story: *Enemy at the Gates* (2010), directed by Jean-Jacques Annaud and written by Annaud and Alain Godard. Set entirely in Stalingrad, it is in English— Jude Law as a top Russian sharpshooter sounds Cockney; and his rival, a German marksman, is delivered by Ed Harris in his sultry, masterminding way, and in right-stuff American.

Obviously it's a war movie, yet it's not. The point is that it is a suspense thriller and a trial-at-arms in which the noise of the city at war frequently falls away for the awed hush of the cat-and-mouse game the two shooters play, tracking each other down as if their single combat will decide everything.

There are big establishing action scenes, with aircraft and a lot of extras filling the screen. But the core of the film is the sonata raptures for a man and his telescopic sights, and in the way of such things, as we attend to the intricate process of aiming, and the squeeze on the trigger, we would like to be firing ourselves. Shooting is so seductive. (Just think of Clint Eastwood's *American Sniper*, 2014, with Bradley Cooper's shooter dead-on at 2,000 yards.)

Enemy at the Gates begins with a violent map of the Nazi stain spreading over Europe. It ends with the jubilation of victory. And it has Bob Hoskins overacting as commissar Nikita Khrushchev, who really was in Stalingrad as an organizer. There is also Rachel Weisz as a dedicated soldier who will end up making love with Jude Law. They are both movie-star lovely, and Weisz has the extra heft of being a very good actress. Still, when they do make love (furtively in a room full of other soldiers) we can't miss her clean white underpants, or the richness of her thighs, which have missed the starvation diet at Stalingrad. The two stars do a good job at what the film requires, but their primed faces seem made of goat-cheese salads more than acorns, rodents, and terror. There was $68 million of Western money behind this project.

The ruined city is largely confined to the abandoned factory-scape where the snipers stalk each other. We have no idea of how the outer battle is proceeding, and the overarching historical perspective is as emphatic yet as hollow as that title—what does *Enemy at the Gates* want to mean? The suspense is effective so long as you take a rain check on knowing which man is going to win. I won't tell you, but you don't need me to give you the answer. As it is, in many ways, this Stalingrad looks like not the worst place to be, not if you're a team player sticking to the rules, with laundry for your undies.

There is one exception to this. The film has a boy of about ten who idolizes the Russian sharpshooter, but then falls for the German, too. And so he becomes a helpless double agent, passing tips and betrayal to both the men, uncertain which one he wants to win. This is a plot mechanism, but it's very perceptive on the urgings in a child driven to hero worship and so romantic as to be unreliable. He ends badly (of course): double agents in such movies are doomed—you can't cheat us. But that deprives us of all the fabulous cheats who have flowered and grown rich and powerful in wartime. A better picture might have this kid coming out of Stalingrad a hero of the Red Army, but morally overwhelmed. Not many people emerge from war feeling their integrity is worth talking about.

Such a character reminds me of another child, the blond boy in Andrei Tarkovsky's *Ivan's Childhood* (1962). This is a fantasy, in lustrous black and white, ashine with enigmatic poetry, about a child who may be dead, or dreaming of how he lived through the war, an orphan and a kind of princeling. Tarkovsky's framework indicates the boy was actually killed, like so many other children, but the body of the picture is alive with his romantic hope that it might have been just a proving adventure. The war in *Ivan's Childhood* is seldom conventionally warlike. There are shots fired in the rural distance. A crashed aircraft stands like a warning cross. There is talk of military plans. But the boy's innocent assertion of his own importance is a touching measure of how children cannot understand war—or not until it's too late.

Better yet than *Ivan's Childhood* is Spielberg's *Empire of the Sun*, though that film belongs as much to J. G. Ballard, whose memoir inspired the picture; and to Christian Bale, who embodies Jim and his ecstatic madness at the age of twelve, a refugee in Shanghai, captive but captivated by haunting side characters like treacherous Americana (John Malkovich), forlorn English gentility (Miranda Richardson), and doomed Japanese heroism (Takataro Kataoka). *Empire of the Sun* is a great film, I think, not just because of Bale but in the feeling of a whole world being broken apart by its madness. At the end, we are unclear what country we are in, or whether any "intelligence" is designing the conflict. It closes on a sense that order can never be regained.

But Spielberg has never been one for losing control. He is a field marshal in the industry. DreamWorks is a fair name for a film studio, but just as good at describing a romantic army. Spielberg hardly notices his own hero worship. I sometimes wish that Captain Miller in *Saving Private Ryan* had more than tremors in his hand. Suppose he is losing his mind. Then reassess Jim in *Empire*, supposedly a victim figure but actually a bit of a demon.

Tarkovsky was a youth in the war years, and the pressure of that history hangs over his films. In *Stalker* (1979), the hero wanders in a rural wasteland that seems postapocalyptic. And in his last film, *The Sacrifice* (1986), the idyllic household of an elderly artist and his family is suddenly threatened by the rush of inexplicable aircraft in the sky. Ever since Guernica, a low-flying plane can be as frightening as a pointed gun.

I DID NOT MEAN TO BE INTIMIDATING WHEN I SAID TOO FEW OF US UNDERstand enough about the war in Russia. Nor was I trying to one-up the rest of the world in its suffering or its contemplation of the dungeon in our culture. But warriors—those who have served, and those who dream of it from armchairs—need to grasp the enormity of the Russian war, not just in proper respect for that much abused country, but as a sighting of our worst instincts and behavior. The war in Russia had appalling casualties, but maybe the worst of all was the damage to the collective soul. If you have not known occupation or its approach, that can be so difficult to imagine.

So I'll end this long chapter with a great and pitiless film, even if it has some problems.

Larisa Shepitko's *The Ascent* (1977) is not merely a war film. It is a Dostoyevskian debate on conscience and betrayal. More than that, it is a film about snow and every metaphor that waits in the cold. It also glories in controlled and rigorous close-ups that put it in a category with the work of Carl Dreyer and Ingmar Bergman.

In black and white (how else can snow be looked at?), *The Ascent* begins with a moaning wind, scenes of desolate snowscape, half-buried telegraph crosses, and then the chatter of machine guns. We are in Belarus in the age of *Casablanca*, an area that lost a quarter of its population during the war.

We are with two partisans, Sotnikov and Rybak, who are struggling through the snow to avoid German soldiers and find some food. Rybak is tough, but weak; Sotnikov is gentler, as much a pilgrim as a soldier. A German patrol sees them and there is a long-range shooting engagement. Sotnikov is wounded and one German is killed. The partisans find shelter in the house of a headman who helps the Germans, and then with a widow and her three children.

All too soon, the partisans are arrested by a platoon of Germans, and put under the interrogation of Portnov, a Russian schoolteacher who has since collaborated with the German occupation. A very ugly situation is in view: the partisans and anyone who seems to have helped them—like the widowed mother—are going to be executed. But in the Nazi protocol, that power must be exerted first through interrogation. That is where Portnov enters into a struggle of will with the partisans. Not that there is any hint of useful information that could be extracted from them. Torture exists for its own sake, and as the armor that Portnov needs to shelter himself from his own guilt.

Portnov may be the most odious and frightening character in this book. And it's hard to say why without accusing the actor. He is thin, unhealthy-looking; he is shabby and nearly bald so he sometimes wears a hat; but his face looms in the film—it is as if he knows the camera is silently aware of his wretched sins and the betrayal of a Russian who is doing this, to survive, to pick up scraps of privilege and insecure company on the edge of Nazi culture, and to exist in his special evil. He is the most deeply felt character in the film, despicable but seductive. So it is important to say that this very bad-looking man, so thoroughly infected by war's compromise, is played by a friend and colleague of Larisa Shepitko, Anatoly Solonitsyn, who was also a leading player in several Tarkovsky films.

He was a great actor (who died young of cancer), and he helps us see that *The Ascent* is an autopsy on the evil that attends collaboration. Is it rash to suggest that any American actor in such a part would betray the ruin in the character with a glow of self-love? Our actors have led sheltered lives. Here is a film made out of an experience of war that cannot shrug off those things or settle for the pluck and fellowship of movie stars. But the film is an ascent, and that may be where the problem begins. Sotnikov is as beautiful a face as Portnov's stands for corruption. It is hard to avoid the feeling that he is Christlike (the actor is Boris Plotnikov, in his first film), and Shepitko gives us a series of rapturous close-ups in which his still, unblinking face radiates light and iconic resignation.

Yes, he is brave (he endures the pain of being branded on his chest with a star-shaped iron). But he is saintly, too, for he has accommodated his predicament in a code of acceptance and spiritual inspiration. He is ascending in a film that inhabits degradation. This is done with utter conviction in both the actor and the director, but it risks seeming heavy-handed when the tenor of *The Ascent* is simply crushing. As spectators, we have been branded by the burning cold—and the film was shot in actual winter, way below zero, so that the severity of the weather and its glare are decor for the parable.

Portnov wants to humiliate the fineness in Sotnikov, to have him see that anyone can succumb to torture and the threat of power. There is no safe citadel in the soul; all its ground has been mined. That is what war and its movies are about once the garden-party exuberance of Dunkirk and even D-Day has been reassessed. Portnov is desperate to hear this imprisoned Christ admit to the failure of humanity. His wickedness depends on it.

The function of the war, and the concentration on its Russian version, is to expose the failure of human conscience, and the jeopardized integrity of the spirit. And in *The Ascent*, that hope stands bravely under the gravest threat of Portnov staring into the camera and our potential. Never mind the flaw; *The Ascent* is a masterpiece. Shepitko, who was thirty-nine at the time (she would die two years later in a car crash), said she could not continue to live without making the film. There may be a vein of dramatics in that, but if we have never had such a test, then we can admit the duress in making a film like *The Ascent* under continued Soviet autocracy when Brezhnev was in charge and Portnovs prowled the corridors in ministries of culture.

So we are out there in the gripping freeze, looking back at the insidious face of Portnov offering cheap vodka if we'll come in from the cold. War provides archives of images of piled corpses, of cities in agony, and of that dazzling light in the sky that the illuminated Jim in *Empire of the Sun* cannot identify yet as Hiroshima. But the haggard, cruel, yet beseeching face of Portnov may be the most disturbing of them all.

War is ruin in the human face, the decay that starts before death. And like a wild creature—the bear mixed in with monstrosity—it was seen first, or reported, in Russia.

So now we have the fresh catastrophes of Ukraine, and Russian behavior—seemingly as cruel as it is irrational—that leaves the West begging to be involved, or waiting for insurrection in Moscow. But are we falling for the "nastiness" of Putin and missing the accumulation of Russian depression? The West is not trained enough in carrying on a hopeless attitude for as long as forever. We want the movie to end.

There are other Russian films on their war—a new *Stalingrad* (2013), and Elem Klimov's *Come and See* (1976)—done in an uneasy mix of self-pity and boasting. I have a different recommendation: as well as the movies, play Shostakovich's 10th Symphony (premiered in 1953). This is a dainty, haunting record of the composer's fear and humiliation under Stalin in those years, exultant yet defeated, a shattering imprint of the Russian ordeal. When you've listened to that music for a few years, go to an extraordinary but nearly forgotten movie, *Testimony* (1988), made by Tony Palmer with the writer David Rudkin. It is a story of Shostakovich's life, with Ben Kingsley in the lead. At 157 minutes, it is a surreal epic that tolerates no prim verdicts about art redeeming the wreckage we leave behind us. Hear that music coming across the night steppes outside.

You see, between 1939 and 1945 we rehearsed the end of the world. And I think we established that we are good at it.

IV

POST-TRAUMATIC STRESS DISORDER

When war becomes climatic there is no need to declare it.

27

THE LOOK ON RYAN'S FACE

In an age of apparent peace, I began to absorb the movies, though in London then we called them the pictures or the cinema.

Of course, neither I nor my parents knew anything about the Russian war that I have just described. The general attitude about the Soviet Union was amiable and fatuous—the study of history sometimes fixes on knowledge, but it has to leave room for the things people didn't know and the myths they lived by instead.

So my dad had a joke about Stalin, or Uncle Joe as he was in the story. You see, in 1947, Uncle Joe came to London on a state visit (to improve relations), and every time he thought of something he wanted to do—like seeing Laurence Olivier onstage, or inspecting the fleet at Spithead—the king, George VI, went to immense lengths to accommodate him, to maintain the hope of friendship with the Reds. Or he did until Joe asked to see Chelsea play Manchester United, soccer at its height. But that game would have to be moved from Manchester to London to suit Joe's travel plans. That's when the king (a modest man) drew the line, because he had picked the game as an away win on his football pools.

This absurd joke grew longer with every telling, probably because I was laughing so much and in love with being Dad's audience.

I didn't know who John Wayne was until my aunt took me to see *Red River* (1948), a turning point in my life because I understood how that film's relationship between Wayne and Montgomery Clift was some secret information on me and Dad. I didn't realize that Wayne had been unusually hard and severe in that Western, and so I had no sense of the reasoning in having him play Sergeant Stryker in *Sands of Iwo Jima* (1949). But I was fascinated by this fearsome yet admirable sergeant, and I knew the example referred to my dad. The people we like on the screen tell us so much about ourselves.

It had to be explained to me what Iwo Jima was, and why, and though I could see that this Stryker was pretending to be a bastard, leaning heavily on his young soldiers, teaching them to suffer in silence and behave the marine way, I could handle it because I knew that Stryker and Wayne were both actors, putting on a show. And doing it pretty well.

I never knew that Wayne had been nominated for the Oscar in *Sands of Iwo Jima*: I had no awareness of those awards. But I understood that his bristling toughie had a heart like mashed potato. That was there in the scene where Stryker, on leave, goes to a bar to get drunk and he picks up a bar girl for . . . well, maybe mashed potato, what did I know at eight? So she takes him back to her place and while she is fixing a drink he hears a sound in another room. He looks in and there is an infant in a playpen, no more than a year old, her son. And suddenly Stryker is touched or humanized. You see, he is separated from his own family and a son; he has been led away by the military life.

Then later, at the climax of the film, on Iwo Jima itself, during the assault on Mount Suribachi, Stryker is shot dead. One of his men, a guy who had hated the sergeant, takes a letter from Stryker's pocket and reads it aloud. It's a letter to the son he hasn't seen in so long, and it's an attempt to explain to the kid why Dad has not been there. But the letter is unfinished. And that pathos hangs in the air as we see a living enactment of the famous photograph where some American soldiers put up the flag on the top of Suribachi.

"That's a picture," said my dad in satisfaction. There are ways in one's cinema history where the fables on-screen were lessons for being someone's son when your dad was away.

Directed by Allan Dwan, a trusty movie veteran, *Sands of Iwo Jima* is lovely hokum, though I'm sure in 1949 most audiences took it very seriously and supposed that it was how the world had been saved. It was all filmed in California, mostly at the marine base Camp Pendleton, but it seemed to contain the wide world, or the one where marines had played the game for real. It was one of the films in the immediate postwar years that either told the stay-at-homes what service had been like, or got them primed for the next war if Uncle Joe and those infernal Reds were determined to be difficult. There was *A Walk in the Sun* (1946), another film by Lewis Milestone; *Battleground* (1949), directed by William Wellman; and *Twelve O'Clock High* (1950), by Henry King.

I can see they are worthy films, living up to patriotic expectations, crowd-pleasers, full of good-looking guys in uniform, helmeted with guns, cracking wise and being characters, but talking and thinking the way sportsmen still talk in live locker-room interviews, running through the clichés of victory and teamwork and one game after another before they've had a shower. If you look at films like that, buttered with message, it's easier to comprehend the unguarded innocence that was still active in 1945.

So as a kid I was not taken to see *Crossfire* or *Act of Violence*. You can argue that neither of those is a war film, but you're walking into a trap. They are films about what soldiering has done to men. And they are too tricky for easy comfort.

Crossfire (1947) opens with a man being beaten to death. A police detective is called in to investigate, played by Robert Young. He interviews a soldier, Montgomery, played by Robert Ryan. And it looks as if the killing involves a group of demobilized soldiers waiting to be released. Montgomery is ingratiating, it seems, but disconcerting. The more he talks, the less you like him. Another soldier, a sergeant (Robert Mitchum), gets in on the investigation and he doesn't seem to trust Montgomery. As written by John Paxton, from a novel, *The Brick Foxhole*, by Richard Brooks, and directed by Edward Dmytryk, this is a famous film noir, shot in lustrous shadows.

Nothing underlines this, but the subtext becomes clear: that there is unappeased violence and buried hostility in these soldiers, so much more interesting than the white lies about togetherness. The man who was murdered was Jewish, and it becomes clear that Montgomery is anti-Semitic. That was not a common topic in postwar movies, but it has softened up the novel for theatrical consumption. In the book, the murder is prompted by hatred of homosexuality.

Mitchum is very good as a cool, laconic sergeant; his presence was a nod to his impact in a supporting role as an exhausted lieutenant in *The Story of G.I. Joe* (1945). Robert Young is steady and phlegmatic, less a real person than a role model. But Robert Ryan as Montgomery seethes with unsettled business. He was nominated as best supporting actor, but lost to Edmund Gwenn playing Kris Kringle in *Miracle on 34th Street*. See *Crossfire* today and Ryan is as present as someone vaguely dangerous who starts up a conversation with you, one you didn't ask for, where you can feel the needle itching to sew. There was no mashed potato in Robert Ryan.

One didn't have long to wait to see more of him. Two years after *Crossfire*, he was the menacing figure who knows the real truth in *Act of Violence* (discussed in chapter 11). It was odd. He was a good-looking man, tall, dark and athletic, an eloquent actor. He had a forthright voice, but it creaked sometimes. Somehow he ended up playing men we had reason not to like or trust. How is it that some players have a look that doesn't quite fit the popular stereotypes? I never met Ryan, but I have known two of his children and talked with them about their father. They both feel they didn't entirely know him. There was something uneasy in him, and he lasts so well now because of that psychological mystery. Films then preferred to believe we understood our parents, but contemporary experience has introduced doubt.

Ryan was not easily cast as heroes, though there's every sign that he was a decent and liberal man. That sort of amiability was not evident in his face. So there he is in Black Rock, waiting for Spencer Tracy, trying to guard the desert's wicked secret. *Bad Day at Black Rock* (1955) is another movie without a battle scene, or anyone in uniform. But it tells you much more about a winning side than Black Rock wants you to know.

A locomotive roars across the colored desert: it might be California or Nevada. We see heat and distance, fluffy clouds in the blue over mountains. Then the train stops at a tiny depot where most trains never pause. This stopping is arranged so that John Macreedy can get off at Black Rock. He is close to fifty; he wears a dark city suit and a hat; he seems what you might call sedentary, and he has lost an arm. He is Spencer Tracy, and it would be a different film if he was Bogart or Gary Cooper because those actors had earned a screen reputation for handling themselves. Can you think of a movie fight in which Tracy had been involved?

He has come to Black Rock in search of a man named Komoko, a Japanese. The few people in the town are hostile or reluctant to talk—a host of great supporting actors: Dean Jagger; Walter Brennan; Russell Collins; and Robert Ryan, who plays Reno Smith, a rancher who runs this wretched place. There's no good reason to live there, or to understand why Ryan keeps Lee Marvin and Ernest Borgnine as his thugs. Unless he's insecure. Black Rock closes ranks against Macreedy. And Ryan gives us the look of a solitary, smart and sardonic, but bleak and scared, someone who can smell trouble and will bring it down himself just to have an advantage. He has a woman (Anne Francis), but he admits no affection or need for her.

Macreedy discovers that Komoko's homestead is burned to the ground, and he realizes that Komoko is no longer alive. Not just sent to an internment camp, like Manzanar, but eliminated. Macreedy lost his arm fighting in Italy and he has come to Black Rock to deliver the medal that Komoko's son earned in saving Macreedy's life.

That is the outline for a thriller in which Macreedy learns that Komoko was murdered out of racist loathing. The film begins in unexplained waiting, but it gets into fierce action and some rather unlikely judo skills from Spencer Tracy, enough to flatten Ernest Borgnine. Such things amount to a stretch, but *Bad Day at Black Rock* is a sun-drenched noir in

CinemaScope that reveals a mean-spirited and paranoid hinterland. This is after the end of the war, but we are being asked to cross-examine so many of the principles handed down to us about the fair society pledged to a just conflict.

You will have guessed, without seeing the film, that the one-armed man does defeat the malignant forces in the ghost town, including Robert Ryan. Maybe Black Rock will be all right then, or maybe without wickedness it will simply vanish, like a pond in the desert. But as ever there was something in Ryan the actor that warned us, *Take care, I will not be as easy to remove as Hollywood pictures want you to think.*

28

IN ALGIERS

Already in 1945 it was clear that while the just war might be officially concluded, the uncertain weather of armed standoff would go on. And the movies would ride along in that overcast, hoping to seem at ease.

In September 1939, Great Britain had gone to war to protect Poland from Nazi ambitions. Six years later, with "peace" declared and distributed, Poland was under the control of another tyrant. In time, the Polish war would be rendered in a trilogy of stirring films made by Andrzej Wajda—*A Generation* (1955), *Kanal* (1957), and *Ashes and Diamonds* (1958). In the postwar era, no films so dealt with the betrayal of Eastern Europe and the ordeal of being occupied. Little wonder that the trilogy was tinged with fatalistic irony as well as the dank horror of fighting in the sewers beneath a Warsaw that the Soviets declined to assist.

In 1945, no one said we must go to war for Poland again, we cannot let that country down. But in the long, slow span of what we called Cold War, the shortfall in history and justice could not be forgotten. The real implication of Cold War was that the hostility or the opposition might last a lifetime. When the war in Vietnam occurred, whether labeled as the Vietnam War or the American war, there was no need to have it formally declared. War was there in the air, as constant as weather. The alleged disorder had become habit. Under the blind eye of Cold War there would be furious engagements and pitiless hatred in Palestine, in Malaya, in Korea, in Kenya, in Iran, in Hungary, in Cyprus, in Ireland, in Cuba, in India, in what had been the Balkans once, in all the parts of the Middle East, in Afghanistan, and in Vietnam. Plus all the other police actions, including those we've never quite heard of.

Like Algeria. That was a kingdom with splendid ruins— Carthaginian, Roman, Berber, Spanish, Ottoman—and the debris of its French annexation. From the 1830s onward France had held Algeria as an overseas territory, and many French people had gone to live there, the *pieds-noirs*. There would be a time when the French were 20 percent of the population of Algeria, and a higher fraction in the city of Algiers. But the Arab population grew restless during the war years, and there were modest massacres to keep them subdued in 1945. The opposition to French rule was centered on the FLN, the Front de Libération Nationale, and its insurgency mounted in the postwar years. By the early 1950s, there was something so like a civil war in process that a movie had to follow.

The Battle of Algiers (1966) is an essential event in this history. I'm not sure it is as great a film as its supporters claim, but its influence is beyond question, for it became, whether it intended this or not, an educational model for insurgent change. Yet it was not made by Algerians. The director, Gillo Pontecorvo, was Italian and Jewish and wealthy. His older brother Bruno was a nuclear physicist who had defected to the Soviet Union. Gillo had gone to Paris in 1938 and he had survived as a tennis instructor, and then as a communist in the Italian resistance to the Nazis. He was so impressed by the neorealist pictures of Roberto Rossellini that he decided on a movie career, and in 1960 he directed *Kapo*, in which Susan Strasberg plays a teenager in a German concentration camp.

Kapo is a good, conventional liberal weepie, almost what might have happened to Anne Frank. It was scripted by Franco Solinas, also Italian, and he and Pontecorvo then agreed to make a film about the insurrection in Algiers.

And it was written and directed, even though in 1966, and ever afterward it has been mistaken for a documentary, or even a rough assemblage of newsreel footage. So part of its originality as a movie is not just telling a revolutionary story, but trading on the ways in which a film's honesty can be misread.

The film is in journeyman black and white: the picturesque possibilities of the Casbah and the Mediterranean are rejected. The mise-en-scène of several sequences is awkward or disjointed, as if only fragments had survived, leaving a problem of fluency. There is nothing like a straight story line, just a series of dated incidents going from 1952 to 1962, thrown together as if in the expectation that we know what happened in Algiers sufficiently to put it all in order.

Then there is the matter of the people. One cannot watch *The Battle of Algiers* without being entranced by its faces. These range from the shriveled features of a gaunt wreck who has been tortured until he talks, to the resolute and confident Colonel Mathieu in charge of the French forces, to Ali La Pointe, the young, handsome insurrectionary, illiterate but determined. Ali is one of the great faces in movie and he is Brahim Haggiag, overwhelming in his first film (though he would make several more). But he was typical of Pontecorvo's casting and his search for striking faces on the streets of Algiers good enough or not too shy to play a big part in a film. The only professional actor in the picture was Jean Martin, who played Mathieu. He had been a member of the French Resistance and then he had served in Indochina. He had also played Lucky in *Waiting for Godot* onstage.

The male faces could be by Daumier or Goya. But then there is a sequence where two young Arab women are assigned to carry bombs to cafés where they will explode at a busy time of day as French teenagers are dancing to a jukebox. These are terrorist outrages in which we are complicit. And the film, like the FLN, chooses pretty women. For the FLN guesses that French soldiers will not stop and search these women because they are so attractive, and because the naive soldiers are too gallant. So they flirt with the women but let them pass unexamined, and thus the bombs are delivered to slaughter unwitting civilians. But the "actresses" flirt with the camera, too, as if they might be Mireille Balin in *Pepe le Moko* (1937), that romantic classic set in the Casbah.

Is it real? On the soundtrack, the ululation of Islamic women is surely authentic, but the insistent drumming, by Pierino Munari, was designed by Pontecorvo, and his composer—none other than Ennio Morricone, who had just done *A Fistful of Dollars* for Sergio Leone. Is it cinema when the Algiers filmed is the real place, or when the hundreds of extras in crowd scenes probably lived through some of the atrocities and demonstrations the film depicts?

In 1966 (with Vietnam underway) *The Battle of Algiers* stopped moviegoers in their tracks. It won the Golden Lion at Venice and it was nominated for the Oscar for best foreign picture (it lost to Claude Lelouch's *A Man and a Woman*). And it was banned in France for five years. It was studied by revolutionary movements all over the world as a kind of training manual. There are many who say it is among the greatest films ever made, that it is inspiring and moving, and like history written in lightning, the remark President Woodrow Wilson is supposed to have made on seeing *The Birth of a Nation* in 1915. (That remark is unproven, but there are documents to record the president's high enthusiasm for the film's celebration of the Ku Klux Klan.) Presidents of Wilson's era believed they were there to rescue the world (or the special take on the world held by their class), but we have realized how, in the past century, another job description has emerged for these personages, that of saying memorable things on television.

Wilson might have known better, and we may now look at *The Battle of Algiers* as the onset of a humbling confusion over the reality or reliability of what we are seeing. Of course, the film was made after the Algerian war, in a time when its result was settled, and aimed at an audience that was generally comfortable with that result. The film could not have been made or shown in the 1950s when Algeria was in the balance. What that means is that countless war films have an imprimatur whereby the outcome of the war is reinforced by the stance of justice we have picked up, allied to a feeling that the institution of cinema stands firm behind the meaning of the story. For example, you can't tease yourself that *1917* and *Dunkirk* are not going to work out OK. Our sitting there safe in the dark implies that everything is going to be all right. The desperation has been undermined by the entertainment of it all. Anne Frank wasn't able to watch *Casablanca*. But major movie corporations pick battles or campaigns over which they can feel good.

Post-traumatic stress disorder supposes that a dire "it" is over and that it left damage from which there may be recovery or adjustment. "All right" may return. But don't we know now that the stress is a resident, not a visitor? Too many things are not going to be all right. Must Ukraine go on, and on . . . ?

So remember the point about a new climate of disorder where warfare carries on regardless of formal political decisions. Do we need to be reminded that Algiers did not emerge as a paradise just because the French elected to leave? In that ongoing vexation, it becomes increasingly necessary to study the texture of film closely if one is not to be swept away in the melodrama. From *Casablanca* to *The Battle of Algiers*, that heady thrill had told us not to worry over the truth or the future of what is happening.

But worry is in our order now, and it carries distrust.

29

THE OTHER SIDE

The onslaught of war movies, as reassessed in a historical overview, reminds us that most of the films were made by the winning side—or by nations that reckoned they were winners. After all, it took serious money to make a comprehensive battle film, even if the investment in celluloid might be deemed frivolous instead of putting it in bricks and mortar, the surgery of facial reconstruction, or attempts to explain the moral indecency in what had transpired.

Still, in the two decades after 1945, it was possible in art house movie theaters in winning nations to get an inkling of the other side's experience. There could be danger in making such films, because sides are not stable or locked in place. When Wajda's trilogy was shown, Poland was still within or beyond the Iron Curtain, with rigid codes of correctness. Its liberty was yet to come. On *Ashes and Diamonds*, at least, set in May 1945, the picture had to tread carefully so as not to offend any regime or influence that might take over the "liberated" Poland (and was still in power in 1958). That's how France resisted *Paths of Glory* at first and then *Army of Shadows* later.

For decades it was not possible to undermine your own country's version of its military glory. *The Life and Death of Colonel Blimp* had run into difficulties because it believed so much in the friendship between an

English soldier and a German. Even as late as Brad Pitt's *Fury*, there is that moment when the young German soldier faces our Norman, hiding beneath his crippled tank, and simply passes on, as if to say what is the point in killing one more of the enemy when enmity is close to being reappraised. We have to let history bring in its fresh harvest of understanding. So years after the sprightly satire of *Oh! What a Lovely War*, Richard Attenborough directed *A Bridge Too Far*, as if soaring on wartime enthusiasm, and ignorance.

Late in September 1944, when it was reasonable to see an approaching conclusion to the war in Europe, there was an airborne invasion in the Netherlands in which 35,000 men (British, American, and Polish) would be parachuted behind enemy lines with a view to breaking into Germany itself to advance on Berlin. This was called Operation Market Garden (as if the British war effort was modest and artisanal), and later in Britain it would become known as "Arnhem," where nearly 7,000 British troops were taken prisoner. You see, Arnhem was a failure, in part because it was too ambitious and too casual about the quality of German opposition, but also because it was a managerial calamity.

But some operations and some movies acquire a wind at their backs. So the producer Joseph Levine put together some $25 million with agreed distribution by United Artists. He gathered gliders and parachutes, uniforms and equipment that would satisfy military buffs. And he assembled a cast that includes Dirk Bogarde, James Caan, Michael Caine, Sean Connery, Elliott Gould, Edward Fox, Anthony Hopkins, Gene Hackman, Ryan O'Neal, Robert Redford, Maximilian Schell, Laurence Olivier, and Liv Ullmann—it is almost simpler to say who wasn't in the film.

The picture delivered value for money. At just under three hours, it was competently made when it must have been as laborious and scary to hold together as the original military mission. The audience more or less lived up to its role in the venture: they could feel it was a big picture about a "recent" historical event. Though the war was thirty years old by the time the film opened. And it seemed more important to identify the stars than understand the fuckup that lay behind "Arnhem." Attenborough did not cheat his subject, or the Cornelius Ryan book on which it was based. But there was a feeling that we were exhausted and a little skeptical before the show began, and rather weary of the way Maximilian Schell (Austrian originally, then Swiss) could be brought in to play a fierce German commander and stand in for the other side.

A fine actor, with smooth English, Schell was "our" Nazi in several films: he was the suicidal officer in *The Young Lions*, the defense counsel in *Judgment at Nuremberg* (he got an Oscar for that), the victor at Arnhem, an SS camp commandant in *The Odessa File*, and then he would be the mad, driven commander in Sam Peckinpah's *Cross of Iron*. Later still (1992), he played Lenin in a TV epic, *Stalin*, where Uncle Joe was . . . Robert Duvall. Schell won a Golden Globe for supporting actor. These matters are like playing solitaire with old cards.

When it comes to movies made by the other side, we are not well endowed. In Germany during the war there were strident propaganda films about the war and escapist romances. We can sneer in advance, without having seen many of those; a similar verdict could be passed on Hollywood in the same era. So films like *Objective, Burma!* and *Bataan* competed with a golden age of comedies that declined to admit the concurrence of war: *The Shop Around the Corner*, *The Lady Eve*, *His Girl Friday*. How frivolous Hollywood was. And how we long for that spirit to return. It was an achievement of American civilization in those war years that it made sublime screwball comedies that refused to see the battle.

There are some exceptions. Hans Detlef Sierck had been born in Hamburg in 1900, to Danish parents. He became a notable theater director who broke into the German picture business in the 1930s. He made some very good films, like *Schlussakkord* (1936), *Zu Neuen Ufern* (1937), and *La Habanera* (1937), the latter two with Zarah Leander, a Swedish actress-singer who became a star in Germany and retreated to Sweden in 1943, and was sometimes attacked for collaboration. But in 1940, he was invited to Hollywood, and by 1942 he was directing *Hitler's Madman*, where John Carradine plays Heydrich. You have to land on your feet. And hope the ground stays firm beneath you.

This was the start of a very successful Hollywood career, mostly at Universal, where Douglas Sirk directed romances, what were called women's pictures—*All That Heaven Allows, Written on the Wind*—and where he helped build the career of Rock Hudson. It was at Universal in 1957 that he made *A Time to Love and a Time to Die*. It came from yet another novel by Erich Maria Remarque (whose *All Quiet on the Western Front* had been a Universal classic). It's the story of a young German soldier fighting on the Russian front. He comes back to Berlin on leave, meets a girl, and falls in love. They marry, and their honeymoon is marred by the ruins of their city as Allied attacks build. (It was shot in Germany, but with art direction re-creating the debris.) Then the man has to go back to the eastern front. He has a change of heart: he sets free some Russian resistance fighters. In turn he is killed by those same partisans. Just like the young hero in *All Quiet on the Western Front*, he cannot sustain hope for the future. Sirk noted that *A Time* did badly in Germany: "They couldn't allow a refugee to give any kind of an interpretation of what life was like in Germany during the war. . . . Everyone was full of self-pity."

It may not seem encouraging that Sirk cast John Gavin as the soldier, and the Swiss actress, Lilo Pulver, as his girl. In addition, the film is in color and CinemaScope, which may not seem ideal for the shattered settings. But it is a touching film, with a well-earned love story and a sense of tragedy—it has Remarque and a young Klaus Kinski in its supporting cast.

Sirk's film had its admirers, notably Jean-Luc Godard and Rainer Werner Fassbinder. It did well enough in 1957 and it is a far better film than *The Young Lions*, which came a year later, with Marlon Brando as a disillusioned German officer and Montgomery Clift as a Jewish soldier abused by his fellow Americans. Gavin and Pulver are too well-fed, and too pretty as the lovers. They come nowhere near the desperate, unbelieving passion of the lead players in *Cold War* (2018), a masterpiece by Pawel Pawlikowski made in Poland, and an unrelenting description of how modern war and occupation have done fatal damage to the sacred hope of romance. Hot war destroys bodies, but cold war has suppressed so much of their vitality. In Pawlikowski's black-and-white picture, worked out over a course of fifteen years, in bliss, separation, and chill, war is an overcast that edges two lovers toward suicide.

Those two films are over sixty years apart, and while this author saw both of them as they opened, he appreciates the minority status that gives him. So is it relevant or just inanely academic to itemize pictures made from the Axis side?

Many people feel awkward over "Nazi" films, or movies ready to examine the cruel mind. This is all the stranger since so many movies feed on cruelty. But some viewers remain uneasy over the insinuating stealth of Liliana Cavani's *The Night Porter* (1974), where a one-time prisoner (Charlotte Rampling) reawakens to her erotic bond with a Gestapo officer (Dirk Bogarde) long after the war has ended. There remains a reluctance to admit how good and disturbing the film is. As if movie isn't made to help us study forbidden states.

As if we are not duty-bound with cinema to face its commitment to fantasy. It is part of the medium's being enthralled by the act of firing that it adores power itself—the heartless command over helpless beholding, and its concomitant: that damage is only a spectacle. So *The Night Porter* admits the erotics in torture and control, and our being horrified at that is not an adequate response to the film's degree of pornography. The sight of Rampling naked but for the mocking traces of a Gestapo outfit cannot be shrugged off or politely disapproved of. I think we need to face the sinister stylishness of the Nazi uniforms and its cult of black leather—those Germans did "costume," that cinematic reconstruction of reality. That remark might seem callous and facetious, or a disgrace, but in 2023 we can look around our world and see the enduring appeal of Nazi regalia. If that is the devil's work we may begin to recognize Satan's complexity. How do we revel in evil? How can that affect our moral progress? Are we the good guys or the other side?

But *The Night Porter* can be seen still. It's so much harder to find *Die Verlorene* (1951), directed by and starring Peter Lorre, who had once made himself available for a German masterpiece, Fritz Lang's *M* (1931). History esteems that picture but has forgotten *Die Verlorene* (*The Lost One*), where he plays a Nazi doctor who has been driven mad by the medical experiments he was expected to conduct for the Reich. Moviegoers have schizophrenic attitudes to madness: it can be a vehicle for great acting or comic exaggeration; or it can be a metaphor for our attraction to very bad things. Peter Lorre the actor was a victim of his brilliance. He could never shrug off the "appeal" of his helpless child murderer in *M*. And I think *Die Verlorene* (a failure in its time) was his attempt to reconcile his own tormented kindness and his reputation for horror.

Sometimes you could not tell one side from another. Roberto Rossellini is a great director (or he was when such judgments meant anything), but he was a heartfelt opportunist (much like a camera, maybe). In the late thirties and early forties, he could have been mistaken as being aligned with Italian fascist filmmaking, at least a conformist. But as war ended, so in the cheapskate filming methods that would be dignified as neorealism, he launched a different career with a series of astonishing pictures.

Rome, Open City was intended as a portrait of different Italian lives in the last days of Nazi occupation. It has a world in which the Gestapo will use any means of torture and extortion to identify members of the Resistance. Filming began not long after the Germans abandoned Rome, and for decades there was a fond legend about how the picture had been made with odd ends and scraps of celluloid. But few pictures have been made without publicity, and in fact it was made from regular film stock. On the other hand, there is no questioning the firsthand experience of several participants. One can't deny or forget the superb mise-en-scène of the passage where Anna Magnani (Rossellini's mistress) is shot down in the street. Rossellini had a big influence on films like *The Battle of Algiers*, and he talked about the authenticity of neorealism as if it might save the world. But authenticity in war is a moveable feast or a bullet that fits many guns.

A better film, or one that cannot be made comfortable, is *Germany Year Zero* (1948), shot in a devastated Berlin, and centering on a twelve-year-old boy who is deranged from the repercussions of war. He has a family to help, but help devolves into prostitution, stealing, and general corruption.

There are neo-Nazis in the wings, and it's worth noting how far another film made at much the same time—*The Third Man* (1949)—manages to romanticize Vienna just as Rossellini has no doubts about the hell left in Berlin. Of course, the zero situation is all the more crushing in that a child is the central character and a suicide in the making (the film was dedicated to Rossellini's own son, Romano, who had died aged eight in 1946).

Rossellini was by 1948 embarked on his notorious affair with Ingrid Bergman, a scandal steeped in irony, for just as she wished to enjoy the creative truthfulness of European film, he longed to get his share of the decadence of the Hollywood she wanted to quit. That passion came and went (and it deserves its own movie). It was 1959, before Rossellini made his finest war film, *Il Generale Della Rovere*.

This is set in Genoa in 1944, with the Nazis trying to eradicate the Italian Resistance. They enlist a small-time crook to impersonate General Della Rovere, a Resistance hero. As such, the crook (played by Vittorio De Sica) enters a prison to infiltrate its Resistance element. But the pretending takes over, and De Sica's character falls in love with the task of acting until he becomes a brother to the fighter he had set out to uncover. It's a stretch to call it a comedy, but aren't a lot of our finest comedies poised on the brink of disaster? Think of Lubitsch's *To Be or Not to Be*, where a company of actors becomes embroiled with the "comic" figure of "concentration camp Ehrhardt." If Germany had won the war (and nothing was too certain in 1942), the courage in Lubitsch's humor would have become fatally apparent.

THE MOST COMPLEX OTHER SIDE IN FILM HISTORY MAY BE THE JAPANESE participation in the Second World War. There are some of us who might say, too quickly, that this is a matter of "Kwai and Kurosawa," an archaic landmark and the most famous Japanese director outside Japan. We've discussed the David Lean epic, and now something has to be said about Akira Kurosawa, if only because he did so much to make us think we understood the grace of samurai prowess. There are plenty of people still who would say that *Seven Samurai* (1954) is the greatest combat film they've ever seen, as seven freelance ronin defend a Japanese farming village against bandit raids.

Why should being a grand master of cinema (and "the greatest Asian of the twentieth century," as one poll estimated) stop the genius of Kurosawa being as opportunistic as Roberto Rossellini, or nearly any other movie director? He was born in Tokyo in 1910 into a family with samurai roots. His father was in charge of physical education in the military. Working first as a painter, Kurosawa shifted toward the film business in the years when Japan was taking on predatory (or apprehensive) attitudes to much of the world. It is a measure of the young man's balance or shrewdness that he did not serve in the military, but developed his movie career. He made what came his way—action films and such profound modern-dress dramas as *Drunken Angel*, and *Ikiru*, or *Living*, the story of a humble bureaucrat who learns he is dying of cancer and resists despair by supporting a children's playground.

But Kurosawa was ambitious and well aware that the exotic aspects of Japanese culture appealed to the West. He made *Rashomon* (1950), a period film, involving contradictory reports of a single story coming from a woodcutter, a samurai, his wife, and a rascal bandit (played with panache by Toshiro Mifune). *Rashomon* won the Golden Lion at Venice, and it was so artful a mix of Western irony (you can't really trust anyone) and Japanese pictorialism from the sixteenth century that it became an emblem of foreign product in art house theaters for the postwar era.

It was also the launch for *Seven Samurai*, a very Japanese film, except that it was the work of a director who loved American Westerns and was as much captivated by the sweep of a sword and the brio of a man on horseback as John Ford or Anthony Mann, essential directors of Westerns. There is a moment in *Seven Samurai* when Kyuzo, the most dedicated and artistic samurai, dispatches an enemy with a sword stroke and the shot goes into exquisite slow motion. This is among the most influential stylistic choices in all battle films. Again, Mifune dominated the cast as a reckless braggart who is not really a samurai, but who gets in on their magnificent act—remember, the Hollywood remake, *The Magnificent Seven*, was only six years away.

That link was not incidental. The rapport between samurai and gunslinger was easily made, and there were Western actors who made a hobby or a fascination out of the samurai code. That reached from Steve McQueen to Steven Seagal, and it prompted Tom Cruise to make *The Last Samurai* (2003), where he is a US cavalry officer who goes to train the Japanese Imperial Army. In 1967, Jean-Pierre Melville wanted to make a film he would call *Le Samourai*, in which his notion of Japanese impassivity and martial splendor would be passed on to an assassin in the French underworld. He proposed this role to Alain Delon; he outlined his sense of how a samurai felt. Whereupon Delon, without a word, motioned Melville to accompany him to a private room in his house. It was a sanctum for the actor's collection of samurai armor and swords.

AT THE CLOSE OF THE SECOND WORLD WAR, THE JAPANESE IMPERIAL ARMY numbered five million. That was one reason why the United States thought to drop its atom bomb, to avert the carnage of a land invasion. But Japan had lost well over two million soldiers. (As a reminder, in all the war, in Asia and Europe, the US lost just over 400,000. Yet again, the war meant different things for different combatants.) But it was America that fought that Pacific war with grievance (something that has not entirely gone away) because of the foul play of Pearl Harbor, something still regarded as part of the Japanese readiness for cruelty and treachery. I think it's plain that the Germans were more cruel (as if they were making a horror film), but they were white and Western, and we should wonder how far that has aided our forgiveness. It is a part of this interpretation that the Japanese—especially their fliers—were prone to "kamikaze" attacks, essentially a suicidal gesture. Seppuku was part of the samurai code: ritual self-immolation when only honor is left. There is a touch of that in the way the young Japanese pilot takes off on a fatal last mission at the end of *Empire of the Sun*, when Japanese defeat is certain.

That character is too poetic for the run of Pacific war films. In 1970 an epic appeared, resolutely old-fashioned, and still trading on anti-Japanese instincts. *Tora! Tora! Tora!* was a saga of the Pearl Harbor attack. And if the word in its title (meaning "tiger") suggested a Japanese point of view, those three exclamation marks were the assurance of action for armchair soldiers and fliers. Kurosawa had been intended as codirector by producer Darryl Zanuck, but the master was "difficult" with the Americans, aloof and demanding: He designed a *Tora!* cap and jacket for all crew to wear—with formal salutes being exchanged. In the end, he "helped" on the screenplay, and two other Japanese directors were there to assist the Hollywood pro, Richard Fleischer. James Whitmore played Admiral Halsey, and So Yamamura was Admiral Yamamoto. The film was full of exciting aerial footage, and it endeavored to cover the diplomatic moves prior to the attack. But it was no more than a board game ending on Yamamoto's warning: "I fear all we have done is to awaken a sleeping giant and fill him with a terrible resolve." As if that wise commander had always known not to mess with us. It was intriguing to see that *Tora!* did rather better with Japanese audiences than with Americans.

Toshiro Mifune was more evident in world cinema: he would play Yamamoto in *Midway* (1976)—that was his third outing with the admiral, after two Japanese films. By then, he was as regular an "enemy" actor as Maximilian Schell. He and Kurosawa had had the sense to exploit the gold mine opened up in *Seven Samurai*. In the following years, they made a run of films together in which Mifune was some kind of warrior in period clothes—as the Macbeth figure in *Throne of Blood*, then *The Hidden Fortress*, *Yojimbo*, *Sanjuro*, and *Red Beard*. They were a franchise, and there's no harm in that.

But out of the blue, another director had cast Mifune in a startling, surreal, and very beautiful comedy of the Pacific war. John Boorman made *Hell in the Pacific* in 1968. We are on a desert island in the war, but it feels crowded. Two soldiers have survived whatever chaos afflicted the area: an American (Lee Marvin) and Mifune's Japanese. They share no language except that of strenuous, expressionistic acting out, and the energy battling to control a landscape. They are unbridled animals, until some simple air of comradeship or bereft fellowship settles on them.

It was shot in the Rock Islands of Palau near the Philippines and filmed by Conrad Hall, who was a master of Pacific light. Marvin had himself been badly wounded in wartime service with the marines at Saipan, and Mifune had been attached to an air unit if not involved in combat. It is the movie that comes closest to my whimsical idea of a modern pentathlon principle—an Olympiad where a single man represents his country and engages with little but cunning and physical endeavor against a man from another country. "Hell" in the Pacific is the expected commercial title for this venture, but the secret grace of the film is in coming close to heaven, too, in its understanding that some boys just have to be boys. One of the functions of official war is to accommodate that youthful limitation and play it for fun. *Hell in the Pacific* lost money, whereas *Midway* earned ten times what it had cost.

Those films from the years 1968 to 1976 may mean more than chance. We are coming up to the crisis of Vietnam, and we should be wary over how uncommon opposition to that war was. There was a spirit in America, and in Hollywood, that was resolved to overlook the bitter facts of Vietnam and the possibility that America might have suffered a loss there. Propaganda can operate without any conscious assumption of that burden. One might break in on the set narrative patterns of *Tora!* or *Midway* by crosscutting its achievements with footage of missteps and calamity from Vietnam. That juxtaposition would make it clearer how the cultural engines of a nation are so often desperate to think well of themselves. And how eagerly audiences leap at that opportunity.

Two other epics deserve attention. In 2005–6, with Steven Spielberg as a fellow producer, Clint Eastwood made back-to-back films: *Flags of Our Fathers* and *Letters from Iwo Jima*. The design was to have the first film a reflection on those soldiers who had raised the American flag at Iwo Jima as if rehearsing for a monument, and then in the companion piece to explore the anguish of Japanese soldiers on the island, living in caves and tunnels as their defeat became more certain. They are both well done, and yet I wondered at the time if the "good idea" in the project, and its refreshing openness to how the Japanese felt, was truly felt, or was it just a high concept of the kind that has often preoccupied Spielberg and Eastwood. Clint is an ideal example of the director as a producer: he intends to get his projects done and banked. But we stay uncertain as to his need, his passion, or even his soul.

Flags of Our Fathers flopped when it seemed nearly un-American to not see the film and salute it. *Letters from Iwo Jima* did better, especially in Japan. Ken Watanabe plays the Japanese commander on Iwo Jima, speaking in Japanese, and he kills himself finally in the dishonor of defeat. *Letters* is a good film, so much so that we have to recognize how far big Hollywood pictures have declined since 2006. If you look at it again, there is the unnerving feeling that this kind of epic cannot work again. Iwo Jima's action needs to be the basis for a video game in which the digital figures sustain the bleak truth—that we don't quite care about them. (Yes, there *are* several video games that use the real battle.)

Those two Eastwood films (made when he was seventy-five) are one epic. The other is something you likely have never heard about—as if there have been wars beyond our alertness. In the years 1959–61, to be blunt about it, there was a work called *The Human Condition*, directed by Masaki Kobayashi. It is three separate films to describe one man and the helpless unfolding of events in his part of the world in the distress of the Second World War. The whole work runs over nine and a half hours, and you may not have anticipated a marathon at this stage of the game, especially one you had never heard of. It is rather as if, in your lifetime, getting to know your neighborhood—a reasonably comfortable, manageable place—you woke up to discover that an immense, unmapped desert lay just over your horizon.

Kaji is an ordinary man, with a wife, a Japanese who faces the onset of war as a challenge to his socialistic humanism. He would prefer to have no part in battle; he would want to lead a calm, good life with his wife. You know that feeling, and the hope that any mindless war is passing by—like driving accidents. To avoid becoming a soldier, he goes with his wife to Manchuria.

You have to know where that was, and what it was. It is 600,000 square miles (bigger than France and Spain together) on the Asian mainland, to the north of Japan, placed awkwardly between what they like to call Russia and China, to maintain some sense of control. It is not exactly samurai territory. Indeed, the romance of chivalry is so hard to find in Manchuria it seems beside the point. It was in 1931 that Japan moved into Manchuria and claimed it as living space and a source of necessary natural materials. This was one of the key invasive episodes in the onset of the Second World War, not least because its crisis proved beyond the inept but well-intentioned reach of the League of Nations, part of the gestures after 1918 that had wanted to say "no more war."

In Manchuria, Kaji is an official in a labor camp for Chinese prisoners, captured and brutalized in the Japanese effort to own and rule Manchuria. Kaji tries to resist this Japanese pressure, so he is identified by the controlling police as a troublemaker or not properly Japanese. He is himself brutalized, beaten, and tortured; he is so un-Japanese that he is ordered to join the Japanese army.

It is felt that Kaji is a communist, and so he is abused and mistreated by his own army. He is an outcast in his own society, and we perceive him as a good man, trying to stand for humane principles. We want him to survive or endure. But Japan is losing the war in its momentous struggle in the Pacific islands. There is a great battle with the Soviet army, a time of slaughter, and the plight of refugees. Let us call it the horror of being displaced.

Kaji is one of those refugees, on the road, except that roads are hard to discern. He and a few fellows are victimized by fascist elements of the Japanese army. They are hounded by the Soviets, and then they run foul of Chinese forces who are obsessed with their own prospect of a Chinese revolution. They want to join Chiang Kai-shek. The chaos is beyond individual understanding—and it is likely that in your history studies you have acquired a very vague and restricted grasp of what happened there then. You owe it to yourself to find useful maps and coherent histories of the era, though you should keep it in mind that coherence can be publicity. This ordeal may come again.

If you are a film buff, you might think of contrasting the naive martial splendor of the Kurosawa movies with the compassionate yet pitiless degradation that is the material of *The Human Condition*. Prowess, honor, and purpose have little agency in this desperate landscape. You can tell already that its story will not end well for Kaji or the world, and yet some veneer of achievement and respectability has been drawn over the ferment of Russia, Manchuria, and China. No war can ever believe that battle has settled the remorseless antagonisms in our condition. So war deserves to be seen as the working model of our forlorn selfishness and our endless failure to make history decent.

The three films opened and played. They won prizes and they had a stunned, respectful audience in Japan, even if Kobayashi was often written off as being "a communist." The trilogy (that term is an attempt at tidy placement) offers no easy way out. You watch it, or you don't. You can make admiring comments about the humanity or the commitment of Tatsuya Nakadai as Kaji. You may observe how in the steady context of an apocalypse, Kobayashi has an eye and an ear and a fondness for "nature"—the devastated places of the action. You can take it on and then tell yourself that you have made it all the way across the desert. You can tell yourself that these actions occurred a long time ago—so that things must be different now, and ready for tourism, with appealing hotels above the burial grounds (not that bodies were adequately buried as opposed to being left to sink back into nature).

I don't think you will ever have a chance to see the three pictures on a large theater screen. But you can purchase the set of DVDs from Criterion for about $40, or stream it. You may come to the conclusion that this is not just the "best" war film, but one of the greatest films ever made.

Critics and historians stumble into that kind of verdict, like people lost in a desert and coming upon a well. Let me just say that the experience of *The Human Condition* is so immense that you may feel inclined to give up watching movies and take a rain check on the next sumptuous display of swordsmanship. But if the critic in me urges you to see *The Human Condition*—nine and a half hours, relentless and dismaying—the historian knows the great work is sixty years old now, and close to being buried. Will you go away and see it, or file it as the past? I'm not sure that Kobayashi's masterpiece can be remembered any more than we maintain daily grief about the losses in the Thirty Years' War or the bitter matter of Jenkins's ear. Some great movies are as phantom yet as awesome as a country railway station as the express hurtles through, loaded with passengers and purposes, but not stopping, not waiting, and guessing its passionate line will soon be abandoned.

"I shook in the wind of that train, Grandad!" But your grandfather is gone. We are two figures at the end of a desolate platform.

There are movies that leave us wistful or ashamed over taking shelter in the screen. Or in deciding, as Americans, that the Vietnam War (next on our screening schedule) was a major event, a lasting wound for America et cetera. Instead of a trivial, vivid exercise. Wasn't that misguided adventure always a movie, and a distraction from our condition?

30

'NAM

We have slippery moments in which experience becomes history—or oblivion—or a movie. So it is that *Casablanca* now stands for the Second World War, not just a lie or a mockery, but a travesty of any hope that we might be in charge of our history, instead of bodies hoping to surf a tsunami. Surfing is important in this chapter; it's a pattern or an energy. Just try to reconcile the fact that Victor Laszlo getting out of Burbank's North Africa coincided with trainloads arriving at Auschwitz. "Mind the gap," a kapo calls out in the dawn fog. Doesn't Victor say he had been in a camp himself?

As I set out on this project, I foresaw at the least a solid, extensive chapter on Vietnam, that well-known modern tragedy, still burned into the American conscience. But then I realized that the United States was out of Vietnam by 1975, and that was forty-eight years ago, long enough for my grandchildren, say, to feel the word "'Nam" was emphatic yet mysterious, and losing its impact as time passed. It is not quite well-known now; it's a word that hints at forgetfulness creeping in. I'm not sure that "Nazi," "the camps," or "Hiroshima" can maintain their currency. Does "Gestapo" mean what it used to? And my grandchildren had a great-grandfather who lived two years in the trenches on the western front, and whose reluctant stories about being there began to reveal how seldom he had ever talked about it. When I shared some of his stories with his daughter, my wife, she said she had never heard them before. The real experience of war may rest in the stories survivors don't want to talk about.

As if anyone can really trust, let alone be in receipt of, "well-known."

By contrast, there is something boastful or cocksure in American movies about Vietnam. In many of those most celebrated pictures, there was a proud air, as if to say, now, the story and the truth can be told, along with the horror and the shame. Nearly every film regretted Vietnam, but *The Deer Hunter*, *Apocalypse Now*, and *Platoon* (all significant event movies) had something of the aplomb with which warriors might show off their scars and make jokes about how they do and don't match their medals. For a generation of filmmakers not short on arrogance or self-dramatization, Vietnam was a peak in their personal emotional arc so compelling or necessary it hardly mattered if the storytellers had never been there.

That is not an accusation; it's simply part of the history of attitudes. But in early 2021, it should be added that our "war" with Covid-19 was sometimes killing five thousand people a day. And that rate was the equivalent of just eleven or twelve days of Vietnam, where America lost 58,000 people over the years, or the period that went from discreet advising to tipping those helicopters off the ships. Isn't that one of the clinching sardonic images of 'Nam, the ending you might have foreseen if black comedy was your thing?

For years, that 58,000 was recited in shocked regard, an emblem of classic American mistake as well as suffering and waste. But usually without the footnote that the South Vietnamese dead may have numbered 700,000, while the losses in the North, or among the Vietcong and their civilian sympathizers, were at least another 700,000 dead. You appreciate that these are round numbers.

WHERE DOES ONE BEGIN? I'D LIKE TO PROPOSE A MOVIE THAT I HAVE NEVER been able to find, but I think it has enormous potential and great appeal for that American appetite for tales about underdogs making good. It could be as winning as "To the Finland Station." This story has a young man from Indochina. He is about twenty-one in 1912, educated, intelligent, and beginning to be radicalized in his feelings against the French colonial control of his country. He wants to see the world. He becomes a ship's cook and sails to France and even to America. In the years of the Great War he works in London hotels as a chef. In the tense decades ahead, he can still conjure up a soufflé or stories about dim sum.

He is watching and learning all the time. Then in the 1920s, he pursues his political education in the Soviet Union and China. I hope you will not be disconcerted by this, but he is drawn to the ideals in communism, as if he can find no other advancement for his Indochina. He marries a Chinese woman. Then in 1941—he is past fifty by now—he goes back to what he calls Vietnam, to oppose or take advantage of the Japanese occupation, and to fight for independence. In that capacity, he gains the support and collaboration of the United States Office of Strategic Services, which is as anxious as he is to overcome the hateful Japanese. As that war ended, he became provisional chairman of a provisional government of Vietnam. He petitioned President Truman for support, but America had become alarmed at radicalism in Indochina when starvation and exploitation had been working fine. America staked its hopes on a restored French government resisting any threat of communism.

Our guy is a likable fellow and his followers sometimes speak of him as "Uncle Ho." Yes, he's Ho Chi Minh, and one would have thought that in a culture of heroic perseverance and achievement, someone would have thought of doing the Ho Chi Minh story as a kind of Spartacus.

That's right, you have been Spartacus in your dreams, and for the moment you can tolerate the risk of being with a red under the bed. Just concentrate on the bed, the locus of dreaming.

Is this imagined wave too wild? With Paul Muni as Uncle Ho? Hadn't he played Chinese in *The Good Earth* in 1937?

Here's another scenario not much less preposterous, but this 1957 film really was made. It was called *China Gate*, written and directed by Samuel Fuller, who never saw or heard of a war without having his creative antennae agitated. This is the plot. We meet a woman, Eurasian, named Lucky Legs, and she is played by Angie Dickinson. She has had an affair with an American mercenary in Indochina, Brock (Gene Barry), who is working for the French army. She has had his son, but Brock rejected them both when he saw that the boy had Asiatic features. However, Lucky Legs is persuaded to help on a war mission. She is to infiltrate the Viet Minh organization of Major Cham (Lee Van Cleef)—a previous lover—to destroy his munitions arsenal. In return Lucky Legs and her son may get to America.

I won't tell you the rest of the story because you might not believe it, and I think you should seek out the movie for yourself. I know, it sounds ridiculous, but it is actually an intriguing story and one that might be remade with advantage. The West screwing the Vietnamese is a plotline with a long history. And while *China Gate* is haphazard or deranged in many ways, it is also a pleasant surprise because of Fuller's dynamic storytelling, his respect for mixed-race relationships, and the crazy casting—I have held back this extra, that Brock has a buddy (they were in Korea together), Goldie, played by Nat King Cole, who can therefore give the picture a title song.

China Gate is casual with its facts. The French control of Indochina had been folded up in 1954, with the siege and the eventual surrender of the French garrison at Dien Bien Phu, a demoralizing event for French military pride but a signal of the future in that a peasant army had overwhelmed a modern, weaponized force. Talk about a wave. Those guys in pajamas and sun hats may have been singing, as they marched, "From the halls of Montezuma to the shores of Tripoli," the marine hymn to music by Offenbach, but learned from a 1951 movie, *Halls of Montezuma*— everyone loved American pictures then.

The Viet Minh had made their way over mountains and through jungle, dragging their antique field guns, in a way that had been beyond French strategizing. People fighting for their homeland have many advantages over professional armies that have traveled thousands of miles on a wave of racial superiority and military condescension. Home field is usually a plus, even if the team will have to fertilize the ground with so many of its dead.

A year after *China Gate*, a film was made of Graham Greene's novel *The Quiet American* (published in 1955). The book is so discerning it had to be overlooked in the 1950s: most American policy-makers, had they read it, would have put their maps of Southeast Asia aside, and played bridge instead of dominoes. It has a Greene protagonist, Fowler, a middle-aged journalist who has been assigned to Saigon by his London newspaper. He has a local mistress, Phuong, eager to be married. But Fowler has a wife, thousands of miles away. Then he encounters the American, Pyle, who is working undercover for American intelligence, granted that that institution is short on its titular faculty. Pyle believes American insight can tidy up Indochina, make it safe and positive. It's a program that depends on ignorance and an absence of irony. The Harvard graduate relies on theory and sincerity and Fowler cannot disillusion him. Phuong now gravitates toward the American. He is certain that America can direct Vietnam. But in the political intrigue of Saigon, Pyle ends up getting killed. Fowler, the eternal cynic, is left to observe the future. His wife in England has agreed to divorce him. Phuong can get her marriage now— "Her excited mouth skated over my face," writes Greene.

The Hollywood movie of *The Quiet American* (1958) was written and directed by Joseph L. Mankiewicz, who was as out of his depth as Pyle. That high-minded idiot was played by the real-life war hero Audie Murphy—it needed the earnest righteousness of a Montgomery Clift. Fowler was Michael Redgrave, the Italian actress Giorgia Moll was Phuong, and there was a cynical French police inspector played by Claude Dauphin, as French influence lingered in corrupt Saigon, where no one expected to be trusted. The film is inept but the novel is still sourly accurate on Western self-deception, and it has a tense sequence where Fowler goes up-country and gets involved in guerrilla action. (There is a remake, from 2002, far closer to the book, directed by Phillip Noyce, with Michael Caine as Fowler and Brendan Fraser as Pyle. At least it cast a Vietnamese, Do Thi Hai Yen, as Phuong.) Neither film flourished, illustrating the handicap in war films that seek to explore the errors in allowing war, instead of satisfying your audience's wish for lively action.

If only America had been more attentive to French experience in Southeast Asia. On the ground and on the screen. In 1965, there had been a film, *La 317ème Section*, directed by Pierre Schoendoerffer and derived from a novel he had written. He had gone to Indochina in 1951 as a cameraman, and on that basis he had joined the garrison at Dien Bien Phu and been taken prisoner by the Viet Minh. *La 317ème Section* was shot with a tiny crew in Cambodia, with Raoul Coutard as its cinematographer, and it was about a group of Laotian soldiers, with French officers, striving to reach Dien Bien Phu. The military historian Antony Beevor has called it "the greatest war film ever made," and it is not without an eye for heroics and combat spectacle. But it is driven by its understanding of a native sense of Indochina and of how the French complacency assured their defeat.

It is filled with respect for that new phrase in the fifties, "guerrilla warfare," which came from the Spanish word *guerra* in a diminutive form, and respect for how ordinary Spaniards had harried the set lines of the Napoleonic invasion with tactics that were not quite fair or conventional—civilian combatants, going without benefit of uniform, ambush, sabotage, hit-and-run, living off the land, cutthroat amateurism, and the overall insight that the only war known to man is total, so throw out the notions of formal conduct and Geneva Conventions. Schoendoerffer and Greene were alike in their belief that if you feel yourself on the brink of war, you need to know as much as possible about the facts of the situation; so skip the theories, for they are the origin of fog.

The *317ème* never played in the United States, but two years later, Schoendoerffer's *The Anderson Platoon* won the Oscar for best documentary. Moreover, its "Anderson" was a black lieutenant out of West Point, to that time maybe the most impressive black soldier to appear on American screens. As a detailed, unvarnished account of search-and-destroy patrols in Vietnam, *The Anderson Platoon* would have a big influence on television coverage of the war. It was photojournalism loosely strung together, the banal mixed in with the desperate, but it was a kind of record not much seen before. It made clear how confusing a trial it was for raw soldiers, meeting Vietnamese in the fields who might be helpless onlookers or patient enemies. The American forces had radiotelephones, and the recommended language for such technology, but you could tell from their harrowed voices that they were lost. And so they said "affirmative that" to everything, like children in the dark calling out to mother. For an hour, the film showed us the input-playback of service, but never asked why these very young men had come so far. It was clear there was no answer. The war could not pass as just or seemly simply because the United States had ordered it. A movie seemed like an executed plan, a mission achieved, but the inner truth was the chaos being ignored.

FOR A TIME, THERE WERE SO FEW AMERICAN VIETNAM FILMS, AS IF HOLLY-wood was worried that the audience was afraid of the subject. The business that makes regular hay out of fabricated fear learned long ago to avoid the wounds of real anxiety.

War on-screen was forbidden for the years in which it reigned, no matter that it was occupying so much time on television newscasts, and in color from the middle of the sixties, with the red and the green adding to the anguish of President Lyndon Johnson. Then in 1968, the year of the Tet Offensive, the My Lai massacre, and the president's decision not to run again, along came John Wayne and *The Green Berets*, anathema to liberals and most critics, but so fully endorsed at the box office that we have to recognize it was in the mainstream, or that diminishing trickle in which Americana and Hollywood still believed they were parts of a unified flow.

The passion in *The Green Berets* was not the war in Vietnam, it was the bitter struggle building in America between the theory of American greatness and power and the seeping realities of confusion and self-criticism. You can say it was a war between the right and the left, between ex cathedra and on the streets. It was also the Duke denying the tremors of deception and indecision in a country trying to face facts. Wayne despised gooks and slants, of course, but his burning animus was directed at Americans who were unhappy with America. That war goes on still, far from cold or open to compromise. The flag of the Confederacy carried through the Capitol on January 6, 2021, was not just in honor of ancient treason, but proof of conflicts that have never been settled.

John Wayne was fifty-nine in 1966, and if he was past his best, a graver problem was that his picture business had lost confidence in itself. He was an immense, archaic screen presence, a monument to insecure confidence, unaware how bogus he was looking to young eyes. He had stood for Hollywood's Old West in John Ford's *The Man Who Shot Liberty Valance* (1962), an awkward gathering of old-timers for a movie proud to approve legend instead of crediting fact, and the last time the upright Wayne could be heroic without facing derision from the audience.

For three decades, he had been his own mesa on-screen, surmounting his hypocrisy: for he had steadfastly resisted service during the Second World War, and then he had won an Oscar nomination as that immense, fierce sergeant in *Sands of Iwo Jima* (1949). He had done great work—*Red River* and *The Searchers*—under the guidance of Howard Hawks and John Ford. But he had become an unashamed believer in what official America told him. He was no fan of Lyndon Johnson, but he had gone to Saigon in 1966, taken a quick look at the war and the "affirmative" chorus, and believed in the Green Berets. Why not? They were as smart, brave, and efficient as any formal military unit on earth. Kennedy had done so much to approve this new force. But their virtues could be undone by guerrilla warfare and peasants with old rifles. How was the Duke to know this when he had been formed by a generation of films in which he was the hero, telling others not to apologize because it was a sign of weakness, and shooting down rogues like Liberty Valance?

He liked the Berets because they did what they did with expertise and seldom asked why they were doing it. That is a recipe for both fighting a war and making a movie. Warner Bros. funded *The Green Berets* (it was a studio film, not a vanity project like Wayne's *The Alamo* from 1960), and they stressed more action, less talk, because in *The Alamo* Wayne had turned dreamy and garrulous over the theory of a Republic. So *The Green Berets* involved Wayne (as Colonel Mike Kirby) not just leading the Berets but teaching a critical journalist (David Janssen) to appreciate his boys. It was always a throwback, and it's well enough made if you take its epic self-love on its own terms. Critics deplored it and said it was absurdly comic. That's really not fair: the failure in the film only emerges if you insist on questioning the purpose and morality of the action. But that is undermining a mainstay of Hollywood in which Wayne had been raised: let action tell the story—or set aside the deeper strains of meaning within the story. The dogged and unforgivable impulse of *The Green Berets* is repeated—with far greater force—decades later in *We Were Soldiers* (2002), which deserves consideration as both a triumph of combat and the most deplorable Vietnam picture ever made, not least in the affirmation that its title relieves us from the job of being thinking human beings.

The small, indignant vocal culture of America regarded *The Green Berets* as a disgrace, but then for the best part of ten years there was no American picture that chose to treat Vietnam in a critical spirit close to Norman Mailer's existential protest in his novel *Why Are We in Vietnam?* That book was published in 1967, and its story involved a young man about to hunt bear in Alaska. The tale is told by that son of a wealthy, domineering father who chooses to hunt with the aid of a helicopter. The son becomes thoroughly disenchanted, but he is himself headed for Vietnam. It's hard to think this novel didn't weigh on the minds of those who made *The Deer Hunter* as a coming-of-age parable.

There were not even Vietnam movies, no matter that the years from 1967 onward mark a new independence in young American filmmakers and a willingness to be critical of their society. This was an era ushered in by *Bonnie and Clyde*, *The Graduate*, and *Easy Rider*, and no one on those very successful movies had dared to serve in Vietnam, or in the armed forces. There were a few exceptions. I have already mentioned the novelty of *Rolling Thunder* (1977), and proper credit should go to the documentary *Hearts and Minds* (1974), directed by Peter Davis and coproduced by Bert Schneider, who had been part of the BBS production team that made *Easy Rider*, *The Last Picture Show*, and *Five Easy Pieces*. In that last film (opening in 1970), Jack Nicholson is a self-conscious outcast against America, but he is not a broken vet back from Vietnam (like Travis Bickle in *Taxi Driver*).

In the films of that very creative era, Robert Altman's *M*A*S*H* (1970) was an artful use of the Korean War to remind viewers of Vietnam. Altman had flown many bomber missions from 1943 onward in the Pacific. He had seen blood and bureaucracy. *M*A*S*H* spoofed military discipline but it did not risk a complete dismantling of the code of the army. As written by Ring Lardner Jr., the film is mocking of the military ethos, but it never challenges the nation's involvement in Korea (nor is it interested in Koreans). Instead, we see two phlegmatic field unit surgeons, Donald Sutherland and Elliott Gould, wisecracking their way through blood and bandages, mavericks who remain attached to the herd while doing humane work.

Not that films of the early seventies were without combat or urban battle. It's not going too far to suggest that the Corleones in the first two parts of *The Godfather* are a small, intense army against all comers in our criminal society. They are very good with guns and all other weapons; they believe in loyalty and strategy and they worship their commanders. Just as much as *The Green Berets* or *We Were Soldiers*, these films adhere to a code in which soldiers do what they have to do, for brotherhood, even if it comes down to having a brother assassinated. Michael Corleone was a marine in the Second World War; that was his training ground for the real struggle for power. And those films were the work of Francis Coppola, who had a Vietnam picture to come, but not just yet.

Directors like Coppola, Bob Rafelson (he had done army service in Japan), Scorsese, Spielberg, Hal Ashby, and Peter Bogdanovich were indignant over Vietnam as much as they were in favor of new liberties with sex and so many other things, including their own careers. But they were not quick to make angry pictures about the war most of them had avoided. Was that their caution, or just the business feeling that the public was not ready yet for pain and loss or something deeper than American glory? The question is more pressing in that during the Second World War, Hollywood was making combat films from the starting gun. There would be a rush of post-Vietnam films, and they coincide with the years that followed Watergate and Nixon's resignation, the most complete collapse of the political right until that time, just as a new president, Jimmy Carter, pardoned those who had avoided the draft by going to Canada or other havens.

All the more credit to the film that headed the rush of Vietnam pictures, and which is still one of the most searching and aware critiques of America's war so far away. I refer to *Go Tell the Spartans* (1978), directed by Ted Post, written by Wendell Mayes, from the novel *Incident at Muc Wa* by Daniel Ford, produced by Allan F. Bodoh and Mitchell Cannold, and motivated by Burt Lancaster, the film's star actor. Post sent the script to Lancaster, who liked it so much he agreed to make it, despite his being in recovery from a serious knee injury—that is evident throughout the film. What does not show is that Lancaster contributed $150,000 to the budget after the film had run out of money.

Lancaster plays Major Asa Barker, a veteran of the Second World War and Korea, a man who has been passed over for higher promotion because of a reckless sexual affair with a senior officer's wife. The limp Lancaster brought to the film fits very well with Barker's weariness. But this is only 1964, and Barker is chief in a group of American advisers trying to sustain the South Vietnamese army. Lancaster's history adds a little here. In *From Here to Eternity* he had played Sergeant Warden, who regards the army as a corrupt bureaucracy and handles it with sardonic equanimity. Barker is where he is because he is too old and demoralized to do anything else. It becomes clear that he is advising a course of action that he sees as self-expressive but futile. When the American army read the script they canceled all thought of helping the production, horrified at its portrait of a desolate fighting force. *Go Tell the Spartans* has no interest in the action of combat; it sees battle as the ultimate manifestation of muddle and compromise. Barker reminisces about the romance of actions from the Second World War, and battles that once seemed necessary and just.

His fellow advisers are misfits, exhausted veterans, or men only interested in making a career. They are older than the recruits of just a few years later, but they do stand for the lack of belief or commitment in troops who did not understand this war. There is a need to discover whether the Vietcong hold a nearby village. In all this, Barker has the bleak advice of Cowboy (Evan Kim), half French, half Vietnamese, who is in no doubt about the climate of treachery. He warns the Americans not to trust the villagers, not even the pretty woman who beguiles them. That advice is ignored.

The Vietcong have unexpected numbers and they overwhelm the American-ARVN contingent. Barker is killed along with all but one of his cohorts. This is 1964 (through the eyes of 1977), but the destiny of Vietnam is laid out in the film's title, which comes from a warning epitaph for three hundred men wiped out in the Battle of Thermopylae in 480 BC: "Go tell the Spartans, stranger passing by that, here, obedient to their laws, we lie." The fatalism makes it clear that this warning may never be heeded. There is so little chance of education. The mechanics of warfare—the bureaucracy and its profits (evident here in corruption in the South Vietnamese command)—will ride over every consideration.

Go Tell the Spartans was respectfully reviewed; it has become a modest cult film; but it is nowhere near as well known as the gaudier Vietnam pictures that won Oscars. Still, it remains exemplary as a pitiless survey of an insane, inept, and criminal incursion on history. You cannot trust that culture to know or acclaim its best movies.

What is lasting in *Go Tell the Spartans* is its hangdog air of dismay, the refusal to fall for ideas about the American soldier being brave or admirable, and the complete suspicion over any way of boosting the Vietnam project. No wonder the army wanted nothing to do with its depressive reappraisal of heroism overseas.

This makes an astonishing contrast with *The Deer Hunter*, which won five Oscars and made a lot of money, and has not the least interest in Vietnam except as a background for the existential melodrama of far-fetched American icons. It is also a quite uncannily affecting film, even if it owes more to a Dostoyevskian tradition of character than to the realities of Southeast Asia. This is about Americans who go to war to find themselves. An intellectual luxury.

This project originated in chaos, also known as greed, egotism, and lies. No one now knows for sure what happened. But Louis Garfinkle and Quinn Redeker had done a script about guys who went to Las Vegas to play Russian roulette. Word of this reached the production company EMI in London, and they managed to get Michael Cimino interested—he had just directed a Clint Eastwood project, *Thunderbolt and Lightfoot*, and turned in an effective genre picture, no more and no less. Someone—it may have been Cimino—thought of transposing the Vegas story to Vietnam. But EMI was convinced that no one wanted to see Vietnam on-screen—this was in the midseventies. Then Cimino got together with Deric Washburn, and gradually a script emerged that gave hints of the final film. Cimino and his producer and girlfriend Joann Carelli dumped Washburn, but then to most people's surprise, EMI gave it all the go-ahead. You cannot count on commanders being sane or businesslike.

The characters were moved around like chess pieces in an end game. It all seemed unlikely until they emerged as Robert De Niro, Christopher Walken, and John Savage, three steelworkers from Pennsylvania who stop work one night, have Savage's Russian wedding next day, go deer hunting in the mountains, and then they're not just in Vietnam, but confined in a water cage and about to play roulette for keeps. No matter that in 1978, the year this extravaganza was released, De Niro and Walken were thirty-five and Savage twenty-nine—far from the age at which kids were being drafted off to Southeast Asia. And it is said that these boys have enlisted.

It feels like a war put on for big actors trying to be characters in some epic novel, as much Russian as Vietnamese. There is no interest in the country or the issue of the war. No one ever accused the North Vietnamese of having a taste for Russian roulette—but the motif was always there as a measure of how adventurous men gamble with life, or some such nonsense. The deer hunt is not a big sequence, but it places De Niro's character in the cockpit of Hemingway and James Fenimore Cooper.

I think this accounting of the film is fair, and I hope it's off-putting. But the experience is more complicated. Cimino had strains of liar and charlatan, and he was a sweet-faced manipulator. (In publicizing the film, he made the false claim of having served in the Green Berets. This was so stupid you feel he must have believed in his fantasy.)

But he had an immense talent, unruly and pretentious, of the kind that sees his own mind as the world and as a dome where movie is being constantly projected. But there are marvels to take account of: the rendering of the dismal Pennsylvania town; the prolonged wedding sequence, with the guys exuberant in a bar, boozing, shooting pool, and singing until the sudden appearance of a harsh army sergeant who assures them war is no game; the blooming presence of a young Meryl Streep, who was allowed to build her own part. To say nothing of the episodes in Vietnam, or what is meant as hell, the suspense of the roulette scenes; and the unequivocal tragedy of Nicky's effective suicide—which is so tautly done, explanation is forgotten, unless the actor sees an Oscar in his gloom? How can a film be so trashy and yet momentous? It's a strange American achievement, made out of a mad romantic arrogance, not far from the visionary blindness that allowed Vietnam to occur.

The Deer Hunter won Oscars for best picture, best director, and for best editing and sound. And Christopher Walken did win for supporting actor. The film earned a lot of money even if some vets were howling at the screen in the confusion of pain and rage. But in the American urge for gratification and attention, *The Deer Hunter* allowed some people to assume that Vietnam had been handled, while others felt it had been trashed by America's yearning for melodramatic glory. It did leave a sense that the war's essential purpose and meaning was to test American heroes. There was fighting at the awards ceremony between the winners' entourage and veterans groups who felt the film was a lie. But Vietnam vets rarely got a fair shake.

Decades later, the film is as muddled and confounding as ever, lurching from deeply felt passages that hardly activate a story line to desperate attempts to wind it up and package it as a signal cultural event. The movie stars seem older than ever; the Americans in Vietnam are white, drunk on rhetoric, posing against horizons and backdrops. The film is so regrettable yet so capable of moving us. Its bravado can only end in self-pity and a lack of interest in the Vietnamese. At the last tableau, with damaged survivors gathering over a halting version of "God Bless America" (a bookend to the lyrical camaraderie of "Can't Take My Eyes Off of You" earlier in the steel-town bar), there is every sense that the nation has lost more than the war or its god. *The Deer Hunter* is a broken, pretentious opera in which implausibility and gesture cannot shrug off the wounds of true feeling. But it is an essential war movie, proof of the madness required in such enterprises. It leaves one with the feeling that Cimino felt a great idiotic vanity (or duty) to deal with Vietnam, and a terrible weakness for seeing it as his own existential fable—instead of a wondering how the world might end.

That rueful verdict is just as applicable to Francis Coppola's *Apocalypse Now* (1979). The cocksure "Now" is incriminating and part of the habit of tragic heroes ready to believe their local demise must bring the whole show to an end. What would Coppola do after the two austere parts of *The Godfather*, and the desolate loneliness of *The Conversation* (in which an expert bugger goes up the river of paranoia)? He had achieved a status in the movie world and in his own imagination that required the largest possible subject. In fact, he was headed for a kind of breakdown in which his exemplary status collapsed. In a few years, he would be "ruined," nearly bankrupt and humbled by his losses. Anyone close to him felt that the downfall had begun in the idea of "going up the river," into a heart of darkness. That interpretation was borne out in *Notes*, the memoir his wife, Eleanor, wrote about the production. The film is a splendid morose pageant, full of ravishing scenes and unhindered overacting. But in hindsight it was evident that the venture had gone rogue as its director fell into the rapture of believing that making a very big picture was the equivalent of all the chaos that had conspired in Vietnam itself.

The film is crucified on the patriotic notion that the apocalypse is happening to an American creative adventurer—be he a movie director, or an ideal but disenchanted officer who has abandoned a good career to go away from it all. Thus, in advance, the apocalypse is magnified yet trivialized as something worthy of a movie star. For all the auspices of Joseph Conrad and the splashy pessimism of John Milius's original screenplay, this is a tale of dead ends for two US officers—Colonel Kurtz and Captain Willard. More or less, Kurtz has gone missing somewhere in the dense jungle of Vietnam. The film is vague about its geography. But the American command (very well embodied in G. D. Spradlin and a young Harrison Ford) is determined to find Kurtz and eliminate him with "extreme prejudice." That is the new language in which ugliness is turned transactional. Affirmative that—out.

It is also close to farce: in reality, the American forces in Southeast Asia were bad at finding anything, so there would be greater wisdom in letting Kurtz stew in the backwater he has chosen until a snake, a fever, or some jungle misadventure solves the problem. But it's a movie trope to play search and destroy, and Willard seems psychotic enough to be a perfect hunter.

Of course, he is Martin Sheen (after Harvey Keitel could not handle the role to Coppola's satisfaction), and Sheen is good at embodying Willard's numb obedience in the face of common sense. He is demoralized as the film starts. The quest is the best thing in the movie, and proof that searching is something the camera and its enveloping technology do so well. Better yet, Willard is equipped with an interior monologue, deadpan getting ready for death, that was written by Michael Herr, the author of *Dispatches* (1977), nearly as good a book about being in Vietnam as Tim O'Brien's *The Things They Carried* (1990). So the journey upriver, with a crew that has Frederic Forrest, Laurence Fishburne, Albert Hall, and Sam Bottoms, is a good portrait of the bizarre assembly of disparate Americans in the army. Note that two of the guys are black (no one was black in *The Deer Hunter*) and all of them are educationally underprivileged. With notable exceptions, the American army in Vietnam was a dumping ground for kids who had failed in the system in a variety of ways. Killing was an area where they might pass.

In *Apocalypse Now Redux* (the revision Coppola released in 2001), the patrol boat finds a haunted French plantation in the fog where Willard stops off for a fine dinner, urbane conversation, and a tryst with the widow of the house (Aurore Clément). That sounds phony, but *Redux* is aware of what Indochina was really like, including its French cultural hangover. There was a motto on the production itself, "Don't let the story get off the boat," because that could lose the narrative momentum. But I appreciate the new sense of Vietnam as a country of many moods and people. Alas, *Apocalypse* still does without Vietnamese characters. American racism was so steady many Americans did not notice it. But these films we are examining begin to suggest an uninhabited country, or one without constituency. As General William Westmoreland once noted, "the Oriental" didn't "put the same high price on life as a Westerner." In that assurance, the commander in chief (1964–68) and chief of staff (1968–72) was bewildered that his opponent, General Giap, was willing to endure such high casualties among the Vietcong.

One can see the problem in advance: great movie searches are best off if they never find what they're looking for—the sled in *Kane* is touching but trite; and a Max Factored Natalie Wood at the end of *The Searchers* does let the Comanche side down. Moreover, everyone knew in advance that Kurtz was going to be Marlon Brando, a weighty and portentous actor and still the Don in the culture of Coppola and Corleone. I don't think Francis was ever sure what his Kurtz would be like, or what he would do. He was trusting the inventiveness and the ego of Brando. But his actor turned up overweight and underprepared and so the two men sank into bitter, disorganized argument over how Kurtz could focus and conclude the narrative. A lot of that meandering doubt ended up on-screen, under the disguise of poetics or a feeling that somehow the subject had become mythological. Instead of a mess.

That's vital to the end product. Coppola was a very organized screenwriter: *The Godfather* works like a sophisticated narrative engine, with sumptuous if horrifying rituals of violence and the hypnotic nihilism of Michael. He is the commanding general going not just insane but malignant, and that is a tidier and more fascist conclusion than Coppola was ever allowed in his screenplay for *Patton*, in which the charismatic tyrant is tamed by consequences and rebuke. Kurtz had no consequences beyond our wondering what the film believed it was about and why it needed to be made. So the promised big bang does end in a whimper.

And what we remember best of all is Bill Kilgore (Robert Duvall), Lieutenant Colonel Kilgore of the Air Cavalry, stripped to the waist wearing a cavalry Stetson from old movies, encouraging his boys to find and exploit a great surfing shore. He is a sublime satirical creation, blessed by having just one emphatic scene, and a witty rendering of the links between war and tourism that have always appealed to American soldiers. Just because the United States has never been occupied doesn't prevent the itch in its guys to get "over there." Kilgore is pathologically averse to the melancholy in Kurtz and Willard, just as he is certain that his tanned barrel chest cannot be impinged on by a bullet from Charlie. He is more lyrically mad than Kurtz and more dangerous, but he has that speech that has passed into our folklore like a knife cutting a throat:

"I love the smell of napalm in the morning. . . . It smells like—victory."

He utters that last word quietly, and it may be true that gasoline and its derivatives often have a pungent, arousing smell, like gin and gunpowder. Still, it is the idea of the line, the reckless American poetry, and the lust for danger we treasure. It is a line as winning as those Clint Eastwood used to pronounce as Dirty Harry. In a film sure that the war is "wrong," Kilgore is a helpless gesture toward martial glory—and to the notion that chaos itself can be tamed by a knockout remark. That's another version of presidents summoning killer lines for TV.

It says something profound about cinema that it permits such devastating shit to be spoken and then repeated over decades. So people who were not alive in 1979 can mimic the rhythm of the line and the way Duvall stands and crouches in the attitude of a strut. Duvall was the son of a rear admiral, raised to military rules and aspirations, and I think he exulted in doing the part. It let him disown the constraint and even the depression he had endured as Tom Hagen in the *Godfather* films.

He could not be Italian there, but now he is the natural figurehead of the regiment. He is resplendent and terrifying. It's as if he might be recommending the smell of burning air in a concentration camp. But we have been taught to think of him as a brave, wild guy, a kind of gorilla who transcends the drab lack of imagination and the coded habits of so many movie military officers. Kilgore has only one brother I can think of: Colonel Nathan Jessup (Jack Nicholson), commander at Guantanamo in *A Few Good Men*, who tells a court that it can't stand the tough truths by which the military conduct themselves. And in doing so he destroys his career—in many military heroes there is that suicidal impulse.

Apocalypse Now is not averse to napalm. The planes Kilgore has called in to clear the beach for surfing drop a line of it in the trees beside the shore, and the aerial view is as lovely as fire rippling through foliage can ever be. Then there is the opening moment when we see a Rousseau jungle (it has a tiger in it, too), we hear the churn of helicopters, there is dust in the air they stir up, then Jim Morrison and the Doors (Morrison was a college-mate of Francis at UCLA) tell us, "This is the end," and the jungle erupts in all the hues of red, yellow, and orange. Erupts like cum in a pornographic movie. This is surfing on beauty. We need to say these things to understand the passion in war and how it thrills us.

Get a load of that napalm even without the smell—cinema can't do everything. It is up to us to remember the black and white imagery from 1972 of a child running naked near Trang Bang after the clinging jelly had set fire to her clothes. Nick Ut took the photo and got a Pulitzer for it.

The girl survived. Her name was Kim Phuc and now she lives in Canada. She has talked about the experience: "In the beginning I was so disabled. My neck, my arm, my hands. It was so ugly. I was not a child anymore. It was not like I was nine years old but like I'm nineteen years old and I just had so many questions at that time: 'Why me? Why am I still alive? What the purpose for my life?'"

THERE'S NO GREAT FUSS OR LAYERING ABOUT *PLATOON*: IT GOES TO THE heart of the matter with unrefined directness about cramming Vietnam into two hours. A young man, a volunteer, arrives in Vietnam and soon heads into open country near the Cambodian border, in a platoon that is itself a preoccupied battleground over which two sergeants seek to exert control. Sergeant Barnes is scarred, mean-spirited, and as ruthless as any code of survival demands. Sergeant Elias is gentler, more humorous, a druggie, a fatalist, and engaging company. Which of them will win the kid's heart and soul? There is an epic Manichaean conflict at work, like the struggle Melville's Billy Budd faces between the best ideals of the navy and his Captain Vere and the oppressive master-at-arms, Claggart.

The young man was Charlie Sheen, Barnes was Tom Berenger, Elias was Willem Dafoe. Two hours in a jungle made iridescent, spooky, and beautiful by the daring cinematographer Robert Richardson, with a heart-break score from Georges Delerue. No one in 1986 could dispute that it was a knockout, destined to win Oscars for best picture and best direction, as well as editing and sound. Berenger and Dafoe were both nominated (they lost to Michael Caine in *Hannah and Her Sisters*). But Pauline Kael was heard to say the film did feel a little overdone. It gave her a sense of being crowded or hustled.

To which the director, Oliver Stone, might have said, *Look, that's the way I am, I'm a movie director, and I was in Vietnam*. Born in 1946, Stone had dropped out of Yale in 1965 to teach English to children in Saigon. He was brave, ambitious, smart, opportunistic, amiable, and possessed by that alarming blend of sincerity and self-dramatization that has marked so many American movie directors. He had a spell in the merchant marine and then, in 1967—as it proved, a very fraught moment—he enlisted in the army and asked to serve in Vietnam. He was in the infantry there for seven months, wounded and decorated, stricken by what he had seen but inflamed about turning it into story.

Platoon is as compelling as a great football game between two outstanding teams who go down to the last play to get the win. But the contest is rather less the United States against Communism than Barnes versus Elias. And you know which side Stone is on. Barnes is hateful, cruel, a tyrant; Elias is amiable, good-natured, and democratic. Barnes shoots a village woman dead to get information. Elias is a beacon of hope.

You have a sure feeling that if Barnes was General Westmoreland, then the war would be fought with unsparing intensity: villagers of uncertain loyalty would be shot as an example to others; prisoners would be executed and tortured and the war would be like an Abu Ghraib with full stress on advantages—not just napalm, but bigger bombs to clear the hillsides and destroy the crops, even all the way to China. Isn't some commander going to inhabit the full logic of America going that far? How can we explain the disgrace of ordering young men to war and not backing them to the hilt?

That thinking was common in America and in the military command. There are still veterans who believe Vietnam could have been won and who do not grasp the principle that it was a war America could only avoid losing by not joining.

Whereas Elias would likely ask for a time-out and begin to make his way toward a peace conference, not with too much faith in it proving efficacious, but held by the drugged vision he had of seeing helicopters tipped into the ocean while desperate collaborators on the embassy roof tried to get on the last flight to leave Saigon. "Mind the gap," Elias might have joked. He was a realist. He was a good sergeant, but his smile had an insight, that the whole thing was a mistake.

You can feel from this the expert scenarist in Stone (he had written *Midnight Express* and *Scarface*), how in doing a screenplay you had to know your *conflict* and your *resolution*, according to the how-to manuals. Beyond that, Stone could bring scenes to life in those days with genuine hunger for action. He created a platoon that was mixed in race and types— the guys included Forest Whitaker, John McGinley, Francesco Quinn, Kevin Dillon, Keith David, Reggie Johnson, and even Johnny Depp. And it all functioned with suspense, fear, horror, and an exhausted realization of what it must have been like—apart from the lack of boredom. Stone did not do ennui; Hollywood regards that mood with plain, moneyed dread. *Platoon* really is a knockout, one of the essential combat films. On a first viewing it could have you trembling and in tears. Not on the second experience, but Stone understood that movies were meant to be seen once.

His commitment to Vietnam did not flag. He would go on to make *Born on the Fourth of July* (1989) with Tom Cruise tortured/exultant as paraplegic Ron Kovic. Then he made *Heaven & Earth* (1993), his least successful Vietnam film but easily the most interesting. It centers on a young Vietnamese woman, Le Ly (played by Hiep Thi Le), who is brutalized and raped by people of the North and the South until she meets and falls in love with an American marine sergeant (Tommy Lee Jones). They marry and he takes her back home to Los Angeles, but he has been so depressed by the violence of the war that their relationship breaks down. When he kills himself she returns to Vietnam to show her homeland to their children (Stone was not allowed to film there by the new Vietnam because his film was critical of the Vietcong). *Heaven & Earth* was poorly reviewed and it became a box-office flop, a lesson that America was more impressed by knockouts than pained explorations of the social reality behind a fight.

IT MAY SEEM QUIXOTIC TO ASK THE AMERICAN PICTURE BUSINESS TO make *Heaven & Earth* more than *Platoon*. It is plain sense to suggest the far-reaching consequences of a policy fixated on knock-out entertainments. So it is worth reminding ourselves that as of 2020 there were close to 1.5 million Vietnamese residing in the United States. Maybe the most far-reaching result of the war is felt in local human terms: in the Vietnamese who came to America, first as exiles or escapees, but then as citizens, businesspeople, and voters in an integrated society or one that is struggling to throw off the shackles of racism. It's worth noting that Oliver Stone's current wife is South Korean. (It's a comic aside, I think, but I notice that my underpants now are "Made in Vietnam.")

Vietnam has been a unified country for forty-five years. I don't mean to sentimentalize it or ignore its flaws and failures in the extent of freedom—but don't we suffer in similar ways in a system where power can be so much more overbearing? Southeast Asia and neighboring areas have not lived through the consequences that hawks and a president warned about. Indeed, a case can be made as an alternative domino theory, that the American agony over Vietnam set off graver, deleterious effects in our national fabric, which materialized in the years of Donald Trump.

Thus, it was disturbing, in 2002, to confront *We Were Soldiers*, written, coproduced, and directed by Randall Wallace, and starring Mel Gibson as Lieutenant Colonel Hal Moore. To be clear: It is a meticulous rendering of sustained combat in which a small band of American infantry hold off a larger force of Vietcong (it is based on the Battle of Ia Drang Valley from 1965). Much of this is hand-to-hand fighting, delivered with the highest standards of action filmmaking and its uncanny mix of horror and enthusiasm for honorable guys (on both sides) doing their deadly thing. These men are all their armies would want them to be, untouched by the pragmatic severity of a Sergeant Barnes. These soldiers say they hate war, but in our dark we long to be with them. That old recruiting trick.

The film is also built around the attitude of a credible Viet Minh officer who begins by wiping out a French patrol in 1954 on the principle that he and his men must kill the invaders until they stop coming to Vietnam. Years later, this man leads the battle against Colonel Moore in an unaltered mood of fatalism. The character, played by Don Duong, owes something to the respect America had acquired by 2002 for leaders like Le Duan and General Vo Nguyen Giap, who had led so many Vietcong campaigns, and lived to be 102.

There are valuable or folkloric elements in *We Were Soldiers*: Sam Elliott is the tough sergeant who is winningly reliable for gruff courage and enduring presence (Elliott had served in the Air National Guard at Van Nuys Airport—they were known as the Hollywood Guard). Barry Pepper is very good as a photojournalist growing up in the fury. And Madeleine Stowe is Moore's wife back home, as functionally attractive as a good rifle, organizing the delivery of telegrams telling other wives that they are widows. All of this would be decent and coherent if its Vietnam was a Pacific battlefield from the Second World War where American troops were uncritical of the decision to put them there. In 1965, most US soldiers supported the war (without wanting to be fighting it), but it's hard for a film made this much later to live in the past. So little in *We Were Soldiers* seemed aware of how misguided the film's central mission was. This was being offered up to the public in 2002 (in the age of Homeland Security and the new war in Afghanistan). And it was consumed with relish. The film took in over $100 million at the domestic box office. Though the zest of combat had been undercut in *Platoon* and *Apocalypse Now*, that energy was back in full force, without doubt or reservation. Nineteen sixty-five had been reheated for a different mood, and so it seemed dishonest.

That was twenty years ago. Should we expect another similarly narrowly focused account of combat in Vietnam? Or are those energies now given over to fantasies in which the dead Vietnamese have been replaced by computer-generated casualties? Sam Elliott is so adorable you want to take him home, but truly he has been manufactured by some automatic scenario in which he tops all the emphatic sergeants we have ever known on-screen, from John Wayne in *Sands of Iwo Jima* to Lee Ermey in *Full Metal Jacket*.

We have a few offsetting movies that take shelter in the discipline of documentary. That is too important to pass over. Surely it is vital for a humane and intelligent society to record what it has done and why, in a documentary spirit? Surely it is a path to disaster to determine that the romance of fiction is the proper way to do history, whether the result is *We Were Soldiers* or *Casablanca*. Both films are superbly made, and catastrophes for history.

As a society on the brink of survival, we should hope that wars are decided on and carried out by informed people working in defiance of nearly everything they have ever learned. In the final crisis in Afghanistan, in 2021, it was a mockery to say America was being prompted by Intelligence. Nearly every intel input at its disposal was mistaken.

Those policy-makers are more important than the warriors, yet our cinema has persistently neglected them. In 1963, George Englund made a strange, well-intentioned movie, *The Ugly American*, in which Marlon Brando played the US ambassador in a fictitious Asian country who aligns initially with the imminent conflict between communism and democracy but then comes to recognize the greater complexities within that formula. It is a bad film, and its commercial failure seemed to discourage any further attention on ambassadors, advisers, government officers, and those civilians who sign off on the slaughter. But they can't teach us more than soldiers.

Robert Strange McNamara was born in San Francisco in 1916. Having graduated from UC Berkeley and Harvard Business School, he served in the Army Air Forces during the Second World War; he rose to lieutenant colonel in the Office of Statistical Control; he was an administrator of war, part of the new managerial attitude to battle. Thereafter he was hired by the Ford Motor Company, where he was renowned for his introduction of new business control systems that made Ford more profitable and efficient. He pioneered computers and spreadsheets, as part of a scientific approach to business activity. He also pushed for the seat belt. He was often described as the kind of executive who could make management work rationally and productively.

He had just become president of Ford when President Kennedy asked him to be secretary of defense in January 1961 (he was offered Defense or the Treasury, and chose the former). It seemed like an enlightened move, in part because while he was highly regarded as a technocrat, McNamara was liked as a man and gave ample evidence of fairness and decency. To be anything else was to risk inefficiency. He was a Republican appointed by a Democratic president, but that was taken as a measure of his rational approach and his dedication to sheer competence more than partisan feelings.

And so, under Presidents Kennedy and Johnson, he was an architect of American conduct in Vietnam. This was far from his objective at Ford: to sell cars at more profit. To "win" in Vietnam was to entertain hopes for a reordering of Southeast Asia that was willfully indifferent to most of the realities in that part of the world. You could not believe in the domino theory without a need to reverse major forces. Years ahead of his resignation McNamara had foreseen a likely abandonment of the war. By 1965, he was advising Johnson that their plan was not working. This wasn't what he had been trained for, just as guerrilla warfare was not easily accessible on spreadsheets. It turned on a quality computers were not ready to identify: the virulent hope for freedom in underprivileged people living under what they regarded as alien occupation. This was not McNamara's kind of job, but that rationale was at first beyond him. By the time it had sunk in, he saw that his only imperative was not to lose—that was sensible, but impossible. All this business scientist had to do was to ignore evidence.

It's a mark of McNamara's education over Vietnam, of his disenchantment and guilt, that he agreed to the request by Errol Morris to sit down for the interviews that would provide for the eventual film *The Fog of War* (2003). Has there ever been a movie so bent on the distress of a smart man, professorial, who cannot stop questioning himself, but who almost longs to disown his power? This helps one appreciate how few American films—of any kind—are focused on doubt. Perhaps the urge to defeat unease is one of the perpetual wars in the American mind. Beware the zeal of those who have overcome doubt.

PEOPLE SAY *THE VIETNAM WAR*, BY KEN BURNS AND LYNN NOVICK, IS UNREAsonably overlong. Its ten episodes ran over seventeen hours as it played on PBS in 2017. It is a chronicle of the war, its origins, and its aftermath, and it has a gallery of people who lived the war and describe their feelings with candor, disillusion, and unforced eloquence. That range of witnesses includes many talking heads and troubled people from North Vietnam, the sort of survivors who had not talked much before and may be guarded still with Novick. And such participants had not been employed in documentary before to the same effect. The war belonged to the Vietnamese, though it was not a gift they had asked for. It turned out that their Asiatic sense of life and death was very like our own—but discovered in deeper and more damaging experience.

It is a measured, conscientious history of what happened over there, and in Washington, DC, and on what we call the home front. It tells of dumb hills taken at savage cost, the corpses piled up against shattered tree stumps, and the hills then immediately abandoned because they had been no more than pinpoints in a diagram called a map. There are portraits of people who were maddened by the war and left with the task of reconciling their distress with the calm dementia of the United States. It left a new sense of how thoroughly America had lost the war in the way its turmoil renewed its old civil war—the unsettled American war.

Burns has always been enthralled by America. In person and in his films, he describes our history in a hallowed voice, and he loves to celebrate such things as jazz, baseball, country music, and Ernest Hemingway. Yet some of those legends have not kept their heroic status in Burns's lifetime. The nation has let him down. So in this chronicle of Vietnam, a bitter insight emerges, without ever being fully addressed, that in a war eight thousand miles away, America set in motion a self-dismantling that has not stopped in the decades since those helicopters were buried at sea.

This *Vietnam War* can feel like a large part of one's life, and its range of sources only teaches us that we could hear from everyone. The film is long, but edited down like any picture. What the series covers lasted from 1945 to 1975 in a succession of Indochinese wars. And that entailed the death of about a million and a half among the Vietnamese. Plus 58,000 Americans (the stars in the death show). That comparison is not intended as sarcasm. Vietnam was a small war by many standards, but it was momentous because it was perceived while it was fought as a contest for our own minds, and as a gradual uncovering of failures in the American idea. It may have been the last complete war, to be replaced only by a constant state of undeclared but insidious hostility. Seventeen and a quarter hours of our time is not too much to ask.

BURNS AND NOVICK CONCLUDE *THE VIETNAM WAR* WITH WHAT AMOUNTS TO a symphonic finale on the Washington Vietnam Veterans Memorial that was completed in 1982 as designed by Maya Lin (born in Ohio, of Chinese descent). Their creative decision was predictable, and it works very well as some of the film's witnesses describe the resolution they felt on seeing the monument with its black granite walls that bear the white names of all the known military casualties. Those walls are beautifully embedded in the ground, and the levels rise and fall, like a gentle sea. The two-acre site is full of grace and shapeliness. It seems a restful place to be.

It also seems to me to be a characteristically PBS saluting place in that its physical elegance, and its air of gravitas, work toward a feeling of closure that is a little movie-like, conservative and sedate, and a proper site for tourist interest. As civic sculpture and silent song it is an assertion of completion, and of a cultural duty having been fulfilled. It's hard to think of Burns and Novick not taking it up as their final set piece. But it's just as hard to feel enough measure of the Vietnam error in those smooth walls.

For myself, I don't find it as challenging as the Memorial to the Murdered Jews of Europe in Berlin, inaugurated in 2005. Designed by Peter Eisenman and Buro Happold, it stretches over 200,000 square feet with 2,711 variegated coffin-like forms done in concrete. There's no need to give out prizes for these works, but they both eclipse the horror I felt in the early 1970s at the vulgarity of the Valley of the Fallen in mountains near Madrid. Conceived and executed under General Franco, this was meant as a religiose and epic tribute to those killed in the Spanish Civil War—or to those who fell on the right side.

The urge to memorialize war, whether in triumph, honor, or remorse, is natural and unending. And sometimes helpless. There is an island in the Pacific, one of the Marshalls, not fit to be returned to because of the toxic remains of war's processes. Nuclear waste waits there beneath a bloated concrete dome. Other monuments are unaware of what history would conclude. The statue of Nelson in London's Trafalgar Square is 169 feet above ground, so loftily surreal that one cannot see the admiral's face, let alone guess his ardor as a spokesman for the slave trade. Will that classic piece of London yet have to be removed, in the spirit that lifted Lee and his horse out of Richmond in 2021?

As with movies, one needs to assess the tone of monuments carefully. For me, the Washington Vietnam memorial is serene and healing, and those are blessed states. I find the Berlin memorial more challenging just because it is founded in a spirit of confusion conveyed in the random variety of its stelae tombs. With the one tribute you can feel that Vietnam is over. But that war deserves more respect or criticism. In Berlin, the concrete labyrinth testifies to doubts that will not go away. It is soul-searching and disconcerting—but that is a measure of soul.

So many war films are based on the American model of feeling settled about ourselves. Of course, you say, but what are movies meant for? That is an American innocence. What makes war so testing as a cultural experience is the instability in which we try to stay ourselves. Books can be memorials, too, and a touch more Berlin than Washington, DC.

31

GIBSON

I wonder what Mel Gibson would have made of the Burns/Novick *Vietnam War*—but that's some admission of how I can't get Mel out of my head. As I wrote in my disapproving way about *We Were Soldiers*, I felt how close he is to the troubling fluctuation in this book, of loathing war while feasting on it. That's the alliance referred to in the title. And it's the foreboding that we know this passion could end badly. So I dislike *We Were Soldiers*—every time I watch it.

This is not a biography of Mel Gibson, and I do not intend to get too deeply into how he has offended so many liberals, or women, or Jews, or people horrified by violence, who feel they can smell a fascist in the morning as well as napalm. But Gibson can be a troubling man, and very likely he is as troubled as anyone else. He has been alcoholic, manic depressive, homophobic, racist, and a bearer of mean temper. Lesser men might have wilted under all those accusations, but Gibson has risen to the challenge. There is a team player in him, a warrior dedicated to the unit: in *We Were Soldiers* he is the commander who cherishes his men, just as the film agrees that the Vietcong were soldiers, too, tough, admirable, and likely to be killed. But there is also a rebel or outcast in Gibson, driven by a fatalistic certainty that men are going to kill one another sooner or later, so why waste time disputing the apparent purpose or need for a war? In Mel's sad eyes, our battlefield has always been there, poised for the lighting of a blue touch paper. We are soldiers, as ants and bees are workers. This is a place where cinema meets anthropology, and the plain bloodlust in audiences—in us—is set free.

He wasted no time in becoming a movie star. So soon after *Mad Max* and *Gallipoli*, he was launched on the *Lethal Weapon* franchise where he and Danny Glover were cops in and out of harness. Gibson's character had been a Green Beret who has lost his wife—he was a tough guy, but soft at the center. Mel was casually good-looking, athletic, adventurous, sympathetic, and cheeky; he had an insolent air ready to make fun of his own films. It was not immediately clear that he had greater ambitions than being a knockout hunk, if much more interesting than Stallone or Schwarzenegger or Eastwood. He was funnier than we care to remember, and adept with women: *The Year of Living Dangerously* had an erotic edge, and *Mrs. Soffel* was on the verge of amour fou, but held back by some unexplained restraint. He had an ease on camera, wry, seductive, and merry; it was angelic sometimes—was that a prelude to being a fallen angel?

He was not yet forty when he played William Wallace in *Braveheart* and carried off the Oscars for best director and best picture. It was a kilted adventure (from a period before kilts were worn), with a beautiful princess (Sophie Marceau) and a wicked king (Patrick McGoohan). It sounded like something Errol Flynn might have made, but it was overwhelmingly postcensorship in its violence, and in its adoration of our habitual moviegoing subterfuge. I say that because screen violence is a practice we would abhor and condemn in life, while luxuriating over in the dark.

Shooting, explosiveness, and intercutting are the mechanics of combat, but they have enabled the instinct of rivalry allied to damage and prejudice. That passes as our innate capacity for violence when we try to believe that those things are wrong and senseless. So we face at least the chance that being right and calm are not necessarily our destiny. And realize that putting violence on-screen tends to be laboriously detailed—boring almost—so that it has to depend on the base emotions that it expresses. Against all reason and training, we are ready to hurt others in a proof of our uniqueness, our competitiveness, and our right to power. Perhaps it is not even readiness, but insistence. This is not easy stuff to process. And so we attempt to lead lives that can avoid the necessity of violence. Until life and death will hinge on an open blade. If we can strike first.

We do things in the dark, or we are accomplice to them, things we could not allow in the light.

I am not saying that Mel Gibson has an unusual taste for violence in his life. But on his (and our) screen he is demonic. In *Braveheart*, heads are bludgeoned and lopped off, arrows strike men in the face, limbs are severed. The murder of Wallace's first love (Catherine McCormack—the best performance in the film) is heartstopping and hideous, tied to a stake and her throat cut; unnecessarily vivid, unless the filmmaker could not live without this surgical thrill. You may say that in the early fourteenth century, war was fought on those terms. But that evades the weight of creative decision-making, just as it begins a pattern that is unmistakably Gibson in his way of seeing. A film selects what it wants us to see. And feel. So Mel Gibson is obsessed with damage and pain, and he would grow into a primitive visionary who sees violence as the essence of our anthropological identity. He does not seem to realize how much he is shocking us—or how much he needs that power. And when the world turned pained eyes on a man it had once liked, that seemed to make him more truculent or vengeful.

We are left wondering what *Braveheart* is about. Is it a chronicle of Scotland's search for independence? Is it a song of hatred toward England? What "freedom" is it that William Wallace cries out for as he is being hung, drawn, and quartered in a prolonged execution scene, as a sadomasochistic ritual? Is it the freedom of the filmmaker to indulge his nightmare of betrayal and cruelty? And how would the creator of the film respond when its exhausting rites of violence won the best picture Oscar?

There was a throwback, in Gibson's *Braveheart*, to the simplistic antagonisms of silent-era epics—he has the energy if not quite the cold eye of Fritz Lang, who had done so much in the 1920s to remind us of the tribal passion of modern society. Like Lang's *Metropolis*, *Braveheart* was sentimental, naive philosophizing, self-pitying, romantic, longing to be poetic, and always exploiting and agonizing over its own power. Looked at again, *Braveheart* seems specious as a tale of Scottish liberty at odds with English tyranny. It is a rhapsody on suffering and slaughter, more intent on the end of the world than improving it. As with *Metropolis*, we totter away from the experience, drunk or sick from the violence.

Gibson only acted in *The Patriot* (2000), directed by Roland Emmerich, but its savagery, and its depiction of a sadistic English officer (Jason Isaacs), had the stamp of *Braveheart* and the same attraction to bright blades cutting flesh. *We Were Soldiers* was 2002, and then two years later Gibson broke away from normal Hollywood production schemes to make *The Passion of the Christ*. There had been so many doubts in advance about this biblical epic using authentic languages (Hebrew, Latin, and Aramaic) but barely restraining its hostility toward the Jews. No studio cared to take it on, so—like a Cecil B. DeMille or a Chaplin—Gibson used his own company, Icon Productions, to pay for the making of the film, and its distribution.

So many previous Christ movies had been sedate, ahistorical, and fit for bourgeois consumption. Gibson was defiant about getting at the real experience—yet the picture turned out to be one more extreme depiction of his own hopes and dreads. If there was to be a crucifixion, then Mel wanted to know how it was done and what it felt like. Wasn't that passion? The result was the most bloodthirsty Christ story ever made—with Christ played by Jim Caviezel (Private Witt from *The Thin Red Line*). Against every prediction of box-office disaster, *The Passion of the Christ* was a colossal evangelical moneymaker. On a cost of $30 million it earned $612 million. It was as if an outlaw had found a way to make the sensationalist factory function again, and it was a triumph for a man facing mounting personal criticism. It is also a horrendous (if brilliant) film, in which mercy and charity have been buried in an apocalyptic sensibility. But its success said so much about the true dread consuming "God-fearing" people, and the size of that following.

Two years later, that feeling was made clear in *Apocalypto*, a fable about early sixteenth-century Mayan society, though the lead role, Jaguar Paw, was taken by the very beautiful, soulful actor Rudy Youngblood, born and raised in Texas, with Hispanic and Native American origins. The contrast between his lovely gaze and the other "savage" faces and bodies came from silent cinema, in which morality and being "good-looking" had formed a devilish pact. The violence was sickening as the rhythm of clubbing enemies to death merged with vicious knives and the hacking out of enemy hearts, all the way to ritual sacrifice. It was beautiful in its way—the red blood and the green jungle, as well as blue body paint (like the woad in *Braveheart*)—and there are memorable moments in the attack of a jaguar, the suddenness of an eclipse, and the awe of Mayans busy slaughtering one another but stopped in their tracks by the sight of Spanish ships anchored in the bay, with conquistadors coming ashore.

It is the most inventive and startling film Gibson has made. If you can keep your eyes and ears open to the rush of brutalism. Other filmmakers, like Quentin Tarantino and Martin Scorsese, praised it, but for every rapt viewer someone else walked out in horror. The descendants of Mayans, and scholars, said it was inaccurate and contrived, a brutal illustration of an epigraph from Will Durant—"A great civilization is not conquered from without until it has destroyed itself from within."

That's glib and convenient, and too readily swayed by the word "great" and the way it masks bloodlust. We have so many civilizations that are other than great. One of them involves the remorseless exploitation of our capacity for brutality, racism, and facile moral mottoes to cover up our fear.

Yes, *Apocalypto* intensifies Gibson's obsession with the violent texture of killing, and that may seem more elemental or acceptable in a mythological nightmare. Realize that Gibson would always rather shoot or suggest a real killing than turn it over to CGI. He is a primitive and originalist. This is a "great," mad film, written by Gibson and Farhad Safinia, but worthy of Homer (if he was doing cocaine and sadomasochistic porn). It has a conventional symphonic score from James Horner, but you might do better to turn that off and listen to the *Rite of Spring* instead. *Apocalypto* makes the entire *Star Wars* franchise feel like paper hats left out in the rain. If you are alarmed but held by Mel Gibson's war with himself, then you need to see this monotonous picture and realize that if cinema was once the light defying darkness, still the darkness is a tide that keeps coming in.

By then, Gibson was a kind of monster on the liberal American scene who may have thought of himself as a drawn and quartered messiah. He had never lost the self-absorption of the fantasist gazing at his dark dream. He is the scariest figure in recent American film—and I can't get him out of my head. It is said that he has moved increasingly toward what is known as the right wing, as if our entity had wings for flight. But you know he sees himself as a true burning center where greatness pulses. This is Trumpian cinema, and you can feel his contempt for us and shudder at the power it may attain.

But Mel is Hollywood cunning, too, a very knowing Mad Max, and so he emerged from his era of dark glory—delivering so many hits and taking in the rewards, while as self-sorrowful as a wounded Kong who nurtures the love of the base. As a "comeback" the prodigal son directed *Hacksaw Ridge* (2016), a torrential display of combat at the Battle of Okinawa in which a conscientious objector (well played by Andrew Garfield) refuses to pick up a weapon but wins the Medal of Honor as a medic saving so many lives (seventy-five, it is said) in an epic attempt to take and hold the Maeda escarpment—"Hacksaw Ridge"—in the spring of 1945.

There was a model for this compromise: enjoying the battle while being high-mindedly spiritual about it—that was *Sergeant York* (1941), where Howard Hawks and Gary Cooper had made hay out of the parable of a saintly sharpshooter, a country boy who mastered the trick of serving Caesar and the Lord. Onward Christian soldiers.

Mel Gibson is only sixty-seven, and just as I can't find a safe quiet room to put him in, so I tremble to think what he may do next in a world that seems more drawn toward acting out his fantasies.

One subject worthy of him is some version of Milton's *Paradise Lost*, where an ultimate war is waged between our best and worst hopes. Isn't that a fitting swan song or Götterdämmerung for cinema, with a Satan pushing seventy and challenging every other vestige of a humanist contract?

32

THE UNIT

There was one significant advance in civil rights during the Vietnam War: for the first time in American history, African Americans were permitted to die in combat without prejudicial restraint. Indeed, the nation was so generous to them in this that some felt black deaths were being arranged so that young white guys could get a break on surviving.

In a film like *Fury*, it would have gone against the grain of history to have an African American in the tank crew. That omission may have troubled Brad Pitt, who has done a lot to support films about black experience. (He was important as a coproducer on *12 Years a Slave*, *Selma*, and *The Underground Railroad*.) But a black crew member would have been invisible in 1944–45.

About 125,000 black servicemen went overseas for America during the Second World War. And 708 of them were killed. If that number seems low, it's because black soldiers were not often put in critical situations. Over half a million black servicemen never left the States. The armed forces were routinely segregated, and General Eisenhower was among those who believed in that policy.

There were exceptional situations, like the Tuskegee airmen, but they were not much celebrated at the time. There was a ten-minute documentary about that group, *Wings for This Man*, made in 1945, and narrated by Ronald Reagan as he became acquainted with history. It was decades before those fliers made it into a feature film: *The Tuskegee Airmen* (1995), an HBO television movie, with Laurence Fishburne, Cuba Gooding Jr., Andre Braugher, and Courtney B. Vance; and then *Red Tails* (2012), directed by Anthony Hemingway, produced by George Lucas, written by John Ridley, and featuring Nate Parker, David Oyelowo, Terrence Howard and, again, Cuba Gooding Jr.

All the more respect to *Home of the Brave*, a picture made in 1949, about a black soldier who has been traumatized not just by war but by the abuse from white soldiers in his unit. In fact, that plot construct irked Arthur Laurents, the original writer on the project. He had written a play that opened in New York in December 1945, about a soldier victimized by his fellows. But that guy had been a Jew (like Laurents, who had served in the Pacific). Stanley Kramer, the producer who bought the rights to the play, and Jewish, told Laurents, "Jews had been done." Laurents knew that there was no such thing in the Pacific as a black guy in a white unit, but he needed the money, so he went along with a revisionist script by Carl Foreman. A very good actor, James Edwards, was cast in the lead role of a black soldier paralyzed by trauma, who is taught by an army psychiatrist (Wendell Corey) to speak out against the abuse he has endured and to walk again. As Laurents himself admitted, *Home of the Brave* worked as a movie, even if its example was not much taken up in Hollywood. President Truman had declared that the military would no longer be segregated in 1948. But the factory town was more obsessed over the metaphor of its other blacklist.

Another exception to the rule occurred as American forces advanced from Normandy and fought their way toward Germany in 1944–45. The racing Third Army under Patton was getting too far ahead. So a system was devised of rapid truck convoys carrying food and ammunition on hazardous nonstop drives. This unit was called the Red Ball Express, and about 70 percent of its drivers were African American. The Express was a marked success, and in 1952 a movie arose to celebrate it. *Red Ball Express* was directed by Budd Boetticher, with Jeff Chandler as the commanding officer. Sidney Poitier had a supporting role, but the studio making it, Universal, was under pressure from the Defense Department to play down black participation. To this day, Spike Lee lists it as one of the projects he would like to make.

But progress is shamefully slow. James Edwards played one of the infantrymen in *Men in War*, but he never got another lead role. In 1970, the year he died, he was cast as the general's valet in *Patton*. Jim Brown was smuggled into *The Dirty Dozen* because he was a revered star in football, one of the other codes cherished by white men, even if its business system can sometimes seem like a new version of the slave trade.

So let us reflect on *Glory* (1989), where a young white colonel (Matthew Broderick) leads a unit of black soldiers that includes Denzel Washington, Morgan Freeman, and Andre Braugher. For 1989, *Glory* was a monument of revisionist decency; it may have seemed noble. And it had been inspired by a real memorial on Boston Common to the 54th Massachusetts Volunteer Infantry as made by Augustus Saint-Gaudens. Directed by Edward Zwick and written by Kevin Jarre, the film was reasonably accurate on the outward facts of the Civil War situation where an integrated military unit was out of the question.

It's a worthy film, with fine performances, even if the white commanding officer seems to get too much attention: it's the story of the 54th viewed too much from the top down. The battle scenes are desperate and they raise an intriguing point: that our cinema has given us too few battle scenes of the Civil War. Is there a searching feature film that explains Gettysburg? Or Sherman's drastic march through Georgia? Why should that be? Is there something sacred still in Southern nobility that we do not want to see the rebels crushed? There are no Shermans or Grants in our movie history with its love of winners. While every kid in America knows there was a Civil War, I'm not sure how many could write a tidy two-page narrative of what happened in that war. Is this just a matter of passing time and forgetfulness, or is there something that the modern America prefers not to know?

Still, it seems a given that a black regiment would fight against the

South, the rebels, in the American Civil War, and it's a major advance on the way films like *The Birth of a Nation* and *Gone With the Wind* made novelettish travesties of black (and white) experience in that war. But those classics shaped the movie business and the glory of box office.

The other *Glory* was well reviewed, but it did modestly. It won three Oscars, including the supporting prize for Denzel Washington. It was not nominated for best picture, an award that went that year to *Driving Miss Daisy*. It's not that *Glory* should have won, it's more that *Miss Daisy* (also with Morgan Freeman) was a complacently genteel or safe fable that saw fit to bring the case for black identity along within cultural speed limits, so as not to alarm white audiences.

But this was twenty years after Vietnam, where black soldiers were far more common, and where some of them asked out loud why should they be fighting this damn war against these people. It reminds me of James Baldwin making the case in *The Fire Next Time* (1963) that while it was necessary and proper for black people to expect equal status in America, why should they have to volunteer for all the iniquitous habits of a white society that had done so much to keep them in servitude? Isn't it possible that in the era of Vietnam, the most valuable service of black soldiers was more mutiny than falling in step? Why were we in Vietnam? In that sense, the most significant black regiment in American history has been the one that took the nation most seriously, the Black Panthers.

This is not simply the prehistory to a reformed situation in which we may feel more comfortable and liberal. By 2021, the nation had General Lloyd Austin as its first black secretary of defense, but would he feel able to oppose white orthodoxies in the Pentagon? So in a full survey of black attitudes to war, it's important to stress what Denzel Washington did in Spike Lee's *Malcolm X* (1992—so long ago), a film that knows where our vital conflict exists. And if it's hard to think of an American movie where a black commander leads our white boys, just remind yourself of Denzel as a leading narcotics detective in Antoine Fuqua's *Training Day* (2001—still too long ago).

Of course, Denzel is not an ideal commanding cop in that film (is that how he got his full Oscar for it?). But we've had scoundrel cops ever since cinema began. So the corruption should be more shared around. It's good to see some pictures attending to the Panthers—like *Judas and the Black Messiah*, where Daniel Kaluuya won a supporting actor Oscar as Fred Hampton.

Better yet—and I use "better" with as much irony as I can muster— I have no doubt about the emphatic, crucial black movie of 2020. It was not full-length; it ran nine minutes and twenty-nine seconds and it showed a knee on a neck, George Floyd and Officer Derek Chauvin. It made for immediate sequels, and something like a franchise of outrage. I use that word because the true work of enlightenment will need a stamina the country has never possessed, and which will require far more than the newsreel footage of people demonstrating on our city streets. That resolution will not come easily. It may commit us to a renewal of our Civil War. But that ordeal was shut down, not settled. There are some questions that cannot be left to endless, polite patience.

More movies now nag at the old wounds. The first script for *Da 5 Bloods* (2020) concerned a group of veterans who return to Vietnam decades after the war trying to find the remains of a lost comrade. Oliver Stone had been set to direct the film, but when that arrangement fell through Spike Lee was invited in, and in a revised script he made the men black (Delroy Lindo, Chadwick Boseman, Clarke Peters, Norm Lewis, and Isiah Whitlock Jr.). I think the film is powerful yet muddled—how could it not be as it tried to show Vietnam as it is today, a place where Americans are noisy and still as lost as Graham Greene's Pyle? But it left a burning question: Why was Lindo's outraged reactionary leader, a man going mad, and teaching us the passion in rage, not even nominated?

Justice comes slowly—and those three words are etched in our benevolent liberal humbug. By the year of that release, 2020, the military was wide open to African Americans, or so it seemed. Black enlisted soldiers were 22.7 percent of the total; they were 16.5 percent of warrant officers. And 11 percent of the officer class. Justice can come down fast, when it wants to.

———

LIFE IN THE UNIT, AND IN THE NATION THAT LIKES TO THINK OF THE UNIT as its pride and glory, becomes ever more complicated. Truly, you can't sustain a military without facing the most awkward questions about democratic rights. Women might not have gone over the top at the Somme, or fought their way ashore on D-Day. But a woman can as easily press this button or that as anyone. A woman can fly a medevac helicopter (Meg Ryan in *Courage Under Fire*, directed by Edward Zwick, who had done *Glory*) or take charge of an enemy anti-aircraft gun to be photographed. In *The Kingdom*, Jennifer Garner engages in furious hand-to-hand fighting in Saudi Arabia. She knows a Wonder Woman routine. Ripley can handle the alien.

It is archaic, in the same chapter, to ask how the unit has accommodated people of color and women. But that is also a measure of the primitive adoration of the unit that resembles the conservatism of a country that is now close enough to fascism so that recent reforms might yet be reversed. The unit ideology has made compromises, and it likes to tell itself it is grown-up now. But in many of its ways of thinking, the unit is still antagonistic toward all the departures in recruitment from a good white kid, like Mel Gibson, John Wayne, and Audie Murphy, buddies who might give you the shivers.

We sensed we had a fight coming with the young Jane Fonda. There was an innate antagonistic urge in her, likely acquired in family upbringing, and a kind of emotional-aesthetic physicality, a stress on health that reminds one of Katharine Hepburn. Her motion was emotional. Long before her epic formation of a middle-aged regiment with *Jane Fonda's Workout* (1982, and a bestseller for over a year), she had had an erotic victory in *Barbarella* (1968) where she took on the fatal sexual pleasure machine and exhausted it with all her orgasms.

She hadn't enjoyed doing *Barbarella*, or being exploited for it by her husband, Roger Vadim, and so she let a surly, combative look take over the face that had lately been willing to be adorable. In *They Shoot Horses*,

Don't They? and *Klute*, she was suspicious and contemptuous of the world. Even with her guy in *Klute* (played by Donald Sutherland), she was wondering whether she could trust her own desire. She scorns it and wants to beat it up. She was about to become a principled toughie and devoutly uningratiating. This was her liberation.

Right after *Klute*, with Sutherland and some pals, she toured a "Fuck the Army" show to military bases, and had the guys rocking with laughter as an antidote to the vacuously positive Bob Hope entertainments. There's a film about the tour, *FTA*, though it vanished as soon as it was made because the Defense Department or President Nixon was so offended. It was rescued and rereleased in 2021.

Fonda became politicized by her Oscar for *Klute*, or given more confidence. Her relationship with activist Tom Hayden had begun, and in 1972 she made a trip to North Vietnam that led to a moment where a still photographer caught her astride an anti-aircraft gun, saying the war was wrong and absurd. She may have been duped, but perhaps she was too smart to be set up. The pictures and the label—"Hanoi Jane"—would hurt her for years, so much so that she often apologized for her reckless action. There is a striking essay film on that event, *Letter to Jane* (1972), made by Jean-Luc Godard and Jean-Pierre Gorin.

But time was on her side. In *FTA* she had kept antiwar feeling at the level of rowdy cabaret. The disapproval and the hatred for Hanoi Jane sprang from the stateside veterans rather than the kids who felt themselves exploited by the Vietnam mission. It's hard to think of a Hollywood celebrity being so candid or effective in just a few frames of film.

I prefer Hanoi Jane to Sally Hyde, her character in *Coming Home* (1978), the film in which she is the dutiful wife of a marine officer (Bruce Dern). As he goes off to Vietnam, Sally—a fully unemployed military spouse—tries to work a little. She helps at a VA hospital and meets the paraplegic Luke (Jon Voight), who has been wrecked in Vietnam.

They become lovers, and the wounded vet gives Sally her first orgasm. When the husband comes home, the confusion is shrill and perilous, until the officer, in shock from his own Vietnam experience, commits tactful suicide, marching naked into the ocean as if under orders still.

Coming Home, directed by Hal Ashby and made for Fonda's production company, was a popular hit. She and Voight won acting Oscars, and the film was regarded as a breakthrough for liberal idealism. Decades later, it feels the most staid and didactic of the films about Vietnam that broke at the end of the seventies. There are other ways to get an orgasm.

It was two decades more before Hollywood felt it could handle the female soldier, and that was in the form of the cunning *G.I. Jane* (1997), by the unstoppable Ridley Scott, with Demi Moore as Jane, buffed and cropped and going through intense training tests to prove a girl could do it. It was a new kind of workout picture, shamelessly sexy in its box-office appeal and very entertaining, but only as feminist as the sweating, Amazonian Demi Moore.

Another twenty years later, there are still moralists in America—like Tucker Carlson on Fox News—who go into fits of disbelief at the thought of female soldiers. Moore won a Razzie for worst actress as Jane, but that dismisses the point—long since absorbed by less sexually inhibited societies—that if the fighting is desperate enough, then women share in it. That is evident in the modern history of Russia in its wars, of the Vietnamese and the Chinese, and even of Anna Magnani's character in Roberto Rossellini's *Rome, Open City*. Or Simone Signoret in *Army of Shadows*. War doesn't behave like a gentleman. Just look at the woman at Kabul airport at the end of *Retrograde*, observing the end of American assistance and contemplating a future where women will have to be combatants.

But the fact of women in uniform can be disarming. As of 2017, women were already 16 percent of the American army, and surely some of them were lesbian or trans, or just interested in being natural born killers. We may recall *Lysistrata* (411 BC) a play by Aristophanes in which the Athenian women decide to stop the Peloponnesian War by withholding their bodies from their men. Better still—and I am earnest—suppose all the armies everywhere were reserved for women soldiers, while the men stayed home and learned to put a hold on their ammunition? The issue has already been raised in America as to whether an all-male draft is unconstitutional.

COULD THERE BE A FEMALE MEL GIBSON? IS IT SENTIMENTAL TO ASSUME or hope that the female gaze and the mind behind it do not inhabit the instinct for making war? Women have directed extraordinary martial pictures, from Leni Riefenstahl in *Triumph of the Will* to Kathryn Bigelow with *The Hurt Locker*. In the former, there is a glorying in ranks of uniformed troops that precedes the fascism inherent in CGI armies. And in the latter, Jeremy Renner presents one of the most plausible and alarming mad soldiers, a warrior who is searching for an explosive device to take him out.

In putting those two films together, I am not trying to suggest that either director is or was fascist, so much as imaginations captive to the passionate mechanics of film. But I am asking us to consider the possibility that war has some roots in our sexual identity. It's telling that in later life Riefenstahl went on to photograph beautiful native bodies (the Nuba) in a way not too far from *Apocalypto*. Then recall that Bigelow would next make *Zero Dark Thirty*, where a bitterly demure and overlooked Jessica Chastain understands the way to Osama bin Laden better than her superior guys. There was controversy over that film: Was it propaganda for Barack Obama? Did it really recommend enhanced torture techniques? Had it got everything factually right?

Of course it hadn't. Movies don't do that. If we want more rightness in our world, we should not trust cinema to get us there.

But are we strong and wise enough for that? Are we prepared to recognize that "the unit" is nothing less than a model for our larger regimental motto, "*E pluribus unum*"? Is there an occasion when the link, or the proposed marriage, between war and movie gets so strained as to be absurd? Or outrageous? Is it possible that the unit is no more than a conceit of nostalgia, patriotism, and show business wishful thinking that will not suffice if we are to think as deeply as our perilous world requires?

On September 9, 2001, HBO premiered the first episode of its ten-part series *Band of Brothers*. The show got a large audience (ten million or so), and it deserved it. That was on Sunday, the television night for new beginnings. Two days later, the sky fell in as the parts of another unit delivered the most significant foreign attack on America's infrastructure and confidence. This was terror and horror. But that mission was a unit, too, not just fired up but carried aloft on spirit and belief, things we esteem and have loved in our movies.

At last, you are saying, your author has come into the open: He is subversive; it's not just that he dislikes war and the mechanism of film; he is wary of the United States, too. Well, yes, I am, but I thought that was allowed when I volunteered for American citizenship. One of the things I liked about our unit and its idea was that the chance to be a critic was welcomed.

I agreed with that first Sunday night audience: *Band of Brothers* was terrific, and there was no pressing reason why a series playing in 2001 could not embody the ethos of 1941–45, if that was the material of its show. The series was based on a book by the popular historian Stephen Ambrose, and it followed a company of the 101st Airborne Division from setup, through the war in Europe, and then on to the Pacific. It was established as a television campaign by Steven Spielberg and Tom Hanks, the unit created just a few years earlier for *Saving Private Ryan*.

It's worth examining that unit, for it has lasted. Hanks and Spielberg would collaborate on *Catch Me If You Can*, *The Terminal*, *Bridge of Spies*, and *The Post*. More than that, they have informed each other: Spielberg needed a rather vague everyman figure for his parables, and Hanks was always edging toward a mix of virtue and amiability, of general decency, that has tended to eclipse his originality and his latent mischief as an actor. They are irreproachable as a team in outward ways; they are good to look at, notionally liberal but solidly conservative. "Earn it" from *Ryan* is a Reaganesque watchword. But by the hardest test, their rooting for goodness, has waylaid two talented and powerful figures in the picture business. They are as radiant and self-limiting as a flashlight: very comforting in the dark but quite hopeless at trying to explain how darkness works.

If you doubt my doubts about such a lovable pair, take another look at *Empire of the Sun*, in which Spielberg has to face up to chaos and mystery; and *The Terminal*, in which Hanks delivers a brilliant, eccentric performance that shows the personality that he has given up on. And both of them could say, *Why complain, when we have made movies that a mass of people cherish, not least* Band of Brothers, *which was so widely honored in prizes and reviews?*

And which itself honors the humbug that America is a band of brothers, so everything will be all right if we stay enlisted. Spielberg and Hanks gave up on the risk of being artists for the gratification and reward of becoming an institution. No one in recent film history has managed it better. And no one, on first impulse, could fail to be moved by *Band of Brothers* and the way it coincided with 9/11. In writing, directing, and acting, the series is a tribute to old war movies, so its nostalgia worked as much on that mood as it did in rekindling the spirit of the just war and its commonplace heroes.

So the series is magnificent—and misleading. It cannot live up to its own aspirations, and becomes a steady gloss on the nature of groups and individuals. It amounts to a genteel advertisement for duty, like padre talk in the Great War. And its bland triumph should not displace the disruptive unease, close to nausea, that you can still feel in reading Joseph Heller's *Catch-22* or Evelyn Waugh's *Sword of Honor* trilogy where white lies do not let us look away from the madhouse of the unit. And don't forget *Fortunes of War*, a 1987 television adaptation of six novels by Olivia Manning (scripted by Alan Plater and directed by James Cellan Jones), in which Kenneth Branagh and Emma Thompson play a young couple tossed about in very untidy war circumstance in Egypt and the Balkans. The ultimate lesson of these comparisons is that *e pluribus unum* is not working. That does not mean the idea is dead, only that it needs critical reappraisal and repair.

How did we ever persuade ourselves that it might work and save us? I think it was the movies that did it.

Warn everyone?

———

THE NATURE OF THE UNIT AND ITS WARS IS TOO DANGEROUS A QUESTION to be left to the military. Every concern over the composition of the armed forces turns into a debate over the structure of society. If teachers can be male or female, or some other variants of gender choice, then doesn't that mean their students have the same opportunity? But no one is quite taken in by the bromides on how modern the services have become, or forget the muffled reports of sexual abuse within the operation.

It is beyond possibility, but within reach of useful discussion, that we might make our armies all female. They could handle the complex machines of war, and if they can't manage all the physical aspects of battle, well so much the worse for battle. How long would it take for female armies to let us see into the mad male supremacy of war at which the men keep on losing? Manliness is so dangerous.

Or watch one of the supreme unit films: Claire Denis's *Beau Travail* (1999), in which we follow the dance-like maneuvers of a male regiment of the Foreign Legion in the desert of Djibouti as a way into the homo-erotic mood of a unit. You can say this film is a daring conceit with a radical agenda. But then look at it beside some more conventional unit studies—Stanley Kubrick's *Full Metal Jacket* (1987), say, or Leni Riefenstahl's *Olympia* (1938), or Jane Campion's *The Power of the Dog* (2021)— and wonder if the essential motif in ranks of men with guns, and the sport of war, might not be exploded as farce—before it blows us up.

33

NO MORE CIVILIANS

In the golden age of war, to be a soldier was an honorable career choice even if, often, it was thought to be the resort of the least talented young men, the ones who might not stand a fair chance in the church, the law, in politics or business, where ambition did not always keep within the rules or the conventions. So the military life ran in some families over centuries, and the feeling spread that whereas war was a matter for political decision, still the fighting itself could be professional, skilled, and codified, and a field for brave managers of the common men who were rounded up one way or another whenever war was declared. This arrangement could seem tidy, and so it fell in line with the larger schemes of class distinction. We trusted military people—because that was a way of regarding them as versions of our better selves. With sound men in charge, weren't the unfortunate, ugly, and demented aspects of war moderated and legitimized? So history determined that war was simply a series of battles leading to a result. Instead of a way of killing and suppressing those outsiders, the civilians.

Occasionally, a film gets at that awkward truth. Tavernier's *Life and Nothing But* is a gradual critique of its apparent hero and an admission that the pomp and fantasy of the search for "the unknown soldier" is a way of escaping shame over the unidentified bodies in the ground and the shabby ways they were unaccounted for. So we have so many battle films from the Great War (some truly spectacular), but not one film that describes the infighting, the corruption, and the callousness that conspired in the Treaty of Versailles and the several pacts that guaranteed more war. Of course, the picture business would say, well, that would never be entertaining enough, and so the travesty and the incest of war cinema continues.

We've seen how thoroughly the movies endorsed that structure in history. And the misguided tidying up after 1918, the Versailles solution, is a measure of how the custom still seemed to apply that those who had won made new rules, while those who had lost took it on the chin, or in any other soft part that was visible.

There was no other field of endeavor in which stupidity, obedience, and dressing up had so much scope for men, and so much room to let them feel like Men.

Of course, this gap between capital letter and lower case is like original sin in the human race. And battle made the gap seem reasonable and honorable, instead of a disaster.

But the Great War had had another lesson, and we can see and feel it in *They Shall Not Grow Old*: that the common soldiers were not a special or professional breed. They were citizens or riffraff who had agreed to be the dead. Does that sound shocking? I agree, but that was their contract, and they had four years to arrive at fulfillment. Their death could be actual and burial-ready. But it was a metaphor, too, in the sense that history had made it clear they would be ignored as they had been in life. What it came to, really, was that any war needed a million or so unknown soldiers.

That was prelude to the deepest lesson of the second war: that there was no longer a distinction between the military and common people. This was a war where the circumstances of conflict meant that anyone was likely to be a collaborator or a resister, or one of the millions of extras, or refugees, who trudged across Europe in search of survival or excuse, in the mass dismay that would be the imprint of the twentieth century. You can be sitting in your hovel, with your dear ones, sharing a meal or a story, and the drone strike explodes your life. That weapon was mistaken, bad luck, but you will never be known. The upsetting error will be erased. There is no more civilian life. That has a corollary: that civilization is disappearing or in doubt.

Yet it, that high *C*, had been the pretext most wars were fought for.

IN THE ONCE UPON A TIME, KINGS WERE OUR CAPTAINS. IN *HENRY V* (Olivier or Branagh), the cloaked king tours his camp before battle. It is a nuance of Shakespeare's stagecraft that the king goes unrecognized so he can chat to his soldiers, man to man, and then next day lead them to victory at Agincourt. Six hundred years later, when he gave up his place in the protocol of royal duties, Prince Harry was upset to realize that he had severed his honorary connections with several regiments (including being captain general of the Royal Marines). He had thought he was a soldier—he had done two tours in Iraq. But now he was oddly alone. He published a book in which he claimed, casually, twenty-five kills. Had he kept count?

The authority in captaincy may have helped encourage Prince Harry in a confusing life. Being obeyed clarifies so much. This might come from being representative of the monarch, but it carries more weight as confirmation of the social eminence shared by royalty and the military. Thus one person may lead so many to their death—often in the name of democratic liberty. It's another class system demanding trust or fear instead of reasoning. In *1917*, General Erinmore has the brusque air of seeming to know what's happening—or has he simply learned not to give the game away by being surprised?

Commanders have to have a front. There is Sam Shepard's officer in charge in *Black Hawk Down*, registering the calamity of the mission, and being so much less decisive than Ridley Scott. There is Tom Hanks saving Private Ryan until he guesses he'll never teach another school class again. So Ryan must be his last student with a life lesson. Captains often seem to have access to the truth, or is it only a plan? There is Wardaddy in *Fury*, a sergeant, but the king in his cockpit, the father of battle, educating his raw recruit. There is Colonel Candy trying to think of the home guard as a frontline operation. I can't forget Nick Nolte's raging Colonel Tall in *The Thin Red Line*. We have Meg Ryan in *Courage Under Fire*, holding her wounded stomach together and shooting down threatening enemy in the dark. There is Denzel Washington's investigating officer in the same film—those two never meet, but his anguish over military determination guides him in making up his mind about her Medal of Honor.

There is Rawlinson on the Somme, not quite getting the point or knowing what to do with it. There is Colonel Nicholson on the River Kwai, caught up in playing trains until he recollects the call of real war. There is the reformist commander (Gregory Peck) in *Twelve O'Clock High* (1949), restoring morale before having a nervous breakdown. That's a kind of surprise. And we should recall Lieutenant Commander Philip Queeg, a model problem skipper from the 1950s.

He is the commander on the *Caine* in the Herman Wouk novel, so paranoid and insecure that he inspires a mutiny at the height of a typhoon. Queeg (Humphrey Bogart) is a nervous wreck; he shouldn't be in charge of anything. But in both the play, *The Caine Mutiny Court-Martial*, and the movie, *The Caine Mutiny* (1954), the officer who defends the mutineers in the court-martial, Lieutenant Greenwald (Henry Fonda onstage, José Ferrer on-screen), tells his clients that Queeg deserved more consideration because he had done his best for years, no matter that he was not good officer material. What is his claim on respect? That he was cowardly, unfit, and inglorious—but that he served nonetheless. After all, he was the captain, and the military are taught to trust and obey their captains, even when they are in error, telling us to lead the next two hundred into the gas chamber, going over the top, or mishandling a typhoon.

The Caine Mutiny is a routine film that does not live up to the insight in Greenwald's view of Queeg. I think Bogart is a limitation in the part. I don't mean he does less than a good job, but Bogart never rid himself of a nasty edge, so he easily becomes unlikable. I wish that Queeg could be recast and made more of a weak nice guy. I'd go for William

Holden in the role: affable, easygoing, a charmer with the other officers, the *Stalag 17* loner, but still a panicker, without the character that his command requires. Holden could have shown us Queeg as a pretender out of his depth—a failure, like just about every officer in every damn war. If Holden could have been persuaded to play weak and unreliable.

In *A Few Good Men*, Jack Nicholson is written to make Colonel Nathan Jessup a bully and a rogue, as well as the intemperate instrument of his own downfall. But do not forget his warning, that we the people cannot stand the truth, that captains are hired to do the dirty work as well as the picture-book stuff. To send in the drones, and then smother the evidence. We can hardly have a military without the resonance of captaincy. Yet it is hard to defend democratic rights in a structure that is unimpressed by those rights. In *Seven Days in May* (1964), General Scott (Burt Lancaster) is convinced that the United States is in such disarray it is his duty to stage a coup and seize control.

Seeing through the rhetoric of an officer and a gentleman was a widespread lesson from the second war. In Evelyn Waugh's trilogy of novels, *Sword of Honour* (1952–61), Guy Crouchback is a muddler but conscientious, fighting real enemies in Crete and the Balkans, but most at odds with the tangle of authority in his own army. There is a fine TV version (1967) of these funny, despairing books, written by Giles Cooper, directed by Donald McWhinnie, with Edward Woodward as Guy. Another version was done in 2001, with Edward Craig as Guy.

The military show in *Sword of Honour* is a black comedy, out of control, but many fraudulent officers carry a designer baton, and expect to be saluted, when they are as disastrous as Colonel Cathcart (Martin Balsam) in *Catch-22*. He is the would-be general who keeps upping the number of missions Yossarian has to fly to get out of his job. (I am recommending the book, not the movie.) In the field, Cathcarts may provoke malicious sniping or booby-traps from their own men. But if you can't erase or contain such men it may be necessary to promote their helpless officiousness—let them be president, or an umpire.

There are fewer privates in the book, as if cinema never expected film stars to play common soldiers. Let's face it, the generality of movies for a hundred years has been shy of showing us the lower classes. Don't we deserve handsome officer chaps who run the show in nicely framed close-ups?

But there have been some ordinaries who command a film. From James Jones, there are Prewitt and Maggio in *From Here to Eternity* and Witt in *The Thin Red Line*. There is Steve McQueen's crazed private in *Hell Is for Heroes* (1962), not just ready to destroy himself, but implacable. John Gilbert plays a private in *The Big Parade*, though he is better looking than most officers. The two men from *1917* are lance corporals, pledged to a vital yet fanciful order, doing what they are told without any notion that they might have a say in the proceedings.

Those two are healthier, fleshier, but they are like the parade of un-distinguished and unnamed soldiers in Peter Jackson's *They Shall Not Grow Old*. The moving thing about that assemblage is that its faces have so little agency or script—they are an army of unknown soldiers. And they put one in mind of the line attributed to the Duke of Wellington: asked if his men might frighten the French, he said he wasn't sure but they scared him. He sometimes called them "the scum of the earth," and expected his friends to think he was amused about this asset. Whereas Wellington's punchy joke could be the cue for education of the scum. Think of it: a war on disadvantage, so that our troops are trained to think and argue.

Most officer classes nurse a lurking worry that the men, the mob, might turn on the gentlemen and simply assert their ordinariness, their privacy. The term "private" refers to the custom of men taken from places beyond the regular army range. Outsiders—or cannon fodder, a term from the era of Napoleon. They were impoverished, uneducated, semi-criminal, without a foothold on the ladder of improvement or a recog-nized place. Universal male suffrage in Great Britain was not established until 1884. The school-leaving age was raised to eleven in 1893. So in 1914 a mass of the men enlisting were inspired by getting education and a place in society, as well as by patriotism. And the privileged classes—

including movie stars—had always been nervous about the uneducated classes if they ever saw through the charade of going to their deaths without complaint.

There is Platon in *War and Peace* (played by John Mills in the 1956 version). He is not a soldier, just some speck of lost humanity picked up in the military slipstream. But he is Pierre's valuable companion, until he is casually shot. Mills was officer class in life, but he often played ordinary blokes. In *Brown on Resolution* (1935), taken from a C. S. Forester novel, he plays Albert Brown, an able-bodied seaman, but a nobody. Brown is a bastard, the result of a fling between a lowly London woman and a dashing naval officer. The mother has raised Albert to be a seaman, and when the Great War comes his ship is sunk in the Pacific and he is taken on board by the crew of the *Ziethen*, a prized German battleship.

The Germans treat him decently, but this prisoner cannot forget his duty, or his "place." When the *Ziethen* puts in at the volcanic island of Resolution to make repairs, Brown escapes with a rifle and ammunition. He finds a shooting site amid the rocks and snipes at the Germans, killing several men. The damage he does delays the repairs, enough for the *Ziethen* to be destroyed by an approaching English squadron, commanded by Brown's unknowing father. Very well: you guessed. In being alone on the island and taking military action Brown becomes his own regiment. He doesn't know his father is coming to the rescue. He has never known about that shadowy figure. The war story is most haunting as a model of lost family ties and fanciful notions of class privilege.

Of course, the gentleman class could hardly have its wars without obedient privates. And under the flag of military adventure, *Brown on Resolution* is loyal to a preserved class system (the Thwaites Glacier that began to crack during the Great War). Put that in the antiwar hopper along with the experimental but determinative use of modern pentathlon, or the giddy policy of only allowing women in the armed forces.

Albert Brown is a test case in another way. He is a humble seaman, without much mind of his own, until he sees the opportunity to take to the island, with a rifle and resolve. At that point, he becomes his own captain. That was over a hundred years ago, but these days we can imagine crises in which privates wake up as one-man armies, out on their own in the wilderness, more set on survival than victory. The lone rider from Western myth could turn into a marauder, the hitchhiker on the highway, a dark figure we are afraid to stop for. That isolation could occur in a country first occupied but then subject to a complete breakdown of organization. *That cannot happen*, we are told. The grid holds firm: every morning our phone is reenergized by it. If not, if that worse came to the worst, surely we could still surrender and go home for dinner?

But suppose dinner is canceled and we are lost in the countryside as night falls, like lambs—or is it wolves?

Henry Fleming is not sure which he is. He is a private, "a Youth," an archetype of heroic desire and rawness. He is with the 304th New York Infantry somewhere in the American Civil War. I don't know how widely *The Red Badge of Courage* (1895) is read now. It's hard to believe parents would still give the novel to their boys. Do we have boys like that any more? But Stephen Crane wrote a terse and stirring book, the more impressive for his never having been in battle.

Henry runs away from combat at first, out of nothing other than fear—and fear is the shadow in war stories. To this day, the general estimate is that we must be brave under fire—and so maybe the useful task of avoiding fire (of organizing our affairs *without* going to war) is often shelved or thought unsporting. But Henry comes through and behaves very well in battle. *The Red Badge* became a bestseller, and in the approaching ordeal of the Great War, it must have been assigned to the young as an encouragement.

By 1951, there were plans to make a movie from the novel: after all, it was filled with action, and it was an inspiration to the military instinct everywhere. It seemed promising to put the project in the hands of John Huston. He had an adventurous air to him, and a fighter's edge. He had been a boxer and an honorary member of the Mexican cavalry. The character he plays in *Chinatown* is one of the most fearsome authority figures in American film, and you feel he relished that part. Living under occupation, I would dread an overseer like Huston's Noah Cross. It was less than farsighted, however, to have the novel as a Metro-Goldwyn-Mayer production. But studio funding was necessary. The movie ended up costing $1.6 million—it was wall-to-wall troop movement.

Huston is a special case in the company of Hollywood guys who put on the uniform. He was more daring than most, and more skeptical of pomp. He carried himself like a pirate, or a captain who would break the rules. There was an Ahab in him (he directed *Moby Dick* in 1956). Moreover, in the war effort, he had made remarkable, subversive documentaries. *The Battle of San Pietro* (1945) had described a spoiled American operation in the Italian campaign, and it did not flinch from pointing out "our" intelligence errors, even as it restaged combat scenes for effect. The War Department was unhappy with the result, but they let it be seen. On the other hand, they forbade screening of Huston's next effort, *Let There Be Light* (1946), a study of the victims of stress and shell shock filmed in a veterans' hospital on Long Island. That pioneering compassion was held back until 1981, and it is one of the best things Huston would ever do.

During the war, Huston read Crane's novel, and loved its uncertainty. But Metro-Goldwyn-Mayer proved another kind of War Department, eager to present unambiguous heroes. You could see it as either the kiss of death or sublime casting, but the studio and Huston chose Audie Murphy as their Henry. Murphy had been born in Texas poverty in 1925, the seventh of twelve children. He grew up slight (five feet five), and never lost what is called a baby face. He was not a profound or versatile actor. But he had one advantage: he had been through three years of infantry combat in Europe, starting as a private, but being steadily promoted. Because whenever he got into action he turned frantic and fearless. He would become the most decorated man in the American army, all the way to getting the Medal of Honor. But he suffered from stress disorder that no one identified at the time. How could a wreck hold the Medal of Honor? He had taken charge of a ruined tank and kept firing its gun at German troops. Wounded himself, he killed close to fifty of the enemy. He was crazy brave. His story makes you think of *Fury*.

By 1948, his reputation had brought him to Hollywood. He began to make Westerns and action films, and no one was sure if he was liked for his screen presence or because he was Audie Murphy the hero. That's how he got *Red Badge*, though he had suggested his pal Tony Curtis would be better casting. Metro had thought of Van Johnson. As it was, on the shoot with Huston, Murphy seemed oddly inattentive, or overawed. Did acting brave leave him cold when he had always needed to be crazy?

The Red Badge of Courage was a commercial failure but it became famous because a seemingly demure journalist, Lillian Ross, was allowed to sit in on the meetings and write down whatever people like Huston and studio boss Louis B. Mayer said. There had never been a book before Ross's *Picture* (1952) that so exposed the indelicacy in moviemaking. Huston shot a rather arty picture, running two hours. He wanted it to be about the mystery of courage. Mayer insisted the story had to be made stronger. He had the director's cut hacked down to seventy minutes, with an imposed narrative commentary spoken by James Whitmore. The studio hated it; they said it was not the way war movies were meant to be made.

A few years later, Murphy had a smash hit in a conventional war picture, *To Hell and Back* (1955), with the oddity that he played himself, killing left and right, taking over a platoon when officers were killed, as if the real Audie had always been Audie the movie star. Murphy had a difficult time in life, and he died in a small-plane crash in 1971. It was said that he could turn intolerably angry, that he lived with a gun at hand, that he drank, gambled, and felt lost. He remains a begging subject for a searching film, about a kid more gloried in than captains but inescapably isolated and at a loss without a battle. In an ideal Murphy movie, I think his character should keep in mind the two Gibsons—Guy and Mel—celebrities who had their own darkness.

The solitude of the private soldier can be poignant. It's the condition of Franz Jägerstätter in Terrence Malick's *A Hidden Life* (2019). He is a poor farmer in the Austrian mountains who determines not to swear wartime allegiance to Hitler, and so brings the weight of disapproval down on himself, with fatal prejudice. Set in the past in another country, *A Hidden Life* is a gentle masterpiece that demystifies military order and rural fascism.

The fear over not doing what authority expects can be as depleting as battle. It's a state in which civilians know they have no cover, just because they are not in uniform. Movies like to say the Resistance triumphs, but no one knows for sure while the history is playing out. Sometimes the Gestapo tortured and executed the wrong person. Some wrong persons screamed not just in pain and terror but from the absurdity of not knowing what to confess. You can't rely on monstrous efficiency. People listen for the tiger's growl, and worry that it is tracking them.

It takes something out of the ordinary to listen to Colonel Jessup's boast about how we the public can't stand the truth of what a resolute captain must do at a place like Guantanamo . . . and instead wonder, *Why in hell are we in Guantanamo?* If we need to torture uncharged prisoners, couldn't we do it in some convenient suburb of DC so that tired interrogators might take a restorative walk in the afternoon at the Vietnam Memorial before going on to their dinner?

34

NO MORE SOLDIERS?

There had been early intimations, the evidence that cinema had always been a special effect, or a finessing of nature. So now we could sit in the cool dark of Duluth, and watch a locomotive in the desert. In *Bad Day at Black Rock* (1955), there was that scene where Ernest Borgnine's character Coley harassed Spencer Tracy's John Macreedy, pushing him into a fight where he might be killed. Borgnine was a bull of a man; only two years earlier he had been the sadist running the stockade in *From Here to Eternity*. While Tracy would have looked like a bank manager, even if he had had both his arms. But then, on a set, with back projection for the desert outside, Macreedy had made a wreck of the thug with some decisive strokes of judo and friendly cutting.

Even in 1955, that scene had a fanciful edge as one looked to see how the film was going to manage its coup. Naturally, it cut a lot of the time, and it shot Macreedy from behind—we weren't seeing Tracy, but a double, a stand-in who seemed like the star if you didn't take too long to study him. And because the double hardly moved. The fight had been fixed or faked, and still it was an astonishing scene, because Ernie did so good a job as a bull reduced to a steer, not just overcome but amazed.

Hadn't movies always done such things to make the dream seem real as well as special? But it was touch and go: the medium did have its contract with nature and actuality, the one in which the camera was supposed to record reality. In *High Noon* (1952), Gary Cooper had a fistfight with Lloyd Bridges that had felt like a desperate physical event from which Coop emerged damaged. Then, and even now, we like to believe we have seen some momentous real thing. We are tricking ourselves, and we know it (and nothing has done more to reduce the passion of movies), but in *Bad Day at Black Rock* our commitment depends on the desert light, the spaciousness of great vistas, the matter-of-fact adjacency of the street and the buildings, and the allure of menace in Borgnine, Lee Marvin, and Robert Ryan. Of course, the business was anxious that Tracy not be hurt. That could mean trouble with the insurance and it might push Spence off on a drunken huff. There were other repercussions: actors in the screen habit of bold fisticuffs became fretful or ashamed of how much they were coddled; they noticed that stunt doubles and stand-ins got the real girls; their male confidence—their trading card—could be undermined. Some of them drank or bullied others to cover self-loathing. Didn't the public know deep down that courage was a sham? Hadn't the audience cottoned to how the whole charade was for shit? Wasn't the secret out, after 1945, that you shouldn't trust a hero? Ask the locals in Saigon or Kabul. The whole American thing was "virtual" long before that everyday genre took over.

Black Rock was 1955, so the dilemma seems archaic now. But things were happening in the technology, and as always in cinema history, the technology was not just a trick, it was an extension of meaning. I said earlier that when I saw *Black Hawk Down* (2001), I had trouble telling one soldier from another. That was because they wore goggles and helmets, but by the turn of the century it was beginning to be possible that a picture could add a few simulacra or lifelike zombies to a photograph, just to make the group feel bigger. This craft was rough at first, so audiences might laugh. But ours is a culture that works at technological improvement like a religion attempting to eradicate sin. The technology is magic—it's that or driving us to nausea.

There will have been a moment for all of you when you gasped in awe and fun to realize that motion pictures had dropped nature and suspended our old contract with the camera. You could plug in however many human shapes you wanted. You could have a war without all the extras and their per diems. You could have bodies come apart and regather, because organisms had given up atoms of human entity for pixels. On *Black Rock*, Tracy had kept one arm cunningly folded away, but sixty years later any body could be magicked into fresh shapes. And the result might be dazzling and beautiful. *You could do anything.* Your moment of realization may have come in the *Star Wars* films, in *The Lord of the Rings*, or whatever. Often the context was trite and devoid of creative character. Technology doesn't care. But sometimes it was enchantingly sinister, like Arnold in *Terminator 2* (1991) being pursued by T-1000 (Robert Patrick), a shape-changing apparition of steel or mercury, endlessly elastic and mocking nature's laws.

Terminator 2 was a turning point, franchising extinction. It wasn't just that Arnold the wishful hero (he might be running one day) had said, *I don't want to be the menace again—let me be the rescuer.* But the surprise was how his baddie replacement, Robert Patrick, needed only minutes to shift from being the nemesis T-1000 to a cute trick that tickled audiences. *Let that freak keep coming.* The battle game of the movie was spelling out how the new gospel of technology was killing photography and telling life to move aside.

There we were in the dark, lapping it up. It was no surprise in May 2011 when we got to play Situation Room. You recall the night when "we" took out Osama bin Laden at that villa compound in Abbottabad? Just days later we got the pictures from the DC situation room of our chiefs watching the drone footage on their screen. There was the pres and the vice, Hillary, and Bob Gates, with the uniformed show-runner, Brigadier General Brad Webb, at the controls. Those guys were just like us, watching a movie. Cinema might be vanishing in 2011, but the cinematic construction of reality was everywhere.

Maybe the situationists said later it had felt very "real," but didn't they cross their fingers? And weren't they already into the state of mind that knew the dreadful real things were "a shot." By then, they and we had seen enough of those night surveillance drone scenes, the ones that tracked a toy car on a desert road, until Puff the Magic Dragon got a hit and a pretty dust storm bloomed? We knew that satisfaction from video games where we watched our kill count flickering in the corner of the frame like a vital sign.

You see, we had drunk the Kool-Aid by then, so battle had gone virtual—and no number of sound-track scenes of casualties howling at the Moon would remove our spiffy safety catch. The being real was virtual. We were compromised. This was the American amendment. Let battle run free.

So no more real soldiers if our technology can bring up these armies for the night? Faceless, fearless, perfect forms, exactly the automata that the cinema's top drill sergeants could hope for? It's a loss, I think, that these armies do not look like Robert Ryan. But pause for a further possibility. The collected film archive of Mr. Ryan could now be programmed into a computer so that fresh images might be generated in which Ryan, with his empty look and cracking voice, is . . . the killer across the courtyard in *Rear Window*, a haunted Prospero, or an implacable Claggart in *Billy Budd*. Tact, taste, and legal impediments may block that muse for a while, but do not doubt our facility for doing whatever technology can do.

We are at a point—and have been for twenty years—where our movie masses are not armies as in the gathering of individual, quirky soldiers, but a smooth force in which we do not detect humanity or damage. Our attitude has been altered, and it has a crucial bearing on battle. Computer-generated fascism. For Stalingrad comes down to a video game. Earlier on, I suggested that our World War 3 (we *still* need a better name) could be a mayhem of virtualness set in an aura of unearned safety for us spectators. That may have seemed comic once, ridiculous, and alien to human nature. That was awhile ago.

This is not just the deviousness of fictional filmmaking. In 2022, when the distress of Ukraine offered daily photographs of damage and slaughter—the old imprint of war—Russian officials laughed at this "mistake." Can't you see, they said, these pictures have been shopped and fabricated; they are the wicked work of propaganda. You can say those Russians were lying war criminals. But they had a point, for all of us knew by then that such subterfuges could be done, without our knowing. It would be up to the victors in the war to determine their veracity, and to distinguish between war criminals and the children of Robert Patrick.

There's a badly neglected film—you even wonder if it was really made, or just proposed. Call it *Good Kill*, and say it's 2014. An Air Force major, stationed in Nevada, gives up actual flying to direct a new drone force. He's very good at it (he's Ethan Hawke?) until he realizes the attacks are being aimed at targets that seem less dangerous to the Air Force than irritants to its thinking. The film is real, written and directed by Andrew Niccol—why not? Didn't he write *The Truman Show*, one of the first films that knew so much of existence had taken refuge in screens?

35

ALL RIGHT NOW?

I try to hear the shy words—"We'll be all right now"—that my mum could have whispered in the spring of 1945, waiting for the last "all clear" siren and the happy return of a band of brothers. If you had had a child of your own in 1945 you might have tried the same reassurance. I know that because you are saying the same words now, in 2023, and telling yourself these are the white lies humans have to repeat.

More than that, didn't it stand to reason that civilization (with or without a capital *C*) was not going to repeat its unfortunate mistake? There had been one great war, reassessed as the First (if only to minimize its gravity), but then it had happened again, with virtually the same alignment of forces. Of course, the vibrato was different the second time. Whereas the Hun had wandered into war in the same haze that befuddled everyone, by 1939 the Nazi had acquired a venom and a dramatic motivation that was unmistakable. They were the worst gang there had ever been. Their plan was to annihilate life, starting with you or me. Really, it was the limit: to think that an esteemed culture had set out to eliminate another with maximum prejudice.

Never again. Right?

As if that fresh motto needed backup, the war had concluded with an astonishing burst of energy—10,000 degrees in Hiroshima. That uses a line from *Hiroshima Mon Amour* (1959), one of the most resonant war movies ever made, the collaboration of Alain Resnais and Marguerite Duras, a film in which a single shot is fired in the French town of Nevers. The larger bang, in Japan, and its second barrel a few days later, showed how clever we were with progress, and how cunningly that had checkmated our boyish urge for battle. How could there be a Third World War when the weaponry was available to spread its prejudice so far and wide?

There was a brief span when, in the imbalance of unfairness, there might have been catastrophe: the West could have wiped out the Soviet Union and China and anyone else impudent enough in those late forties. It was a further proof of man's wisdom that as soon as possible a mutually deterrent power was made available to the USSR. In our storytelling we said this was an intelligence disaster, the result of appalling treachery, betrayal, and espionage, but that indignant smokescreen was farcical. So some spies were executed, such a short time before they became oddly sympathetic figures. Which side are you on—Ethel Rosenberg's or Roy Cohn's? It was like shifting from outrage to the amusement we feel for Claude Rains in *Casablanca*, the one realist in that romance. There had to be balance if "never again" was to function. Affirmative that.

Smokescreen was the future. Espionage and treachery were our new foreplay. So in an inversion of strategic reality, the West persuaded itself that our recent ally—impoverished by the war, devastated by its losses, and without a Bomb to bid with—was a deadly threat to the most vulnerable greatest nation on earth. Don't say we aren't ingenious: making that Bomb was no more impressive than conjuring up the decades-long scenario of a Cold War. That phrase was initiated by the financier Bernard Baruch in a 1947 speech to mark the deteriorating relationships between former allies. I was going to say it would last until Mikhail Gorbachev, the dismantling of the Berlin Wall, and the deflation of the Soviet Union. But that interpretation is wishful thinking. Just as there never was a need for cold war, now it seems we cannot rid ourselves of the chill. In 2023, we still live in loathing of Russia and that blank-faced former KGB officer, Vladimir Putin, a man raised to ask questions in theater lobbies.

Putin makes one think of John le Carré's Karla, the longtime chess player in a match with George Smiley. This seems credible. Wasn't le Carré himself a spy for us—surely he knew the rules of the crooked game? Very well, let that entertaining cult persist, but perhaps le Carré is a po-faced satirist making hay out of gloom. His dignified and dishonest circus of British men in the game wants to be taken seriously; they need to believe that the matters at hand are hinges for the world's destiny. But are they any more than chess problems, and isn't the solemnity of those guys fit for mirth?

Le Carré functioned in the shadow of two wars, the last and the next, until you get the feeling that that combat is music for his minuet of intrigue. He is a master of the cold war as smothered comedy. It's true he gets buried in his own gravitas too often—and he is not always lucid as a writer. But he did give us the warning anguish of Richard Burton and Claire Bloom shot dead as they climb the Berlin Wall at the end of *The Spy Who Came in from the Cold* (1965). That's a cheerless movie. I prefer the romance of *The Russia House* (1990), a film that goes from authentic Russian locations (one of the first films to use them) to end in Lisbon sunlight. It also had the wit to make Sean Connery shabby, while tempting Michelle Pfeiffer into smiling.

Connery is crucial to the steady deactivating of cold-war movies. His Captain Ramius in *The Hunt for Red October* is a model of expert reason—maybe the last time on-screen when an officer was so humane and so correct in his reckoning. Without that Connery, there would have been less pleasure in 007. Little of his edge exists in Ian Fleming's wintry texts or in the glum body doubles who followed in Sean's dancing steps. But in those first films, fucking and gadgeting his way out of boredom, and never regarding Soviet plots as more than flimsy screenplays, Sean Connery presided over the cultural dead end of James Bond and its gentler persuasion that the Cold War was a silly diversion from our more complex struggles—like the endless gap between rich and poor. One passionate lesson in Vietnam was that in the crisis of survival, the poor might have it in them to exhaust the rich.

If you are shocked by this heresy (millions still sentimentalize 007 and the equation of gadgets and virtue), so be it. A serious examination of war ought to be shocking now and then. All I am trying to suggest is how far the artifice and corruption of the movies has compromised the plain intensity of war. Don't forget that the holy terror of October 1962 (also known as the Cuban Missile Crisis) has degenerated into the insouciance with which we now sport in the aura of Armageddon (should that still take a capital *A*?), like the London kids dazzled by the light show of the Blitz in John Boorman's exuberant *Hope and Glory* (1987), one of the best films for putting war in its place. As decor and fireworks.

In the first age of Cold War, filmmakers breathed a sigh of relief about carrying on with battle. Their material and their market were not to be put away. It might seem vulgar right after 1945 to make immense films about slaughter. In which case, the hell with tact. We have seen how martial energy never falters, and we know its zeal and its aim rely on our polite bloodthirstiness. One calm triumph after another, with many of them adopting the camouflage of being antiwar movies—that smug song.

Here is a magisterial war film that respects its infantrymen and seems to forgive war for being futile and addictive. It has a generic title: *Men in War* (1957), written by Philip Yordan and directed by Anthony Mann. We are in Korea, with a platoon of American soldiers led by Lieutenant Benson (it's Robert Ryan again), who is ordinary and doing his best. But to have Ryan being "ordinary" is to be downcast. The platoon is trying to reach a hill where they may "link up" with other American forces. Linking up is a recommended thing in war. It is the outward gesture toward brotherhood.

When I saw the film at sixteen, I was moved by its grace—Anthony Mann could shoot battle as if Vermeer was its showrunner. But the film feels no need to ask why these guys are risking their lives in Korea. It immerses itself in the abstract gestures of duty, or troop movement. The Pentagon refused to cooperate with the filming because it detected hints of fear or disorder in the platoon.

The film is black and white, in a Korea found in Bronson Canyon, a part of Griffith Park in Los Angeles. The platoon is full of supporting actors we knew and trusted in 1957—Nehemiah Persoff, Phillip Pine, James Edwards, Vic Morrow, L. Q. Jones, among others. But most of them are scared.

Then the platoon confronts a jeep, driven by Sergeant Montana (Aldo Ray) and carrying the hunched figure of a shell-shocked colonel (Robert Keith). Montana has made it his vocation and his need to look after the mute colonel, and that places him outside the normal chain of authority. In other words, he is not necessarily obedient to Lieutenant Benson. His name suggests the pioneer America.

The enlarged group makes its way across country, suffering through minefields, artillery barrage, and the stealth of assassins. That's how James Edwards is dispatched, taking off his boots to relax as an enemy knife comes out of the long grass. It is a kind of pilgrim's progress. But these men can hardly identify an enemy.

As they advance, so an antagonism emerges between Benson and Montana. The lieutenant wants to go by the book, but Montana is single-minded about surviving and winning. For once, Ryan lacks energy or impulse on-screen. But Montana might be the father of Sergeant Barnes from *Platoon*. In the end, the remains of this 1957 platoon will win its designated hill because Montana goes beyond infantry style and takes a flamethrower to the enemy. The gasps of white fire sweep across the ground like a local fireball. Only three men survive the action, so Benson and Montana take a container of medals (as if.standard equipment) and toss them down the burnt hillside.

Such nihilism reached its peak in the late fifties and early sixties, when it seemed poor taste to keep boosting the "cold" war. Until in October 1962, over Cuba, Kennedy and McNamara called the bluff of severe prejudicial seriousness and it became possible to glimpse the scary farce. Stanley Kubrick did his best to catch that mood in *Dr. Strangelove (or How I Learned to Stop Worrying and Love the Bomb)* but the sharpest comedy could come minute by minute, clinging to TV's breaking news as its matter-of-fact voice edged into surrealism: "There may be images in this newscast that disturb some viewers. . . ."

Men in War is not as well known as *Black Hawk Down* or *Saving Private Ryan* (though Benson is a forerunner of Tom Hanks's captain in the latter). But it is a work of uncommon beauty—and you know that word is not out of line in talking about war movies. It is the bonus we are ready to take with a ticket to watch the fight. So it is sometimes hard to remember that in Korea, sixty years later, there is still a vexed border where infant tyrants glare at each other.

If we were to remake *Men in War* today, there would be no taking of that deserted hill. The men would wander Korea in circles, enduring attrition and old age, never seeing an enemy. We would need a Samuel Beckett to write the sparse dialogue—affirmative that.

In the fifties, there were still reiterations of the Second World War that encouraged defense budget imperatives: Be Ready for the Next Battle. We bankrupt ourselves to be strong, and ration help for the poor. US military expenditure for 2022 was reckoned to be $773 billion. Only Social Security and relief packages cost more—but they could be squeezed. There are still such films, from *A Bridge Too Far* and *Pearl Harbor* to *Fury*, *World War Z* or *X-Men: The Last Stand*, that receive support from a Department of Defense or a War Office and which let us scheme over a tabletop battle, just like ancient supporting actors replaying the Crimea.

To be sporting, our governments diverted this martial spirit into smaller, more "controllable" wars and so the films spill out, a lot of them etched in the latest startling realism, and conscious of the overlap between correct martial disposition and pathology. In the growing spread of the Middle East wars go on forever: the troubles in Afghanistan were twenty years old, officially—time to quit? But there are Afghans who recount tales of hostility from the 1830s, just as in many countries of the "Middle East" there are citizens who regret the loss of friends and relatives, civilian casualties, not counted or owned up to at the time. So we have desert incidents, the children of *Lawrence of Arabia*, where one sandstorm blurs with another.

We are more than ever aware that our men in uniform, our protectors (soldiers and cops), are falling in the gap between duty and going too far.

In 2020–21, we saw so many figures of law and order on American streets, from local police to National Guard, swollen with thirty pounds of gear and equipment, so often helmeted and faceless, steadily torn apart by the pressures of security and insecurity, but sometimes on their way to prayer. Doing war while saying it's antiwar. Keeping hands on all the guns—as if the remorseless hardware needed to be justified.

We ask too much of our captains and our privates, because we prefer not to get too invested in the battleground they patrol. That's not just steering clear of the bullets. Our films have also encouraged us to overlook causation and consequence; that is what the merry popping of guns is for. But this is seldom a contest between simple Freedom and Unfreedom, goodies and baddies. It is the constant undeclared wars between races, and between those who have power and those who don't. This is how the United States is organized on the principle of civil war—an exam it has never yet completed.

SO IN THE SEVENTY-FIVE YEARS AFTER THE END OF THE SECOND WORLD War, we worked it out that we had played "sincere" war to the end of its rope. Vietnam was therefore a throwback to the idea of a showy running pitched battle for justice, or keeping our dominoes in order; in fact, firepower and sophisticated command modules had been defeated by implacable poverty. There could be no showcase war after Vietnam, just the endless hostilities of the Middle East spreading out into toxic and grisly police actions. It was more apparent that battle was a means of stress disorder for soldiers and humiliation for commanders. There had been an era in which we had mixed feelings over George C. Scott's *Patton* or Jack Nicholson's Colonel Jessup in *A Few Good Men*, a bastard and a liar, but isn't he more our captain than Tom Cruise's gaudy but empty lieutenant? Jessup is a career soldier, pledged to do our dirty work. Cruise's Danny Kaffee is so untouched by dirt he's absurd. Retreating from Mariupol, do you want Kaffee or Jessup as your commander?

A faith in duty cracks after 1945. In his inane but elegiac novel of wishful thinking, *Across the River and Into the Trees* (1950), Hemingway had enshrined a last lost captain—Colonel Richard Cantwell—reminiscing on wars to his daughterly beloved while engaging with her in the bed of a gondola, and replaying the scorecard on Allied generals of 1939–45. Cantwell was clinging to the grave romance of war, and going out of his mind with stuffed maleness as he waited on a heart attack. But those heroes were over, or about to be assigned to pampered, arthritic movie stars trying to hold off the ant hordes of computerized armies.

Those classic battles were antiques, pieces of fancy furniture in the culture's last palaces. But the guerrillas about to evolve would not allow anything like a stately battle that later generations could visit, have their pictures taken at, and where they could purchase souvenir hats.

The last battle pictures could not come close to dealing with the calamitous lesson available in 1945. That the alleged just war had been overwhelmed by the evidence of humanity behaving so badly it was beyond redemption.

There had been banner-bright victory parades, as if the world was a pompous Rome (or a Caesars Palace). There was a big pageant in London in the summer of '46, with Sikhs, Gurkhas, and Africans marching, peoples who were about to reject British imperial authority and benefits. That mood coincided with Uncle Ho realizing that America was going to let him down.

There was another parade with scraps and vestiges of people in pajama suits, standing by the barbed wire, blanching in the fresh air—and these were the survivors, in the lines judged fit for our polite newspapers. How had it been a just war when millions of such scraps were like tufts of human hair on the rusted wire? Not only the famous six million, but the millions more who were gone in Russia and Asia, beyond the counting procedures then available? This was before the computer, when we still did math in our heads.

How were we to live in the example of how ready we had been for death and the squandering of justice? How could we forget Anne Frank waiting for the sounds of boots on the staircase—or abide by the pretty Millie Perkins in the 1959 film, the forlorn expression of a society that had escaped so much? Or put aside the principle that people who longed for everything to be "all right" had been occupied by secret police, Gestapo (or whatever the local name was), surveillance, torture, and the pressure to be obedient, or to discard so many traits of human independence?

In all of this, people—so many of us—had been compromised, trying to survive or endure, instead of advancing like Rick or Ilsa and Victor Laszlo. We assumed quietly that some of us could be as two-faced as Captain Renault, though without his wit and flourish, or his merry lines about rounding up the usual suspects and being shocked to discover there was gambling going on, while pocketing the banknotes he had won. We chuckled, because we liked movie stars being cheeky like Robert Patrick. They made our day as much as Dirty Harry with his gun.

Claude Rains turned Louis into such a sweetheart, still a jaunty captain, despite his regimen of self-protection, corruption, and the selfishness any survivor has to learn. How badly must we behave to get through this wretched story?

Rains was only fifty-four in 1943, still handsome, what everyone called "urbane" or "dashing." The actor was then on the fourth of what would be six marriages, endearing to the public no matter that his own romances were a shambles. But compare his Vichy captain in *Casablanca* with Culture Minister Bruno Hempf in East Berlin in *The Lives of Others*, Florian Henckel von Donnersmarck's film from 2006. Here is true brutishness. As played by Thomas Thieme, Hempf is fifty-eight, overweight, coarse, and loathsome—he uses his power to fuck the unwilling actress (Martina Gedeck), and then to impose himself on Georg Dreyman (Sebastian Koch), the handsome but weak writer who wants to oppose the Stasi scrutiny in East Germany.

Let that film stand for thousands that describe the unstitching of humanism under the pressures of occupation, surveillance, and all the systems we have created to keep ourselves insecure. Remember that the pivotal character in *The Lives of Others* is Gerd Wiesler (Ulrich Mühe—

the actor had once been an East German border guard at the Berlin Wall), who is expert in sound recordings to provide evidence against everyone and anyone. In *The Lives of Others* we have to see how the others can be ourselves. And all we need to do while we are waiting is prepare the moral adjustment for ourselves so that—if necessary—we grumble about how were we to know what was going on, or question that odor on windy days from the establishment down the road?

I am thinking about our not being as upright as Private Ryan or Rick, or all the assured models from battle films. But of equal concern is the deeper failure of the movies in flinching from manageable ways of saying we were—and will be—craven, corrupt, treacherous, and human. That is part of the menu humanism has to feed on. Part of that corruption, and the pattern of lies we have told, is to make a dreamworld of battle stories, as if we might be ennobled by them. Or saved in victory.

This is daunting stuff, to be sure, so recall how in *The Lives of Others*, the insignificant Wiesler, the story's expert and discreet bugger, does decide to restrict his own surveillance. That is how Dreyman survives, no matter that his lover kills herself out of horror at her betrayal of him, and it is Wiesler (officer HGW XX/70) who lets Dreyman stay free and to whom Dreyman the author dedicates his eventual book.

There is hope. Keep your eyes and your soul on that gap. It seems small, but it has room for all of us. (Or is it just the officers and gentlemen and their ladies?)

There is the possibility that ashamed citizens may set out to define and reform the virulent hostilities within their life-support system instead of playing pretty war games.

The Lives of Others is not obviously a battle film, or even a war story. No shots are fired. But it has a society in which hostility and insecurity have supplanted official war. The world is occupied by fear, where the enemies are mirrors of ourselves. That was then: the film is set in 1984, the age of the Stasi, who are no more—so we like to believe. We tell ourselves that in countries imprisoned by cold war, people had a very hard time, without quite admitting how in our alleged prosperity and self-confidence a similar chill is setting in. Isn't our America poised over the intimidatory pressures of mistrust and loathing?

Wiesel's sinister technology has been replaced by degrees of sur-veillance that begin to be built into our very bodies—how long before a phone is implanted in the hand—like the way, once upon a time, kids made six-guns with their fingers? How long before the eye is threshold to a set of files, with a delete button for those nostalgic for triggers? Open carry could become the modern manifestation of liberty and alertness.

It is increasingly far-fetched that we will gather planes, ships, and in-genious weaponry to mobilize for some foreign battleground. Such actions feel as quaint as cavalry charges and duels fought in the name of honor. The current hostility over Taiwan will have to be finessed, or do we trust the big boys to be "sensible"—as in the summer of 1914? Can Taiwan be played at the level of a video game? Isn't there a television genius in wait-ing who can find a way to keep its slaughter virtual?

There are going to be a few real casualties? Very well—we can handle the numbers. We've always done them.

So we keep our wars for metaphor: we talk of campaigns on drugs; on crime; on racism, dread, and poverty; on cyber technology, plastic bags, and the firearms some clutch for security. There is even a war against the decline in our sperm count. Is our elemental explosiveness at last in doubt? These are wars we have little history at winning. But we should heed the omens on our public screen, the outbursts of fear and loathing, and the passion for violent excitement. For years we have told ourselves we are against violence; but in the same time our taste for it has been cultivated and sharpened beyond the ancient limits of censorship. Think of a movie called *January 6th* (2021, available for streaming on all platforms). Try not thinking of it. Consider how a day may come when that film could be shown in schools to honor the tradition of our deranged militia spirit. You know about "militia" from the Second Amendment.

The war film to match the nation after the sixth, the one I am ending with, is a haunting epic that goes some way to offset the exuberance that made *The Birth of a Nation* and *Gone With the Wind*. It lets us see how little those Hollywood monsters would admit about the real America. I am thinking of Barry Jenkins's *The Underground Railroad*, adapted from the novel by Colson Whitehead.

Not that it is comfortable viewing, but how can we feel we deserve ease or amusement? The nature of slavery was that of power and brutality, so you will have to watch a man flogged to a point where his skin is in tatters, and then he is roasted over a wood fire, lynched, charred, and ignored by a white society at its complacent picnic on a nearby lawn.

The series (ten episodes, over ten hours) is set in the nineteenth century, yet it has a disarming way of omitting particular dates and even the Civil War—so a referee could claim it is not exactly a war film. But you are too smart now for that escape. You realize that "history" was a white construct, a forest or an "into the woods," in which blacks were always lost children. Jenkins has made a movie about a country under wartime occupation where white society resents the intrusion of black people on its peace and its moral authority, while those blacks live in an extensive imprisonment that skips from casual to cruel as a man might flick at a horsefly on a hot day.

Until *The Underground Railroad* I had never properly seen the South on-screen or felt its light, its humidity, and its growth. Jenkins knows to be wary of human nature, but that only sucks him into the profusion of countryside so that slavery seems more repugnant for occupying paradise. Thus the "railroad" is as spinal and elemental as hope, or justice. There were not many actual railroads in that nineteenth-century underground. But in Jenkins's film, the possibility of a railway, buried like a tomb, is a metaphor and a myth, like the Beast that may become a prince or the echo of hymns in the music of Charles Ives.

So *Underground* cannot be simplified or localized as a war film. That only tells us how far war has reached. Here in plain view is America the occupied country, a ravaged Eden, a dream of hope for the world that became its nightmare. This book alludes to a time when men went to war as a place fit for their adventure, their honor, their manliness. When battle seemed as handsome as a smart uniform. It is part of that tradition that good-natured, peaceable people—like us—can watch *Black Hawk Down*, *The Thin Red Line*, or *Zulu* as if eating a deserved meal. Our composure is astonishing.

That halcyon genre, the war movie, will not go away. But in living with it, we face a dire consequence: that battle *has* become us and wounded our thinking. In freeing ourselves from slavery, we have to rehabilitate not just the slaves but the Gestapo masters who were also crippled by the contract. As battle becomes us, so many are left shamed and limping, like humans pursued in the forest, preoccupied by fear. We will kill to survive, like wolves who believe they are lambs.

As for the cinema, we accept a far-reaching error by agreeing on a narrow genre of war films when the warring instinct consumes so much more of our activity. When a teenager on our city streets can carry an assault rifle illegally, kill two strangers, and be acquitted in the name of self-defense, then the readiness for combat—our triggering—has overtaken so many aspects of what it might mean to be a citizen.

Things are not all right, Mum. We are cells in some disenchanted organism, furious, and ready to knock our heads off as well as the hats.

36

LOOKS LIKE THERE'S A WAR ON....

I warned you, wars and chapters ago, of a time in an expensive hotel room, with a man and a younger woman. . . . He is a swaggering brute; he seems to be dying—he is coughing up his guts; but he has abused her verbally and raped her. We should have got out sooner, the way people were advised in '38 or '39 to leave Vienna, when there was a safe wherever to go to. The woman, her name is Cate, gazes out of the window, and says, "Looks like there's a war on," as if it has started to rain.

This is not a movie; I don't think it would be filmed even in our depraved now. It is a play, *Blasted*, by Sarah Kane, that opened in 1995 at the Royal Court Theatre Upstairs, in London. Very soon in the play, a soldier appears at the hotel room with a sniper rifle. He does not seem part of any official army, operating under codes or orders. He is a soldier because that is all his time has left scope for. The brotherhood thing has been retired.

There is worse to come. A mortar bomb hits the hotel. The man is blinded. The soldier kills himself—that indicates the lapse from any line of duty. Cate finds a baby, but the baby dies. The blind man eats the dead baby. Cate earns bread, sausage, and gin on the street, trading herself in return, and feeds the blind man. He thanks her. Black out.

So things are not quite all right, because the untended chaos of our situation lets us know there will be no Nuremberg trial to set things straight. No one is in charge to be judicious. *Blasted* caused a stir of outrage when it opened. It was declared a work of filth. The fury over its offense was inseparable from the dread that its premonition might come to pass.

Rain falls throughout the play, nothing remarkable in 1995, but rain means more now, including a future affliction that no umbrella will withstand. What looks like war is a dark light on our horizon, an ultimate crisis but calm and banal, one in which our captains may turn so desperate they make *Patton* seem like a showoff infant.

Blasted was so long ago, and Sarah Kane is no longer with us to protect or direct the play (she killed herself in 1999)—as if she ever believed in protection. But in the years since, the formality of movies in theaters has declined. The battle is in our own governance and in our homes, where the screen is like a lodger we can't get rid of. The friction of sport has been joined by the hysteria of tribal dispute—as if that racketing din could persuade us that we still have useful politics. And television's craze for contest has been fed by franchises like *The Hunger Games*, or *Game of Thrones*. No massacre is out of bounds if the glow of "games" goes with it.

So if I imagine a fresh production of *Blasted*, I would have the entire play taking place in the same hotel room but with this addition: a gorgeous wall screen is playing stuff all the time. We can turn its sound off in order to hear the actors speaking Kane's lines. Still, it will be apparent that the screen is playing something like *Squid Game* on an endless loop, with its spasms of triumph and execution as a terrific pinball background. Don't forget terrific.

With bread, gin, and sausage from room service. Plus any other delicacies.

Somehow we should have got out earlier, before we had to face that we had been living under occupation all along.

37

DO YOU REMEMBER?

Things are out of order. People are behaving more strangely. Unkindness and loss of memory are taking us over. "World war" was not a particular announcement, or event. It was a way of characterizing "world."

Do you recall how in the early stages of composing this book, I worried in the dawn hours about some action or hostilities breaking out over Taiwan? That island seemed to be poised for its moment. There was a likelihood that "they" and we would soon declare it as a war. Or skip the formality and just have damage happen.

I don't mention this in a proprietorial way, no matter how premature I was. We have to think ahead; that is where dread marries hope. And I retain allegiance to Taiwan as a pregnant situation. Fear of it needs to be kept in mind, all the more so in the blast of Ukraine. After all, if our home cracks open, rats will emerge from fissures we never imagined were there. I see no reason to assume the pressure of Taiwan has gone away. War is always waiting.

So as I was finishing this book—authors like to feel a sense of closure and moving on—the map of Ukraine exploded on every front page, with reports of catastrophe and then the first cautious photographs of bodies in the street—or what looked as if they had been streets once. I say "cautious" because a degree of restraint hovers over dead bodies, even if the fatal numbers are boasted about. There is a blurring of the faces—or are they already erased from the blasting? Eyeless buildings, scorched and naked; the grid of streets ironed out. *Official warning: some of these images may be disturbing.* As if the safeguard of officialdom still holds. Then Sergey Lavrov, the foreign minister of Russia, is saying that the pictures of corpses; the reports of rape, torture; tethered men shot in the back of the head—whatever—these were all fake and enemy propaganda. Because it is so easy now to fabricate such emotional images.

One day early in April there was a color picture on the front of the *New York Times* in which an elderly woman was standing over three dead bodies in Ukraine: two of them were half concealed by rubble, but one was seen in a way that raised the possibility of decapitation. There were also ideas in the air of peace talks with the very people who had both made the dead and then suggested they were unreliable.

The picture in the *Times* was not quite clear. In the Lavrovian philosophy, the old woman might be an actor with the three corpses just lie-ins or photoshopped stooges. Lavrov may be a scoundrel, complicit in war crimes, but in the infectious undermining of modern war he might be right, so that we cannot be sure of anything. Unless we are there and in the early stages of our own death, where a scent of decay may be originating in ourselves like songs or smoke. Even then, we may wonder. We have all of us always been dying, and we won't be here to ensure that history tells the truth about us. We can say that the Russian attack has been iniquitous, but the victors will write the history books to tell blank centuries what happened. Or what can be forgotten. And we cannot assume we are cast as the victors.

We may believe we know the outlines of the evil that took effect in Ukraine, but I am not confident about spelling it out. You have made up your mind, and you are as smart as I am in wondering if—by the time you read this book—the burial pits in Ukraine may be sleeping (like the graves at Stalingrad) while the outrage of a war in Taiwan monopolizes the damp newsprint. *Fresh breaking news today.* It is more the point of this book to assess Ukraine as a new kind of movie, a bleak pageant, or some frenzy on a screen.

Is that thought unbearable, on top of our need to accommodate and repair the destruction in Ukraine? I am only trying to describe how we come to perceive these things, and how a narrative settles in. We can agree that Ukraine has been wronged. We knew that would happen. NATO, the European Union, and the United States had intelligence that this conflict was coming. It could be measured in the assembly of Russian troops and equipment. And maybe there were secret reports that supported the drone-observed lineup on the board game. The United States warned Russia that this was a very bad thing, that it would lead to immense sanctions against Russia and ignominy in the eyes of the world. President Biden read speeches about this, and was sometimes so horrified at what he was saying that he stopped short and blurted out an anguished ad lib.

But he and "we" did not deploy a modest force—say 50,000—in Ukraine at the invitation of that threatened government. Fifty thousand trained soldiers with the best high-tech firepower—or 25,000, if you want to be economical, with Winchester 73 rifles, and some George Patton type in charge. (A rough rider with a cool head. Now we're talking movie!) We did not do that because we reckoned it could be a provocative act of war, capable of prompting what would have to be called World War 3, and the use of nuclear weapons.

The strategy is for armchair strategists, and it's beyond me. But I have a basic instinct that force does speak to bullies and monsters. Ukraine was about to be invaded and devastated. A reasonable defense group— just 10,000, with Bowie knives, Sioux arrows, and a certain Eastwoodian grit—might have been a deterrent. Because if we are afraid of nuclear weapons, then surely the Russians share that anxiety. They are cowards, too, with a history more steeped in fear than ours.

Never mind the academic military debate. Just recognize how far our backing away made the war a spectacle, movie-like, for which we were helpless onlookers, aghast but without agency or responsibility. The predicament of Ukraine's Western neighbors was to watch and count the damage. And there was pain, fury, and humiliation in that diligence. As it happened, much of the spectacle was of a good old-fashioned war, with tanks, aircraft, and infantry. The weaponry was smarter and more lethal, but the conflict was like the one seen in *Fury*, and in the final battle for Europe in 1944–45. The pictures in the paper were as up-to-date as being in color, but they depended on verbal news reporting to interpret what the pictures meant. Pictures are eloquent, yet dumb, so often at the mercy of feeble captions. But there was this extra subversive realization: that we no longer trusted the pictures in the way we did in 1945. And the more moral conviction is withdrawn, the less it exists.

To be cast as mere spectators, under orders to be still or calm, was demeaning and a further depletion of our chance to be actual people. But this shrinkage is not new; it is something we have been acquiring in our movie dark.

Our futility was exacerbated by mounting reports of "war crimes" committed by the Russians in Ukraine. In some places, civilians seemed to have been abused, tortured, and executed in hand-to-hand intimacy. Such things are hideous and shameful, but they were only a specific of the cruel indifference that had been demonstrated in artillery onslaughts, bombing raids, and the destruction of homes and buildings known as places of communal gathering. "War crimes" may pale against the serene criminality of war, and the apparent Russian ambition of degrading the country it had said it was setting out to liberate.

Of course we take sides; that is what battle is about, no matter that every significant human controversy demands talk, evidence, reasoned argument, and compromise. But this book is an attempt—written in dismay—to describe how what we call the media have drawn up an order of battle and turned us from hurt or outraged citizens into numb spectators somewhere between safe and helpless. The community of movie people—the makers and the watchers—may not like to face this, but the condition is inescapable. Film and the media are weapon systems now—and the agony and impotence in being watchers will intensify.

———

YET QUAINT FANTASIES AND WAR GAMES PREVAIL. AS I WAS WRITING THIS coda, in April 2022, there came jubilant publicity for a forthcoming movie, and its antique attitudes. That May, something called *Operation Mincemeat* would be delivered to the world. It was a movie about the ineffable British cunning in 1943 through which the plan to invade Sicily was "disguised" by a storybook plot to let Jerry think the attack would go through Sardinia. This was a way of diverting German and fascist Italian attention from a Sicilian opening. You could do worse now than look at a map, to realize that taking Sardinia then would be nearly as marginal as making the remote isle of Skye the focus of an invasion of the United Kingdom. The attack had to go through Sicily, bloody and painful as that would be. We knew it; the Germans knew it; the Sicilians knew it. That invasion of Sicily worked very well, with George Patton playing a key part in it.

The only people with any other view of that campaign in 1943 were the aging schoolboys who dreamed up wizard schemes and promoted them as wishful entertainment. So there was an elaborate plot to have a corpse wash up on the Spanish shore with fake documents (created with glee and ingenuity) announcing target Sardinia. That information would surely pass into German hands. This was the brainchild of Ewen Montagu, a lawyer and a yachtsman who was employed by British intelligence. He thought of the corpse, found a viable body, and ran the whole crazy ruse. In *Operation Mincemeat* Montagu is played by that admirable English actor Colin Firth (the king from *The King's Speech*).

I knew this story already because as a youth I had kept a respectful straight face sitting through *The Man Who Never Was* (1956), directed by Ronald Neame and written by Nigel Balchin. Clifton Webb had played Montagu then, and the enterprise was presented as one more flourish in how British wit won the war and treated it as about as dangerous as French cricket with bare shins and a hard ball. That film had a pro-German Irish spy, too, entirely fictitious, even if Stephen Boyd looked real in the role.

He had scenes with Gloria Grahame playing an Englishwoman—there was an undertone of espionage or playacting throughout.

That was sixty-seven years ago, an interval in which we say war has changed out of recognition. But here was the old dance dressed up again, directed by John Madden and scripted by Michelle Ashford. It had Matthew Macfadyen as Montagu's sidekick Charles Cholmondeley, and Simon Russell Beale as yet one more Churchill. This film was set to open in a world that would be discovering the habit of war crimes in Ukraine as that war became a continuous performance and an ordeal for heartbroken liberals. I saw a trailer for *Operation Mincemeat*, and glimpsed Kelly Macdonald as attractive female decoration—some bright assistant. No, I did not see the whole picture, but time is crowded and you appreciate by now that I have a skeptical disposition. I may miss this version of the tale of the magical corpse and stick around for the next one, conceived possibly in some bland concentration camp as a refreshing jape.

On almost the same day, the *Guardian* ran a stricken report from Ukraine detailing the evidence of war crimes. Now our Risk game included the threat of rape, even in front of one's own children (they could be slaughtered if the sight was too much to bear). One woman told the *Guardian* that she could no longer live in the heady spirit of old movies. Was that fantasy indecent at last? But it seemed unlikely then that the blithe romance of *Operation Mincemeat* could reach cinemas in Kyiv or Mariupol (or any that were standing).

The picture business has always known how war fucks up the foreign market.

Why was there this war? Why had there been that war in 1914? The declared objects of the Ukraine adventure seemed specious or insulting. How could Nazi methods be part of a de-Nazifying pilgrimage? Was there then an unspoken purpose of the battle? Had it been arranged to distract the lazy world from the graver problems it usually ignored—the poverty, the racism, the fear, fire and flood, and the perpetuity of our stupidity?

It is fear that drives most wars, and so war movies celebrate courage.

Imagine a movie where war has become so general it hangs in the rainy air. Think of Christian Petzold's *Transit* (2018). This is taken from a 1944 novel by Anna Seghers in which a German refugee has slipped away to Nazi Paris. Anxious to blur his own identity, he pretends to be a writer who has just died. Can he escape to Mexico? Are there letters of transit more comforting than a gun, or cyanide pills? Will the Americas be safe?

Petzold pulls a sweet trick in his movie version. He films in the Paris and Marseilles of 2018. But vans drive by full of police, their sirens howling. People are stopped to show their papers. Of course, those cities are free today, or open; though I've seen side streets in Paris crammed with silent armed police, just in case. What case?

Petzold has found a simple way—comic yet sinister—to remind us that we are accustomed to forms of occupation by now, the systems that ask for passwords and insecurity. And while some complain at that, others feel reassured. That is war's weather system, the idea of being under control. Oppressed, yet sort of safe? Warn yourself.

ACKNOWLEDGMENTS

I was raised in a house in south London close enough to a main railway line to be hit by German bombs. It may seem bizarre to give thanks for that but throughout this project I felt the benefit of the experience. There were rats in our garden, in the rubble of a part of the house that had to be chopped off because a bomb had left it unstable. These rodents horrified my mother, but at two or three I was more impressed by the steady approach of our black cat, Mackie, who delivered a dead rat most days as if it was his rent.

I am not complaining; I don't think I was afraid until much later, when I understood what had been happening. We were not invaded, or put out on the street as refugees; we were not sent to camps, though for a couple of weeks Mum and I were evacuated to a mining village in Nottinghamshire to escape the bombs. It didn't work: Mum felt the outside earth lavatory was more undermining so she took us back to London.

That's comical or matter-of-fact, and that's how the war impressed me as a child. I didn't dread it, not at that time; I assumed that that was how life was. Later on, I slipped into seeing that education as invaluable, for it taught me how a state of war had always been there. And I don't think it will go away. Our outrages were very small compared with those that were available not far away.

So I did not feel damaged, or whatever the word should be—not until my grannie showed me a newspaper picture of inmates who had been "relieved" from one of the concentration camps. The look on those faces was more lasting than the sequence of dead rats, the bomb sites, and the times we had to try to eat whale meat. What happens to you in your first four or five years is decisive: for me that was a hardship I never noticed, and a custom of bleak English jokes about it all, culminating in the post-1945 insight that we might have been better off losing the bloody affair. War was what we had—and I was told ruefully that it was what we had had some twenty-five years earlier.

I was sheltered, and we actually had a bomb shelter in the house, made of iron, with pockets of water and rations in case the house fell down on it. I remember lying there, awake because of the great noises in the sky: they were more likely massed flights of our Allied bombers than German planes, but I think there were flying bombs, too, the V1s and the V2s. Even so, the noise was like the sound effects of thunder in a pantomime. For kids, war can be a show—and thus the alliance of war and movie had begun.

Later on I heard stories from my uncle (Reg Birchett) who had been a prisoner of war in Italy and then Germany, and who had come back too weak to climb stairs; and from my best friend's dad, Tommy Hamilton, who had been in France after D-Day and liked to tell us it had been one big lark of the kind boys would appreciate. In war boys often have to become men, but sometimes men have to insist on remaining boys.

Later still, I had a father-in-law, Robert Evans, who had been on the Western front for two years in the Great War and he told me horrific stories in a calm voice, no matter that he had not told these stories before to anyone. I think like many people who have seen dreadful things he had not wanted to upset others, and had reckoned or hoped he would not be believed.

It's in that spirit, maybe, that war stories gain ground—I mean stories in which it was a lark, with the boys brave but shy about it, and everything working out all right. That nonsense; that helpless way of ensuring that war will go on and on. For me that nonsense included the postwar movies, British and American, and the great danger that young idiots would believe them and accept their theory of war. I have discussed a lot of these films in this book, but anyone my age knows there were many more films, and many of them shamefully worse than the "classics." In the late 1940s and '50s, there was a legend that the war had been a very bad thing, but the mainstream of war pictures nonchalantly denied that and said it had been fun. It's in that experience that this book begins. It's central to my point that war is one of the large things we tell lies about—and that is an inescapable part of our movie tradition.

So, I owe a great debt to the novels I started to read about the war. Not that they were always more reliable than the films. But they did stress the thing that my first years had indicated: that war was usually the same old life led under heightened pressures. And the people in books are often more interesting than those in films. Every movie enthusiast needs to face that unrelenting condition.

For me, more or less in the order I read them, the formative novels were James Jones's *From Here to Eternity* (1951); Herman Wouk's *The Caine Mutiny* (1951); Irwin Shaw's *The Young Lions* (1948); Norman Mailer's *The Naked and the Dead* (1948); and the best book of them all, Joseph Heller's *Catch-22* (1961). In the English voice, I would discover Graham Greene with *The End of the Affair* (1951) and *The Quiet American* (1955). And then a rush of books: Evelyn Waugh's *Sword of Honor* trilogy (1952–61); *The Heat of the Day* by Elizabeth Bowen (1948); Olivia Manning's series of books set in the Balkans, *Fortunes of War* (1956–64); and the *Parade's End* (1924–8) novels by Ford Madox Ford. As recently as 2018, Second World War novels made a return with Michael Ondaatje's *Warlight*, a wonderful evocation of the home front, and the mysteries of wartime authority.

That brings me to a number of personal acknowledgments. Michael Ondaatje is a friend, and we talked about *Warlight*, British films on the war, and many other things. In a similar way, I benefited over the years from knowing Michael Powell and talking about *The Life and Death of Colonel Blimp* with him, from talking to John Boorman about *Hell in the Pacific*, *Hope and Glory*, and *Queen and Country*. I was fortunate to be able to talk to Nicholas Ray and Samuel Fuller, and I did interviews with Ken Burns and Lynn Novick about their documentary epic, *The Vietnam War*. I was able to show Bertrand Tavernier what I had written on his war films, and I then benefited from his notes in response. I had talks with Spike Lee about *Da 5 Bloods* and with Barry Jenkins about *The Underground Railroad*. I was able to talk to Tom Luddy about his friendship with Larisa Shepitko, and there is hardly a film matter I haven't discussed with Tom over forty years. For so many of us, he has been the essential link and connection in movie matters. Much the same feeling extends to my friendship with Phil Kaufman, wry but fond observer of the right stuff.

At different stages in my work, I shared the text with two special friends—Mark Feeney and Mary Pickering—the one outstanding as a cultural commentator, the other as a professor of history. They were so generous with their time and the care in their comments; the book would have been much less without them; it would have been more of a mess than is the case (but you should not expect a book about war to be tidy). Mark and Mary are not responsible for any of the views in the book, but I have been lucky to have their friendship and their assistance. I also had a characteristically astute reading from my agent, Steve Wasserman, who had done so much to set the book up as a publishing venture.

There are other debts I recall: talking with Kieran Hickey about *Men in War*; being at film school with a man who had worked on *The Bridge on the River Kwai*—I think his name was Vu Di, so we called him "Woody"; visiting the beaches and the cemeteries in Normandy; taking my own children to the Imperial War Museum and living in imagination in its recreations of the trenches on the Western Front and London in the blitz— more theater, of course; discovering the work of Humphrey Jennings at the National Film Theatre in London; being exposed to Alain Resnais's essay film, *Night and Fog*, as if it was acid for my metal; realizing slowly that William Wyler's famous war film, *The Best Years of Our Lives*, had actually omitted the war; then long after its events, seeing that the film *Fury* (2014) had conveyed what it was like to be inside a tank—something I had heard from Tony Godwin, a tank commander in north Africa, my boss at Penguin, my publisher, and a flag for so many hopes. It was at Penguin that I edited Martin Middlebrook's book *The First Day on the Somme* (1971) and learned so much from it.

All those details from the screen in a genre that often mocked its own cause of realism, and made war like an insane romance. There's the subject again.

Above all these names and influences, I thank Jonathan Jao for his work as editor on the book. From the start he was a force of enthusiasm and confidence. Then as the book came into being he was tireless, alert, and ingenious in finding ways to improve and extend the book and to make it feel more of a whole. Most of what we did together was in telephone calls during Covid (8 a.m. my time; 11 a.m. his in New York). He was a model of clarity, utterly familiar with the book, and sensing where it was weak or too strong. He eased the book in different directions and saw connections that were waiting. Editing, I fear, is going out of fashion, but Jonathan Jao lived up to a model and would have made Tony Godwin appreciative. Thank you, Jonathan.

I am also grateful to David Howe for his care over production of the book.

NOTES ON SOURCES

There are sources like movies and books, but a more extensive and profound background has to do with objects, procedures, words and sounds, and other things from life. So, as a five- and six-year-old, I saw movies like the Olivier *Henry V* (1944) and *Courage of Lassie* (1946), in which our dog assists in the war effort, and where (I think) he or she is pursued by German soldiers. The word "Courage" was often stressed; it seemed to have been as important as the basic supplies of war, like ammunition, uniforms, dried egg, and the American flier's helmet that I treasured for a few days. My mother showed it to me: It was soft leather with some fur inside. I put it on. I loved its fragrance. And then it vanished. When I asked about it, my mum seemed to have forgotten its existence. How did she have it for a few days? I don't know. But I have never stopped wondering. Also, she said it was American, and in 1944 or '45 it might have been. The helmet is a source, as valuable as the movies or the books about Biggles—James Bigglesworth, the pilot hero in a series of adventure stories by Captain W. E. Johns (though Johns was never a captain). I suspect the books are misleading, but I'm not going back to check it out. The stiff upper lip has a way of taking over the rest of the head.

1 | IMITATE THE ACTION OF THE TIGER

I am referring to *The Banshees of Inisherin*, as mysterious a film as it is satisfying. It says there is a war going on on the Irish mainland, with sounds of gunfire coming across the water. The year is 1923. So there might be hostilities in Ireland then, if nothing as complete as war. But I think the director Martin McDonough wants us to feel how some wars smolder on for decades, and nearly a century later it is possible that the calamity of Brexit could breathe upon the embers. Such thoughts put me in mind of a novel I love, *Troubles*, by J. G. Farrell (London, 1970), a book I found in her apartment while my wife and I were the guests of Diane Johnson. It can mean a lot to find a book like that among several thousand. In *Troubles*, in 1919, Major Archer, just discharged from the army, arrives in Wexford and enters a world of breakdown. The idea of a gentleman unhinged by the war is a vital link in British history, no matter that it may be wishful thinking.

The end of the Kabul involvement comes from many hours and fragments of television reporting, and from Matthew Heineman's film *Retrograde* (2022). I suspect there will be more, and I will not be surprised if one day we are back in Afghanistan telling stories as high-spirited as *Charlie Wilson's War* (2007, though it feels as if from the nineteenth century).

Warn the Duke is just one of the brilliant shafts of light, memory, and imagining from E. L. Doctorow's *Ragtime* (New York, 1975), a book always on my desk while doing this book.

2 | AT EASE

In my childhood, John Buchan was a touchstone, the author my father recommended most often. It was decades before I realized that this very influential author (1875–1940) was and is an imperial racist. But the history of war teaches us that there is no abandoning of our awful ancestors. It's not as if *Greenmantle* (1916) is simply out-of-date. Bad books last as well as the good ones.

Equally, I have watched leftish children (my own) playing Risk with zeal. (Risk was created in 1957 by the filmmaker Albert Lamorisse—for decades, its "Ukraine" was a territory that included most of Russia.) The alignment of territories on its map is so archaic it's a wonder the game is popular still. But it has shaped us as much as Monopoly or bridge or tennis. Nearly every good game is a model of warfare. Thus, at five, it seemed natural that the mocking gift of tennis balls in *Henry V* was a prelude to total war.

3 | **OPEN FIRE**

As I write this (February 2023), Alec Baldwin has just been charged with involuntary manslaughter in the *Rust* accident. I suspect this story could outlive me. But the most lasting source or influence it reveals is a subject we have neglected: the curious fulfillment that a hand feels in holding a gun. I mean the conjunction of physicality and ideology, and the tendency in men to grab hold of precious things.

Norman Mailer was often very discerning on our relationship with objects or instruments, and this insight from early on in *The Deer Park* (New York, 1955) is a hint toward the quality of that book and the cultural gap between aiming and understanding.

4 | *BLACK HAWK DOWN*

There seem to be few books about Ridley Scott. This is surprising at first, but I think it's proper: he is productive to a high degree, hugely skilled, yet endearingly impersonal. There is *Ridley Scott Interviews* (Jackson, Mississippi, 2005), which makes clear the character of his voice and his dislike of fuss. There is an admiring book by Ian Nathan, *Ridley Scott: A Retrospective* (2020). But nothing says as much as the work itself, or his unshakable gruffness over duty and service. He is as natural and inexplicable as Howard Hawks or Fritz Lang. As he keeps going back to battle we have to recognize that his first full film, *The Duellists*, is one of the most arresting debuts in the field, and proof of how beguiling military mania can be. Harvey Keitel's bristling presence in that film is one of the genre's landmarks in duty's nightmare. The question of how the best trained paragons can go crazy hangs over the future of the military and many police actions.

5 | **IN THE HEART OF NATURE**

I have quoted from the screenplay of Godard's *Pierrot le Fou* (London, 1969) and I recommend Richard Brody, *Everything Is Cinema* (New York, 2008). On Samuel Fuller, we have Fuller, Christa Lang Fuller, and Jerome Henry Rudes, *A Third Face: My Tale of Writing, Fighting and Filmmaking* (New York, 2002).

The quotation from Ford Madox Ford is *A Man Could Stand Up* (London, 1926), p. 581 in the Vintage edition of *Parade's End* (1979). Added to which, Ford's great work is *The Good Soldier* (London, 1915), without battle, but full of the tortured selfhood of a man retired from and shaped by the military—Captain Edward Ashburnham. The novel is set just before the Great War and Ford had wanted to call it "The Saddest Story." But by 1915, the publisher reckoned readers needed cheering up and so the grumbling Ford came up with *The Good Soldier*, as if knowing there could be no such creature. Christopher Tietjens in the *Parade's End* books has no pretense about being good at his command job. It's just that he has the wit to see what the war is doing to civilization. One of Ford's most discerning and disturbing strokes is in treating Ashburnham as a man of wayward destructive passions who cannot express himself beyond the narrow terms of good form. So Ford describes a personality who can never find a critical faculty or emotional liberty, while standing for a soldierly ideal. It is a kind of bipolarity.

On James Jones, there is Frank McShane, *Into Eternity: The Life of James Jones, American Writer* (Boston, Massachusetts, 1985).

On Terrence Malick, there is a profusion of writing that includes Thomson, "The Wonder of Terrence Malick," *Liberties*, Volume 1, number 1, 2020.

6 | 1914, SUMMER

On the delivery of a full war in 1914, see Barbara Tuchman, *The Guns of August* (New York, 1962); A. J. P. Taylor, *War by Timetable: How the First World War Began* (London, 1969); Samuel Hynes, *The War Imagined: The First World War and English Culture* (New York, 1991); and Stefan Zweig, *Beware of Pity* (New York, 1939).

Those books will lead you to so many valuable historical studies. But don't forget that in 1918, James Joyce was writing *Ulysses*, Willa Cather published *My Antonia*, and Booth Tarkington published *The Magnificent Ambersons*. The year saw the delivery of war poems by Apollinaire and the eventual publication of the poetry of Gerard Manley Hopkins (including

"The Wreck of the *Deutschland*"), who had died in 1889. Another work of that year was *Married Love*, by Marie Stopes. Bartok's second string quartet was premiered and the Original Dixieland Jazz Band had a hit with the Tiger Rag "Hold That Tiger!" Egon Schiele painted "Die Familie." The movie *Tarzan of the Apes* opened. The list could go on and on (indeed, the list became an essential literary form), and we are left to ask whether there is progress here or chaos, humanism or chance. Few questions so arose during the Great War or have lasted as long. The influenza, first detected in Kansas in early 1918, would spread across the world: estimates of its death toll range from 17 million to 100 million. The statistical compromise is happy enough with 50 million (more than twice the service personnel who died in the war). No one is sure how the pandemic started.

7 | ERROR AND HENRY RAWLINSON

See Rodney Atwood, *General Lord Rawlinson: From Tragedy to Triumph* (London, 2018).

8 | THE MG 08

See Arthur Hawkey, *The Amazing Hiram Maxim: An Intimate Biography* (London, 2001); Malcolm Browne, "100 Years of Maxim's 'Killing Machine'," *New York Times*, November 26, 1985.

See also, Calvin Tomkins, *Duchamp: A Biography* (New York, 1996).

9 | SHOULDER ARMS/SHOULDER CAMERA

See Charles Chaplin, *My Autobiography* (London, 1964), pp. 218–19; Kenneth S. Lynn, *Charlie Chaplin and His Times* (New York, 1997), pp. 221–3.

On Wilfred Owen, see Jon Stallworthy (ed.), *Collected Poems* (London, 2004); and Stallworthy, *Wilfred Owen: A Biography* (London, 1974).

10 | THEY

See interviews with Peter Jackson: *3aw*, November 11, 2018; *Flicks*, November 10, 2018.

On the people mentioned at the end of the chapter, George Harvey Bone is the schizophrenic composer in Patrick Hamilton's novel *Hangover Square* (London, 1941), who is being drawn toward murder as the next war dawns. Jimmy Gatz is Jay Gatsby in Scott Fitzgerald's *The Great Gatsby* (New York, 1925)—when he first met Daisy he was in uniform. James Allen (Paul Muni) is the lead character in the film *I Am a Fugitive from a Chain Gang* (1932), a man who comes out of the Great War a hero but despite his dedicated hard work ends up an outcast; and John Hume Ross is the pseudonym adopted by T. E. Lawrence after the wartime events that had made him famous. He joined the Air Force (Captain W. E. Johns of the Biggles books was the recruiting officer), as John Hume Ross—later he changed his alias to T. E. Shaw. The reality of this Lawrentian afterlife seems to me worthier of a good film than the desert adventures. Among other things, Lawrence was persuaded to dress up as his desert image in a stage version of his story (instigated by the journalist Lowell Thomas, but agreeing to it). All leading to his motorbike crash in 1935, still only forty-six.

II | **A TERRIBLE PLACE**

On *The Four Horsemen of the Apocalypse*, see Liam O'Leary, *Rex Ingram: Master of the Silent Cinema* (Dublin, 1980); Emily Leider, *Dark Lover: The Life and Death of Rudolph Valentino* (New York, 2003).

On *Paths of Glory*, see Vincent LoBrutto, *Stanley Kubrick: A Biography* (New York, 1997).

On *The Big Parade*, see King Vidor, *A Tree Is a Tree: An Autobiography* (New York, 1953), p. 111; Vidor, *On Film Making* (New York, 1972); Raymond Durgnat and Scott Simmon, *King Vidor: American* (Berkeley, CA, 1988).

On *All Quiet on the Western Front*, see Marvin J. Taylor, *The Life and Writings of Erich Maria Remarque* (New York, 2011).

On *Heroes for Sale*, see William Wellman Jr., *Wild Bill Wellman: Hollywood Rebel* (New York, 2015).

On *Act of Violence*, see Zinnemann, *Fred Zinnemann: An Autobiography* (New York, 1992).

On *Rolling Thunder*, see Kevin Jackson (ed.), *Schrader on Schrader* (London, 1990), in which Schrader admits that in his first vision, the central character had himself been racist trash, so that the final slaughter was a metaphor for what had happened in Vietnam. But the studio preferred to soften this point, and so, as Schrader says, "Once you take out the perverse pathology of these characters, rather than films about fascism they become fascist films" (p.121).

On Virginia Woolf, beyond the key place of *Mrs. Dalloway* (London, 1925), there is the larger matter of how far her legendary "madness" is complicated but made more understandable by the extent of her sexual abuse as a child and a youth. The damage of her early life, and the overcast of male superiority, is explored in Louise DeSalvo's *Virginia Woolf: The Impact of Childhood Sexual Abuse on Her Life and Work* (New York, 1990). If anyone is seriously interested in ending warfare, they might set up a study on the relationship between battle or shooting and thwarted and misdirected desire in men. When Woolf took her own life, in the River Ouse in East Sussex (March 1941), we "know" from the film of *The Hours* how she put heavy stones in her pockets. That may be so, but it is also the case that, in apprehension of a German invasion, she and her husband, Leonard, had poison tablets in their pockets.

I have found one addition to the Septimus Smith wounded brigade. In 2013, the writer Peter Moffat began what was meant to be an epic TV series for the BBC, *The Village*, the history of a rural family reaching from 1914 to 2000. At the outset a young man enlisted for the Great War, and then came back to his Derbyshire village on leave after the Somme. He acted fit at first but he was scrambled by shellshock. He deserted, was recaptured, and then he was executed.

I should also add the two versions of Vera Brittain's *Testament of Youth*, her 1933 memoir on being a nurse at the front, losing two lovers in the procession of death. The first was a TV series, for 1979, with Cheryl Campbell as Vera. Then in 2014 it became a movie, directed by James Kent, with Alicia Vikander as Vera. As seen through the disturbed gaze of the nurse, the combat seemed more ghastly for being pointless.

By the way, *The Village* was too good, or trenchant. The brave show was discontinued after two seasons: it never got past the 1920s.

12 | FUNNY OLD WAR

On Joan Littlewood, see "The Birth of Oh! What a Lovely War", *BBC News Magazine*, November 12, 2011.

On Richard Attenborough, see Attenborough and Diana Hawkins, *Entirely Up to You, Darling* (London, 2008). Vincent Canby's estimate is from *New York Times*, October 3, 1969.

On *1917*, see Matthew Moore, "Sam Mendes's film *1917* is a Personal Battle," *The Times*, August 7, 2019; Justin Chang, "*1917* is a Mind-Boggling Technological Achievement—But Not a Great Film," *Fresh Air*, January 18, 2020.

13 | THE GALLIPOLI ADVENTURE

See John Tibbetts (ed.), *Peter Weir Interviews* (Jackson, Mississippi, 2014), pp. 94–96, 244–52.

14 | APRÈS LA GUERRE

See Bertrand Tavernier and Jean-Pierre Coursodon, *50 Ans de Cinéma Américain* (Paris, 1970). Also, there is Tavernier's documentary film, *My Journey Through French Cinema* (2016).

15 | A BRIEF ILLUSION

The best book is Nicholas Macdonald, *In Search of La Grande Illusion* (Jefferson, North Carolina, 2014). See also Jean Renoir, *My Life and My Films* (New York, 1974) and *The Notebooks of Captain Georges* (London, 1966).

16 | HORSE FEATHERS

On the Spitfire, see Alfred Price, *Spitfire: A Complete Fighting History* (London, 1992). On Leslie Howard, see Estel Eforgan, *Leslie Howard: The Lost Actor* (London, 2010).

On the Korda family and its own empire, nothing surpasses Michael Korda, *Charmed Lives*: *The Fabulous World of the Korda Brothers* (New York, 1979).

Winston Churchill's letter to the Duke of Marlborough is September 29, 1898, Library of Congress Marlborough papers and exhibition, "Churchill and the Great Republic."

The Omdurman charge was re-created in Richard Attenborough's film, *Young Winston* (1972), where Simon Ward plays Winston and the ubiquitous John Mills is Kitchener. Seven years after his death, the Churchill legend was set: He was a stalwart and a rebel, a wise man yet a rash youth, the most influential British icon of modern times, embracing all the actors who tried him on—but resolutely distant from the actual opportunist and careerist. That portrait is still to be made. But large biopic movies may be dead before any filmmaker summons the nerve to try one.

There is also a BBC documentary film, *Churchill and the Movie Mogul* (2019), directed by John Fleet.

On *The Charge of the Light Brigade* (1936), see Alan K. Rode, *Michael Curtiz: A Life in Film* (Lexington, Kentucky, 2017), and another film, Tony Richardson's *The Charge of the Light Brigade* (1968), where Trevor Howard and John Gielgud are outstanding as Cardigan and Raglan, alarming lords whose hostility overshadows the reasons for the Crimean War and sustains the theory that wars require helpless victims led by madmen. The 1968 version shows the army as a shambles, officered in the most inept but flamboyant ways. It forsakes any sense of order or elegance in the battle. So it's worth noting that the film opened in a bad year for the war in Vietnam, and was written by enemies of obedience, Charles Wood (who had served in the army, and had many military writing projects) and John Osborne. Most war pictures are made as some other battle is looming in the audience's mind.

17 | MASSES

Pandemonium, 1660–1886: *The Coming of the Machine as Seen by Contemporary Observers* was published at last in London in 1985.

On Mass-Observation, see Charles Madge and Humphrey Jennings, *Mass-Observation Day Surveys* (London, 1937); Madge and Tom Harrison, *Britain* (Harmondsworth, 1939).

On Humphrey Jennings, see Kevin Jackson (ed.), *The Humphrey Jennings Film Reader* (London, 1993); Jackson, *Humphrey Jennings* (London, 2004).

On Septimus Warren Smith, see Virginia Woolf, *Mrs. Dalloway*, an example of a writer imagining someone they cannot know. Woolf could have met men back from the war, but she has given Smith her own uneasiness. In planning the novel, Woolf had once considered having Mrs. Dalloway kill herself.

On John Grierson, see Jack C. Ellis, *John Grierson: Life, Contributions, Influence* (Carbondale, Illinois, 2000).

On the "Why We Fight" series, see Mark Harris, *Five Came Back: A Story of Hollywood and the Second World War* (New York, 2014).

18 | BLIMP

See Michael Powell, *A Life in Movies* (London, 1986), pp. 398, 409; A. L. Kennedy, *The Life and Death of Colonel Blimp* (London, 1997); Ian Christie, *The Life and Death of Colonel Blimp* (London, 1994).

On *Went the Day Well?* see Penelope Houston, *Went the Day Well?* (London, 1992).

19 | DAMN FINE SHOW

On Olivier's *Henry V*, see Laurence Olivier, *Confessions of An Actor* (London, 1982); Terry Coleman, *Olivier* (London, 2005).

There were several popular books in the postwar years, which led to films, and provided an interpretation of the war that was invariably misleading: these include Paul Brickhill, *The Dam Busters* (London, 1951); P. R. Reid, *The Colditz Story* (London, 1952); and Bruce Marshall, *The White Rabbit* (London, 1952), the story of Wing-Commander Forest Frederick Yeo-Thomas, who was parachuted into France, captured, tortured, and then, by misadventure, became an inmate at Buchenwald. This was a story in which the customary British nonchalance edged into true horror. *The Dam Busters* was filmed with Richard Todd as Guy Gibson (1955). *The Colditz Story* was a film, starring John Mills. And *The White Rabbit* waited until 1967 to be a TV series, with Kenneth More as Yeo-Thomas.

On Guy Gibson, see Richard Morris, *Guy Gibson* (London, 1994).

On John Mills see Mills, *Up in the Clouds, Gentlemen Please* (London, 1980).

20 | **KWAI**

See Natasha Fraser-Cavassoni, *Sam Spiegel: The Biography of a Hollywood Legend* (London, 2003), pp. 177–201; Kevin Brownlow, *David Lean: A Biography* (London, 1996); Stephen Silverman, *David Lean* (New York, 1989); Gene D. Phillips, *The Life and Films of David Lean* (Lexington, Kentucky, 2006).

See also, Russell Braddon, *The Naked Island* (London, 1952).

On *Bitter Victory*, see Patrick McGilligan, *Nicholas Ray: The Glorious Failure of an American Director* (New York, 2011).

21 | **THE BASTARDS AND THEIR DEMON**

See Carlo D'Este, *Patton: A Genius for War* (New York, 1995); George Patton, *War As I Knew It* (Boston, Massachusetts, 1947).

22 | *FURY*

See Belton Y. Cooper, *Death Traps* (New York, 1998); David Fletcher, *The Great Tank Scandal* and *Universal Tank* (London, 1989); Leland Ness, *Jane's World War II Tanks and Fighting Vehicles* (New York, 2002).

23 | *THE BEST YEARS OF OUR LIVES*

See A. Scott Berg, *Goldwyn: A Biography* (New York, 1989); Axel Madsen, *William Wyler* (New York, 1973).

24 | SAVING SAVING PRIVATE RYAN

See Joseph McBride, *Steven Spielberg: A Biography* (New York, 1997); Molly Haskell, *Steven Spielberg: A Life in Films* (New Haven, Connecticut, 2017); Richard Schickel, "Saving Private Ryan," *Spielberg: A Retrospective* (London, 2012).

25 | ON BEING OCCUPIED

On Melville, see Ginette Vincendeau, *Jean-Pierre Melville: An American in Paris* (London, 2003).

On *The Sorrow and the Pity*, see Stuart Jeffries, "A Nation Shamed," *The Guardian*, January 22, 2004.

26 | RUSSIA

To be brief and all-encompassing, anyone's venturing here could begin with a double-bill of Tolstoy's novel and Clive James—the latter in James, *The Guardian*. February 13, 2016, while remembering an epigraph James quoted in his *Cultural Amnesia* (New York, 2007), from Benedetto Croce—"All history is contemporary history."

On Larisa Shepitko, see *Larisa* (1980), a short film by Elem Klimov.

27 | THE LOOK ON RYAN'S FACE

There are two books on this remarkable actor, so we have a portrait of a decent man that does not fully explain the actor's instinct for menace: Franklin Jarlett, *Robert Ryan: A Biography and Critical Filmography* (Jefferson, North Carolina, 1997); J. R. Jones, *The Lives of Robert Ryan* (Middletown, Connecticut, 2015). Is this just a sign of how movie pretending can bring out the worst in us?

On John Wayne, see Scott Eyman, *John Wayne: The Life and Legend* (New York, 2014).

On Robert Mitchum, see Lee Server, *Robert Mitchum: "Baby, I Don't Care"* (New York, 2001).

On *Bad Day at Black Rock*, see Glenn Lovell, *Escape Artist: The Life and Films of John Sturges* (Madison, Wisconsin, 2008).

28 | **IN ALGIERS**

On *The Battle of Algiers*, see the various essays included with the Criterion release of the film (2004).

29 | **THE OTHER SIDE**

On the Arnhem adventure see Cornelius Ryan, *A Bridge Too Far* (New York, 1974).

On Douglas Sirk, see Jon Halliday (ed.), *Sirk on Sirk* (London, 1971), pp. 125–8.

On *The Night Porter*, see Annette Insdorf, essay included in Criterion release, 2000; John Coldstream (ed.), *Ever, Dirk: The Bogarde Letters* (London, 2008).

On Peter Lorre, see Stephen Youngkin, *The Lost One: A Life of Peter Lorre* (Lexington, Kentucky, 2005).

On Roberto Rossellini, see Peter Bondanella, *The Films of Roberto Rossellini* (New York, 1981); Peter Brunette, *Roberto Rossellini* (Berkeley, California, 2022).

On Japan, see Noël Burch, *To the Distant Observer: Form and Meaning in the Japanese Cinema* (Berkeley, California, 1979); Stephen Prince, *The Warrior's Camera* (Princeton, New Jersey, 1999).

On Kobayashi and *The Human Condition*, see Philip Kemp, essay with the Criterion release, 2009.

30 | **'NAM**

On the general history of how this war was filmed, there is Gilbert Adair, *Hollywood's Vietnam* (London, 1989), all the better in that Adair was the least belligerent or militaristic man you could hope to meet. The filmography in his book is unexpected in many cases and demonstrates that the blood and anxiety of Vietnam reached everywhere: his list includes *American Graffiti, Billy Jack, Cutter and Bone, Hair, Ice, Model Shop, The Stunt Man, Who'll Stop the Rain?*, and *Zabriskie Point*.

On the history, see Stanley Karnow, *Vietnam: A History* (New York, 1983); William J. Duiker, *Ho Chi Minh: A Life* (New York, 2012); Geoffrey C. Ward, *Vietnam: An Intimate History* (New York, 2017), the book derived from the Ken Burns and Lynn Novick television series.

The fiction may be more striking, so it's hard to understand how few saw that history was being written or forecast live in Graham Greene, *The Quiet American* (London, 1955). See also Norman Sherry, *The Life of Graham Greene: Vol. II: 1930–1955* (London, 1994).

On *La 317eme Section*, see Sara Ferguson, "Return to Dien Bien Phu," *Sight & Sound*, December 1991. Antony Beevor's estimate ran in *The Guardian*, May 29, 2018.

On *Go Tell the Spartans*, see Daniel Ford, *Incident at Muc Wa* (New York, 1967); Kate Buford, *Burt Lancaster* (New York, 2000).

On *The Deer Hunter*, see commentary by Michael Cimino and F. X. Feeney on Blue Ray DVD, 2020.

On *Platoon*, see DVD commentary by Oliver Stone, 2001; Stone and Richard Boyle, *Oliver Stone's Platoon and Salvador* (New York, 1987); James Riordan, *Stone: The Controversies, Excesses, and Exploits of a Radical Filmmaker* (New York, 1996).

On *Apocalypse Now*, see Michael Herr, *Dispatches* (New York, 1977); Peter Cowie, *The Apocalypse Now Book* (New York, 2001); Eleanor Coppola, *Notes* (New York, 1979); John Milius and Francis Ford Coppola, *Apocalypse Now Redux* (New York, 2001).

31 | **GIBSON**

Without Dostoyevsky or Ayn Rand, it seems improbable that we will get the novel that Mel Gibson deserves. It is also likely that an adequate biography would come to grief in the courts and still end up beyond belief.

32 | **THE UNIT**

On *Home of the Brave*, see Arthur Laurents, *Original Story by Arthur Laurents: A Memoir of Broadway and Hollywood* (New York, 2000); Laurents, "A Life in Musicals," *The Guardian*, July 31, 2009.

On Leni Riefenstahl, see Steven Bach, *Leni: The Life and Work of Leni Riefenstahl* (New York, 2007).

This chapter also had the benefit of conversations with Spike Lee and Barry Jenkins. On the red ball express, see David Colley, *The Road to Victory: The Untold Story of World War II's Red Ball Express* (Lincoln, Nebraska, 2000); Sean Axmaker, "Ride Lonesome: The Career of Budd Boetticher," *Senses of Cinema*, February 2006.

See also Matthew F. Delmont, *Half American: The Epic Story of African Americans Fighting World War Two at Home and Abroad* (New York, 2022).

33 | **NO MORE CIVILIANS**

On Commander Queeg, see Herman Wouk, *The Caine Mutiny* (New York, 1951), and the play *The Caine Mutiny Court Martial* that opened two years later. The film followed in 1954, with Bogart as Queeg. It was a role he wanted and for which he was supported by Harry Cohn, the head of Columbia. The film was just a few years ahead of that other study of flawed command, *The Bridge on the River Kwai*.

On Evelyn Waugh: his war service was unhappy but extensive and it led to the three Guy Crouchback novels—*Men at Arms* (London, 1952); *Officers and Gentlemen* (London, 1955); *Unconditional Surrender* (London, 1961)—known as the Sword of Honor trilogy. Though less familiar now than *Brideshead Revisited* (1945), they are essential reading and unrivaled in assessing the desperate farce of war, not least in its generating bureaucratic disorder.

On Albert Brown, see C. S. Forester, *Brown on Resolution* (London, 1929). It has inspired two movies—*Forever England* (1935), with John Mills as Brown, and then *Sailor of the King* or *Single-Handed* (1953), with Jeffrey Hunter as a Canadian Brown. In this version, Brown is awarded the Victoria Cross for his action.

On *The Red Badge of Courage*, see the novel by Stephen Crane (New York, 1895).

On the movie and John Huston, see Lillian Ross, *Picture* (New York, 1952); Huston, *An Open Book* (New York, 1980); and Mark Harris, *Five Came Back: A Story of Hollywood and the Second World War* (New York, 2014).

On Audie Murphy, see Don Graham, *No Name on the Bullet* (New York, 1989)—that biography's title comes from a Murphy Western from 1959. Murphy's gravesite at Arlington is the second most visited in the cemetery: John Kennedy is number one.

On *A Hidden Life*, see Thomson, "The Wonder of Terrence Malick," *Liberties*, vol 1, number 1, 2020.

34 | **NO MORE SOLDIERS?**

It is not a matter of sourcing the ways in which technology has altered war, and undermined our "decent" response to it. Consider this: today (and dailiness is becoming more compelling), February 24, 2023, there is a color picture on the front of the *New York Times*. It is credited to Tyler Hicks, a *Times* photographer, and my good will does not doubt it any more than I have given up the *Times*. But look at it closely: It is a photograph of about a dozen soldiers piled together on top of a troop carrier. They wear uniform, helmets and a grim tiredness; they are looking into the camera without apparent dissent or criticism. If I knew more about military apparel, I might know which side they are—Russia or Ukraine. But I do not know, and I think that is because the silhouette, and the facial intensity of soldiery are universal. The caption says "Indelible Images of War" and this cover picture is the introduction to a gallery inside the paper, pp. A10–13.

It is not just natural, but unuttered, that this picture must be of Ukrainian soldiers—so the strongest face, the most accusatory, with a lean, staring gaze, and gloved hands at the ready, is likely to be Ukrainian. Why? Because that is "our" side, the *Times*'s side, and so we are looking at heroes, or in the mirror.

But don't ignore the openness of the image, or the way all soldiers look so alike that they might be CGI figures. As I say, I trust the photograph, but I am like all of us in that I wait to have this ultimate alliance (me and the picture) confounded. This picture might be fake, artful, well-intentioned. We have become fatally separated from reality.

35 | **ALL RIGHT NOW?**

On Claude Rains and the ambivalence in *Casablanca,* start with Aljean Harmetz, *Round Up the Usual Suspects*: *The Making of Casablanca* (New York, 1992) and David J. Skal, *Claude Rains: An Actor's Voice* (Lexington, Kentucky, 2008), and then imagine a remake of *Casablanca* (it could be set in Kabul) in which our Renault is the central character, doing all it takes to survive and wondering which of his lovers he will have to leave behind.

Equally, think of *The Lives of Others* as a story free-floating in so many conflicts. That film is widely regarded as a classic now, but in its moment it was declined by several important film festivals. When it opened, some complained that it was not correct in its treatment of the Stasi operation. Then some viewers (like William F. Buckley and John Podhoretz) said it might be one of the best films they had ever seen. Sydney Pollack and Anthony Minghella had thoughts of remaking it, but they both died too soon. What I am trying to indicate is that its climate of surveillance, confined liberty, and insecurity is not simply a measuring of our side and theirs. It is in the baleful condition of our machines of self-examination.

36 | **LOOKS LIKE THERE'S A WAR ON. . . .**

Sarah Kane's play *Blasted* can be found in her *Complete Plays* (London, 2001). That edition, by Methuen, had a cover picture of a Tommy from the Second World War, in a helmet with a rifle, looking back at the camera to give us a bravado grin. He is one of ours, we think; he is giving a V for Victory sign with his hand; but it is up to us to realize that that sign means "Fuck off" too, in Britain.

37 | **DO YOU REMEMBER?**

Something unexpected happened in the winter of 2022–23. It had been felt that the Academy Award for Best Picture was a matter for *The Banshees of Inisherin, Tar,* and *The Fabelmans.* But then it was said that another film, as yet like gunfire beyond the horizon, might be worth seeing: I mean the German remake of *All Quiet on the Western Front.* As people began to see that film, they said, well, yes, it was well done, and even as upsetting as Erich Maria Remarque had intended in 1928. So maybe it could win best foreign or international picture. (How clumsily America adjusted to the rest of the world.) But then at the BAFTA awards in London in February, it won not just that prize, but best picture of any kind. Wisdom said that this movie was benefiting from the proximity of the war in Ukraine. Could that edge carry it to the Oscars, and even the highest award? And some irony was attached to that sophistication, as if the voters were to be forgiven for their emotional gesture. But in a sinister yet undeniable way war had won; it had taken us over, and reduced winning and losing to technicalities, like the football results.

INDEX